Medieval Imagination

MEDIEVAL IMAGINATION

Rhetoric and the Poetry of Courtly Love

Douglas Kelly

THE UNIVERSITY OF WISCONSIN PRESS

Published 1978

The University of Wisconsin Press
Box 1379, Madison, Wisconsin 53701

The University of Wisconsin Press, Ltd.
70 Great Russell Street, London

First printing

Printed in the United States of America

For LC CIP information see the colophon

ISBN 0-299-07610-5

Publication of this book was made possible in part
by a grant from the Andrew W. Mellon Foundation

for Borghild David and Stephen

Le texte 'contient'-il son sens, cette pluralité jaillissante?
Voici que la question rebondit et se démultiplie. Tout, dans
le système du poème comme tel, est-il traductible en langue? La paraphrase est-elle jamais terminable? Plus nette-
ment encore: le poétique, quoique *fait* (substantif et par-
ticipe) de langue, ne comporte-t-il pas une part irréductible
de non verbalisable?
　　　　　　　　　—Paul Zumthor, *Langue, texte, énigme*

Contents

Preface

C. S. LEWIS ASSERTS in *The Discarded Image* that "no medieval author mentions either Phantasy or Imagination as a characteristic of poets." Nonetheless, the cognitive function Lewis is referring to—the *vis imaginativa*—is an explicit feature of invention and composition for the Chartrain poets, the medieval arts of poetry, and medieval French literature from the thirteenth century on. This is especially true of courtly literature, but applies also to other kinds of writing. Villon exclaims in the scatological spoof of Chartier's Scholastic terminology that concludes *Le Lais:*

> Tout le sensitif s'esveilla
> Et esvertua Fantasie....

Villon's *Fantasie* is not *vera imaginatio*. But they are complementary characteristics of poetic invention, important to works ranging from farce through courtly idealism to moral and religious literature. A study of the significance of Imagination in medieval poetics is overdue.

The time necessary to complete this study was made available through the generous support of the University of Wisconsin Research Committee and the Institute for Research in the Humanities, where I spent the year 1967–68 getting started on the project. The opportunity to teach late medieval literature during the intellectually exciting sixties—Alas! now all gone—to several classes of critical, demanding students forced me to clarify and deepen my reading of most of the authors examined here. I had the opportunity of presenting the results of some of my studies at the 1972 meeting of the Modern Language Association (parts of chapters 2 and 3) and at the 1971 meeting of the Medieval Institute at Western Michigan University (chapter 6). The honor of having as colleagues both Professor Eugène Vinaver and Professor Jerome Taylor has been of great benefit in my study of medieval poetics; I derived especial satisfaction from the course Professor Taylor and I gave together in 1976 on Chaucer and his French contemporaries. This study also owes much to Professor Julian Harris, who first started me out on the Imaginative search for what medieval literature is. Finally, and most important, a personal truth, but true nonetheless: those named in the dedication are the source of the experience by which I understood enough to write this book.

Where good translations exist for citations in the original, I have used them. In a few cases I have made minor changes in the translations, which are put in italics. All translations not identified by source are my own. For Charles d'Orléans, I have used the Middle English version attributed to him when there is one; for my purposes it does not matter whether Charles actually prepared, supervised, or even reviewed the translation. I have not translated passages in modern French or in Middle English, or material cited in the notes or in the Appendix.

Introduction

Pel bruoill aug lo chan e'l refrim
E per q'om no men fassa crim
    Obre e lim
    Motz de valor
    Ab art d'Amor
Don non ai cor qe'm tuoilla.
                —Arnaut Daniel

    Vielle relique en viel satin.
              —Charles d'Orléans[1]

TWO FACTS ARE OBVIOUS to students of courtly literature: the constant union of art of love and art of poetry, and the durability of the subject of courtly love and the forms used to express it. Arnaut Daniel's words cited above were as valid for him and his contemporaries as for courtly writers in the time of Guillaume de Machaut and Jean Froissart. Courtly love was the subject demanded by an aristocratic public refined enough in taste and worldly enough in spirit to appreciate its qualities. As interest in courtly love continued, a keener awareness of the faculties of thought and sentiment became manifest in courtly poetry. No doubt the emergence of the cleric to complement and eventually to supplant to a large degree the aristocratic poet[2] facilitated accommodation and adaptation of the cognitive faculty known as *imaginatio* to courtly poetry. The success of a literature of Imagination in twelfth-century philosophical poetry influenced the authors of the twelfth- and thirteenth-century arts of poetry; from them it was borrowed by the clerical poets trained in that tradition, who wrote in the vernacular for aristocractic audiences interested in matters of courtliness and courtly love. *Ymagination* was widespread as a word and as a feature of courtly poetry by the time of Guillaume de Machaut.

The notion of Imagination has not been studied in its theoretical and practical applications to courtly literature. When scholars come across the word, they tend to treat it in the modern, Romantic sense of free, at times capricious, even foolish writing: "chasteaulz en Espaigne et en France." Imagination is a

xi

mental faculty. It governs the invention, retention, and expression of Images in the mind; it also designates the artist's Image, projected as it were into matter. I shall refer to it in this study with the capital in order to avoid confusion with its senses today.

Machaut's is the most thorough blend of the earlier theoretical and practical uses of Imagination. And his writing evinces a commitment to courtly love as subject matter. He thus epitomizes Imaginative writing before and after him, from Guillaume de Lorris and Huon de Mery through Froissart to Oton de Grandson, Chartier, and Charles d'Orléans, as well as Chaucer and Gower. These authors began with courtly love as a typical subject handed down from the twelfth century and utilized the forms and styles characteristic of the art and aesthetic of the Second Rhetoric. Although Machaut and Froissart are the central figures, Chaucer described most clearly and succinctly the essential features of Imagination.

> Now harkene wel, for-why I wille
> Tellen the a propre skille
> And a worthy demonstracion
> In myn ymagynacion.[3]

The invention of Images in courtly literature is both a *skille* and a *demonstracion*. This literature is based on techniques of argument familiar in rhetoric.

The courtly poet did not create a poem, he found its parts and put them together—he was a *trouvère*. This fact is fundamental to courtly literature, and explains both its fascination and, to a certain extent, that peculiar beauty which escapes so many modern readers. The elusive charm of the chanson and balade, a lost *merveilleux,* is accessible, it appears, only in privileged moments. "Combien de médiévistes n'ont pas éprouvé un jour l'illumination produite par un vers du XIe, du XIIe siècle où soudain, merveilleusement, pour reprendre l'image de Henry Bremond, 'le courant passe'?" Paul Zumthor continue judicieusement: "Certes, cette expérience a peu de valeur discriminatoire en elle-même, et dépend, pour une grande part, des aléas de sensibilités individuelles. Du moins nous assure-t-elle de la permanence d'un certain dynamisme; nous suggère-t-elle que l'acte poétique, au cours des siècles, n'a point changé de manière radicale; et que le mot de poésie, d'un bout à l'autre de cette histoire, s'il est équivoque, l'est moins par son sens même que par les associations différentes qu'il éveille."[4] The "univers mental nécessairement provisoire" of medieval poetry imposes on the reader applications foreign to "les associations différentes" peculiar to modern literature. Courtly love is one of those applications. The urging to *fin' amors* is itself sufficient to make most of us draw back, as if we had touched something weird and possibly perverse, which it would be embarrassing to take seriously.[5] This is the shock of "distanciation"—surely a dramatic experience!

There have been attempts to bridge the gap between medieval and modern attitudes to courtly literature. Some have argued that we cannot appreciate the poetry without its music. (Most writers until after Machaut were both poets and composers.) In Northrop Frye's opinion, music confers on abstract language an affective quality lacking in the words: "The words of a singable lyric are neutral and conventional, ready to be absorbed into a musical structure."[6] Music therefore would provide the emotional experience adumbrated by courtly language purposely abstract, intellectual, conventional. The explanation will not do. First, it is belied by medieval accounts of the experience of music and poetry. Second, anyone listening to modern recordings of balades and rondeaux may well find them aesthetically satisfying, but I have yet to meet anyone swayed by the verbal argument merely because it was sung. Furthermore, the poets themselves stress the importance of the words in judging the quality of their writing. Even *trobar clus* was meant to convey, and convey well, a significant message.[7] Dante's *De vulgari eloquentia* mentions music only in passing. This fragmentary treatise is about vernacular eloquence, not vernacular music or even lyricism, though Dante is dealing with French and Provençal poets who set their chansons to music. There are manuscripts without a note of music, or with empty staffs, as if the music had been forgotten. Most of the fixed forms in the manuscripts whose preparation Machaut himself supervised are without notes.[8] And poets after Machaut continued to use the earlier subject matter and forms, when their conventionality would suggest that something more might have been required to quicken the reader's interest in such "neutral" and "conventional" writing.

The formality and conventionality of the literature are not marks against it. When writers like Villon and Deschamps speak of things other than courtly love, we readily respond to their "greater lyricism," "sincerity," concern with "realism" and "true" art. Yet their language and forms are demonstrably formal and conventional: no literary historian has difficulty identifying their tradition. Or, to consider the question from another angle, perhaps the one poem by Jean de Garencières—a conventional, often facile poet—that may evoke ready response today is a balade describing his imprisonment.

> Mes yeux sont tournez en tristesse,
> Tant suis de plaisir desconfis;
> Car a riens je ne prens lyesse.
> Je ne voy que ras et souris;
> Poux, punaises comme formis
> Et pulces sont devant mes yeulx,
> A quoy me fault mettre delis
> En esperance d'avoir mieulx.
> (vv. 9–16)[9]

[My eyes have turned sad, so separated am I from pleasure; for I take delight in nothing. I see only rats and mice; lice and bedbugs are before my eyes like ants and fleas, wherefore I am constrained to take delight from the hope of later improvement.]

Yet beyond the fact that the poet's circumstances are more readily imagined, and perhaps inadvertantly romanticized—we like to think we understand prisons today, that to speak of them makes a poet more sincere than when he writes of noble love—there is little in these lines that is not as conventional, as clichéd as Jean de Garencière's courtly lyrics.

> Dedens l'abisme de douleur,
> Sont tourmentées les povres ames
> Des amans; et, par Dieu, mes Dames,
> Vous leur portez trop de rigueur.
> (Rondeau CXL)

[Within the abyss of sorrow the poor souls of lovers are in torment; and, in God's name, ladies, you are too harsh on them.]

Did Charles d'Orléans or his audience feel the same shock we do between the Image of the ladies and the metaphysical abyss in a single precious context?

Perhaps then our ears are no longer attuned to the formal perfection attained by the *trouvères* and the poets of the Second Rhetoric. It would follow that retuning our ears to subtle semantic resonances or variations in form should enhance our appreciation of this poetry as pure poetry.[10] We are often more aware of similarities than of differences among courtly poems. A considerable effort is required to recognize subtle nuances, let alone enjoy them, in reading successive poems. Even scholars who have studied these poems long and carefully, and are therefore aware of their variations, confess that the pleasure found in reading them is fugitive, their subtleties rarely satisfying. How many medievalists spend an evening reading Machaut or Froissart? Yet Pierre Bec is surely correct in asserting that "il n'y a pas d'art sans échelle de valeurs et le lecteur moderne, retrouvant les anciennes lignes de clivage, peut et doit arriver aisément à une discrimination esthétique qui ne soit pas anachronique."[11] And indeed, the question of reading pleasure does not confront us for Renaissance, Metaphysical, or Baroque poetry.

I suggest that our difficulties derive from the universality of courtly love as subject matter in, by medieval standards, the best vernacular poetry. It is not the conventional language of the poetry, but our indifference and, in some quarters, aversion to courtly love that impedes our appreciation of the finesse of *fin' amors*. Yet the emphasis on courtly love is a historical fact in the canso and the chanson, just as it is in the balade, rondeau, and virelai. Dante's addition of prowess in arms and moral fortitude in the *De vulgari eloquentia*[12] is a desideratum hardly met by the French and Provençal poets who inspired the treatise. *Fin' amors* is the subject par excellence of courtly poetry.

Why did medieval poets choose to express love as such a high aspiration? The question touches on a historic and literary, and psychological, phenomenon so prominent as to cry out for understanding. There is no longer an aristocracy in the medieval sense, and the bourgeoisie does not seek to emulate it. Love today, besides having been fixed by Romantic notions, no doubt for a long time to come, only seems to confirm Andreas Capellanus' opinion that courtly love is for the high-born few. That statement is not a value judgment. It recognizes the separation between us and the courtly mentality. Such separations are legitimate subjects for historical and philological study. For courtly love was certainly no passing fad, romantic aberration, or Byzantine solemnity preserved for its own sake. It was a durable, and thus serviceable, aristocratic ideal. Indeed, its durability suggests that a profound human need continued to be met and satisfied by *fin' amors*. Perhaps its significance is finally accessible only by reference to some unconscious stratum in the human mind, a level on which "le courant passe."

But there are reasons other than different mentalities and psychic regions for our consternation before this poetry. The expression *courtly love* has been misunderstood and misused, largely because of the laudable desire to clarify it by definition and identification of the rules peculiar to its art. In this we forget that love is more an idea than a concept, and that an art is a skill, not an etiquette or a book of manners.

Imagination is a fundamental feature of the conception of art prevalent from the twelfth to the fifteenth century. It is particularly striking in dealing with courtly love. My purpose here is, first, to describe the character and origins of the art of courtly literature in its poetic, amorous, and, to a lesser extent, musical manifestations. Second, in studies of Guillaume de Lorris, the Second Rhetoric, and the decline of late medieval poetic art, I shall describe further the salient characteristics and principal styles and modes of courtly literature that uses Imagination. The stress on courtly love accounts for the absence or relative subordination of authors like Jean de Meun, Rutebeuf, Deschamps, and Villon, despite the fact that Imagination is a feature of their art. To that extent my choice of material is selective. To include these authors any more than has been done would burst the bounds of an already long and complex subject, and destroy its conceptual unity as well.

The inclusion of the Latin beginnings of courtly literature—Chartrain thought and literature, classical and medieval rhetoric, the medieval arts of poetry, Andreas Capellanus—is justified by their seminal influence on the art of the French writers, particularly their use of an aesthetic founded largely on Imagination. Their influence would be just as prominent on the literary tradition represented by Jean de Meun, Rutebeuf, Deschamps, and Villon. But the two traditions make different adaptations in conformity with their different subjects. Of course, there is much of Jean de Meun's esprit in Christine de Pisan and Chartier, as well as in the English writers who belong to the tradition of the Second Rhetoric; they do not consider their amorous works to be their most significant writing. It is noteworthy that they contribute more to the breakdown of the courtly tradition than to its maintenance, despite their efforts to keep love as a living ideal in aristocratic society.

The mode adopted in later courtly literature has commonly been termed allegory, and the works abstract and commonplace. No doubt these designations are accurate enough. "Si nous voulons, en effet, comprendre l'usage qui est fait de l'allégorie, il faut se référer à une conception du monde unitaire, qui cherche à tous les niveaux de l'être la ressemblance, et considère celle-ci non comme une simple vue de l'esprit, une perspective, mais comme une participation réciproque à une commune réalité."[13] The essential characteristic of such allegory is the comparison of two intersecting semantic planes. The intersection constitutes a *tertium quid,* the *tertium comparationis* that makes allegory possible and, by its cogency, effective. No wonder that this common element became the focus of concentrated attention, and the literature remarkable for abstraction transcending not only individuality and originality, but also the two intersecting planes which realize the allegory. The mental process by which this is possible is Imagination. Imagination is a function of memory, and as such it is part and parcel of prudence. Alain de Lille shows Prudence capable of transcending the different levels of the universe to bear Nature's message to the Divinity. The return of Prudence leads to the invention of a new, perfect man. That man's struggle, a psychomachia of good and evil qualities, measures the man's potentialities for good and evil and suggests a hierarchy of possibilities for achievement. The new human being styles a whole literature by his perfection.

Medieval Imagination

1

Rhetoric and Poetry

THE SECOND RHETORIC

The Second Rhetoric covered vernacular prosody.[1] Just as the *artes versificatoriae* taught the principles of Latin versification in the medieval classroom, so did the *arts de dictier* provide the nobility with the rudiments of verse writing in French.[2] As such they were by and large manuals for amateurs. But amateurs were eager to write in the new forms because remarkable poets had perfected them, inspiring study and imitation. Guillaume de Machaut had a decisive influence on the Second Rhetoric. The last of the great poet-composers, he lifted fixed forms like the balade, rondeau, virelai, and lai above the secondary level to which Dante consigned them in the *De vulgari eloquentia* and gave them a prominence they retained through the fourteenth and fifteenth centuries in France. Like the canso and chanson, the balade after Machaut was *nobillissima* because it possessed "illud . . . quod totam comprehendit artem" (II.iii.8) [that which comprehends the art in its entirety].

Machaut's conception of art embraces the three traditional prerequisites to mastery: *natura, ars,* and *exercitatio*.[3] He presents his ideas and elaborates on them in the opening lines to the *Remede de Fortune:*

> Armes, amours, autre art ou lettre.
> Car chose ne puet si forte estre,
> S'il vuet, qu'il n'en deveingne mestre,
> Mais qu'il vueille faire et labeure
> Ad ce que j'ay dit ci desseure.
> *(Remede, vv. 40–44)[4]*

[Arms, love, or any art or kind of writing. For no subject can be so difficult but that one may become master of it, given the will to do so, and the desire to achieve and labor at those things I have indicated heretofore.]

Machaut's discussion is therefore applicable to the arts of music, poetry, and love.

By *natura,* or *ingenium,* Machaut understands natural talent, inborn inclination. The artist should practice that art "ou ses cuers mieus se tire / Et ou sa

3

nature l'encline" (*Remede,* vv. 4–5) [to which his preference goes, and towards which he is naturally inclined]. *Ars* as technique requires instruction or "doctrine" (*Remede,* v. 16) from a competent master. In return the master may expect love (v. 9), honor, obedience, and service (v. 11), all proffered with humility (v. 16). The training and practice demand effort and perseverence (vv. 18–20). "Soing, penser, desir de savoir" (v. 21) [care, application, a desire to know], as well as an early start in study (v. 23), complete the summary of prerequisites for mastery in an art.

Machaut's *Prologue* applies this skeletal plan to the arts most important for the Second Rhetoric: poetry, music, and love. As one of Machaut's last compositions,[5] the *Prologue* represents a mature consideration of the arts he practiced most. The work has two principal parts. In the first, Nature and Love in turn present their gifts to the poet in four elegantly constructed balades. In the second part, the poet reflects and elaborates upon these gifts in rhymed octosyllabic couplets.

Thus Machaut places his work under the aegis of Nature and Love. Nature provides him with the poetic skills: *scens, retorique,* and *musique.* Love furnishes the subject matter: *dous penser, plaisance,* and *esperance.* Machaut provided a complete and systematic analysis of love in the *Remede.* He considered love to be the only subject worthy of his poetry, and the *Remede* became inspirational and decisive for the Second Rhetoric because of its authoritative examples of the prominent fixed forms.[6] He generalizes in expressing thanks to Love in the *Prologue* for her gifts:

> Vous et vos enfans moult esclarci
> M'avez ces fais que j'ay a ordener,
> Pour lesquels arriere tous mis
> Seront autres, puis qu'a ce sui commis,
> N'a autres fais jamais jour n'entendray.
> (IV, vv. 13–17)

[You and your children have greatly clarified the subjects that I am to treat, for which all others will be put aside, given that I am committed to this one; and I shall apply myself to nothing else.]

Machaut's opus bears out the truth of these lines. Only love makes his writing worthwhile: "Et s'a autre chose pensoie, / Toute mon oeuvre defferoie" (V, vv. 41–42) [And were I to consider any other subject, I should undo all my work]. Thus, by dint of perseverence, the poet strives to gain the approbation of the ladies, those high arbiters of taste and excellence for whom he writes (V, vv. 176–80). Even his religious poems are directed to the Virgin Mary. To understand and appreciate Machaut and his peers, we therefore must attend to their arts of poetry, music, and love.

Dante defines poetry as "fictio retorica musicaque poita" (II.iv.2) [rhetorical invention set to music]. Brunetto Latini, Dante's mentor, stands at the watershed between the trouvères and the Second Rhetoric. As rhetoric, he could take up the composition of the chanson together with the art of letter-writing in a discussion based on Cicero and Geoffrey of Vinsauf. In all the specific applications of rhetoric, he asserts, the great thing is to persuade or dissuade.[7] Just as the epistle is written to argue for or against some proposition or action, so is "la chançons dont li uns amans parole a l'autre autresi com s'il fust devant lui a la contençon. . . . Et tous contens sont apertenant a rectorique" (*Tresors,* p. 322) [the chanson by which one lover speaks to another, as if standing before him in debate. . . . And all debates come under rhetoric]. Brunetto Latini is more detailed in his Italian treatise *La Rettorica,* but nothing fundamental in the statement in the *Tresors* is changed. To illustrate the *tencone,* he refers to the fact that "uno amante chiamando merzè alla sua donna dice parole e ragioni molte, et ella si difende in suo dire et inforza le sue ragioni et indebolisce quelle del pregatore" (p. 101) [one lover asking mercy of his lady proffers many words and arguments, and she defends herself by her words and supports her own reasonings while weakening those of her suitor]. Thus the poet "intende ad alcuna cosa che vuole che sia fatta per colui a cui è la manda. Et questo puote essere o pregando o domandando o comandando o minacciando o confortando o consigliando; e in ciascuno di questi modi puote quelli a cui vae . . . la canzone o negare o difendersi per alcuna scusa" (pp. 101–2) [strives for something that he wishes to have done by the one he addresses. And he may do so by entreaty, request, command, threat, comfort, or compromise; and in each of these ways the recipient of the chanson may refuse or defend herself through some justification]. This is precisely what one discovers in Machaut's *Voir-Dit,* as well as in clusters of two or three poems he constructed as exchanges between a lover and his lady in *La louange des dames.*

The *Voir-Dit* recounts a love that includes exchanges of letters and poems. Both the man and the woman take part in the exchanges, and the style, commonplaces, and situations are conventional. Errors, fears, complaints are evident on both sides. The sole distinction between Machaut's correspondence and poetry and that attributed to Péronne d'Armentières is the author's sex: the poems by Péronne are *chansons feminines.* But she is hardly the modern stereotype of the silent lady atop a pedestal (a figure rarely found as such in romance or chronicle, and perhaps not really intended in most shorter verse), but one of the two lovers. The silent one is usually on a pedestal, always a threat to the person writing, a hyperbolic representation conforming to the excellence attributed to the loved one by the lover. In the *Voir-Dit,* whatever the sex of the writer, the love poem is an expression of sorrow and joy, of entreaty, argument, or self-defense. The rhetorical character of such poetry will permit the composition of poetic exchanges between two lovers. Christine de Pisan will make such exchanges into narrative cycles.

Machaut's fixed forms offer incipient exchanges between two persons.[8]

5

The poems are distinguished according to the circumstances of composition and the sex of the author: *chanson desesperee, balade de desconfort, lai de plour, chanson feminine.* Each satisfies a rhetorical intention.

> Certes mes dous amis fu nez
> En aoust, je ne m'en doubt mie,
> Car il est de tous deboutés,
> Et s'a valour et courtoisie,
> Et dignes est d'avoir amie,
> N'il n'a en li que reprochier:
> Pour ce l'aim je de cuer entier.
>
> (Bal. XC, vv. 1–7)

[Surely my sweet love was born in August—I doubt it not—for everyone rejects him despite his valor and courtesy; and he is worthy of a sweetheart, for he is in no way blameworthy. That is why I love him with all my heart.]

The shifting situations allow for variant elaborations dependent on the obligations felt by the writer towards Love—including the responsibility to the honor of one's sex—and the need to argue one's case through the poem. For example, a lady asserts in Balade CCLIV:

> il n'apartient que dame à son ami
> Doie mercy ne grace demander;
> Car dame doit en riant refuser
> Et amis doit prier en souspirant.
>
> (vv. 33–36)

[It is not proper for a lady to ask mercy or grace from the man she loves; for a lady is supposed to refuse with a smile, and the lover beseech while sighing.]

But the argument becomes merely a foil for her inability to adhere to her role, and strong evidence of the sincerity of the entreaties she lapses into in spite of herself.

> Et je te pri souvent et en plourant.
> Mais en toy truis, quant plus sui esplourée,
> Cuer de marbre couronné d'aymant,
> Ourlé de fer, à la pointe asserée.
>
> (vv. 37–40)

[And I beg you often and in tears for your love. But in you I discover, when most tearful, a marble heart crowned with diamond, ringed with iron, with a steel point.]

This is a refreshing variant to the lady on a pedestal. Her appeal anticipates the appeals of ladies in Christine de Pisan's cycles. But her comportment is not remarkably different from that of men in "masculine" poems. Both Bernart de Ventadorn and the Countess de Dia would have recognized that in rhetoric every commonplace includes its opposite.

6

Recognition of the place of rhetoric in medieval poetics still leaves open the problem of music in the lyric verse. Indeed, the rhetorical function of moving an assumed audience appears to have something in common with the function of music. What relationship obtained between the musical and the rhetorical in medieval chansons and balades?

MUSIC AND RHETORIC

The only important difference lies in the sad situation that those who collected troubadour chansons seem to have had less interest in collecting the melodies along with the poems.

—Hendrik van der Werf[9]

The rhetorical entreaty points to an apparent contradiction in Machaut's *Prologue*—and it brings us to the art of music as well. While allowing that a poem may contain "matiere dolereuse" (V,v. 79), Machaut denies that music does: "Partout ou elle est, joie y porte" (v. 91) [Everywhere it brings joy in its train]. Music, "divers et deduisans" [varied and entertaining], makes the *faits,* the poems, "frique" (I, vv. 14–16) [lively]. Even when the words are melancholy or sad, the music lightens the air and diffuses joy. But, as the notes are played and the words pronounced, may one feel joy and sadness at the same time? What is the relation between verbal and musical expression in Machaut's poetry?

Attempts have been made to resolve the problem in favor of one art or the other.[10] Or a historical solution is proposed: for Machaut and his predecessors, who were composers, the music was fundamental, whereas with Deschamps and Froissart, who did not write music, the word came into its own.[11]

Several facts militate against such simple, decisive solutions to the problems. First, for the majority of the fixed forms by Machaut himself there is no music, nor is any space left in the manuscripts for music to be added, even in manuscripts whose copying he supervised.[12] It would appear that he envisaged some poems being sung, but not all or even most of them. Or rather, as in the *Prologue,* he foresaw the possibility of both reading and singing. An example from the *Remede de Fortune* makes this point implicitly. The lai in that dit is set to music in the manuscripts; however, Machaut *reads* it to his lady in the text.

> Tant que par aventure avint
> Qu'en sa presence cils lais vint
> (Et venus y estoie aussi,
> Dont j'os puis assez de soussi)
> Qu'elle me commanda au *lire.*
> Si ne li osay escondire,
> Eins li *lus* tout de chief en chief,

7

> A cuer tramblant, enclin le chief,
> Doubtans qu'il n'i eüst meffait,
> Pour ce que je l'avoie fait.
> Et quant je li os tout *leü*
> Et elle l'ot bien conceü,
> Me demanda qui fait l'avoit.
>
> (vv. 689–701; emphasis mine)

[Until, as chance would have it, this lai happened to come before her (and I was present as well, which caused me subsequently a great deal of trouble), and she requested that I read it. And I dared not refuse; rather, I read it from beginning to end, my heart aflutter, my head bowed, fearing lest it contain something improper—for I was the author! And when I had read it through and she had grasped its contents, she asked me who wrote it.]

There is reason in his reading the poem when sad or fearful; for music, to Machaut's mind, is joyful, and could not express fear and anxiety.

> Et mes cuers moult s'y deduisoit,
> Quant ma dame a ce me duisoit
> Qu'a sa loange et a s'onnour
> Me faisoit chanter pour s'amour.
> Car chanters est nez de leëce
> De cuer.
>
> (*Remede*, vv. 419–424)

[And I derived sincere pleasure whenever my lady brought me to sing out of love her praises and her honor. For singing is born of heartfelt joy.]

Moreover, it is not true that after Machaut the poets no longer concerned themselves with music. Even Charles d'Orléans may have intended the chansons—as distinguished from the rondeaux—in his autograph to be set to music.[13]

Froissart is the best example of a poet who was not a composer but who wished some of his poems to be both read and sung:

> A ma dame vint li recors
> Dou virelay que je recors:
> Bien li pleut, si le volt avoir,
> Che dist, pour aprendre et savoir.
> Elle l'aprist et le chanta.[14]

[The virelai I have copied came to be recited before my lady; it pleased her greatly, and she wanted a copy, she said, in order to learn and know it. She did learn it and she sang it.]

Later he explains how this was possible: the poem was set to a known melody (*Prison amoureuse*, vv. 963–70).[15] In this scene, a counterpart to that in

Machaut's *Remede,* the poet who is not a composer has his poem sung. Hence in both Froissart and Machaut one perceives an awareness of two functions, musical and poetic. The music predominates on festive, joyful occasions when large numbers of persons are present for song and dance (*Prison amoureuse,* vv. 400–411); the poem itself is for more solitary, retrospective, or introspective moments, or for communication.

The two purposes may even contrast dramatically.

> La fu mon virelay cantés
> Et moult volentiers escoutés.
> Mes a painnes peut il fin prendre,
> Quant ma dame en volt un reprendre
> Qu'onques mes je n'avoie oï.
> Mes noient ne me resjoï,
> Ains me fist merancoliier;
> Pour ce ne le puis oubliier;
> Bien le retins, mieuls le notai,
> Encor ens ou coer le note ai.
>
> (*Prison amoureuse,* vv. 419–28)

[There my virelai was sung and listened to willingly. But it had hardly come to an end when my lady wished to hear one performed which I had never heard. But it did not please me at all, but rather made me melancholy. That's why I can't forget it; I remembered and marked it well, and the music is still ringing in my memory.]

The virelai describes the satisfaction a lady takes in her *ami*'s melancholy, because she believes he derives contentment from dreams and sweet thoughts. This explains the contrast between the effect of the music on everyone but the lover, and the effect of the words on him.

> Tout chil et chelles qui oïrent
> Che virelay s'en resjoïrent,
> Et fu moult grandement prisiés;
> Mes je voel que vous escripsiés:
> Onques ne me peut resjoïr.
>
> (vv. 461–65)

[All who heard that virelai liked it, and it was highly esteemed; but you may record: it can never please me.]

The words of these songs, as abstract and impersonal as they may seem, had significance for private lives, or at least were credible in an appropriate context. It could be when the listener took to heart the words of another's poem:

> Je le lisi sans plus d'atente
> Et grandement y mis m'entente
> Pour ce qu'elle assés s'arestoit

9

> Sus la matere qui m'estoit,
> Selonch mon fet, vive et propisce,
> Sans empecement et sans visce.
> (vv. 707–12)

[I read it without delay and applied myself to it diligently, for it dwelt at length on the subject which was real and appropriate for my circumstances, without hindrance and without fault.]

Or when the lover composed his own poem:

> Encores entrepris a faire
> Un lay, quoi que fust dou parfaire,
> Selonc le matere et le tamps
> Le quel j'estoie adont sentans.
> (vv. 2122–25)

[I undertook again to write a lai, however it might succeed, in conformity with the subject and the atmosphere that fitted my feelings at that time.]

The situations are contrived, but there is no reason to suppose that they are not representative of actual practice. Rather, they reflect and enlarge upon circumstances discernible in the arts of the Second Rhetoric, which are practical guides to the composition of love poems. The oldest such art, Deschamps' *Art de dictier,* will serve as an illustration.

Deschamps distinguishes between *musique artificiele* and *musique naturele.* The former is music stricto sensu: music as the art of composing in notes for instruments or singing. The latter is the art of the spoken word, or rhetoric, and therefore distinct from music as such (or in Deschamps at least, derivative from it and therefore separable). It is not taught as an art, but rather springs from an inner urge to verbal expression (*naturele*). It is poetry "de volunté amoureuse a la louenge des dames, et en autres manieres, selon les materes et le sentement de ceuls qui en ceste musique s'appliquent" (pp. 270–71) [of amorous intention in praise of ladies, and in other ways, fitting the subjects and the feelings of those who apply themselves to this kind of music]. Deschamps is therefore concerned with eloquence, not song: "Les faiseurs d'icelle ne saichent pas communement la musique artificielle ne donner chant par art de notes a ce qu'ilz font, toutesvoies est appellée musique ceste science naturele, pour ce que les diz et chançons par eulz faiz ou les livres metrifiez se lisent de bouche, et proferent par voix non pas chantable" (p. 271) [The latter writers do not usually know artificial music, nor how to make song by musical composition for what they write; nonetheless this natural knowledge is called music because the words and songs they write, or their books in verse, are read aloud and uttered by a voice that does not sing]. In fact, the puys and other poetic contests required dual presentation of poems submitted for competition, first as song, then as eloquence: "Portoient chascun ce que fait avoit devant le *Prince du puys,* et le recordoit par cuer, et ce recort estoit appellé *en disant,* après qu'ilz avoient chanté leur chançon devant le Prince" (p. 271) [Everyone brought what he had written before the Prince of the poetic contest, and recited it by heart, and such recitation was termed *by speaking,* after they had sung their song before the Prince]. *Musique artificiele* lends itself to public performance, whereas *naturele* is more intimate, suitable for communication of sentiments and desires or for private expression of joy, distress, or consolation (p. 272). Such poetry conforms to the rhetorical function described by Brunetto Latini; it fits the example of Machaut reading the lai to his lady in the *Remede;* and it is confirmed by the practice illustrated in the romances and dits that incorporate short pieces into their narrative.[16]

Music is therefore not essential to the enjoyment or appreciation of thought and sentiment in the poetry of the Second Rhetoric, nor is it ancillary to the art of poetry. Rather it is a parallel and independently valid art. One may listen to the poem for its music, which is conducive to joy. Or one may listen to the poem for its rhetoric, which is meant to direct thought and sway emotions.

The third gift from Nature in Machaut's *Prologue* is *scens.*[17] Nature describes *scens* as that which provides the subject matter of the poem: "Par Scens aras ton engin enfourmé / De tout ce que tu vorras confourmer" (I, vv. 10–11) [With *Scens* your mind will be provided with all that you may wish to express in verse]. It describes the capacity for topical invention. Hence *scens* is "matere a faire ce que Nature li a enchargié" (III, p. 4) [subject matter with which to write what Nature has imposed upon him]. In limiting *scens* to the sole subject of love, Machaut is in fact fixing the parameters of his own invention. His *scens* contrasts with that of Deschamps, for example.

From the formal point of view, Machaut construes rhetoric as metrics. He stresses the ornamental and technical quality of versification suitable to the fixed forms illustrated in the *Remede.* This sets the scope of the treatises of the Second Rhetoric. There is a description of rhetoric in the first *Prologue* balade: "Retorique n'ara riens enfermé / Que ne t'envoit en metre et en rimer" (I, vv. 12–13) [Rhetoric will contain nothing which she fails to commit to you in metrics and in rhyme]. Subsequently, Machaut mentions the usual fixed forms: lais, motets, rondeaux, virelais, complaintes, balades (*Prologue* V, vv. 13–16). But with the balade he introduces a certain flourish: "balades entées," that is, balades using a rondeau as refrain. The variety represents a *maniere joieuse* corresponding to rhetoric's pleasing and instructive argumentation:

> Retorique versefier
> Fait l'amant et metrefier,
> Et si fait faire jolis vers
> Nouviaus et de metres divers.
> (V, vv. 147–50)

[Rhetoric makes the lover write in verse and meter, and compose poems that are diversified and in varied meters.]

Rhyme may therefore be "serpentine," "equivoque" "leonine," "croisie," "retrograde;" embellishment by tropes and figures provides "maniere plaisant et sage" (V, vv. 151–58). This is not the joy associated with music, but the satisfaction derived from hearing a case argued with distinction and elegance. One need not be judge, jury, or defendant to apprehend the quality of the argument, any more than one need live under the Roman Republic to appreciate Cicero's orations. Though the poem is ostensibly written for one person, it may well be applicable to many who find the situation, sentiments, or manner of expression pleasing. Thus the poem written for a specific lady will redound to the honor of all ladies (V, vv. 17–23)[18] Nonetheless personal sentiment is the point of departure: "Car qui de sentement ne fait, / Son ouevre et son chant contrefait" (Remede, vv. 407–8) [For he who does not write from a sincere heart falsifies his work and his song]. That would be sophistry.

With the exception of the Confort d'ami, the best of Machaut's dits and most of his short pieces are written for love and for ladies. Nature, he says, made him "a part, pour faire par toy fourmer / Nouviaus dis amoureus plaisans" (Prologue I, vv. 4–5) [different, so that you might compose new and pleasing poems about love]. The rhetorical intention in the fixed forms is sustained in the dits. The Jugement dou roy de Behaingne and the Jugement dou roy de Navarre present full-scale debates; the more philosophical and moral dits like the Remede and the Fonteinne amoureuse synthesize argument in abstract or universal terms. The rhetoric brings us to the problem of the relation between the art of love and the art of poetry. For, as we know from Andreas Capellanus, elocutio is essential to both.[19] Pertinent to the study of that relation is the subject of allegory, and, more specifically, of Imagination as applied to courtly love.

2

Allegory of Love

Sapienter amare poterimus, quod tamen rarum est, cum quidam
dixerit: 'quis unquam sapienter amavit?' Nos vere sapienter amare
poterimus.
           —*Epistolae duorum amantium*

For loves lawe is out of reule.
      —Gower, *Confessio amantis*[1]

MUCH OF THE CONFUSION and disagreement about what may be termed allegory of love, or, more precisely, the use of the allegorical mode to represent courtly love, derives from confusion and disagreement as to what allegory and courtly love are. At the root of the problem is the desire to reduce each to a single concept, a clean and neat definition. However, allegory was a polysemous term in the Middle Ages.[2] A number of modern notions of allegory and courtly love add to the confusion. And there is now an effort to deny that allegory was used for purposes other than moral and theological ones, and that courtly love is applicable as a term to medieval literature. Yet there was an expression *fin'amors*[3] in medieval French, and there were corresponding synonyms; other medieval languages had analogous terms. The modern English equivalent for all of them is courtly love, the modern French *amour courtois*. I shall therefore use the term courtly love for the different meanings attributable to *fin'amors* as eros.[4]

Medieval French literature constantly brings up *fin'amors* and its cognates, not only in works usually considered courtly, like romance and chanson, but also in farce and fabliau, and in a variety of contexts ranging from love for Christ and the Virgin Mary through friendship, conjugal affection, and courtly love to infatuation, passion, and lust. We must therefore determine the distinctive characteristics of *fin'amors* in its usual sense of courtly love. The medieval theory of material style will assist us here.

Material style was a misuse of the classical theory of the three styles. It stressed the quality of *matière* as determined by its relative "nobility" in specific class terms. Dante incorporated material style into a classification of subjects based on hierarchical notions of excellence derived from Aristotelian thought and the poetry of the troubadours and the trouvères. He found three *matières* suitable for the most noble poetry: prowess in arms, love, and moral fortitude. The three covered the tragic style, the *superior stylus* of the poets (*De vulgari eloquentia* II.iv.5). This style is appropriate only for noble love, corresponding to modern notions of courtly love and also the *fin' amors* of the French and Provençal chanson. Dante is following the medieval idea that qualitative differences in style correspond to real class distinctions. As Richart de Fornival alleges, "li cuer des amans doivent estre plain de noblece"[5] [the lovers' hearts must be full of nobility].

FIN'AMORS AS COURTLY LOVE

Current difficulties with the expression courtly love arise from two contrary tendencies in contemporary scholarship. The more traditional one seeks a definition and a code for courtly love covering, with hardly any latitude for variation in detail, all important amorous writing typically classified as courtly, such as romance, chansons, narrative and lyric lais, etc.[6] The expression is thus taken to be a term. The other tendency is to question the utility of the concept courtly love for medieval literature, seeing in it a misleading expression better dropped from serious critical discussion.[7] Both tendencies are essentially reductionist, based upon the tacit assumption that there is, or should have been, a common, explicit meaning for *fin' amors* from the twelfth into the fifteenth century, when it was current in French. In fact, thinking on courtly love in those centuries was quite subtle, supple, and diversified.[8]

The author of the Commentary on the verse *Echecs amoureux,* surveying the subject and literature of love from a fifteenth-century vantage point, admits a variety of ways in which it may be understood. In the poem itself, Diane urges the more nearly chaste love extolled by Geoffrey of Monmouth, Wace, and Andreas Capellanus, and typical of the best Arthurian romance.

> Car selon ce que nous ensaigne
> L'istoire de la Grant Bretaigne,
> Les cheualiers qui lors s'armoyent
> Lëaument par amours amoient
> Les dames et les damoiselles.
> Les dames auoient lors [*sic*]
> Les cuers de si noble franchise
> Que dame, tant fust fort requise
> Ne tant le sceuïst on proyer,
> Ne daignast s'amour ottroyer
> A cheualier tant fust vaillans,
> S'il ne fust si bien bateillans
> C'om l'euïst esprouué anchois
> Es fais d'armes aumains trois fois.[9]

[For according to what the history of Great Britain tells us, the knights who then bore arms loved their ladies and maidens faithfully and in courtly fashion. Ladies then had hearts of such nobility and aristocracy that none of them, no matter how much she might be courted or suited, would deign to grant her love to any knight, however worthy he might be, who had not fought so well that he had proven his mettle at least thrice in combat.]

The Commentator glosses this passage in discussing love in Arthurian romance: "Et ne doit mie estre oublié que l'acteur en son livre dont nous parlons n'entent pas a reprendre la bonne amour loable et honnourable, mais tant seullement l'amour folle ou les amans ont trop desraisonnablement l'ueil a charnel delict et le cuer et l'entente"[10] [And you must not forget that the author, in the book we are treating, has no intention of berating love that is good, praiseworthy, and honorable, but only foolish love wherein the lovers fix their attention immoderately on carnal delight]. He then divides love into three kinds (fols. 296v–297v). First is carnal love, "amour... commune au monde" whose principal goal is "delict," the "amour folle" condemned in the preceding citation. Second is conjugal love. Third is *fin'amors,* which is like "l'amour qui est et qui doit estre en mariage, combien qu'elle puist moult bien estre entre personnes frances qui par amours s'entreayment" [love which is and ought properly to be conjugal, although it may well exist between single persons who love in courtly fashion]. The Commentator then discusses the merits of *fin'amors:* "Et de ceste amour voulons nous quant a present parler, et l'aultre amour laissier qui en mariage a son lieu" [And we wish to speak for now of the last kind of love, setting aside conjugal love for the time being]. For him good lovers "ayment et premierement leurs amyes pour le bien qu'ilz voyent en elles comme sont beaulté et simplece et les aultres graces plaisans qui a amour attrayent, et le delit apres secondement" [love their sweethearts principally for the qualities they see in them, like beauty, sincerity, and all the other pleasing qualities that inspire love, and only secondarily for carnal delight]. The Commentator's classification is by no means unique.[11]

   Huon de Mery distinguishes between fornication and love "sanz vilanie" in the *Tornoiement Antecrist.*

> Par cest mot fornicacïon
> Ici nule descripcïon
> Ne vos en faz, par foi je non:
> Amours n'a pas si vilein non!
> Non! C'amours nest de courtoisie.
> D'amor, qui est sanz vilanie,
> Aillors est la descripcïon.
>   (vv. 1057–63)[12]

[By the word fornication I do not designate it in any way, no indeed! Love's name is not so villainous. No! For love is born of courtesy. Of love that is not villainous you will find the description elsewhere.]

That description, beginning in verse 1713, allies Love with Proesse, Cortoisie, and Largesse; Love leads Proesse, as in Arthurian history, and all three provide Love with arms.[13] "L'escu a une passe rose / Asise sour or floreté" (vv. 1726–27)[14] [The shield bears a "rose surpassing" set in flowered gold]. Huon stresses the close relation between Cortoisie and Love, a relation essential to Love's place in the army of Christ.

> Pour ce, se j'ai amour descrit
> Ci entre la gent Jhesu Crit,
> N'est il mie toz jours des suens,
> Fors tant com il est fins et buens,
> Si comme en maint païs avient:
> Ce que l'en doit, ce qu'il convient,
> Doit l'en amer courtoisement.
> Qui aime bien et lëaument,
> Il est de la gent courtoisie,
> Ou se ce non, il n'en est mie.
> (vv. 1813–22)

[Although I have described love as being in the army of Jesus Christ, he is not always on His side, but only when he is courtly and good, as happens in many a country. Where it is proper and suitable, one is to love in courtly fashion. He who loves well and faithfully is in the army of courtesy; otherwise, he has no place in that army.]

Such "courtly loving" opens Christ's ranks to the knights of the Round Table; like the author of the *Echecs amoureux,* Huon de Mery perceives their love not as *fole amor* (vv. 1975–2030), but as the superior *fin'amors* deriving from Cortoisie. That is, courtly love.

However, when Venus and Cupid unite to uphold fornication—when we pass, as it were, from the world of Guillaume de Lorris to that of Jean de Meun—the quality of love changes from an expression of Courtesy to foolish surrender to carnality. The new context changes the affective value of the abstractions as they enter into new configurations. Esperance is virtually lust (vv. 2657–63), and thus quite different from her appearance later as hope for salvation (vv. 2986–90). The tale of the now hapless lover is no longer "fins et buens": it has become a farce, and the story of the lover's foolishness while serving Venus and Cupid in the name of fornication and despairing hope is laughable (vv. 3298–3311).[15] Like Andreas Capellanus before him, Huon de Mery makes qualitative distinctions among different kinds of love. He eschews the condemnation in Andreas' third book, since the criticism of love in the *Tornoiement* is directed against *fole amor,* not *fin'amors.* Of course, this may be true of Andreas' condemnation as well.[16]

Huon de Mery includes Lancelot among the knights of the Round Table fighting on Christ's side (vv. 1991 and 2343). He and Andreas make distinctions among lovers which parallel the loves of Lancelot in the Lancelot-

Grail prose cycle:(1) *amor mixtus* with Guenevere in the *Lancelot* Proper; (2) *amor purus* with the "demoiselle guérisseuse," also in the *Lancelot* Proper;[17] (3) *amor simplex* or *fole amor* with Guenevere in the *Mort Artu;*[18] (4) a kind of conjugal relation with the daughter of King Pelles, by whom he begets Galaad, ignorant of what he is doing and for the sole purpose of procreation;[19] and (5) *caritas* sublimating his love for Guenevere in favor of service to God in the *Queste* and, perhaps, the conclusion to the *Mort Artu.*[20] His affection for Galaad is paternal.[21] A review of most of the other knights in the cycle would reveal this same hierarchical scheme. The distinctions within the Arthurian frame are no doubt what the authors of the *Echecs amoureux* and its Commentary have in mind when they associate *fin'amors* with conjugal love even when adulterous.[22]

Between the composition of the *Echecs amoureux* and its Commentary, Christine de Pisan criticized what she considered the one-sided view of love in Jean de Meun's continuation of the *Roman de la rose:* "Puis qu'il [Jean] vouloit descripre entierement amours, il ne la deust mettre si extreme a une seule fin, voire fin si deshonnestement touchiee"[23] [Since he (Jean) wished to describe love fully, he should not have reduced it to a single purpose, and indeed a purpose treated so outrageously]. She countered with contemporary examples conforming to what the *Echecs* Commentator calls *fin'amors.*

Et ainsi cuides tu que je croye tous ceulz, qui ont esté ou sont bien amoreux, que toute leur felicité soit de tendre a couchier auec leur dames. Certes ce ne croys ie mie, car ie croy que pluseurs ont amé loiaument et parfaictement qui oncques n'y couchierent, ne oncques deceurent ne furent deceuz, de qui estoit principale entencion que leurs meurs en vaulsissent mieulx. Et pour celle amour deuenoient vaillans et bien renommez et tant que en leur viellesce ilz louoient dieu qu'ilz auoient esté amoreux. (p. 94, ll. 446-54)

[And thus you presume me to believe that all who have been or are truly in love find their entire happiness in striving to lie with their ladies. I certainly do not believe this to be so, but rather that a goodly number have loved faithfully and wholly who never lay with them, nor ever deceived or were deceived; and whose principal purpose in loving was to render their conduct more worthy. And for that love they became valiant and renowned, so much so that in their old age they praised God for having loved.]

Her assertion that love may be good reiterates a commonplace going back to Geoffrey of Monmouth and Geffrei Gaimar. It recalls the ideal of *amor sapiens* which Andreas Capellanus raised above *amor simplex* and *nimia voluptatis abundantia.*[24] In the quarrel itself, Christine distinguished between the two parts of the *Rose* on the basis of their representations of love. Jean Gerson supported her reading of the two parts of the *Rose.*

Ne fu pas un mesme acteur, ainçois fu cil sur le commencement du quel cest acteur de qui je parle edifia tout son ouvrage; pieça les fondemens estoient gettez par le premier, et de sa propre main et matiere, sans mendier çà et la, et sans y assembler telle vilté de boe et de flache puante et orde, comme est mise ou soumillon de cest ouvraige. Je ne sçay se le successeur le cuidoit honnourer; s'il le creoit pour vray, il fut deceu, car a ung commencement qui par aventure se pourroit assez passer selon son fait, mesmement entre crestiens, il adjousta trés orde fin et moien desraisonnable contre Raison.[25]

[The author was not one and the same person. Rather the author I am speaking of constructed his entire work on the beginning made by the first author. The foundation had already been laid by the first author, using his own art and subject matter. He neither went begging for material here and there nor collected together such vile filth, such a sewer of stench and offal as one finds contained in the conclusion to this work. I know not whether the continuator presumed to honor his predecessor; but if he did so presume, he deceived himself. For, to a beginning whose contents could perhaps be received even among Christians, he appended a vile conclusion and an unreasonable central section directed against Reason.]

There were, of course, two sides in the quarrel that occupied the royal court for three or four years.[26] Pierre Col insisted that Jean de Meun intended merely to "poursuir la matiere commensee et touchee par Guillaume de Lorris, et en ce faisant parler de toutes choses selonc leur estat au proufit de creature humaine, tant a l'ame comme au corps" (p. 71, ll. 635-37) [continue the subject begun and treated by Guillaume de Lorris, and in so doing to speak of all things according to their place for human advantage, for the soul as much as for the body]. He implies that the manner and conclusions of the two authors are congruent, except that Jean amplified in the interest of clarity and moral profit what Guillaume had developed too briefly. "Des qu'il [Jean] commensa ceste escripture, il entre en raison et dieu sceit combien il se tient, a paine se peut il oster. Aussy ne s'i estoit gaires tenu le premier aucteur" (p. 61, ll. 212-15) [As soon as he (Jean) began this work, he took up reason—and God knows how he held to the subject: he could scarcely leave off! Moreover, the first author had hardly touched on it].

Around the year 1300 Gui de Mori noticed the different intentions of the two authors and conceived his adaptation of Guillaume de Lorris in light of Jean de Meun's continuation.[27] The *Echecs* Commentator himself implies differences when he recommends that good lovers follow the god of love's commandments in the first part of the *Rose*.

Car vraye amour . . . fait les vrays amans vivre aussi come chastes;[28] car chilz qui ayment d'amour vraye et loyalle a a celle qui l'ayme son cuer et sa pensee toutte si enthierement mise qu'il n'en vouldroit nulle souhaydier tant fust belle. Ains lui seroit toutte aultre abhominable ou regardt d'elle. Ainsi encline les amans honnourables a pluiseurs vertus belles et les fait habonder en pluiseurs bonnes meurs selon ce que ly amoureux dyent communement. Et ce est voir, se doit estre entendu d'amours qui est bien par raison rieulee et adrechie. Ly amans n'ont pas trop excessivement l'ueil ne leur cuer au delict que on y quiert; car on ne doit pas querre l'amour pour le delict, comme dit est, mais a rebours le delict pour l'amour. . . . Finablement il doit tous les commandement[s] d'amours a son pouoir garder et acomplir ainsi qu'ilz sont escript ou *Rommant de la rose* et es aultres livres aussi d'amours. (fol. 300r)[29]

[For true love . . . makes true lovers live as if they were chaste; for he who loves truly and faithfully has fixed his heart and mind so intently on the loved one that he could not wish for another, no matter how beautiful she might be. Rather, any other person would be abhorrent to him in comparison to her. Thus do worthy lovers incline to a number of fine qualities, and they abound in good conduct, as lovers themselves frequently assert. And this is true, if it is to apply to love that is directed and controlled by reason. The lovers do not fix their gaze overmuch on the delight sought in love; for one must not love for delight, as it is said, but rather seek delight out of love. . . . Finally, he must keep and follow, to the best of his ability, all love's commandments as they are set forth in the *Roman de la rose* and in other books about love.]

The recommendation to follow the instruction of the god of Love in Guillaume de Lorris' *Rose* shows that the Commentator was as aware of the different conceptions of love held by Guillaume and Jean de Meun as were Christine de Pisan, Jean Gerson, and Gui de Mori. He repeats their disavowal of Jean de Meun's narrow view of love.

Of course, Jean de Meun may just possibly have included good love under *amistié,* a notion which he took largely from Cicero and Aelred de Rievaulx.[30] The possibility is borne out in the *Epistolae duorum amantium.* The Vir formulates a definition of love in Letter XXIV based on those two authors, and frequently emphasizes the at once egalitarian and elevating character of love.[31] But if Jean was aware of such love, it is not the subject of his *Rose,* and neither side in the later quarrel seems to notice it.

The different conceptions and classifications of love evident in the two parts of the *Rose* and in the ambivalent attitude to the *Rose* of the verse *Echecs amoureux* and its Commentary are not peculiar to relatively late writers. Rather, they illustrate a diversity of views confirmed everywhere one looks. This diversity is prominent in the representation of *fin'amors* in the Vulgate Lancelot-Grail cycle, especially in the judgment of Lancelot's love in the *Lancelot* Proper, where it is usually extolled, the *Queste,* where it is condemned, and the *Mort Artu,* where it is finally sublimated; in the thirteenth-century prose cycle of the Seven Sages of Rome, whose readers were apparently not made uneasy by the juxtaposition of the viciously misogynist *Marques de Rome* and the courtly, semi-Arthurian *Laurin*; in the distinction between fornication and love free from villainy in the *Tornoiement Antecrist*; in the emphasis on the equality of lovers rather than domination in Richart de Fornival's *Bestiaires d'amours;*[32] behind the debate about Chrétien de Troyes' opinion of love in his separate romances; in the identity of love and reason Jean Frappier has demonstrated for Thomas d'Angleterre's courtly version of the Tristan legend;[33] in Wace's interpolation into his adaptation of Geoffrey of Monmouth of the disagreement between Cador and Gauvain, who, like Jean de Meun and Guillaume de Lorris a century later, disagree on the value of leisure, or *uisdive,* and love;[34] and in the "schools" postulated by some scholars to account for differences among the troubadours on what constitutes good and bad love.[35]

The frequently mentioned incompatibility of love and marriage is in many ways a false problem as far as courtly love is concerned. Guenevere's argument in *Cligès,* for example, that marital love is happier than extramarital is simply common sense. She and Lancelot, Tristan and Iseut would no doubt have married, had circumstances made it possible. Cligès and Fénice did so. There may be factors distinguishing conjugal affection and courtly love, as we read in Andreas Capellanus; but Andreas is a rigorist. Other works indicate a search for a kind of friendship, an equality, in marriage which Andreas recognizes in *amor* but not in the marital state.[36] But even his presentation of the problem through debate indicates doubt and uncertainty. But where there already was a Christian marriage, divorce was not the easy, or even safe, recourse it is today!

All these examples and scores of others like them bear witness to the vigor, the variety, and the anguish of thought on courtly love during the four centuries when it was of literary and social concern. And they demonstrate the difficulty, indeed the impossibility, of achieving a single, meaningful definition of love suitable for all medieval literature. To understand the curious ambiguity, vacillation, and disagreement regarding courtly love among so many works and writers, we must examine the expression *fin'amors* itself.

Fin'amors as used in the Middle Ages and *courtly love* in modern parlance are not always synonymous. The difference lies in the divergent connotations of the adjectives *courtly* and *fin.* Courtly love commonly suggests arts of love, rules and directives prescribing specific conduct and fixing sentiment within an exact mold. It is held to be essentially deductive, functioning as an elaborate etiquette covering every conceivable circumstance and action. That which is *fin* evinces finesse. Finesse characterizes "la puissance intuitive," as one critic has put it, "la faculté de saisir confusément la réalité profonde des objets concrets,"[37] that is, the essential and indicative elements of experience. But experience is subject to variation and thus to the constant shifting of the experiential data. No human code, law, or a priori order is absolute, though common beliefs and maxims may help the individual to understand the significance of particular circumstances.[38]

Finesse has a place in social history extending back through the sixteenth century into the Middle Ages, thus linking *fin'amors* to Pascal's *esprit de finesse,* a notion he himself took from the aristocratic milieu of seventeenth-century France and its variety of "courtly love" evident in *préciosité.* Justification for the link with Pascal's *esprit de finesse* is found in medieval usage of *fin* and its derivatives in social and literary parlance evident as far back as the fifteenth century for *finesse* and the thirteenth for *fin.*

Car li plus verai fausseront
Et verai li plus faus seront,
S'iert faus voirs et voirs faus sera,
Lues que fine amors faussera,
Qu'estre ne puet; tant a de fin
En bonne amour.[39]

[For the most faithful will be false, and the most untrue true, and false will be true and true false, as soon as courtly love is false. For that cannot be, so much *fin* is there in good love.]

In this sense *finesse* blended with the earlier notion of *superior quality, ideal,* then expanded semantically to include *duplicity, deception,* and *deceit.* The latter meaning occurs in farces. In "Le procès d'un jeune moyne et d'ung viel gendarme devant Cupido," Cupid advises a girl:

Belle, se vous prenez amy
Par amour, au jour la journee,
Vous serés vestue, aournee
Autant a l'endroit qu'a l'envers,
Et s'on vous dit rien de travers,
A Dieu jusque au revenir.
(vv. 73–78)[40]

[Belle, if you take a lover in a courtly manner, from day to day, you will be dressed and adorned fore and aft; and if he says anything you don't like—so long till we meet again!]

Semantic extension of *amour par amours,* a synonym for *fin'amors,* permits Jean de Meun's irony.

Au deu d'Amours e a Venus,
Qui m'orent aidié meauz que nus,
Puis a touz les barons de l'ost,
Don je pri Deu qu'il ja ne l'ost
Des secours aus fins amoureus,
Entre les baisiers savoureus
Rendi graces dis feiz ou vint.
(vv. 21753–59 [21723–29])

[I rendered thanks, among the delicious kisses, ten or twenty times, first to the god of Love and to Venus, who had aided me more than anyone, then to all the barons of the host, whose help I pray God never to take away from pure lovers.]

However, real finesse had always been associated with notions like courtesy, honor, and friendship. Like them, *fin'amors* is susceptible of interpretation and refinement, of ideal realization contingent on the mind and actions of the individual and the exigencies of argument. No wonder argument and rhetoric play such a prominent part in medieval poetry and in Andreas Capellanus.[41]

Under *passio* Andreas groups a variety of loves, each representing some facet of *passio* in diverse and carefully scaled contexts. One context is that of *amor sapiens,* or reasonable love. This is a suitable Latin equivalent for courtly love and the art of *honeste amandi.* Andreas chooses to treat the nuances of *amor sapiens* in a series of discussions and debates on its quality and the conduct suitable to its realization for various social levels and situations. Earlier, the so-called *Epistolae duorum amantium* had emphasized the subject of *sapienter amare* founded on virtue, *probitas, honestas,* discretion, prudence, secrecy, intimacy, and delight.[42] These are characteristics Andreas insists on as well. Furthermore, Andreas relies on eloquent and artful use of cogent maxims and authorities of recognized discernment to assist and advance argument, as would any good rhetorician.[43] This *amor sapiens* compares in seriousness with Dante's *amoris accensio,* by its nobility a worthy subject for the best poetry.[44]

The dignity of courtly love stems ultimately from what John Steadman has called the decorum appropriate to the aristocratic society for which it was intended.[45] Courtly literature contains a whole range of words suggestive of aristocratic prerogatives: *jovens* and *prouesse, courtoisie, bonté, mesure,* and others, all used together with *fin' amors.* At a given historical time such words may have a number of meanings and nuances, varying according to the context and the quality of individual finesse. And they have that deeper meaning made manifest through the concrete evidence of the allegorical mode. It is precisely on the diversity of the literal that the finer characteristics, the nuances of a given abstraction depend. The propensity to treat abstractions not as terms, but as semantic fields, facilitated the adaptation of allegory to courtly love.

ALLEGORY AND LOVE

> Und sold ich dir glîch nâhen sîn
> der lieben, werden vrowen mîn,
> dâ für næm ich niht den grâl,
> den der küene, werde Parcifâl
> mit ritterlîcher arebeit
> alsô kumberlîch erstreit.
> —Ulrich von Liechtenstein[46]

Exegetical commentary and the principle of the *integumentum* and the *involucrum* in both exegesis and poetics inspired the accommodation of amorous literature to religious and moral truth, from Fulgentius down to the scholars whom Judson Allen has called the "friar critics" and to the *Ovide moralisé.*[47] This tradition, together with works of a general moral import and the usual practice and training in grammar and rhetoric, accounts for the emergence in the thirteenth century of an "allegory of love" employing on the literal level personified abstractions, mythological figures, and bestiaries. The *Ovide moralisé* is typical of the attempt to preserve secular literature often condemned in the Middle Ages for its mendacity, its advocacy of sin, and its worldliness. "The pagan worldliness of much of [secular literature] clashed with Christian otherworldliness, and those who loved the ancient poets were hard put to defend their poetry. The only way out, as the accessus and glosses to many a classical and pagan work show, was to argue strongly for the *utilitas* of such literature, and *utilitas* meant finding a moral meaning."[48] Accordingly, the *Ovide moralisé,* like its Latin predecessors, begins with a vindication.

> Tout est pour nostre enseignement
> Quanqu'il a es livres escript,
> Soient bon ou mal li escript.
> Qui bien i vaudroit prendre esgart,
> Li maulz y est que l'en s'en gart,
> Li biens pour ce que l'en le face.
> (I, vv. 2–7)[49]

[Everything written in books is for our instruction, however good or bad the writings may be. If one were to consider them carefully, the evil is there so that we may learn to eschew it, the good that we might do it.]

Similarly, the *Queste del saint graal* derives a Christian moral from the worldly Arthurian legend by condemning the love/prowess ideal, fostered since Wace and Chrétien de Troyes, in favor of a heavily ascetic, otherworldly idealization of knighthood. It does so by a thorough allegorical reading of the grail Image and the quests leading to it. Despite the need to incorporate an already elaborate and complex narrative, the *Queste* successfully avoids the pitfalls and constraints of imposed allegory that often render the *Ovide moralisé* flat and simpleminded.[50] The imposition of a more typological conception of Arthurian history deepens the traditional aristocratic notion of the transmission (*translatio*) of chivalry and courtesy from the past to Arthur—it is the significance of the grail that the Arthurian world should absorb—and sends reverberations back over the preceding narrative in the *Lancelot* Proper. In the *Queste,* successful imposition is attributable to what Rosemond Tuve has called "proper allegorical ambiguity"—the shifting of meanings through nuance, adaptation, elaboration, changing connotations.[51] Such imposition occurs in Richart de Fornival's debate with his lady in the *Bestiaires d'amours* and the *Response au Bestiaire;* the lady, anticipating the *belle dame sans mercy,* turns his reading of the literal Images against the lover by her own contrasting glosses.[52]

Those who sought to preserve courtly literature had now to defend it not

23

only against traditional rigorism,[53] but also from formidable attacks in their own language like the *Queste* and, soon after, Jean de Meun's *Rose*. Guillaume de Lorris showed the way with personifications and settings adapted to the idealization of courtly love. In so doing, he carried to its conclusion the tendency of romance to move from history towards Imaginary dream worlds, replacing historical veracity with allegorical truth[54] and romance with dit.

One nagging problem in the adaptation of allegory to courtly love is the question of personification allegory. Personification is common in allegory. It is justifiable for purposes of classification to regard personification as characteristic of some allegorical writing. It is prominent in romance and dit throughout the French Middle Ages, and was indeed more successful than bestiary figures or apocalyptic scenes like the psychomachia in Huon de Mery's *Tornoiement Antecrist*.[55] But personification has also been taken to be allegory as such. This is, of course, a misrepresentation, though one not so gross as often argued. The function of personification on the level of *sententia* tends to transform it from literal metonymy into an allegorical figure, from a near synonym into a figure with two or more discrete levels of meaning. The ease with which metonymy becomes allegory derives from the fact that both are forms of transferred meaning. The distinction depends on the form of the transfer. The *Ovide moralisé* gives a varied allegorical reading for the personified abstractions, gods and goddesses, and external or emblematic signs which rhetoricians classified under metonymy.[56] And the distinction between allegory and metonymy is rarely sharp: metonymy as a manner of speech denoting one thing by another closely akin to or deriving from it (*verba immutata*) maintains in practice a hazy frontier with allegory as a manner of speech denoting one thing by the letter of the words, but another by their meaning (*verba translata*). For example, when Matthew of Vendôme reads *superbit* as meaning *fastidit,* or cause for effect, it is a moot point whether the word is an allegory or a metonymy. Matthew seems to consider it metonymy, but his words are not clear: "Dictio poterit esse alterius vicaria, cujus significatio ad significationem alterius antecedit" (p. 187, §§ 27–31)[57] [One word can take the place of another if its meaning *denotes a condition preceding that of* the other (p. 88)]. In both cases personifications tend to use concrete objects to represent something immaterial. The close study in chapter 4 of the figures depicted in the wall of the Garden of Deduit will show how standardized and, with minor exceptions, how undifferentiated, how close to true allegorical figures they are. We depend on tags to understand the import of their epithets, their conventional *attributa personis et negotiis*, as Matthew of Vendôme calls them (pp. 118–51).

Because the distinction between metonymy and allegory as rhetorical devices and in extended metaphorical discourse was not always discernible, authors easily slipped from one into the other.[58] We need not, therefore, feel

24

compelled to substitute metonymy of love for allegory of love because of the widespread use of personification. In fact, personification can act upon the varied literal meanings in a word's semantic field, and thus provide *materia* for a richer allegorical reading.

Attention to the meanings and synonymy of words was a fundamental task in grammar and rhetoric.[59] In the *Roman de la rose,* the Rose obviously cannot have the same signification when it is plucked, sniffed, kissed, or walled up. Just so, Dangier may realize in a given episode any of the various meanings C. S. Lewis found for the word in the late Middle Ages;[60] it is not necessary for the critic to impose a single one as an explanation for Dangier variously benevolent, asleep, and brandishing his club. This is the lexicographical counterpart to the "ambiguity" Tuve pointed to in the *Queste del saint graal.* Alain de Lille's *Distinctiones* show that the Bible itself encouraged such semantic adaptation in conformity with usage, context, or intention, and Alain availed himself of the possibilities in his own writings.[61] The discriminate reading of a word's possible connotations, of the *vis verbi,* provides the personification with fields of action that may be appropriate to the sustained reading of its allegorical signification. It is this very ambiguity that made possible Jean de Meun's adaptation of Guillaume de Lorris to his own understanding of love. The medieval propensity for rhetorical etymologies provided a technical foundation for "this habit," as Tuve calls it, "of coming at the nature of a thing by observing facets of it."[62] Hence the finesse of the best allegorical writing on love. That finesse is possible as Imagination.

In the Middle Ages, Imagination does not have the sense of free inspiration or invention, nor, strictly speaking, that of idle fantasy. As a mental function and a poetic principle, it neatly bridges and thus eliminates the terminological problem of metonymy and allegory, and has the advantage of being used more frequently than they were to designate metonymic and allegorical inventions. It acquires prominence in treating courtly love in the *Rose* of Guillaume de Lorris, and that prominence is sustained throughout the writings of Machaut and Froissart. For both these poets the notion of Imagination is fundamental to the allegory of love and the invention of figures suitable for its expression. Its history in the twelfth and thirteenth centuries helps explain the dearth of an allegory of love before Guillaume de Lorris.[63]

3

Imagination

omne adeo genus in terris hominumque ferarumque
et genus aequoreum, pecudes pictaeque volucres
in furias ignemque ruunt: amor omnibus idem.
—Vergil[1]

THE SOURCES

Image and Imagination in their spiritual and moral senses have been the object of considerable study lately, especially as a result of the writing of Robert Javelet.[2] The subject of Image and Imagination is complex. The use of these words in Patristic and Scholastic writing is not immediately referable to courtly literature. Man as the Image of God (his spiritual state) and man seeking to be like God (his moral life) preclude the courtly lover and love service. Yet there are similarities with courtly paradigms.[3] The following brief survey outlines the adaptation of Image and Imagination to courtly literature.

The hierarchy of cognitive functions includes Imagination as the perception and retention in the mind of the forms in visible things. Twelfth-century writers in particular elaborated a new poetry by the projection of Images formed in the Imagination. This poetry described creation and man's moral responsibilities by Images representing ideas and archetypes as they had been traditionally understood in Neo-Platonic thought.[4] This technique parallels the invention of topoi and exemplification in rhetoric. The instruction in the arts of poetry, derived both from this poetry and from traditional rhetoric, made the Image into an imitative representation of a mental archetype. Abstracted from religious, scientific, and moral concerns, Imagination could be applied to secular subjects, including courtly love.

Et ainsi ont parlé communement les sages alkimiens, et aussi font les astronomiens aulcunnesfois, et ceulz qui font prenostiquations et prophezies ou ilz voellent parler des choses advenir, et pluiseurs aultres sages. De ceste maniere meismes de parler par paraboles et par figures faites use souvent l'Escripture sainte comme il appert es Canticques Salomon et en l'Apocalipse et en pluiseurs aultres lieux. Et ainsi ont aulcun

26

parlé de leurs amours et de pluiseurs aultres manieres secretement. (*Echecs* Commentary, fol. 14v)

[And thus did the wise alchemists commonly speak, and so do the astronomers sometimes, and those who make predictions and prophecies whereby they seek to treat things to come; and many other wise men do so as well. Holy Scripture also avails itself of the very same way of speaking through parables and contrived figures, as is evident in the Song of Songs and in the Book of Revelation and in several other places. And some have also spoken of their love in this way, and in many other ways secretly.]

The courtly authors, especially after the thirteenth century, demonstrated their awareness of the adoption and adaptation of Imagination to their subject by references to *ymagination* and its effects.

The specifically medieval conception of *imaginatio* was a hoary one in the twelfth century. It went back to the Church Fathers in ecclesiastical Latin,[5] and acquired the sense of a specific kind of cognition very early through Boethius' immensely influential *Consolation*. "Ipsum quoque hominem aliter sensus, aliter imaginatio, aliter ratio, aliter intellegentia contuetur. Sensus enim figuram in subiecta materia constitutam, imaginatio uero solam sine materia iudicat figuram. Ratio uero hanc quoque transcendit speciemque ipsam quae singularibus inest uniuersali consideratione perpendit. Intellegentiae uero celsior oculus exsistit; supergressa namque uniuersitatis ambitum ipsam illam simplicem formam pura mentis acie contuetur."[6] [Likewise sense, imagination, reason, and understanding do diversely behold a man. For sense looketh upon his form as it is placed in matter or subject, imagination discerneth it alone without matter, reason passeth beyond this also and considereth universally the species or kind which is in particulars. The eye of the understanding is higher yet. For surpassing the compass of the whole world it beholdeth with the clear eye of the mind that simple form in itself.] Since each cognitive faculty may comprehend any inferior faculty, reason fulfills an important function for Imagination (as will *intellegentia* in authors like Bernardus Silvestris and Alain de Lille). "Ratio namque cum quid uniuersale respicit, nec imaginatione nec sensibus utens imaginabilia uel sensibilia comprehendit" (V.Pr 4. 104–6) [Likewise reason, when it considereth any universality, comprehendeth both imagination and sensible things without the use of either imagination or senses]. The same holds later, for example in Bernardus Silvestris (*Commentum*, p. 53, ll. 15–18). Reason defines and classifies the species whose form is apparent in discrete material objects or as abstracted from them in the figures of Imagination, and thus obviates confusion and error. Macrobius used Imagination as well for the objects of intellection: "Siquid de his adsignare conantur quae non sermonem tantum modo sed cogitationem quoque humanam superant, ad similitudines et exempla confugiunt"[7] [When they wish to assign attributes to these divinities that not only pass the bounds of speech but those of human comprehension as well, they resort to similes and analogies]. Macrobius is here anticipating Martianus Capella and the Chartrain poets. Imagination is thus an eminently metaphorical mode, the source of what G. Raynaud de Lage describes as the "perpétuelle génération de métaphores"[8] in the writing of authors like Alain de Lille. Where reason is a source of concepts and definitions, Imagination provides representations by description and other rhetorical devices that function as amplifications.

Reason and Imagination come to the fore in the debate between Reason and Guillaume in Jean de Meun's *Rose*. Reason presents love in two ways. The first, by Imagination, is a description relying on oxymoron and antithesis (vv. 4293–4358 [4263–4328]). It is an appropriate use of Imagination by Reason; the shape of love emerges by abstraction and incremental repetition as the *imaginabilia* comprehending love's diversity. With Reason's assistance, Imagination as a mental faculty is able to sort out typical manifestations of love in conformity with rational understanding of love as an idea. The second way is definition. The lover, confused by so many "contraries" in Imagination (v. 4364 [4334]),[9] asks for a clear definition of love (vv. 4371–75 [4341–45]). It is entirely within the purview of Reason to make definitions, and she does so by citing Andreas Capellanus.[10]

The hierarchy of cognitive functions was accepted in principle by twelfth-century thinkers.[11] Hugh of Saint Victor included Imagination as "memoria sensuum ex corporum reliquiis inhaerentibus animo, principium cognitionis per se nihil certum habens"[12] [sensuous memory made up of the traces of corporeal objects in the mind; it possesses in itself nothing certain as a source of knowledge (pp. 66–67)]. *Imaginatio* provides a mode of expression, as Hugh explains. "Spirituum namque et animarum natura, quia incorporea et simplex est, intellectibilis substantiae particeps est. sed quia per instrumenta sensuum non uniformiter ad sensibilia comprehendenda descendit, eorumque similitudinem per imaginationem ad se trahit, in eo quodammodo suam simplicitatem deserit, quo compositionis rationem amittit" (p. 26). [For the nature of spirits and souls, because it is incorporeal and simple, participates in intellectible substance; but because through the sense organs spirit or soul descends in different ways to the apprehension of physical objects and draws into itself a likeness of them through its imagination, it deserts its simplicity somehow by admitting a type of composition (p. 63).] In poetry, *imaginatio* pointed to an ineffable reality lying beyond the reach of the senses, and made possible "the discovery and, as it were, the personification of natural forces and processes"[13] through representations formed in the mind according to what the mind could know of them. The method was essentially rational, although it treated for the most part suprarational entities. Appropriate visual representations gave access to ideas and sentiments which ultimately defied rational scrutiny and analysis.[14]

In this way epistemology joined with rhetoric to become poetry. The *fabula* became an *integumentum* or an *involucrum,* and it revealed historical, scientific, and moral truths.[15] We shall find it still alive at the end of the Middle Ages among the mythographers, especially in the *Ovide moralisé,* and in the *poetries* of the Second Rhetoric.

POETRIA

> Tum durare solum et discludere Nerea ponto
> coeperit et rerum paulatim sumere formas.
> —Vergil[16]

Rhetoric facilitated the application of *imaginatio,* as conceived in the epistemology of Boethius and other writers, to literary invention. Traditionally, *imaginatio* provided evidence in discourse and debate.[17] It derived from *imago,* which in Latin meant either a mental picture, frequently fictitious, or an actual picture or representation and in rhetorical terminology meant a kind of metaphor, usually a simile.[18] The *Rhetorica ad Herennium* defines *imago* as convergence of forms, "formae cum forma cum quadam similitudine conlatio" (IV.xlix.62)[19] [the comparison of one figure with another, implying a certain resemblance between them]. Invention of an *imago* is *imaginatio,* the invention of a true or credible illustration in narrative, discourse, and argument.[20] The *imagines* as persons, objects, and actions bring before the mind's eye an *imaginaria visio,* as Matthew of Vendôme calls it.[21] The procedure is amplified to include the entire *fabula* in narrative: "Fabula est oratio ficta verisimili dispositione imaginem exhibens veritatis"[22] [Fable is fictional discourse showing forth by credible arrangement an Image of truth]. The relation between *fabula,* dream, and truth acquired authority in Macrobius' commentary on the *Somnium Scipionis.*[23] There was thus a bridge between rhetorical and ecclesiastical usage which allowed for greater freedom in glossing, interpretation, and original invention.

> O noua picture miracula! Transit ad esse
> Quod nichil esse potest picturaque simia ueri,
> Arte noua ludens, in res umbracula rerum
> Vertit et in uerum mendacia singula mutat.
> (I.122–25)[24]

[O painting with your new wonders! What can have no real existence comes into being and painting, aping reality and diverting itself with a strange art, turns the shadows of things into things and changes every lie to truth (p. 49).]

Eventually this freedom extended to the two main kinds of vernacular narrative: historical and allegorical romance. Its final flowering was the late medieval dit. Here too the Poet, Nature, and God unite to fashion an exemplary human being in the beloved, as we read in Machaut's *Dit dou vergier* (vv. 75–108).

Where Roman orators sought to make the past visible to the mind's eye, the poets of the Middle Ages sought to make the invisible visible. All founded demonstration on analogy. The medieval arts of poetry combine traditional rhetoric and the poetics of twelfth-century philosophical poets like Bernardus Silvestris, Alain de Lille, and Jean of Hauville.[25] These authors, like Hugh of Saint Victor, adopt a version of Boethius' hierarchy of cognitive powers, always including Imagination, for poetic invention.[26] In their writings, Imagination is explicitly the making of poetic *picturae*. Alain's Nature illustrates through Images her otherwise hidden actions in the world, thus metonymically advancing effect for cause: "Virgo varias rerum picturaliter suscitabat imagines" (*De planctu*, p. 445) [The virgin ... called up and pictured various images of things (p. 19)]. Alain relies on Imagination to express the wonders of Nature through the extensive description in the *De planctu:* "Viroris smaragdo oculis applaudebat. Haec autem nimis subtilizata, subterfugiens oculorum indaginem, ad tantam materiae tenuitatem advenerat, ut ejus aerisque eandem crederes esse naturam, in qua, prout oculis pictura imaginabatur, animalium celebratur concilium" (p. 437).[27] [It gladdened the sight with the greenness of the emerald. Moreover, spun exceedingly fine, so as to escape the scrutiny of the eye, it was so delicate of substance that you would think it and the air of the same nature. On it, as a picture fancied to the sight, was being held a parliament of the living creation (p. 11).] This is part of the lengthy inventory of the birds that adorn Nature's costume. But "haec animalia, quamvis illic quasi allegorice viverent, ibi tamen esse videbantur ad litteram" (p. 439) [these living things, although as it were in allegory moving there, seemed to exist naturally (p. 19)]. The material is evanescent; the forms survive in each new creation. Alain's descriptions preserve the forms in generic shapes that appear as *imagines*.

The poetic imitation of Nature's handiwork is set forth by Bernardus Silvestris.

> Si sensu fortasse meo maiora capesso,
> Mollius excudi silvam positoque veterno
> Posse superduci melioris imaginem formae,
> Huic operi nisi consentis, concepta relinquo.
> (I.i.7–10)[28]

[Though what I seek to realize be beyond my comprehension—that Silva be made more malleable, that she cast off her lethargy and be drawn forth to assume the image of a nobler form—yet if you do not consent to this undertaking I must abandon my conceptions (p. 67).]

The Image verbally depicted represents an archetype apprehendable only by intellection. The *imago* is thus the visible correlative to the real, permanent archetype. For example, Alain's Nature "mentali intellectui materialis vocis mihi depinxit imaginem, et quasi archetypa verba idealiter praeconcepta, vocaliter produxit in actum" (De planctu, p. 449)[29] [depicted for my mental perception the image of a real voice, and by this brought into actual being words which had been, so to speak, archetypes ideally preconceived (p. 24)]. The agents of God's will are personified Images that function like artists. "Illic Oyarses quidem erat et genius in artem et officium pictoris et figurantis addictus. In subteriacente enim mundo rerum facies universa caelum sequitur sumptisque de caelo proprietatibus ad imaginem quam conversio contulit figuratur" (De mundi, II.iii.91–95). [For the Usiarch here was that genius devoted to the art and office of delineating and giving shape to the forms of things. For the whole appearance of things in the subordinate universe conforms to the heavens, whence it assumes its characteristics, and it is shaped to whatever image the motion of the heavens imparts (p. 96).] Hence "sensilis hic mundus" is "mundi melioris [the archetype] imago" (II.x.9) [this sensible universe (is) the image of an ideal model (p. 113)]. The artist thus invents as God created. Comprehension of the ideas by the intellect conforms to the Boethian hierarchy of cognitions.[30] The authors extend metaphorical Images that lead the mind to the contemplation of abstract truths and ideas, giving access through word pictures to the ineffable. Such ideas may even have been construed as having "personal" existence; Alain de Lille, at least, seems to have understood the ideas to be angels.[31]

An object of intellection is Bernardus Silvestris' Endelechia. The incorporeal archetype becomes through its verbal reverberation—vocis imago—a metaphorical Image. "Huiusce igitur sive vitae sive lucis origine vita, iubar et rerum endelechia quadam velut emanatione defluxit. Conparuit igitur exporrectae magnitudinis globus terminatae quidem continentiae, sed quam non oculis verum solo pervideas intellectu. Eius admodum clara substantia liquentis fluidique fontis imaginem praeferebat inspectorem suum qualitatis ambiguo praeconfundens, cum plerumque aëri plerumque caelo cognatior videretur" (De mundi I.ii.167–75).[32] [From the very source, then, of this our life and light, there issued forth by a sort of emanation the life, illumination, and soul of creation, Endelechia. She was like a sphere, of vast size yet of fixed dimensions, and such as one might not perceive visually, but only by intellect. Her shining substance appeared just like a steadily flowing fountain, defying scrutiny by its uncertain condition since it seemed so closely akin to the atmosphere, and at the same time to the heaven itself (p. 74).] Velut, conparuit, liquentis fluidique fontis imaginem—these words suggest the verbal representation of an essence existing only in ineffable harmony and number, "quae consonantiis, quae se numeris moveret" (I.ii.175–76) [that mode of being which emerges from harmony, from number (p. 74)]. Thus does the artistry of the writer effect an act of prestidigitation—"quodam quasi praestigio veram imaginem fraudaretur" (I.ii.177) [deluded as if by magic as to its true aspect (p. 74)]—"fraudulently" demonstrating through a true Image (*veram imaginem*).

Such "mendacity" is part and parcel of the *fabula,* wherein the artist imitates Nature's opus in fashioning his own. His Imagination, in its place and on its own plane, is a mirror of God's, "de semblance ne mie de hautesce," as the author of the *Queste del saint graal* might put it. This is the foundation for the opening lines to Geoffrey of Vinsauf's *Poetria Nova.*

> intrinseca linea cordis
> Praemetitur opus, seriemque sub ordine certo
> Interior praescribit homo, totamque figurat
> Ante manus cordis quam corporis; et status ejus
> Est prius archetypus quam sensilis. Ipsa poesis
> Spectet in hoc speculo quae lex sit danda poetis.
>
> . . . .
>
> Opus totum prudens in pectoris arcem
> Contrahe, sitque prius in pectore quam sit in ore.
> Mentis in arcano cum rem digesserit ordo,
> Materiam verbis veniat vestire poesis.
>
> (vv. 44–49, 58–61)[33]

[The measuring line of his mind first lays out the work, and he mentally outlines the successive steps in a definite order. The mind's hand shapes the entire house before the body's hand builds it. The mode of being is archetypal before it is actual. Poetic art may see in this analogy the law to be given to poets. . . . As a prudent workman, construct the whole fabric within the mind's citadel; let it exist in the mind before it is on the lips. When due order has arranged the material in the hidden chamber of the mind, let poetic art come forward to clothe the matter with words.]

Geoffrey is describing Imagination as Matthew of Vendôme understood and adapted it from the Chartrain poets. Matthew links the *imago* to topical description, and thus makes it central to invention. "In poeticae facultatis exercitio praecedit imaginatio sensus, sequitur sermo interpres intellectus, deinde ordinatio in qualitate tractatus; prior est sententiae conceptio, sequitur verborum excogitatio, subjungitur qualitas scilicet materiae, sive tractatus dispositio" (p. 180, § 52)[34] [In the exercise of the poetic faculty a mental image of the perception comes first; utterance, which expounds the meaning, follows; and finally, arrangement ensues in the nature of the treatment. The first is the conception of the meaning, next is the invention of words, and finally we have the nature of the subject matter or the disposition of the treatment (p. 84)]. Imagination, verbalization, stylization and disposition: this is composition in the Middle Ages.

The use of Imagination for other than philosophical and theological subjects[35] derived from philosophical speculation going back from the twelfth-century poets to Plato's *Timaeus,* as the Commentary on the *Echecs amoureux* points out. And the same Commentary grants the extension well beyond philosophical and theological speculation to a wide spectrum of intellectual activities in which "on n'en pouoit pas bien la verité conclure par raison naturelle" (fol. 13v) [one could not correctly arrive at truth by natural reason]. Such "ymaginaire vision" (fol. 14v) is widespread in literature and science, and is prominent in love poetry, especially after Guillaume de Lorris and Richart de Fornival. The *merveille* as union of Image and meaning accounts for the appeal of such works, "car les choses qui sont subtillement faittes ou dittes font plus esmerveillier l'entendement et par consequent deliter, car les choses mervillab[l]es sont par nature desirables. . . . Pour ce se delite on es Fables de Ysopet et de Renart et de pluiseurs aultres escriptures amoureuses meismes . . . pour la fainte maniere de parler soubtille et raisonnable soubz laquelle est enclose une sentence plaisant et delictable et moult souvent une moralité qui est de grant prouffit" (fol. 14v). [For those things which are made or expressed with subtlety cause the understanding to marvel and thus to delight in them; for marvels are by nature desirable. . . . Thus we enjoy the Fables of Aesop and of Renart and several other writings about love itself . . . because of the simulated way of speaking, which is subtle and reasonable, and beneath which is found a pleasing, delightful lesson and often a moral of great profit.]

The *Echecs* Commentator compares artistic invention to God's creative activity in a way reminiscent of the twelfth-century Chartrain poets and the arts of poetry that combine their learning with traditional rhetoric.

Es choses que nous veons par art faittes . . . nous veons que l'ouvrier qui voelt aulcunnes choses raisonnablement faire entent premierement et conchoit par devant en sa pensee la fourme de la chose qu'il voelt faire. Et puis vient apres la fantasie ou la fourme dessusditte est imprimee et pourtraite. Et puis la main et la doloire apres ou le pincel qui la chose parfait en la vertu des choses dessusdittes. Car tout aussi que la doloire du carpentier ou le pincel du paintre se met a la similitude de la main qui l'adresce, et la main le remeult a la similitude de la fantasie et la fantasie oultre aussi a la similitude de la figure ou de la fourme que l'ouvrier principal entent. (Fol. 16r)

[In the objects we see made by art we perceive that the craftsman, desirous of making certain objects in a reasonable manner, first applies his intention and conceives beforehand in his mind the form of what he wishes to make. Then follows Imagination, wherein the aforesaid form is impressed and portrayed. Then the hand and chisel come, or the brush, which complete the object in conformity with the aforementioned steps. For just as the carpenter's chisel or the painter's brush conforms to the hand that directs it, the hand moves in accordance with the Imagination, and the Imagination in conformity with the figure or form which the principal craftsman intends.]

Writers like Alain de Lille and Bernardus Silvestris used Imagination as a cognitive faculty suitable to the verbal representation of abstractions not immediately accessible to the senses but perceptible by reason or intellection.

33

They proceeded to the invention (*trouve*) of appropriate Images conforming to their intention, usually personifications or mythological figures. Such are the *fabulae* that Macrobius admits into serious philosophical disquisition. The process is allegorical in the rhetorical sense, although the nature of the transfer may not be strictly allegorical in the second term of comparison, but metonymic. More important than the terminological problem is the distinction between true and false *imaginatio*. False Imagination has no substance, but is merely the stuff of empty dreams. "Infruniti homines in hoc opus sensus proprius non impingant, qui ultra metas sensuum rationis non excedant curriculum, qui iuxta imaginationis sompnia aut recordantur uisa, aut figmentorum artifices commentantur incognita" (*Anticlaudianus,* p. 56). [Let not men without taste thrust their own interpretations on this work, men who cannot extend their course beyond the bounds of sense-knowledge, who, in the wake of dreams of the imagination, either remember *idle fancies* or, as contrivers of figments, discuss what they have never learned (p. 42).] Only those capable of inventing Images that accurately represent ineffable ideas possess the quality termed *ingenium* in rhetoric.

The traditional school exercises, including practice in invention and amplification, provided the training for the Imagination of which Matthew of Vendôme speaks. Just as allegory is extended metaphor, so *usus* or *chria* is *commemoratio,* that is, amplification of words and actions as description. Techniques related to disposition and Geoffrey of Vinsauf's *interpretatio* appear in Priscian's examples in the *Praeexercitamina.* Subsequent categories in the same work contain instruction pertinent to the dilation of Images: *locus communis, laus, comparatio, allocutio, descriptio, positio, legis latio.* All illustrate *enargia,* the illustration and presentation of evidence as subsumed by Priscian under *descriptio:* "Descriptio est oratio colligens et praesentans oculis quod demonstrat" (p. 438) [Description is discourse that gathers together and presents for observation that which is being proven]. The arrangement of such descriptions provides the topical elaboration of poem and dit in late medieval literature. Person, place, and time fix the context. All are linked to *enargia* as Imagination in a late treatise on ornamentation: "'Ενάργεια est imaginatio, quae actum incorporeis oculis subicit et fit modis tribus: persona, loco, tempore"[36] [Enargia is Imagination which represents an action in the mind's eye, and does so in three ways: by person, place, time].

The Imaginative process is thus the use of metaphor to make incorporeal and abstract sentiments and qualities visible and thus comprehensible. This was true in Roman rhetoric as well. The representation of past actions in descriptive Images provided interpretation of motive, passion, premeditation. The complexity of the human soul—"non simplex natura hominis," said Prudentius—was resolved by representing each facet in its unique and essential simplicity. "Neque enim omnimodo simplex dici potest, quod composito

34

simile est" (*Didascalicon,* pp. 26–27). [For nothing that resembles a composite can, strictly speaking, be called simple (p. 64).] To analyze and comprehend man's composite soul, Prudentius broke it up into the qualities and defects that contest for mastery over it, then abstracted, personified, and correlated the qualities and defects antithetically. The result is a construct formed in the mind and then projected into words as the description that makes up almost the entire *Psychomachia.* "Quando nomina haec non communiter ad totam interiorem hominis partem, sed determinate et distincte ad quasdam ipsius referuntur virtutes, tunc, ut diversae voces, ita et diversae solent esse significationes, secundum quas res eis subjectae discernuntur, non modo a se, sed a mente."[37] [When these names refer not in general to the whole inner part of man, but specifically and distinctly to certain of his qualities, then like diverse words they have as a rule diverse meanings by which the things subject to them are discernible, not in themselves, but in the mind.] Similarly, the Vir in the *Epistolae duorum amantium* likens the Mulier's memory to a *similitudo* because of its *imagines* (Letter XVI). The Mulier herself analyzes the *imago* by describing its parts. "Quippe qui rem quamlibet assumit laudare, debet tandem in partes distribuere singularumque partium qualitates summa cautione pensare et quamque secundum dignitatem congrue laudis celebritate conorare" (Letter XXIII).[38] [For he who proposes to praise anything must nonetheless separate it into its parts and weigh the characteristics of the single parts with great care, and then distinguish each according to its dignity by extolling them with apposite praise.] The entire process is a rational ordering and distribution of parts which, after careful scrutiny, are subject to amplification. It presupposes a mind in full possession of its faculties.

One type of amplification, personification, is the most common mode of representation, but bestiary figures and mythological examples are also sources of Imaginative representation. In fact Richart de Fornival explicitly links word and Image (*parole* and *peinture*) in the elaboration of his *Bestiaires d' amours*. This is normally taken to be a reference to the illuminations added to the text. But not all manuscripts are illuminated.[39] Richart himself suggests that the Image rises up in the mind from the words rather than from the illuminations (p. 4, l. 6 –p. 5, l. 5). The illuminations thus become *aides-mémoire.* This kind of conceptual separation and classification is not just an intellectual or academic system, but corresponds to common expectation in character analysis. The finished analysis is remarkable less for its thoroughness than for its "integrity." That is, the abstract elements and their disposition form a coherent whole consistent within its own context. The vernacular authors understand this as *entier* (from *integer*). Their descriptions are thus extensive, but also differentiated, configurations of *teches* or characteristics.[40]

The usual criticism of such Imagination is that it is simplistic, excessively categorized, or dehumanized, and that its rhetorical function makes it tendentious and one-sided. The procedure is indeed basically simple. In the *Psychomachia,* for example, Prudentius uses a sequence of seven combats between Virtues and corresponding Vices, followed by a victory celebration. However, to understand the poem is not so simple; active participation of a rather complex sort is required of the reader. Prudentius himself implies as much, by reference to the usually complex nature of internal conflict. He was well aware of the diversity of emotions and drives in the human soul; but that diversity (and thus for us moderns psychological complexity) derives from sin. The conflict represented is not only psychological, but moral as well, and its moral character is preeminent. Morality is the imposition of order on human conduct for the sake of correcting evil and fostering the good through improvement. It is concerned more with ethics than with ethos. The victory of the Virtues over the Vices in the *Psychomachia* brings order and clarity into the human soul—"simplicity" in the medieval sense of openness, forthrightness, and sincerity. The violence of the Virtues in combat is mental sharpness triumphing over diversion, confusion, and ignorance. The description is an ideal hardly met in mundane conduct, which is customarily beneath such moral simplicity and excellence; but on a level where dwell saints, Galaads, Alain de Lille's New Man, we witness only clear decision-making and ready triumph. Thus could the rational mind show order in the soul's confusion, and permit it with Christ's aid to move towards a perfection and simplicity not fully attainable.

> dissere, rex noster, quo milite pellere culpas
> mens armata queat nostri de pectoris antro,
> exoritur quotiens turbatis sensibus intus
> seditio atque animam morborum rixa fatigat,
> quod tunc praesidium pro libertate tuenda
> quaeve acies furiis inter praecordia mixtis
> obsistat meliore manu.
>
> (v. 5–11)[41]

[Say, our King, with what fighting force the soul is furnished and enabled to expel the sins from within our breast; when there is disorder among our thoughts and rebellion arises within us, when the strife of our evil passions vexes the spirit, say what help there is then to guard her liberty, what array with superior force withstands the fiendish raging in our heart.]

The intention is clearly didactic, but its effectiveness depends on the reader's reflection on the state of his own soul.

Froissart and Gower conclude the *Joli buisson de jonece* and the *Confessio amantis* by looking into a mirror and finding each his own face. Thus they realize what separates them from the ideal in their Imagination. That distance is what much late medieval literature is about. A perfect human is a fascinating subject for speculation and invention, whether imitable or not. The popularity of hagiography not only attests to a hope for saintly intercession and salvation through the good offices of those closer to God than the rest of mankind; it also suggests the appeal of such Images. Even our bemused or indeed dramatic alienation today from such personification allegory is an unwitting revelation of such comparison, and an acknowledgement that Prudentius' moral principles, in particular his notion of sin, no longer obtain. These are no marks against Prudentius. His principle of imposition was effective when Fides was actually at war with Veterum Cultura Deorum in many souls.

The principle of imposition was adaptable to courtly love. In the *Roman de la rose,* Guillaume de Lorris is struck by Love's five good arrows. But it is obvious that other combinations of arrows were feasible. Different narrative lines and conclusions are possible—rhetorically possible, and thus arguable. Robert O. Payne found similar compositional possibilities exploited in Chaucer, even in poems like *Troilus* which employ exemplification rather than personification and dream vision. "It is also worth noting that a fair share of the illusion of reality comes not from the actual processes of characterization, but from the affective immediacy of the moral and emotional problems within which the existences of the characters are defined. . . . The two most striking results are a great increase in attention to characters and a simultaneous broadening and intensification of their representativeness, their typicality."[42] The reader is aware of the distance separating him from his own perfection. He is a more or less faithful *imago* of the perfect self visible in the mirror of his own soul. Whatever the idealized context the author has chosen, one finds direction to life and meaning by consideration of the goal as perfection. Imagination as Memory is thus linked to Prudence; and Prudence, as we read in the *Anticlaudianus,* is the sole agent able to approach God and consider His perfection, his "diuinam psichen,"[43] at least in a mirror. That mirror can only show things as Prudentius does. The prudent inspector will thus experience a *laetus horror,* an awful and exuberant horror before the abyss of separation.

The expression *laetus horror* is borrowed by the Vir from Statius to express the effect of the love he conceives for the Mulier in the *Epistolae duorum amantium.*[44] That love too has its diversity, its slippings into disarray and self-alienation, the flights of the soul into *diversa* because of impinging cares, worries, and difficulties (Letter LXXXV). The difficulties may be caused by external interference (Letter XCI) or inner uncertainty: "Nullus nobis infelicior est, quos amor et pudor in diversa rapiunt" (Letter XCIII; cf. CVII) [Nothing is less happy for us whom love and shame draw in opposite directions]. Diversity is not at all incompatible with rhetorical characterization.

37

Criseyde's separate loves, and her self-doubts before and between them, derive from such alienation.[45] The important consideration for the author is the idea that provides characterization and context; the representation in *matière* is an Imagination combining idea and substance, no matter how "realistic" it may appear. The Imagination may include the reader himself or his projection into the author's experience. The impact on the reader follows reflection on a fixed and imposed system of values as revealed in the attributes and relations of the characters depicted in the text and contrasted with the reader's own moral simplicity or complexity.

But it is not diversity itself that medieval writers prefer to stress, but the exceptionally good or the exceptionally bad. The significance of such confrontations, the *laetus horror* which the best inventions evoke, is related to both matter and meaning. Even in Statius' passage employing the expression, the omen of the gods takes on the import of a *somnium,* with its blend of mystery and significance—the *horror* is fruitful in yielding meaning, *laetus* because the meaning is productive of understanding which relieves uncertainty.

> sensit manifesto numine ductos
> adfore, quos nexis ambagibus augur Apollo
> portendi generos, vultu fallente ferarum,
> ediderat.
>
> (I.494–97)

[He felt that they had come, led by heaven's clear prompting, whom prophetic Apollo in riddling obscurities had foreshown to be his destined sons-in-law, under the feigned guise of beasts.]

The result is restoration and revitalization of a soul formerly lost in perplexity (I.500–504), a change evident in the joy and celebration that break out in the ruler's palace.

The knights in the *Queste del saint graal* have similar experiences of *laetus horror,* the ultimate being Galaad's. "Et si tost come il i ot regardé, si comence a trembler molt durement, si tost come la mortel char commença a regarder les esperitex choses. Lors tent Galaad ses meins vers le ciel et dit: 'Sire, toi ador ge et merci de ce que tu m'as acompli mon desirrier... ' " (pp. 277–78). [And he had no sooner looked in it than he began to tremble greatly, as soon as mortal flesh began to look upon spiritual things. Then Galaad raised his arms to heaven and said: "Lord, I adore and thank thee for having accomplished my desire... "] Such *laetus horror,* the celebration of mystery and truth, dominates the literature of Imagination in the Middle Ages, and accounts for its fascination. Meaning blends with mystery, order and simplicity emerge from ambagious diversity. Combat and quest, the rose and Ovidian *fabulae* are some sources that amply sustained it. But so long as a moral principle remains absolute, its workings rather than those of the individual

38

soul are paramount. Its fascination lies not in originality, specificity, or uniqueness, but in excellence that transcends even abstract expression, unites all qualities in integrity, and generates Images in the reader's mind.

A central theme may be named, or its meaning may escape specificity, like the grail in the *Queste* or the rose in Guillaume de Lorris. In either case, Imagination is the visual correlative to elucidation (*descriptio*) of ideas. Abstract conceptual relationships determine the choice of material for the Image; description is the sum of these relationships, static if they are placed in a state of inertia, dynamic if the relations are shown as they shift.[46] Each such Image is in effect a "complex."

A simple illustration of static description as Imagination is Raoul de Houdenc's *Roman des eles*. Starting with the idea of Prowess, Raoul seeks an Image to represent the elevation of Prowess. Since "la prouesse monte," it can be pictured as a bird in upward flight. *Monter* is literally possible by means of wings, and Largesse and Cortoisie become the wings of Prowess' upward flight (vv. 139–41). From each wing are drawn seven characteristic feathers (vv. 146–49). Raoul conceives of Imagination in terms of *deviser-aviser*. The metaphorical Image is drawn out by descriptive amplification (*deviser*), then interpreted for each part of the description by proverbs or abstractions (*aviser*). For Largesse Raoul sets forth seven *sententiae* corresponding to the wing's seven feathers. The first feather is an admonition to be forthright in the practice of largesse; the second, to eschew avarice and covetousness; the third, to give without ulterior motive; and so on. The transition to the wing of Cortoisie restates the *deviser-aviser* formula.

> Bien ai de Largece avisées
> Les.vii. penes, que devisées
> Les ai en ele. Or recovient,
> Por ce que volenteis me vient,
> Ke de l'ele de Cortoisie
> Les.vii. cortoises penes die
> Coment ont non, quel doivent estre.
> (vv. 269–75)

[I have interpreted well the seven feathers of Largesse, for I have described them on the wing. Now I should, since I am so inclined, relate the names and the appropriate attributes of the seven courteous feathers on the wing of Courtesy.]

For Cortoisie, abstractions replace proverbial generalizations. Each succeeding abstraction is dilated more than its predecessor. The final and longest amplification is for love, suggesting the primacy of love in Cortoisie. Raoul has applied Imagination to a chivalric subject, treating in part *fin' amors*. He never defines Prowess, Courtesy, or Love; rather he arranges each idea in an abstract system made coherent by coordinating the literal (*deviser*) and the abstract (*aviser*) structure of the Image.

39

The function of relationships in a dynamic structure is conspicuous in the allegorization of Branch XXIV of the *Renart*. Aesopian and Renart fables were traditionally allegories.[47] In the prologue to Branch XXIV, a relational system is constructed on the opposition of Adam and Eve. Adam strikes the water to bring forth domestic animals friendly to man, while Eve's blows produce wild animals that become man's enemies.

> Entre les autres en issi
> Le gorpis, si asauvagi:
> Rous ot le poil conme Renarz,
> Moult par fu cointes et gaingnarz:
> Por son sens toutes decevoit
> Les bestes qantqu'il en trovoit.
> Icil gorpis nos senefie
> Renart qui tant sot de mestrie.
>
> (XXIV.77–84 [vv. 3827–34])[48]

[Among the others there issued forth the fox, and he became wild. His fur was red like Renart's hair, and he was smart and thievish. By his wits he deceived all the beasts he could. This fox represents Renart to us, for he was such a sharper.]

Three Images stand in systematic and basic relation: Eve as the source of evil, and the fox and Renart as, respectively, animal and human Images of evil.

> Tot cil qui sont d'anging et d'art
> Sont mes tuit apele Renart.
> Por Renart et por le gorpil
> Moult par sorent et cil et cil.
>
> (vv. 85–88 [3835–38])

[All those who are cunning and tricky are henceforth called Renart; through Renart and through the fox they all learned a lot.]

The extension of the Images to all individuals of the type is summed up in an *interpretatio* that identifies a large group of persons/animals constelled about and "emanating" from the notion of deception, like the feathers and wings of Prowess for Raoul de Houdenc. "Se Renart sot gent conchier, / Le gorpix bestes engingnier" (vv. 89–90 [3839–40]) [If Renart knew how to screw people, the fox knew how to cheat beasts]. Where Raoul used wings to organize his Image, the *Renart* uses the lines of lineage: "Moult par furent bien d'un lignage / Et d'unes meurs et d'un corage" (vv. 91–92 [3841–42]) [They were both of one family, one conduct, and one heart]. The system opens through family ties to different degrees of deception in other wild animals, much as abstractions operate through family connections when personified in dream visions. All the wild animals descend from Eve and are thus sons and daughters of Evil more or less closely linked by their common vice

40

Deception: the wolf/Ysengrin, the she-wolf/Hersent, etc. Ysengrin is Renart's uncle.

The juxtaposition of human and animal attributes presents an unusual admixture on the literal level, as one world alternates with the other in often dazzling succession. However, there is no inconsistency within each literal Image. Despite the constant shift in the literal Imagination from the human to the animal world and back, the subordination of both to the abstract *senefiance* of what is going on keeps order in the Image; reference is not from human to animal and vice-versa, but from both to their common abstract correlative. For example, the rape of Hersent:

> Onc ne fina [Renart] d'esperonner
> Jusques au recept de Valcrues.
> Quant il i vint, si entra lues,
> Quant vit dame Hersent s'amie
> Qui vers lui vint si esgramie:
> Et de lui n'a il huimais garde.
> La fist Hersent trop que musarde.
> Apres Renart en la fosse entre
> De plein ellais de ci au ventre.
> Li chastiaus estoit granz et fors:
> Et Hersent par si grant esfors
> Se feri dedenz la tesniere
> Que ne se pot retraire arriere.
> (II. 1248–60 [v. 5924–36])

[Renart didn't stop spurring on until he reached the keep of Valcrues. When he arrived there, he went straightway in; suddenly he perceived lady Hersent his beloved, who was coming towards him in full heat. She had no more worries about him. There she acted very foolishly. After Renart she flung herself into the hole up to her stomach. The castle was big and strong. And Hersent by dint of such a great thrust started into the lair such that she couldn't get back out.]

The abrupt, virtually paratactic shifts between the human and animal *accidentia* present no problem to the reader aware of the parallel relationship between the human and animal world as well as the abstract moral sense elicited by the felonious knight Renart and the lustful Hersent on the one hand and the treacherous fox and the she-wolf in heat on the other. Careful use of literal and figurative qualifiers and epithets, the interpenetration of the two literal narratives and the allegorical sense in a coherent system—one is tempted to say fugue—holds everything together. Proper names have become epithets, and their elaboration as narrative brings all elements and levels of discourse into order.

The *Echecs* Commentator uses the same method to elucidate mythological *fabulae* by comparing them with one another. This facilitates the allegorical elucidation of two or more discrete narratives. The *Queste* does the same with vision, dream, and literal adventures. We shall see Froissart combine features of several Ovidian tales to invent new ones more suitable to his intention. Such *conversio,* as Bernardus Silvestris calls it (*De Mundi* II.iii.93), extends and incorporates into Imagination Geoffrey of Vinsauf's instruction on conversion and determination.

Conversion permits the adaptation of a simple statement or idea to the most effective expression of authorial intention, and determination provides suitable qualifiers that explicate and specify that intention. As such, conversion and determination are techniques that render a given thought at once explicit and ornate. Conversion makes changes from one part of speech to another; determination seeks appropriate modifiers for nouns and verbs. Both strive for precision, clarity, ease of understanding, finer approximation to the thought that is to be conveyed. "Sic enim gradatim descendendum est, donec inveniat animus in quo resideat et in quo complaceat" (*Documentum,* p. 307, §123).[49] [For thus step by step one continues until his mind finds that in which it will abide and in which it might take pleasure.] Variant statements of a given subject may constitute so many gradual approximations to the thought. The accumulation of conversions and determinations, the variation in parts of speech amounting to nominal description alternating with verbal narration and episodic variety is *frequentatio.*

Frequentatio is a rhetorical figure.[50] The definition in the *Ad Herennium* reads: "cum res tota causa dispersae coguntur in unum" (IV.xl.52) [when the points scattered throughout the whole cause are collected in one place]. It therefore precludes *alienatio*—internal distraction, confusion, loss in the diversity of conflicting impulse, and ultimately what we might call coma and courtly poets death. In Geoffrey of Vinsauf, *frequentatio* becomes: "Singula rursus in unum / Conveniunt et quae sunt undique sparsa resumit" (*Poetria nova,* vv. 1242–43) [Single details are brought together, and [it] gathers up points that had been scattered through the work]. The figure had special significance in the twelfth century because of its relation to philosophical speculation on emanation.

Emanation is the creative process an author imitates when using *frequentatio.* In Bernardus Silvestris, *frequentatio* is the elaboration of divine principles as the forms in matter. Nature is the agent effecting the union of matter and form. Manifold variety is brought back to God through appropriate intermediary channels which cause the formal aspects of objects to converge, through Imagination and morphological specialization, on their intellectual First Cause.[51] The imposition of meaning onto matter is known as Imagination. Just as the manifold abundance of creation could bring the beholder back to God through greater and greater abstraction and intellection, the multiplication of the manifestations of an abstract idea served to reveal more and more of the significance of the abstraction. The Imagination thus dominates the dispersed elements the poet relates systematically by *frequentatio*. The affinities of the technique with *interpretatio* and *expolitio*, fundamental to amplification in the arts of poetry and thus to poetic invention, are patent. The frequent binding together of Bernardus Silvestris' *De mundi universitate* with Geoffrey of Vinsauf's *Poetria Nova*[52] suggests an awareness early in the thirteenth century of the close relation between the former's understanding of emanation as *frequentatio* and the latter's application of it to composition. Faral demonstrated the link between *frequentatio* and *interpretatio*.[53]

In Geoffrey's *Poetria, expolitio* follows immediately after *frequentatio* in the inventory of figures of thought, and is described as a special kind of emanation.

> In replicando frequens, iterum variando colorem,
> Dicere res plures videor; sed semper in una
> Demoror, ut poliam rem plenius et quasi crebra
> Expoliam lima, quod fit sub duplice forma:
> Dicendo varie vel eamdem rem, vel eadem
> De re. . . .
>
> (vv. 1244–49)

[By turning a subject over repeatedly and varying the figure, I seem to be saying a number of things whereas I am actually dwelling on one thing, in order to give it a finer polish and impart a smooth finish by repeated applications of the file, one might say. This is done in two ways: either by saying the same thing with variations, or by elaborating upon the same thing.]

Geoffrey then refers to the *Ad Herennium*,[54] where three kinds of synonymy and seven varieties of incremental elaboration are set forth in detail: *commoratio, contentio, similitudo, exemplum, imago, effictio,* and *notatio* (*Poetria nova*, vv. 1249–64). The elevation of *interpretatio* and *expolitio* to the role of amplification establishes *frequentatio* in poetics. Indeed, *interpretatio* subsumes the other varieties of amplification,[55] many of which are related to the seven from the *Ad Herennium*.

Interpretatio and *expolitio* elucidate literal abstractions, mythological figures, and bestiaries. As amplification they acquired a narrative function denied to the more humble figure, but this did not change their characteristic features:

> sententia cum sit
> Unica, non uno veniat contenta paratu,
> Sed variet vestes et mutatoria sumat;
> Sub verbis aliis praesumpta resume; repone
> Pluribus in clausis unum; multiplice forma
> Dissimuletur idem; varius sis et tamen idem.
>
> (*Poetria nova*, vv. 220–25)

[Although the meaning is one, let it not come content with one set of apparel. Let it vary its robes and assume different raiment. Let it take up again in other words what has already been said; let it reiterate, in a number of clauses, a single thought. Let one and the same thing be concealed under multiple forms—be varied and yet the same.]

Since *interpretatio* and *expolitio* include the *imago,* the *imago* as Imagination is prominent in amplification. Given the scope of *interpretatio* and *expolitio,* the *imago* could absorb such specific kinds of amplification as description, digression, periphrasis, comparison, apostrophe—figures with which it had already been associated in rhetorical instruction and forensic oratory, as we have seen in the example above from Priscian's *Praeexercitamina.* The diverse subjects and objects drawn together by *frequentatio* form a composite Image as a verbal constellation or system of references. Through that system the idea is seen to emerge as if by emanation. The theory fits this succinct description of Imagination from an anonymous treatise: "Per ymaginationem non est in istis sed secundum ista" (Alain de Lille, *Textes,* p. 313) [Through Imagination it exists not in these things but in accordance with them]. And it harks back to Macrobius' use of similitudes and examples to speak of supernatural subjects.

The similarity between the artist's craft and God's creation is a medieval commonplace that appears in Hugh of Saint Victor, Bernardus Silvestris, Alain de Lille, and Geoffrey of Vinsauf.[56] That is why Geoffrey described the poet's opus as moving from the mental archetype as idea to verbal expression in *materia:* "Status ejus / Est prius archetypus quam sensilis" (*Poetria nova,* vv. 47–48)[57] [Its mode of being is archetypal before it is actual]. The archetype becomes a mental model the poet imitates by finding suitable words and bringing them together into a whole that manifests the archetype: the poet is indeed a trouvère, and his first responsibility is the invention of Images that imitate archetypes. This conception of imitation, which hardly begins to emerge in classical *imitatio,* comes into its own in ecclesiastical Latin, especially in conjunction with the Fathers' use of *imago* as an allegorical figure. Jean de Ghellinck has identified this new sense of *imitatio.*

C'est celui, non pas de l'imitation proprement dite d'un acte ou d'une personne, qu'on prend comme modèle concret, vécu [as in classical Latin], mais celui de la reproduction d'un modèle théorique, idéal, entrevu dans sa pensée, qu'on se propose soi-même de réaliser. Le modèle qu'on veut copier ou reproduire n'existe pas au concret: il n'a de réalité que dans l'esprit qui le conçoit et l'effort de l'"imitateur" tend à le réaliser concrètement, comme un artiste tâche d'exécuter l'idéal entrevu.[58]

The use of Imagination for allegory and metonymy is obvious. The twelfth-century philosophical poets demonstrated the applicability of the method to the expression of philosophical, theological, and moral thought; the allegorizations of Ovid extended it to concerns of popular moral instruction and religious faith. Both bequeathed to vernacular literature a mode that was, for two centuries and more, in Guillaume de Lorris and his successors, to attain distinction as an expression of *fin' amors*.

YMAGINATION

Poëma loquens pictura, pictura tacitum poëma debet esse.
—*Rhetorica ad Herennium*

Ille sollicite scribat, qui non habet, ut quod non habet, reperiat.
—*Epistolae duorum amantium*[59]

A highly complex, if irregular,[60] psychological vocabulary existed at the end of the twelfth century and continued in use, despite adaptation to changes in philosophy and world-view, to the end of the Middle Ages. However, variation in technical usage, the lack of appropriate words in French that were not explicit Latinisms, and the generally low level of discrimination prevented the use of a coherent cognitive vocabulary before the thirteenth century. The studies of Bechtoldt and Koenig reveal the uncertainty and confusion in specificity and categorization.[61] Neither discusses Imagination as such, even under the Latin terminology (Bechtoldt touches on it only under *memorie*[62]). Nonetheless, authors trained in the schools were clearly aware of the function of Imagination; if they scarcely used the word except in the sense of "statue" or "painting" or as man in the Image of God, they did use the function to represent thoughts and feelings as projections. The troubadours[63] and trouvères correlated feelings of the heart with projected settings and dramatizations.

> tan ai al cor d'amor,
> de joi e de doussor,
> per que'l gels me sembla flor
> e la neus verdura.
> Anar posc ses vestidura,
> nutz en ma chamiza,
> car fin'amors m'asegura
> de la freja biza.
> (XLIV.9–16)[64]

[In my heart I have so much love, joy, and sweetness, that ice is for me a flower, and the snow verdure. I can go about without clothing, bare in my shirt, for courtly love guards me against the cold blast.]

In *Yvain*, Chrétien de Troyes experimented with Imagination as projection of abstract notions and sentiments through the personified thoughts of Yvain and Laudine in love or falling in love as well as the psychomachia, in which Yvain and Gauvain do battle while Love and Hate dwell separate but at peace in the

45

edifice of their hearts. Similarly, Perceval is transfixed by the drops of blood in the snow that become the Image of Blancheflor.

Thomas d'Angleterre also invented some striking projections that foreshadow the later adaptation of Image and Imagination in French. For Tristan, the appeal of Iseut White Hands is, first, the possibility of projecting into her as his wife the love he feels for Iseut the Blond. Second, by the fact of marriage, he sees the possibility of understanding how Iseut the Blond can remain married to Marc and still continue to love Tristan even during a long separation. Tristan's discovery of his own impotence, real or imposed, does in fact permit him to understand Iseut the Blond's emotional and sexual life with Marc. The Image is worthy of Bernart de Ventadorn. So is Tristan's next expedient, the construction of a statue qua Image of Iseut the Blond in a cave.

> Por iço fist il ceste image
> Que dire li volt son corage,
> Son bon penser et sa fole errur,
> Sa paigne, sa joie d'amor,
> Car ne sot vers cui descoverir
> Ne son voler, ne son desir.
>
> Fragment Turin[1], vv. 45–50[65]

[He made this statue because he wanted to open his heart to it, and give expression to his noble thought and his mad confusion, his pain, his joy in love; for he knew no one to whom he could discover his will or his desire.]

The extension, under Latin influence, of affective vocabulary continued into the thirteenth century, when the powerful examples of Arthurian prose romance and the *Roman de la rose* will furnish substance for Imagination, and the development of the dit an adequate vehicle for its poetic expression.

By the end of the thirteenth century, Imagination is a well-known concept in French literary vocabulary. A *Salut* by Philippe de Remi, sire de Beaumanoir, illustrates the various connotations of Imagination as the mental achievement of perfect, idealized form and its verbal projection.

> C'est que la biauté que devis
> Et son maintien et sa maniere,
> Soit pres de li u bien arriere,
> Avra en soi en liu d'ymage.
> D'ymaginier lor le fas sage:
> Si iert en son cuer enformee
> Sa forme que ja desformee
> Ne sera, ains enfourmera
> En son cuer cele ki fourme a
> En soi de la plus bele forme
> Qui onques fust fourmee en fourme.
>
> (vv. 556–66)[66]

[It's because the beauty I depict will have in itself as Image her conduct and her qualities, be she near or rather far away. I shall teach him how to Imagine them. Her form will be so impressed in his heart that it will never be undone, but rather she will give form in his heart, she who has within her the form of the most beautiful form ever moulded into form.]

The archetypal figure of the lady appears in the poet-lover's heart as an Image of perfect abstract beauty. He then exteriorizes the inner form in a suitable Image: "Est prius archetypus quam sensilis." (Geoffrey of Vinsauf, *Poetria nova*, v. 48) The Image becomes a convincing, because accurate, rendering of the ideal qualities the poet discerns in the integrity of his lady's form. The movement from sight to memory to verbal Image rehearses both the *gradus amoris* described by Andreas Capellanus and, in reverse order, the stages of invention set forth in the *Poetria nova*.

The use of Imagination in Beaumanoir's *Salut* is characteristic of Imagination in most short poems. The Image is briefly sketched, abstract, conventional in its components, literal, and idealized—it is *bone et bele*. Machaut's "Lay de l'image" contains a hyperbolic, laudatory description of the lady with topical metaphors.

> La rose et la flour
> De biauté et de douçour,
> Tout en mi
> Le cuer de my,
> Com vo douce ymage.
> (XIV.96–100)

[The rose and the flower of beauty and sweetness, right in the middle of my heart like your sweet Image.]

The *ymage* is both an "exemplaire" (v. 142) of Nature's idea of beauty, and a "pourtraiture" (v. 187) of the lady in the poet's heart. Similarly, the description in Balade CLXXIII is an abstract realization of the heart's Image (cf. Geoffrey of Vinsauf's "sitque prius in pectore...").

> Gente de corps et tres bele de vis,
> Vraie de cuer, d'onneur la souvereinne,
> Ymage à droit parfaite, à mon devis,
> La grant bonté de vous, entiere et seinne,
> Le scens, le pris, la maniere certeinne
> Et vo douceur vous font estre en ce monde
> M'amour premiers et ma dame seconde.
> (vv. 1–7)

[Noble in person and with a very beautiful face, true in heart, sovereign in honor, Image exactly perfect—in my estimation—your great goodness, whole and sound, your wit, renown, assured manner, and your sweetness, make you here on earth my love first and my lady second.]

The posture of the lover in adoration before his lady's perfect Image (Balade notée IX.11–17) recalls Pygmalion: "Je puis trop bien ma dame comparer / A l'image que fist Pymalion" (Balade CCIII) [I can quite well make a comparison between my lady and the Image Pygmalion made]. In it Imagination is metaphorical and hortatory—the balade is conceived as a *prière*—and the two rhetorical intentions fuse in the poet's hope that his lady, like Pygmalion's, may come to life through love. The Image elicits mirror play between portrait and lady that we shall see elaborated upon in the *Voir-Dit*.

Rarely do Images in the shorter pieces become truly metaphorical, since metaphor usually demands elaboration more suitable to longer narrative or the dit; in the latter the heart's Image can be transformed into a dream vision expressive of courtly poetry's continuing quest for ideal love. However, there is some variety of Images among the shorter poems. The lady may be perceived as her properties (Lai XXI.131–40). This is *imaginatio:* "Cum in quadam sensibilium ad que sensus exierat rememoratione, anima penes se quasi quodam memoriale exemplum inscribit, ut tota animalis intentio preter sensibilium de quibus cogitat presentiam, in eorundem ymaginationem comparabiliter videatur esse suspensa"[67] [When, through a certain recall of sensual perceptions, to which the senses have gone out, the soul inscribes in itself, as it were, an exemplum in memory, the entire attention of the soul, removed from the presence of the sensible objects upon which it reflects, seems to be suspended figuratively in the Imagination of them]. Machaut, similarly:

> Car Dous Pensers en recoy
> De sa biauté l'exemplaire
> Doucement me monstre au doy.
> C'est pourquoy
> Loing et près toudis repaire
> Joye en moy.
> (Lai XXI.49–54)

[For Sweet Thought in secret points out to me in a gentle manner the exemplar of her beauty. That is why Joy always dwells in me, be I near or far.]

The abstraction of the properties in the Image, a metonymic and synecdochic process in the fixed forms, expands into exemplary metaphorical narrative or argument in the dits. Being rhetorical, the method is eminently rational and meaningful. The expression, elaboration, and intention of the Image and the conceptual originality of the author are described in the *Response* to Richart de Fornival's *Bestiaires*.

Aussi comme fait meïsme li lions, qui giete, si comme j'entenc[h] de vous, une pieche de char quant il faonne, et dont li sanle que par raison n'est mie bien maullee a

48

s'ymage: dont va entour et le fourme a le langue tout autel comme il doit estre. Aussi bee je a faire, sire maistres, que s'il avient que dire me couvient aucune cose que je n'aie mie bien conchut, c'est pensé, que je voise entour et le meche a sens et a raison par bonne doctrine que je puisse aprendre en vos dis. (p. 115)

[Just as even the lion does, which throws out, as I hear you tell, a piece of flesh when it bears young, flesh which seems to it not at all rightly moulded in its own Image. Therefore it goes over it and shapes it with its tongue into the form it should have. So do I seek to do, my lord and master. For if it happens that I should express something that I do not clearly understand, that is, have not thought out clearly, I go over it and make it meaningful and reasonable with the help of the sound instruction imparted to me in your words.]

The Image in the dit is a *merveille* fashioned in accordance with an intention that may be the author's or may be imposed by the specific role of the figures in context. Thus in the *Response* the same matter treated in the original *Bestiaires* receives more often than not a new reading that subverts the latter's meaning.

After Guillaume de Lorris' adaptation of allegorical personification to courtly literature, few attempted to emulate his subtlety in the use of personification. There are historical explanations for this apparent anomaly. One is a movement towards exemplification; another is the popularity acquired by Ovidian figures, especially after the *Ovide moralisé;* finally, there is a trend towards didacticism and classification at the expense of Imagination. But most significant of all, abstractions themselves became less and less expressive. Richard Glasser, in his important study of the history of personified abstractions in Romance languages, especially French, has traced a gradual semantic paling of personifications after the thirteenth century. The loss of semantic flexibility and clarity precluded subtlety. This was fatal to a mode of representation which depended on semantic clarity and adaptability.[68] The decline was due in part to indiscriminate use of common abstractions, without care for sharp discrimination in meaning and nuance. Thus the fault lies partly in the widespread use of *frequentatio. Frequentatio* as *interpretatio* and *expolitio* was, as we have seen, at the origins of Imagination in composition. The powerful examples of both parts of the *Roman de la rose* provided additional incentive to adapt these principles in the dit. But indiscriminate accumulation of abstractions blurs the source of *frequentatio* and finally loses it. The system of interrelationships among the diversified elements of a *frequentatio* is undone, leaving only clusters of abstractions whose relationship is arbitrary or commonplace. Discursive explanation, even explicit definition, became necessary to convey meaning through abstractions and their personifications. This explicitness produced primary colors less amenable to the subtleties and nuances of immediate apprehension characteristic of Imagination.

The evidence of greater discursiveness appears already in Machaut. But he avoids the more serious pitfalls of cloudy abstraction by the use of mythological examples. The adventures of gods and heroes were sufficiently varied, and the Ovidian or mythographic originals could be adapted; thus when the abstractions were no longer serviceable, the old fables were readily taken up and adapted in retelling to authorial intention. The use of Ovidian moralizations had become widespread by the thirteenth century. John of Garland, the last of the important authors of *poetriae*, composed a very popular one. Such material was rendered into French early in the fourteenth century by the *Ovide moralisé*, which, despite its length, never lost appeal, judging by the number of manuscripts as well as borrowings and allusions to it which have been identified by modern scholarship. And it inspired one or more commentaries.[69] Ovidian material, together with Biblical exempla, was incorporated into the arts of the Second Rhetoric as the *poetries:* lists of personages and places with brief summaries of their character and attendant actions that could be used for Imaginative writing.[70]

The use of Ovidian material tends towards both exemplification and true allegory. For although the personages and events are more unique than personified abstractions, and are also in a sense historical and were often taken to be so by euhemerization, the separation between their literal meaning and the author's imposed meaning is wider. Personification is metonymic. It thus retains a certain ambiguity in transfer that permits the author to avoid the deliberate imposition of meaning characteristic of the *Ovide moralisé*. Ovidian material and its consequent discursive mode, which quite distinctly— even schizophrenically—divorce poetic *delectare* from doctrinal *prodesse,* replace discernment with definition. Reason's gain is Imagination's loss. We may still observe the Image as Ovidian example and personified abstraction in Machaut's use of the word.

Machaut frequently uses *ymage* as a visual representation: portrait, statue, figurine, the "image que fist Pymalion," "une ymage en pointure" (*Confort,* v. 2771) like that of Péronne d'Armentières in the *Voir-Dit. Figure* also appears in this sense: "Nabugodonosor figure / Qu'il vit en songe une estature" (*Remede,* vv. 1001–02) [Nebuchadnezzar imagines that he dreamed of a statue]. Two facts are striking about the statue: one, its appearance in a dream; two, Machaut's new interpretation of its meaning. The dream fits the statue seen by Nebuchadnezzar into the phenomena represented in the *Roman de la rose,* and, by extension, into any visual representation in the mind. This includes the lady herself and the Lover's mental homage to her.

> Lors dois avoir l'impression
> De ceste ymagination
> Et de ceste douce figure
> Que Dous Penser en toy figure,

S'en dois en ton cuer une ymage
Faire, a qui tu feras hommage.
(*Confort* vv. 2185-90)[71]

[Then you must have the imprint of this imagination and of this sweet figure which Sweet Thought represents in you, and you must make an image in your heart to which you will do homage.]

In the *Voir-Dit,* the portrait of Péronne and the Image in the poet's mind are projections onto the lady herself, and the three fuse in the poem. In fact, the portrait as Image comes to life in a dream and turns away as if it were the real lady (*Voir-Dit,* p. 213); later it speaks in a dream (pp. 315-17). In a third instance the portrait is linked to Venus, becoming a representation of both Venus and Péronne: "Maintes fois la comparay / A Venus quant je l'aouroie" (vv. 1393-94) [Often I compared her to Venus when I adored her]. In one episode Machaut and Péronne share a bed enveloped by Venus' cloud. The interrelation, the virtual "interreplaceability" of Venus, Péronne, and the *ymage* recalls the blending of different literal Imaginations in continuous narrative sequence observed in the *Renart:* they are contextually coordinated representations.

Quant je vi sa coulour vermeille,
Et sa biauté qui n'a pareille,
Son dous vis, sa riant bouchette,
Douce plaisant & vermillette,
Et sa gorge polie & tendre,
Je m'agenouillay sans attendre
Et encommençay ma priere,
A Venus, par ceste maniere:
'Venus, je t'ay tousjours servi,
Depuis que ton ymage vi.... '
(*Voir-Dit,* vv. 3704-13)

[When I saw her reddish complexion and her beauty unparalleled, her sweet face, her laughing little mouth, sweet, pleasant, and slightly ruddy, and her smooth, tender throat, I knelt down forthwith and began my prayer to Venus in this manner: "Venus, I have ever served you since I first saw your Image.... "]

Qualitative separation of the person and his or her Image is also possible, as in the striking contrast between the idealized portrait (*imago picta*) personified in the dream (*imago ficta*) and the real Péronne allegedly untrue to the poet (vv. 7719-72).[72]

Mental Image is the most frequent sense for *ymage* in Machaut's dits.

Car la trés douce imprecion
De son ymagination

51

> Est en mon cuer si fort empreinte
> Qu'encor y est et yert l'empreinte,
> Ne jamais ne s'en partira,
> Jusques a tant qu'il partira.
>
> (*Lyon,* vv. 207–12)

[For the most gentle impression of her imagination is impressed so firmly in my heart that it is still there and ever will be; nor will it take leave of it until death.]

Similarly, regarding the god of Love in the *Vergier:*

> Grace et loange li rendoient
> Et comme leur Dieu l'aouroient.
> Et quant j'eus tout cela veü,
> Ymaginé et conceü,
> J'en os en moy moult grant frëour.
>
> (vv. 191–95)

[Thanks and praise they gave to him, and worshipped him as their god. And when I had seen, imagined, and conceived in my mind all of that, a great shudder came over me.]

Laetus horror! Machaut's Imagination parallels Matthew of Vendôme's *voir-ymaginer-concevoir* as well as Raoul de Houdenc's *deviser-aviser.* Solomon used it to write Ecclesiastes, according to Machaut:

> il demoustre en sa page
> Que, quant il a tout conceü,
> Tout ymaginé, tout veü,
> Esprouvé, serchié, viseté
> Le monde, c'est tout vanité.
>
> (*Jugement Navarre,* vv. 130–34)

[he shows in his writing that, after having conceived, imagined, seen everything, tested, investigated, examined all, everything is vanity.]

The lady's Image in the poet's mind may be a source of consolation and hope.

> Encor y a maint ressort:
> Ramembrer,
> Ymaginer
> En dous plaisir
> Sa dame vëoir, oïr,
> Son gentil port,
> Le recort
> Dou bien qui sort
> De son parler
> Et de son dous regarder.
>
> (*Remede,* vv. 445–54)

[There is still many a recourse: remembrance, imagination of the sweet pleasure of seeing, hearing his lady, her noble bearing, the recall of the good that springs from her conversation and from her sweet gaze.]

The Image of the lady moves here into the allegorical mode, for just preceding these lines from the *Remede*'s lai is the abstract description of the lady's qualities. That Image of the lady is "miroir et exemplaire / De tous biens desirer et faire" (*Remede*, vv. 171–72) [mirror and exemplar for desiring and doing all things good]. The comparison links the Image to its type, a notion itself peculiar to *figura* as the stamp to the stamped Image.[73] It also accords with the idealization of the lady as her qualities, and makes her serve an eminently allegorical function representing the qualities she incorporates.

The *Prise d'Alexandrie* illustrates the application of this principle to narrative composition and even biographical writing. The blend of personification allegory, chronicle, and romance requires careful preliminary elaboration of the subject (vv. 1–228).[74] Machaut chose Pierre de Lusignan, a knight in whom he saw a remarkable union of prowess in arms and nobility in love. The personifications bring these two qualities to the fore.

> Si supplierent à nature
> Qu'el feist une creature
> Le mieus & dou milleur affaire
> Qu'elle porroit ne saroit faire.
> Lors de Mars & de Venus ensamble [*sic*]
> Fist conjunction, ce me samble,
> Et la creature crea
> Si bien, qu'à chascun agrea.
> (vv. 69–76)

[They besought nature to make a creature of the best and finest quality she could or knew how to do; then she conjoined Mars and Venus, it seems to me, and created the creature of such quality that it pleased everyone.]

Pierre de Lusignan approximates the more idealized portraiture of action and sentiment typical of adventure romance.[75]

In the *Fonteinne amoureuse,* the lady's Image is the source of the complainte (vv. 1003–18), especially its artistry.

> Cent rimes ay mis dedens ceste rime,
> Qui bien les conte.
> Prises les ay en vostre biauté qui me
> Tient sans dormir dou soir jusques a prime.
> (vv. 1021–24)

[You will find by careful count that I have employed a hundred rhymes in this poem. I drew them from your beauty which holds me sleepless from even till morn.]

53

Such adoration raises the specter of idolatry. D. W. Robertson, Jr., has made much of this feature of courtly love, to such an extent as to argue from it that nothing like courtly love could have existed in medieval literature.[76] Imagination can connote idolatry, the making of an idol like Pygmalion's, even if it reigns only in the heart, as Machaut and Froissart point out;[77] they illustrate it in the adoration of the lady and love frequent in their fixed forms and dits.[78] But I have avoided the word idolatry because Machaut and Froissart obviously did not equate it with true Imagination, and almost never use *ymage* to refer to *ydole*. Machaut uses *ydole* to refer only to what pagans and sinners (not *fins amants* like him!) worship,[79] and then only literally. Like homage, worship is an allegory for love service, the acquisition of the lady's grace through imitation of her qualities. Idolatry as such is false Imagination, the substance of *insomnia* and *visa*, as Radulphe of Longchamps points out.[80] Machaut consistently employs *ymage* to designate his lady. In the *Voir-Dit*, he prays to God, Love, and Venus.[81] The hierarchy is explicit in the *Confort d'ami*, where Charles the Bad's duties to God, his lady, and his family are enunciated and assigned worth in relation to each other.

> Mais, pour chose que je te die,
> Garde toy bien que t'estudie
> Soit adès tout premierement
> En servir Dieu devotement,
> Qu'il n'est amour qui se compere
> A s'amour, foy que doy saint Pere,
> Ne chose, tant soit pure, eu monde,
> Ne que riens contre tout le monde,
> Ou comme une ymage en pointure
> Contre une vive creature.
> (vv. 2763–72)[82]

[But, whatever I may tell you, take care ever to apply yourself above all else to serving God, for there is no love comparable to His love, by the faith due Saint Peter, nor anything on earth like it, no matter how pure; the latter is like a speck compared to the whole earth, or like a portrait compared to a living creature.]

And the description of Machaut's lady is usually a fragmentation into spiritual and corporeal abstractions less redolent of idolatry than expressive of the idea of noble love, the relative or actual sublimation characteristic of his understanding of *fin' amors*.[83]

Since there is a wide variety of applications for the notion Image, the adaptation of the technique of *ymagination* to courtly writing was to be expected. The word connoted generally the realization, at least in the mind, of a certain intention leading to action.

54

> Mais pluseurs fois ymaginay
> En mon cuer, & determinay
> Que je penroie un homme estrange. . . .
> (*Voir-Dit*, vv. 1756–58)

[But several times I Imagined in my heart and determined to hire a foreign man . . . .]

In an amorous, and more abstract, context:

> Mais la belle prist à sourire
> De sa tres-belle bouche, au dire;
> Et ce me fist ymaginer,
> Et certainement esperer
> Que ce pas ne li desplaisoit,
> Pour ce qu'elle ainsi se taisoit.
> (*Voir-Dit*, v. 2291–96)

[But the lovely girl's most lovely mouth began to form a smile at what was said; and this caused me to imagine, and certainly to hope that this was not displeasing to her, given the way that she held her silence.]

Or:

> Et, sans cesser,
> Ymaginer
> A li porter
> Foy, sans fausser.
> (*Voir-Dit*, vv. 4227–30)

[and unceasingly to imagine keeping faith with her, without falsehood.]

The movement from understanding to visualization of what is understood, that is to *ymagination,* is evident in the following lines:

> Véu avés le dous escript
> Que ma douce dame m'escript.
> Et aussi je l'ay bien véu,
> Ymaginé et concéu.
> Et certes quant je bien l'ymagine,
> Je la compere à la roÿne
> Qu'on appelloit Semiramis.
> (*Voir-Dit*, vv. 4563–69)

[You have seen the sweet writing from my gentle lady. And I too have seen, imagined, and conceived it in my mind. And indeed when I fix her clearly in my imagination, I compare her to the queen called Semiramis.]

Imagination moves from matter to meaning through form and metaphor. In the subsequent development of the above comparison, the lady herself becomes the model for an actual portrait of Semiramis commissioned by the people of her country (vv. 4679–86). Mythological figures as well as the Bible provided *poetries,* a rich source of Images made significant according to the author's intention, and effective by the quality of his artistry. Machaut himself concludes the tale of Orpheus and Eurydice in the *Confort d'ami* by: "Mais selonc la poeterie, / Telle fu sa mort et sa vie" (vv. 2631–32) [But according to *poetrie,* such was his life and death]. Machaut's invention of bestiary figures in the *Alerion* illustrates the range of possibilities traditionally associated with Imagination. Indeed, the portrait of Péronne commissioned by her countrymen permitted Machaut to understand Semiramis as representing her qualities, just as Richart de Fornival used traditional bestiary illuminations to represent his love. Semiramis, Eurydice, Polixène, Pygmalion's statue and lady—these figures and others like them emerge from an idea that each serves to express. The poet's lady is in turn raised and abstracted onto that plane by Imagination. The distance separating the authorial ego from realizing the qualities in the Image are the hope and despair of courtly poets. The acquisition of those qualities enhances their love, and earns them esteem for the capacity to know and express a worthy love. This broad survey must now be deepened by a more careful study of some principal contributions to Imaginative courtly literature.

4

Guillaume de Lorris and Imagination in the *Roman de la rose*

C'était un lieu commun; il n'en répondait pas moins chez lui à une
pensée sincère.
—Jean Frappier[1]

GUILLAUME DE LORRIS' ROMANCE is a product of Imagination. As Radulphe
de Longchamps says in his commentary to Alain de Lille's *Anticlaudianus*,
"Sub imaginatione quodammodo continetur somnium" (p. 52) [under imagination is classified *somnium* in a certain sense]. Radulphe's discussion of
somnium as *imaginatio* is based on Macrobius' authoritative classification of
dreams in the commentary to Cicero's *Somnium Scipionis*—Guillaume de
Lorris' authority on the veracity and prophetic value of dreams (vv. 3–10
[ibid.]). There are two kinds of false dreams: *insomnium*—the wish-fulfilment
dream and the nightmare; and *visum*—fantastic Images which appear between
waking and sleep. They are unworthy of serious consideration, "cura inter-
pretationis indigna . . . quia nihil divinationis adportant" (Macrobius 1.3.3)
[not worth interpreting since they have no prophetic significance]. They are
therefore not *vera imaginatio*, but rather belong to what Radulphe terms
"confusa imaginatio" (p. 51). The forms of objects are obscure and incom-
prehensible or out of joint; they have neither substance nor truth, and thus lead
to error and melancholy.

> Al is ylyche good to me—
> Joye or sorowe, wherso hyt be—
> For I have felynge in nothyng,
> But, as yt were, a mased thyng,
> Alway in poynt to falle a-doun;
> For sorwful ymagynacioun
> Ys alway hooly in my mynde.
> (Chaucer, *BD*, 9–15)[2]

The *insomnium*, which reflects in sleep the hopes and concerns of waking life,
includes among other subjects the "amator deliciis suis aut fruentem . . . aut
carentem" (Macrobius, 1.3.4) [lover who dreams of possessing his

57

sweetheart or losing her]. But neither Chaucer's "sorwful ymagynacioun" nor Macrobius' *insomnium* describes Guillaume's dream. For the dream may be "senefiance / Des biens as genz e des enuiz" (vv. 16–17 [ibid.]) [*a sign of* the good and evil that come to men]. Guillaume's own dream turns out to be prophetic.[3]

> Mais en cel songe onques rien n'ot
> Qui trestot avenu ne soit
> Si con li songes recensoit.
>
> (vv. 28–30 [ibid.])

[But in this dream was nothing which did not happen *entirely* as the dream told it.]

In Macrobius' classification, Guillaume's dream is a *somnium proprium,* that is, it reveals events that actually take place later in the dreamer's life. But as a *somnium* it "tegit figuris et velat ambagibus non nisi interpretatione intellegendam significationem rei quae demonstratur" (1.3.10) [conceals with strange shapes and veils with ambiguity the true meaning of the information being offered, and requires an interpretation for its understanding]. Imagination provides the figures and actions that show forth the truth of the dream. For Guillaume's romance is neither a mildly erotic *locus amoenus,* nor a Napoleonic code of love, nor a conventionally stylized setting for ironic presentation of "true" love. The substance and truth of the dream behind the "matire . . . bone et nueve" of his Imagination is the "Art d'Amors" (vv. 38–39 [ibid.])[4]

Guillaume's *Roman de la rose* contains as Images three groups of personifications: first, the Images painted into the wall of Deduit's garden and illustrating defects that impede courtly love; second, the personifications participating in the song and carol inside the garden and representing qualities essential to the *fin amant;* and third, the personifications, gods, and goddesses appearing in the narrative proper centering on the Rose and depicting the adventures[5] of and changes in the Lover in his pursuit of the Rose.

THE IMAGES IN THE WALL OF DEDUIT'S GARDEN

The defects painted outside the garden are static descriptions.[6] The noncourtly world is represented by means of an elaborate *distributio* that clashes with an otherwise lovely spring morning.

Each portrait represents a defect by underscoring physical ugliness, poor dress, and baseness. The ensemble—Haine, Felonie, Vilanie, Covoitise, Avarice, Envie, Tristesse, Vieillesse, Papelardie, and Povreté—precludes joy, and thus love. For each personification there is a simple, typical description. The meaning of the personification is an elaboration upon an idea accessible through the Image: "Si vos conterai e dirai / De ces images la semblance" (vv. 136–37 [ibid.] [And I shall recount to you and tell you the appearance of

58

these images]. The *semblance* is the representation of an abstraction in an Image. Each description is identified by name. The technique is the same as that of Raoul de Houdenc in the *Roman des eles*. It has the advantage of being explicit and readily comprehensible as the description unfolds. This simplicity is suitable for public reading, which tends to preclude reflection and reconsideration of difficult or abstruse passages. Jean de Meun makes this point in his continuation.[7]

> E pour tenir la dreite veie,
> Qui bien voudrait la chose emprendre,
> Qui n'est pas legiere a entendre,
> Un gros essemple en pourroit metre
> Aus genz lais, qui n'entendent letre,
> Car teus genz veulent grosse chose,
> Senz grant soutiveté de glose.
>
> (vv. 17390–96 [17360–66])

[If one wanted to understand the matter and stick to the straight way—and it is not an easy thing to understand—he could *present* a rough example to lay people, who don't understand writing. Such people want something general, without any great subtlety of a gloss.]

The method renders the thought accessible to those untrained in the subtleties of abstract ideas but still able, by Imagination, to appreciate the implications of careful and clear illustration.

The Images are on the whole more similar than different. Topical are: the characteristic, typical, or emblematic pose; the recurrence of green and yellow; the insistence on the wrong done to *proece* and the nobility; hyperbole and anaphora; etymological word-play; clothing and physical ugliness. Only the nominal designation permits any consistent distinction among the Images and gives specificity to the otherwise formal, inexplicit descriptions. We may illustrate this by the first three Images. The first,

> Qui de corroz et d'ataïne
> Sembla bien estre moverresse;
> Corroceuse e tençonerresse,
> E pleine de grant cuvertage
> Estoit par semblant cele image;
> Si n'estoit pas bien atornee,
> Ainz sembloit fame forsenee.
> Rechignié avoit e froncié
> Le vis, e le nés secorcié;
> Hisdeuse estoit et roïlliee;
> Et si estoit entortilliee
> Hisdosement d'une toaille.
>
> (vv. 140–51 [ibid.])

59

[Who certainly seemed to be the one who incites anger and strife. In appearance the image was choleric, quarrelsome, and full of malice; it was not pleasing, but looked like a woman crazy with rage. Her face was sullen and wrinkled, with a pug nose; she was hideous and covered with filth and repulsively wrapped up in a towel.]

It would be difficult to identify Haine as the subject of this description were she not named before the description proper begins: "Enz en le mileu vi Haïne" (v. 139 [ibid.]) [In the middle I saw Hatred]. The description proper is not meant to be discriminating except referentially. Indeed, Guillaume immediately transfers it to Felonie.

> Une autre image d'autel taille
> A senestre avoit delez lui;
> Son non desus sa teste lui:
> Apelee estoit Felonie.
>
> (vv. 152–55 [ibid.])

[Beside her, to the left, was another image of the same size. I read her name, Felony, beneath her head.]

He then transfers the same description to Vilanie!

> Une image qui Vilanie
> Avoit non revi devers destre,
> Qui estoit auques d'autel estre
> Con ces deus e d'autel faiture.
>
> (vv. 156–59 [ibid.])

[I looked back to the right and saw another image named Villainy, who was of the same nature and workmanship as the other two.]

Guillaume merely adds a few epithets of the kind used for Haine: "male creature" [a creature of evil], "outrageuse / E mesdisant e ramponeuse" [an insolent and unbridled scandal-monger], "chose vilaine" [a truly contemptible creature], "d'afiz pleine" [full of all sorts of defamation], "petit seüst / [D'enorer ce qu'ele deüst" [knew little of how to honor what she should] (vv. 160–68 [ibid.]). The technique is synonymic repetition or *interpretatio,* not incremental repetition.

The complementary descriptions of Covoitise and Avarice illustrate Guillaume's descriptive technique in two complete portraits. Guillaume begins each with the name: "Après fu pointe Covoitise" (v. 169 [ibid.]) [Covetousness was painted next] and

> Une autre image i ot assise
> Coste a coste de Covoitise,
> Avarice estoit apelee.
>
> (vv. 195–97 [ibid.])

60

[There was another image, called Avarice, seated side by side with Covetousness.]

The ensuing descriptions vary, but their diagnostic value is low or nil except by reference to their common informing idea. For Covoitise, Guillaume begins with the anaphora sequence "C'est cele" in order to suggest by disparate examples how Covoitise acts among men.

> C'est cele qui les genz atise
> De prendre e de neient doner,
> E les granz avoirs aüner.
> (vv. 170–72 [ibid.])

[It is she who entices men to take and to give nothing, to collect valuable possessions.]

Covoitise is suggested by three characteristic actions: *prendre, neient doner, avoirs aüner*. More explicitly, we have the usurer,

> C'est cele qui fait a usure
> Prester mainz por la grant ardure
> D'avoir conquere e assembler;
> (vv. 173–75 [ibid.])

[It is she who, in her great passion for heaping up treasure, loans money at usury to many.]

the thief,

> C'est cele qui semont d'embler
> Les larrons e les ribaudiaus;
> Si est granz pechiez et granz diaus,
> Qu'en la fin maint en covient pendre;
> (vv. 176–79 [ibid.])

[*It is* she *who* excites thieves and *wastrels* to theft; and it is a great evil and sorrow that in the end many of them must hang.]

the embezzler,

> C'est cele qui fait l'autrui prendre,
> Rober, tolir e bareter,
> E bescochier e mesconter;
> (vv. 180–82 [ibid.])

[It is she who causes people to take the goods of others, to rob, to ravish, to commit fraud, to keep false accounts, and to tally falsely.]

and finally, the perjurer

> C'est cele qui les tricheors
> Fait toz e les faus plaideors,
> Qui maintes foiz par lor faveles

61

Ont as vallez e as puceles
Lor droites eritez tolues.
(vv. 183-87 [ibid.])

[It is she who leads people to the trickery and trumped-up litigation by which boys and girls have often been defrauded of their rightful inheritances.]

The complete passage exhibits three salient characteristics. First, the classification is not exhaustive. Second, it is not systematic. The *ribaudiaus* intrude among the thieves, who as a group are not necessarily covetous. But the thieves reappear in a second group as part of a gradation centering on embezzlers: *rober, tolir, bareter, bescochier, mesconter;* indeed, *bareter* is applicable to the perjurers in the final group, a class not always motivated by covetousness either. Third—and most important, because it reveals Guillaume's intentions—each example emphasizes the ignobility of the covetous towards love (*ribaudiaus*) and nobility (defrauding *vallez* and *puceles* of their inheritance). By anticipation, Guillaume is making the description of the exterior comprehensible in opposition to the noble figures inside the garden.[8]

Il ne li tenoit d'envoisier
Ne d'acoler ne de baisier;
Car qui le cuer a bien dolent,
Sachiez de voir qu'il n'a talent
De dancier ne de queroler.
(vv. 331-35 [ibid.])

[She took no interest in enjoyment, in embraces and kisses, for whoever has a sorrowful heart—know it as the truth—has no *desire* for dancing or caroling.]

Thus over and above the name of the abstraction looms a larger context, the praise and vituperation of qualities respectively noble and ignoble. The Images in the wall inspire vituperation; their positive opposites will be lauded in the description of the garden itself.

After the "C'est cele" sequence, Guillaume introduces an emblematic description of Covoitise that continues to use the particular to reflect and manifest an abstract idea giving meaning to the whole Image complex. "Recorbelees et crochues / Avoit les mains icele image" (vv. 188-89 [ibid.]) [This image had hands that were clawlike and hooked]. The description closes with three repetitive statements which underscore the notion of covetousness as a desire to possess what belongs rightfully to others.

Si fu droiz, que toz jorz enrage
Covoitise de l'autrui prendre;
Covoitise ne set entendre
Fors que a l'autrui acrochier;
Covoitise a l'autrui trop chier.
(vv. 190-94 [ibid.])

[(This is) appropriate to Covetousness, who is always in a fever to get the possessions of another. She understands nothing else, but esteems most highly what belongs to another.]

Throughout this description we learn the obvious about Covoitise; her ultimate significance derives from conventional attributes randomly selected but made to conform to the context of Covoitise. The descriptive elements are of universal application, and thus they are topical adaptations of the universal to the particular attribute, or rather of the generic to the special.

The same method is used for the description of Avarice, but not the same features or rhetorical devices. Variety in detail should render the expression of the simple idea clear by restatement, but without monotony: "Attributis tam negotii quam personae non superfluit exemplorum pluralitas, ut, si duo vel plura inducantur exempla, primum evidens, secundum evidentius, tertium evidentissimum esse perpendatur. Majoris etenim firmitatis est aedificium cui columnarum diversitas accommodat fulcimentum. Prodest etiam exemplificanti exemplorum opulentia" (Matthew of Vendôme, p. 150, § 114). [The numerous examples of attributes of action and of person are not redundant: if two or more examples have been adduced, let the first be considered clear, the second clearer, the third clearest. That building is more solid which is supported by a diversity of columns. Abundance of examples also assists the person supplying the examples (pp. 79–80).] An accumulation of vituperative epithets shows Avarice to be inherently vicious: *laide, sale, folee, maigre, chaitive, vert come une cive, descoloree, enlangoree, morte de fain.* The notion of avarice gives these words and expressions a sense, and they in turn provide an affective judgment. Their combined effect is as bitter as the taste of hermit's bread;[9] the necessities of the good life are wanting, and want is seen as a defect in the wall Images. Guillaume then introduces a brief description of Avarice's wardrobe: "Iert... povrement vestue" (v. 207 [ibid.]) [She was... poorly clothed]. Her *cote*

> viez et derompue,
> Come s'el fust as chiens remese,
> Povre... e esrese
> E pleine de viez paletiaus.
> (vv. 208–11 [ibid.])

[old..., torn as if it had been among dogs, poor... and worn out and full of old patches.]

The *mantiaus* hangs from a narrow little rod, as does another *cote de brunete* she owns. The cloth is inelegant, "sleazy" (Dahlberg), but the older robe is still used after ten years lest the newer one be worn out too soon: Avarice would not willingly buy another. An emblem shows Avarice holding her purse so tightly that it would be difficult to open even if she wished to (vv.

227–31 [ibid.]). But Avarice has no intention of taking anything out of the purse anyway. The emblem complements Covoitise's crooked hands in the preceding description.

Perusal of all the Images in the wall reveals the same characteristics: variety in details and in rhetorical embellishment, but synonymic or unsystematic incremental repetition for the amplification of each idea personified. The Images are therefore not discursively analytical, but rather the expression or "emanation" of their idea. In the literal narrative, the cumulative effect is to awaken in Guillaume the desire to flee the ignoble world of Haine, to escape into the garden where the birds sing, and only those not defective in quality may dwell—"uns vergiers, / Ou onc n'avoit entré bergiers" (vv. 469–70 [467–68])[10] [a garden where no shepherd had ever entered].

THE IMAGES IN DEDUIT'S GARDEN

If the descriptions on the outside wall resemble one another, those on the inside are even more alike. As on the outside, designation of the personification is the source of differentiation: Oiseuse (vv. 582 and 1251 [580 and 1249]), Cortoisie (v. 780 [778]), Deduit (v. 801 [799]), Leece (v. 832 [830]), the god of Love (v. 866 [864]) with Douz Regarz (v. 905 [906]), Biautez (v. 992 [ibid.]), Richece (v. 1017 [ibid.]), Largece (v. 1127 [1125]), Franchise (v. 1191 [1189]), and Jonece (v. 1260 [1258]). Except for Oiseuse, each personification is introduced by its name. Oiseuse appears at the gate of the garden only as a "pucele" (v. 525 [523]); her name is given at the end of the description. This may be a means of preserving some initial suspense regarding the garden and its inhabitants. But the other descriptions are virtually identical.[11] They adhere to standard head-to-toe physical and vestmental descriptive techniques, employing accumulation of epithets with a laudatory intent that contrasts with the vituperative intent of the Images in the outside wall.

Such conventional description in the thirteenth century can astonish. Even the description of Oiseuse, whose name is held back for over fifty lines, is the usual laudatory catalogue of feminine parts: hair, skin, forehead, eyebrows, and so on to the breasts and, in conclusion, her overall corporeal beauty (vv. 525–50 [523–48]). The same conventionality holds for her apparel and accoutrements, including garland, mirror, sewed sleeves, and comb. Choice of descriptive material stresses her ease and nobility: "une pucele . . . assez . . . gente e bele" (vv. 525–26 [523–24] [a very sweet and lovely girl].

> . . . el n'avoit soussi ne esmai
> De nule rien, fors solement
> De soi atorner noblement.
>   (vv. 572–74 [570–72])

[She led a good and happy life, for she had no care nor trouble except only to turn herself out nobly.]

Her nobility comes as an abrupt and effective contrast to the villainy rampant just outside the gate she opens. Nonetheless, the subordination (by artificial disposition) of her characteristic features to the idea she personifies betrays the same technique evident in the Images in the wall.

Every figure in the garden is given a conventional laudatory description like that of Oiseuse, including both physical traits and attire. One might have expected analysis or at least meaningful synthesis, but the descriptions are, if anything, less distinctive than those on the outside. Deduit, whose garden it is and who is the origin of the entire *locus amoenus*—"Ce est cil cui est cist jardins" (v. 591 [589]) [who owns this garden]—has no distinguishing characteristics in his description. Oiseuse informs us that he spends a good deal of time with his companions "en joie et en solaz" [in joy and comfort] listening to the song of the birds (vv. 603–8 [601–6]). He is "biaus e lons e droiz" (v. 801 [799]) [handsome, tall, and straight], a "bel ome" (v. 803 [801]) [handsome man]; this is true of his face, eyes, mouth, nose, hair, shoulders, waist. Indeed, like the opposed outside figures,

> Il resembloit une pointure,
> Tant estoit biaus e acesmez,
> E de toz membres bien formez.
> (vv. 812–14 [810–12])

[He was so elegant and full of grace, so well formed in all his limbs, that he looked like a painting.]

His attire is conventional, even to the rose garland (vv. 820–30 [818–28]). His *amie* Leece is no different except in gender; for her too we have the conventional anatomical catalogue and the rich clothing, including "un chapel d'orfrois tot nuef" (v. 857 [855]) [a brand new chaplet of gold embroidery]. Generally speaking, the other personifications fit the pattern. Noble in bearing, splendid in multicolored, gold- and jewel-bedecked apparel, wearing garlands of flowers around which singing birds fly, they move with ordered grace about the garden or in dance, speak properly, display gentle manners. The same epithets return with an insistence that would be monotonous were it not for Guillaume's consummate skill in hyperbolic *interpretatio: gente, bele, riche, cointe, envoisiez, vaillant, debonaire, plaisant.* Finally, almost every personification has an exemplary companion.

The few characteristics applied to any one personification are broad enough to be interchangeable, and are thus implicitly suited to all the personifications, again in conformity with the technique used to trace the figures outside the garden. A rapid survey of these passages will demonstrate their function as

65

ornamental restatement rather than analytic specification and differentiation. Oiseuse is the most specialized. "En sa main tint un miroer" (v. 557 [555]) [in her hand she held a mirror], and

> Il paroit bien a son ator
> Qu'ele estoit poi embesoigniee.
> Quant ele s'estoit bien pigniee,
> E bien paree e atornee,
> Ele avoit faite sa jornee.[12]
> Mout avoit bon tens e bon mai,
> Qu'el n'avoit soussi ne esmai
> De nule rien, fors solement
> De soi atorner noblement.
>   (vv. 566–74 [564–72])

[It certainly seemed from her array that she was hardly busy. By the time that she had combed her hair carefully and prepared and adorned herself well, she had finished her day's work. She led a good and happy life, for she had no care nor trouble except only to turn herself out nobly.]

Oiseuse's own words rehearse these lines in part of a *sermocinatio:*

> S'ai d'une chose mout bon tens,
> Car a nule rien je n'entens
> Qu'a moi joer e solacier,
> E a moi pignier e trecier.
>   (vv. 585–88 [583–86])

[And I have a very good time, for I have no other purpose than to enjoy myself and make myself comfortable, to comb and braid my hair.]

Yet she is scarcely different from the other figures in the garden in this respect; her quality blends into the total setting.

> Maintes foiz por esbaneier
> Se vient en cest leu ombreier
> Deduiz e les genz qui le sivent,
> Qui en joie e en solaz vivent.
>   (vv. 603–6 [601–4])

[Many times Diversion and those who follow him, and who live in joy and comfort, come to this place to have a good time in the cool shade.]

Cortoisie invites Guillaume to join the carol. But it is hardly surprising to find Cortoisie being courteous. In the description itself the notion of courtesy predominates, as in the following *oppositio:*

> El ne fu ne nice n'ombrage,
> Mais sage e entre, senz outrage,

De biaus respons e de biaus diz;
Onc ne fu nus par li laidiz,
Ne ne porta autrui rancune.
(vv. 1235–39 [1233–37])

[She was neither foolish nor distrustful in her fair replies and fine speeches, but wise and reasonable, without excess. She never gave anyone cause to feel injured, nor did she hold rancor toward anyone.]

These traits are echoed in the description of the knight accompanying Cortoisie: "Acointables e biaus parliers / Qui bien sot faire enor as genz" (vv. 1246–47)[1244–45] [easy to know and pleasant of speech, and who knew how to accord due honor to people]. The entire group is characterized by such aristocratic "humanism": "bele est cele compaignie / E cortoise e bien enseignie" (vv. 629–30) [627–28] [this company is fair, courteous, and well instructed]. It stands in topical contrast to the outside figures.

The god of Love's description is typical of love, but also conventional in its adaptation of Ovidian and courtly topics. It is he

qui depart
Amoretes a sa devise.
C'est cil qui les amanz jostise,
E qui abat l'orgueil des genz,
E si fait des seignors sergenz,
E des dames refait baesses,
Quant il les trueve trop engresses.
(vv. 866–72 [864–70])[13]

[who apportions the gifts of love according to his desire, who governs lovers, and who humbles the pride of men, making sergeants of seigneurs and servants of ladies, when he finds them too haughty.]

Otherwise the description fits the pattern evident in Deduit and Leece. Douz Regarz, the god of Love's companion, is not described. He carries the bows and arrows with which Love does his work (vv. 904–56 [ibid.]), and these are named and described briefly. Some distinguishing traits make the bows and a couple of the arrows the most explicit part of the entire description of Deduit's garden. Of the two bows, one is finely polished and smooth, the other knotty and twisted; the arrows are distinguished by their names. Two have epithets more explicit than the others, when referred back to the noun they qualify. Compagnie is "pesant" (v. 945 [ibid.]) [heavy] and thus effective at close range. The amplifications stress this property of the abstraction.

El n'estoit pas d'aler loing prete;
Mais qui de près en vosist traire,
Il en peüst assez mal faire.
(vv. 946–48 [ibid.])

67

[(It) was not prepared to travel very far, but if anyone wanted to fire it at close range he could do a lot of damage.]

Biaus Semblanz is the least grievous arrow:

> Neporquant el fait mout grant plaie;
> Mais cil atent bone menaie
> Qui de cele floiche est plaiez;
> Ses maus si est bien empleiez,
> Car il puet tost santé atendre,
> S'en doit estre sa dolor mendre.
>
> (vv. 951–56 [ibid.])

[Nevertheless, it made a very large wound. However, he who is wounded by this arrow may expect good grace: his pain is of good use, for he can soon expect health, and by it his sorrow must be cured.]

There is no suggestion as yet of the special kind of love, particularly courtly love, that one might have expected in the *Rose* as an art of love. Like Andreas Capellanus, Guillaume begins with a general statement, and reserves the distinctions for later. For Guillaume himself is not yet in love.

> Mais ne dirai ore pas toute
> Lor force ne lor poesté;
> Bien vos en iert la verité
> Contee e la senefiance,
> Nou metrai pas en obliance,
> Ainz vos dirai que tot ce monte,
> Ançois que je fine mon conte.
>
> (vv. 978–84 [ibid.])

[But I shall not now tell all about their force and power. I shall indeed recount to you the truth about them and their significance, and I shall not forget to do so; before I finish my story I will tell you what all this signifies.]

This statement refers to the episode where the god of Love shoots his arrows at Guillaume. It precedes as well the god of Love's extensive lecture, which is, in a sense, the real "art of love" in the *Rose,* as the *Echecs* Commentator pointed out in recommending it to the reader interested in *fin' amors.* The god of Love loves Biautez, who is beautiful, like all the "plus beles genz" (v. 615 [613]), the "bele . . . compaignie" (v. 629 [627]).

The description of Richesse stresses her power on earth (vv. 1017–52 [1017–50]), her clothing and jewelry (vv. 1053–1108 [1051–1106]), and her companion (vv. 1109–26 [1107–24]). The first part is the most circumstantial; in it Guillaume stresses Richesse not only as wealth, but also as the power and authority deriving from *richesse* in its sense of nobility and aristocracy:[14] "Une dame de grant hautece, / De grant pris e de grant afaire" (vv. 1018–19 [ibid.]) [a lady of great dignity, worth, and moment]. Particular stress is laid on the nefarious influence *losengiers* may have on her, corrupting her nobility (vv. 1034–51 [1034–49]).[15] Jean de Meun will draw a Richesse deriving only from wealth. The beneficial aspects of Guillaume's Richesse can be seen in her attire: nobility in the purple portraying the lives of illustrious kings and dukes, curative powers in the medicinal stones that are her most valued possessions, a free and willing exercise of largesse. Unlike Jean's version, she exudes wealth, she does not require it. Richesse is thus the source of the aristocracy that permeates the garden.

The portrait of Largesse is also standardized. She wins honor and friends for her followers. The description centers on a missing collar clasp which Largesse gave away. An Arthurian knight is her companion. But he is not Arthur[16]—since it is not the knight's largesse, but his prowess in tournaments that Guillaume underscores, prowess demonstrated for the sake of his *amie* Largesse (v. 1185 [1183]). Tournaments were occasions for largesse in the distribution of booty, as we see not only in scores of Arthurian romances, but in more nearly historical writing like *Guillaume le maréchal* and *Jehan de Saintré*. Tournaments guarantee as well the strictly aristocratic character of largesse.[17] Guillaume construes largesse in the same manner as did Young Henry Courtmantle.

Franchise is *franche,* and we get little more concerning her that is not applicable to Cortoisie, who follows. Both have abbreviated physical stereotypes for description; both are correct, helpful towards others. Franchise wears a *sorquenie* that suggests her character as "douce e franche" (v. 1222 [1220]) [sweet and open]. Each has a companion.[18] Jonece is the last figure in the carol. She is a mere twelve years old, and unabashedly embraces her *ami* before others.[19]

Guillaume can generalize regarding all the figures in the garden:

> Franches genz e bien enseignies
> E genz de bel afaitement
> Estoient tuit comunement.
> (vv. 1282–84 [1280–82])

[All together they were warm, open people, well instructed and beautifully trained.]

Not only is Biautez beautiful, Cortoisie courteous, Richesse rich—all are beautiful, courteous, rich, young, all are in *deduit.*

Why did Guillaume draw so many repetitious descriptions that seem to add nothing to the quality of the personifications? Is he one of those authors whom Henri d'Andeli criticized for composing five hundred lines on a fig leaf?[20]

AMPLIFICATION OF DEDUIT'S GARDEN

Some twenty or thirty years before Guillaume wrote the *Rose,* Geoffrey of Vinsauf—certainly no innovator—put aside typical descriptions of human beauty because they were already overworked and therefore of less interest:

"Formae descriptio res quasi trita / Et vetus" (*Poetria nova,* vv. 622–23)[21] [The description of beauty is an old and even trite theme]. A more original artist, Chrétien de Troyes, consistently excised, reduced, or hid such descriptions from *Cligès* on.[22] The explanation for Guillaume de Lorris' apparent conservatism lies both in the character of amplification itself and in the real intention of the description of Deduit's garden. Despite the similarity of the separate personifications, the description of the garden itself is not entirely conventional, not empty of significant features that explain the import of the stereotyped personifications.[23]

Amplification as a compositional device taught by the twelfth- and thirteenth-century arts of poetry, and as used in romances and the *Roman de la rose,* is not merely additional material added to no obvious purpose;[24] rather it lays stress on a given subject, dwells upon it in order to elicit the sense desired by the author. Matthew of Vendôme makes much of normative and exemplary description in the *Ars versificatoria.* He demands emphasis on the characteristic in keeping with context and authorial intention. "Verbi gratia, si agatur de virilitate alicujus personae, de inconstantia mentis, de appetitu honestatis, de fuga servitutis, sicut habetur de rigore Catonis apud Lucanum . . . , describenda est virtus multifaria Catonis, ut, audita morum elegantia et multifario suae virtutis privilegio, quicquid sequatur de negligentia Caesaris, de observatione libertatis, auditori *facilius* possit intimari" (pp. 118–19, § 39).[25] [For example, if our concern is with the manliness of any person, the constancy of his mind, his desire for virtue, his flight from servitude—as we read in Lucan on the moral rigor of Cato . . . —we must describe the manifold virtues of Cato, for example, so that, having heard the grace of his character, and the manifold preeminence of his virtue, the audience may *the more easily* divine what may follow regarding the negligence of Caesar, the observance of liberty.] Similarly, Jupiter's love in Ovidian adaptations is made credible by description of the desired woman's beauty (p. 119, § 40). This is obviously rudimentary psychology as motivation, for which the elementary level of Matthew's treatise is only a partial explanation. The technique recurs repeatedly in romances, dits, and shorter verse forms throughout the Middle Ages. To see psychological observation in such amplifications is anachronistic. For Matthew and Geoffrey of Vinsauf, description is not psychological, but topical. Description represents a person, place, object, action, or idea by its most obvious, appropriate, and characteristic features, in close conformity with both the demands of the *materia* and authorial intention. Through descriptive attributes the reader may more easily—*facilius*—perceive the author's meaning.

Since the preceding discussion questions "psychology" as a means of interpreting medieval literature, it may be well to dwell on the point. Can one speak of psychological observation, of credible character analysis in medieval writing? Of course, the word "psychology" was not in use in the Middle Ages,[26] nor had Freud, Jung, or even Racine written anything. But the notion could have been current even if the word or the modern science was not. But we must identify the language in which the notion was expressed. For literature, rhetoric provided the terms. They are the ones used to describe topical invention as description. The thrust of topical invention was not, however, individualization, but rather normalization and typology. This holds not only for the Latin arts of poetry and the rhetorics associated with them; it is evident as well in the treatises of the Second Rhetoric. For example, in the prologue to the late medieval *Jardin de plaisance* the author gives instruction on narrative composition, "pro misteriis compilandis cronicis romanicis et hystoriis"[27] [on compiling mystery plays, chronicles, romances, and histories]. He emphasizes topical representation of characters.

> S'en personnaiges l'on veult faire
> L'on doit penser et minuter
> Quans personnaiges il fault traire,
> Sans superfluité porter
> Ne diminucions traicter;
> Puis considerer quelle forme
> A chascun conuient assorter
> Selon quel peult estre conforme.
> (fol. cii r)

[If you propose to write about persons, it is necessary to think through and detail how many persons are required, with neither too many nor too few; and then consider the form suitable to each, in conformity with character.]

The form that is "conforme" to the characteristic harks back to Matthew of Vendôme's treatment of description. Class and status in life, appropriateness of description for elucidation and substantiation of customary actions in the *materia*—these are concerns common to the twelfth-century schoolmaster and the fifteenth-century rhetorician.

In Matthew's treatise description and *interpretatio,* as Geoffrey understands them, come together in the instruction on the use of epithets. Epithets are not analytic devices for Matthew. They refer to the type represented by the individual. "Debet . . . quaelibet persona ab illo intitulari epitheto quod in ea prae ceteris dominatur et a quo majorem famae sortitur evidentiam" (p. 120, § 44)[28] [Any person ought to be designated by that epithet which overshadows all the others and from which he receives the clearest mark of his renown (p. 66)]. Thus epithets provide a taxonomy that classifies their subject; they do not individualize it in the modern sense. All attributes that distinguish the subject from others of the same class must be ignored. Matthew gives illustrations of the technique: Caesar as emperor, Ulysses as wise counselor, etc.

(pp. 121–32, §§ 50–58). The description of Helen fits particularly well into the class of the personifications in Deduit's garden, whereas the ugly and disreputable figures painted in the wall correspond to the villainous Davus. For nothing in their descriptions individualizes Caesar, Helen, or Davus. The epithets are referential only to their type. "Igitur aliter ponenda est descriptio alicujus ecclesiastici pastoris, aliter imperatoris, aliter puellae, aliter veteranae, aliter matronae, aliter concubinae vel pedissequae, aliter pueri vel adolescentuli, aliter veterani, aliter liberti, aliter conditionalis, et aliarum proprietatum variationes in descriptionibus debent assignari, quae ab Oratio . . . colores operum nuncupantur" (p. 120, § 46). [Henceforth descriptions we set down must be different for a pastor of the church, an emperor; a girl, an old woman; a matron, a concubine or a waiting-woman, boy or young man, old man; freedman, slave; and thus must we represent in description the variations of other characteristics, which Horace calls the shadings of the work (p. 67).] The *colores operum* refer to Horace's treatment in the *Ad Pisones* of poetic decorum. "In the medieval rhetorical concept of poetry, 'affective' must involve judgment reached through emotional conviction, not simply emotional response."[29] Thus Matthew insists on choice of affective epithets deemed fitting for each type of person or action.

To assist his students, Matthew schematized the choice of epithets and descriptive material according to the properties each may have (*attributa*): condition in life, age, public position, sex, class, and so forth (p. 119, § 41). The same is true for things and actions (*negotia*) (pp. 143, § 93; 147–48, § 110; 149, § 112). These are in fact conventional formulae for topical invention. Synonyms have an important place in the instruction (p. 150, § 114). It follows from Matthew's instruction that Guillaume de Lorris does not seek to differentiate through descriptive amplification, but merely to contrast those on the outside of the garden of Deduit with those on the inside. Each separate figure is, by *interpretatio,* a restatement of defect or quality as manifested in, respectively, villainous or noble settings. Deduit, Oiseuse, Richesse, Jonece, and the others are synonymous in a way that Caesar and Helen of Troy are not: they all have the same attributes, and thus are representative of the same type. They all shine with the same golden splendor, just as the outside Images are all twisted in the same green hatred.

Matthew of Vendôme also teaches that the descriptive epithet does not have an absolute sense. Its meaning and signification are determined by context. In the last analysis, the choice and meaning of attributes are determined by authorial intention and the exigencies of his *materia.* "Amplius, si in eodem exemplo incidat attributorum diversitas, referendum est non ad effectum sermonis, sed ad *a*ffectum sermocinantis. Verba etenim notanda sunt ex sensu quo fiunt, non ex sensu quem faciunt. . . . Unde exempla ad mentem exemplificantis debent retorqueri" (p. 150, § 115). [Further, if diverse attributes fall within the same example, we must refer not to the effect of the discourse but to the intention of the speaker. For words are to be perceived according to the sense out of which they are made, not according to the sense which they make. . . . Hence examples are to be referred to the intention of the person supplying them (p. 80).] My correction of Faral's text from *effectum* to *affectum*, as italicized in the citation, is justified by their use elsewhere in the *Ars versificatoria* for determining epithets. For example, the student is enjoined to give special attention to the examples of description: "Etenim contemplandus est non effectus sermonis, sed affectus sermocinantis" (p. 132, § 60) [For we should consider not the effect of the speech but the intention of the speaker]. Matthew goes on to explain: "Igitur quod dictum est de summo pontifice, vel de Caesare, vel de aliis personis quae sequuntur, ne nomen proprium praeponderet ceteris personis ejusdem conditionis, vel aetatis, vel dignitatis, vel officii, vel sexus, intelligatur attributum, ut nomen speciale generalis nominis vicarium ad maneriem rei,[30] non ad rem maneriei reducatur". [Hence the attributes assigned to the Pope, or Caesar, or the rest, must be understood in such a way that the particular name does not outweigh the relevance of these attributes to other persons of the same condition, age, dignity, office, or sex. The particular designation should be taken to stand for a general designation according to the nature of the subject, and not according to the subject used to exemplify that nature.] This point can not be stressed too much. The epithets derive their significance, their import, from authorial intention (*affectus sermocinantis, ad maneriem rei, ex sensu quo fiunt*) rather than from their sense independent of context (*effectus sermonis, ad rem maneriei, ex sensu quem faciunt*). This is consistent with amplification as *interpretatio*. The author fully aware of the abstract senses, the *vis verbi*, including "dictionary" meanings and more figurative connotations, uses his vocabulary in conformity with his intention and the word's semantic possibilities.[31] The result is a convincing statement.

It has been known for some time that the figures in the wall and those in Deduit's garden were traced after medieval notions of amplification.[32] But because the use of amplification itself has rarely been properly understood or even studied, it has not been possible to appreciate Guillaume's accomplishment in the garden description, certainly one of the most extensive examples of a *locus amoenus* in medieval French, and of considerable importance within the *Rose*, as it takes up, in its entirety, close to half of the extant romance. Amplification as a compositional device taught in twelfth- and thirteenth-century arts of poetry, and as used in romances and the *Roman de la rose*, is not mere filling or additional narrative material. It is stress given to a subject by dwelling on it, eliciting from it a meaning or affective value

73

suitable to authorial intention.[33] It is thus a kind of repetition, since the same thing is said more than once by description, digression, apostrophe, circumlocution, or whatever specific device is used.

> Sic surgit permulta seges de semine pauco:
> Flumina magna trahunt ortus de fonte pusillo,
> De tenui virga grandis protenditur arbor.
> (*Poetria nova*, vv. 687–89)

[In this way, plentiful harvest springs from a little seed; great rivers draw their source from a tiny spring; from a slender twig a great tree rises and spreads.]

But the large still derives from the small and thus depends on the small for its origins: the description expresses the word. It is expression of meaning in the etymological sense, like the artist's movement from the idea towards the idea's verbal representation by Imagination. Amplification is, like the tree in the seed, realization of potential in conformity with authorial understanding and intention.

This being so, *interpretatio* and *expolitio* are fundamental to formal and material amplification. Description by *interpretatio* reveals the essentially prismatic character of amplification: the same light shines with different colors. The author's task is to determine to what extent certain parts of his *materia* require amplification, and what form it should take. Emphasis and precision result from restatement. Such emphasis, in amplification, accentuates the normative and exemplary.

These considerations are important to a proper understanding of the marginal reference to Matthew of Vendôme found in one manuscript of the *Rose*.[34] The resemblance is not in the content,[35] but in the method of topical invention. Matthew's treatment of description sets forth the technique of topical invention and the questions pertinent to such amplification as suit the author's purposes. This is the identification of the *maneries rei*. As D. Thoss points out,[36] the vernacular, courtly tradition provided substantive elements that Guillaume adopted, then combined and adapted to his interpretation of the *locus* suitable to Deduit. The figures in the wall evoke sadness, which Guillaume shuns in favor of Deduit on the inside (vv. 331–38 [ibid.]). This initiates narrative progression to which thematic and affective progressions run parallel. In the garden part of this reverse *oppositio* (the negation precedes the affirmation), Deduit holds sway. The affective function is explicit: "Por la grant delitableté / Fui pleins de grant joliveté" (vv. 683–84 [681–82]) [full of gaiety as I was over the garden's delectable charm]. Oiseuse is "en ce deduit" (v. 687 [685]). The form and content of the descriptions of Deduit's companions, their affective value, derive from the *deduit* they evoke by their splendid and richly adorned clothing, their ideal beauty, their harmonious disposition and movement in dance, the configuration of abstractions appropriate to, and thus properties of, Deduit. Splendor, light, beauty, and proportion are the traits of the garden of Deduit. They give form and content to its personifications and lift the quality of the garden above *deduit* as mere *delict,* or lust. Like the *chambre de beautés* in Benoît de Sainte Maure's *Roman de Troie,*[37] the *locus amoenus* realizes an earthly paradise nonetheless redolent of spiritual grace.

> ... je cuidai estre
> Por voir en parevis terrestre;
> Tant estoit li leus delitables
> Qu'il sembloit estre esperitables;
> Car, si come lors m'iert avis,
> Il ne fait en nul parevis
> Si bon estre come il faisoit
> Ou vergier qui tant me plaisoit.
>   (vv. 635–42 [633–40])[38]

[I thought that I was truly in the earthly paradise. So delightful was the place that it seemed to belong to the world of spirit, for, as it seemed to me then, there was no paradise where existence was so good as it was in that garden which so pleased me.]

The comparison recurs throughout the description of the garden: the birds sing like "ange esperitel" (v. 664 [662]); the personifications seem to be "anges empenez" (v. 725 [723]) [winged angels], especially the god of Love: "uns anges / Qui fust tot droit venuz dou ciel" (vv. 902–3 [ibid.]) [an angel come straight from heaven]. The full realization of joy in this paradise is love, "Qu'il n'est nus graindres parevis / D'avoir amie a son devis" (vv. 1299–1300 [1297–98]) [since there is no greater paradise than to have one's beloved at one's desire]. The drift of *deduit* towards love (vv. 1291–94 [1289–92]) prefigures the movement of Guillaume towards the Rose.

The most consistently recurrent topic in the entire description of the garden of Deduit is the song of birds. Birds are commonplace in idyllic and amorous poetry, where their singing is conducive to joy.[39] Even outside the garden their "douz chanz piteus" (v. 83 [ibid.]) [heart-felt songs] accompanied Guillaume on his meandering promenade to the garden, and awoke in him a longing to escape from sadness into joy (vv. 497–500 [495–98]). Their song is "piteus" (v. 485 [483]), harmonious, "Mout estoit bele l'acordance" (v. 484 [482]) [The harmony of their moving song was very good to hear], conducive to joy (vv. 486–88 [484–86]). The music and singing in the carol are inspired by the birds' song (vv. 494–96 [492–94]). The singing gives rise to dance because it is *musique artificiele* in Deschamps' sense. The birds are grouped in choruses or "escoles" (v. 647 [645]) according to their species (vv. 645–60 [643–58]; and their performance includes forms recognizable in the repertory of courtly lyric.

Lais d'amors e sonez cortois
Chantoient en lor serventois,
Li un en haut, li autre en bas.[40]
De lor chant, n'estoit mie gas,
La douçor e la melodie
Me mist ou cuer grant reverdie.
(vv. 703-8 [701-6])

[They sang love lays and elegant songs, one high, the other low. Without joking, the sweetness and melody of their singing brought great joy to my heart.]

Leece picks up the song and begins the carol.

The source of the music is the idealized, immaterial essence of the garden, an earthly paradise, "delitables" and "esperitables" (vv. 637-38 [635-36]). Hence the quality of the birds' singing:

Qu'onc mais si douce melodie
Ne fu d'ome mortel oïe.
Tant estoit cil chanz douz e biaus
Qu'il ne sembloit pas chant d'oisiaus,
Ainz le peüst l'en aesmer
A chant de sereines de mer,
Qui, por lor voiz qu'eles ont saines
E series, ont non sereines.
(vv. 667-74 [665-72])

[For mortal man never heard so sweet a melody. It was so sweet and beautiful that it did not seem the song of a bird; one could compare it rather with the song of the sirens of the sea, who have the name *siren* on account of their clear, pure voices.]

Guillaume de Lorris here anticipates Machaut's *Prologue,* which juxtaposes the sacred song of David and the profane song of Orpheus. The birds' music makes joyful noise, and thus inspires the dancing in the garden; and it determines the quality of the common joy. The elegant and luminous clothing, the wonderful domestic and foreign plants and animals that are also part of the ordered setting, add to the affective value and quality. The affinities among the personifications complement this intention. Deduit listens with pleasure to the birds (vv. 607-60 [605-58]); corresponding to the birds who sing like "ange esperitel" (v. 664 [662]) is the angelic beauty of the personifications.

Que, quant je les vi, je ne soi
Don si trés beles genz pooient
Estre venu, car il sembloient
Tot por voir anges empenez.
(vv. 722-25 [720-23])[41]

[When I saw them, I did not know where people so beautiful could have come from, for, in absolute truth, they seemed winged angels.]

Every part of the description evinces joy as a predisposition to love. This is the sense of the entire configuration of Images.

Joy is fully realized in love.[42] The carol terminated, the birds and personifications withdraw.

> Les queroles ja remanoient,
> Car tuit li plusor s'en aloient
> O lor amies ombreier
> Soz ces arbres, por doneier.
> Deus! com menoient bone vie!
> (vv. 1291–94 [1289–93])

[Already they were stopping the carols, for most of them were going off with their sweethearts to shelter under the shade of the trees in order to make love. God! What a good life they led!]

Only Love remains alone, without his partner. I shall return to this fact.

But it is first necessary to consider the significance of the configuration of personifications in the garden of Deduit. We may begin with the question, raised by Genius in Jean de Meun's continuation, as to the real quality of the garden. Following a brief, but not entirely faithful, resumé of Guillaume's description, Genius continues:

> Les choses ici contenues,
> Ce sont trufles e fanfelues.
> Ci n'a chose qui seit estable,
> Quanqu'il i vit est corrompable.
> Il vit queroles qui faillirent,
> E faudront tuit cil qui les firent.
> Ausinc feront toutes les choses
> Qu'il vit par tout laienz encloses.
> (vv. 20351–58 [20321–28])

[The things contained here are trifles and bagatelles. There is nothing here that can be stable; whatever he saw is corruptible. He saw carols that will pass away; all those who dance them will disappear, and so will all the things that he saw enclosed therein.]

For death ends all earthly joy. In the context of Jean's allegory, the joy in Deduit's garden is not conducive to the propagation of the species, as Genius and Nature desire, and as Reason counsels.[43]

One should recall at this point Matthew of Vendôme's pronouncement that words should be understood "ex sensu quo fiunt." That sense is not the same in Guillaume de Lorris and Jean de Meun. Guillaume is concerned with courtly love and courtliness in this world. This is apparent in the noble and courteous personifications that people the garden, and especially in the precise groupings of abstractions without regard for Christian morality. These groupings provide significant clusters of qualities and defects. Such a world will always exist where Love is idealized.[44] Jean, on the other hand, is concerned with simpler and more stringent moral values broadly valid for all humanity. This distinction helps to explain why the words vice and virtue are inadequate to characterize the personifications. Poverty is no vice, but it is a defect in a nobleman, as Chrétien de Troyes and Marie de France had shown.[45] Poverty is no ironic reminder to stay out of the garden, since it is aligned with Envy, Hatred, Felony, and a number of other crimes and sins—including Hypocrisy! Outside the garden, in Guillaume's scheme of things, are defects conducive to Tristesse, the opposite of Joy, the enemy of song and love and nobility—just as it will be in Machaut's *Prologue*. Inside the garden, in the company of Deduit, are precious few virtues, but many recognizable aristocratic qualities: Franchise, Cortoisie, Largesse.[46]

Oiseuse obviously presents a complex problem for a courtly reading of the *Rose* personification. Fleming's iconographic evidence for reading her as lechery[47] is largely supported by lexicography. However, there is evidence in courtly, as distinct from moral or didactic, writing that *oiseuse* and its cognates were adapted to include feats of arms and acts of courtesy. We have already noted the quarrel in Wace's *Brut* between Cador and Gauvain. Moreover, the attributes of bed, comb, and mirror are not always assigned to Lust or the Whore of Babylon, as depicted in the Angers Tapestry. In *Durmart le galois* the hero is treated and brought back to health by a maiden encountered in the woods, a maiden "sage et vaillans" (v. 3302). She is seated in a red tent (vv. 3061–62) on a bed (v. 3074).

> Un pigne d'ivoire tenoit
> La pucele qui se pignoit;
> Devant li sert une tosete,
> Une mout jone meschinete
> Cui li servirs mout bien avient.
> Devant la damoisele tient
> Un mireor, ce m'est avis,
> Dont ele mire son cler vis.
> (vv. 3089–96)

[The maid held an ivory comb with which she was combing her hair; before her serves a young girl, one whom service became very well indeed. Before the maid she holds a mirror, it seems to me, in which the former looks at her bright face.]

Durmart liberates the maiden and her *ami* from the *dangier* of the arrogant, discourteous Fel de la Garde (cf. the earlier reference to "De deus orguilloz le dangier," v. 2849 [the dominion of two haughty persons]), who becomes courteous as a condition for Durmart's mercy.

> Jamais n'iere se cortois non;
> D'or en avant me vera om

78

> Dames et puceles amer
> Et les chevaliers honorer.
> Ma felenie guerpirai;
> Ne jamais rien ne forferai
> Vers gentil home en mon vivant
> Se ce n'est sor moi defendant.
>
> (vv. 3589–96)

[Never will I be other than courteous; henceforth I shall be remarkable for the love I show ladies and maidens, and for the honor accorded knights. I shall quit my felony; nor shall I ever wrong a nobleman as long as I live, unless it be against my will.]

"Ce sachiés," remarks the anonymous romancer, "bien s'aaisierent" (v. 3213) [rest assured . . . , they had a good time—not with the *aise* of lust, but of "grant compaignie et grant solas"] (v. 3319). The art of the illuminator has no doubt influenced this representation, as has that of the rhetorician. Arriving on the scene, Durmart places his sparrow-hawk on the olive tree, ties his horse to a laurel, and seats himself under an oak in a Welsh forest (vv. 2990–3003): the illumination is clear. But the meaning is not determined by the illumination; its art is at the service of narrative context.

This is true as well of the context into which Oiseuse introduces Guillaume. She is only the gatekeeper, and he advances to join the group of refined, aristocratic qualities. Is it not then possible to say that Oiseuse represents for Guillaume's aristocratic audience what *otium* did for Cicero's readers—"in otio cum dignitate"?[48] Despite Fleming's assertion that Christine de Pisan did not understand the *Rose,* she provides the only explicit parallel of *oiseuse* and lechery I have come across in later courtly literature. The "gens oyseux" (v. 4187)

> . . . veulent tenir la vie
> De quoy nul preudoms n'a envie:
> C'est d'oyseuse et de lecherie,
> Qui de nul vaillant n'est cherie.
>
> (vv. 4190–94)[49]

[want to lead a life which no worthy man wishes, that is, one of idleness and lechery, which no worthwhile person holds dear.]

But envy opposes her *oiseuse* to the *preudom.* It thus falls into the company of those outside the garden. Jean Acart de Hesdin brings out the value of good and bad *oiseuse* by stressing the necessity of using it in the right way (vv. 183–206); for him, *oiseuse* is a feature of *compaignie.*[50]

Compaignie is important in determining the affective value and significance of the components in a given configuration. For example, the description of Oiseuse in René d'Anjou's *Livre du cuer d'amours espris* does not use the attributes of Guillaume de Lorris, but retains her courtly quality by the associations given her—the company she has—in Love's palace. Richly apparelled, she bears not a mirror and comb but a falcon "gentil et mignonnet."[51] Oiseuse also figures prominently in Love's tapestry as the source of aristocratic pastime.

> Mon droit nom est Oyseuse, qui tousjours voys premiere,
> Pour cela que je porte d'Amours, voir, la benniere,
> Comme celle qui mieulx la puet et doit porter;
> Car ma plaisance n'est fors a me depporter,
> Faisant incessamment joyeuse et gaye chiere,
> Toudis preste a chanter, dancer et bouhorder,
> Aussi par Jeunesse ma grant queue porter,
> Laquelle a moy servir ne se moustre estre chiere.
>
> (§ 250, vv. 2-10; cf. § 266)

[My right name is Oiseuse, who always precede because I bear the banner of Love as she who can and ought to bear it. For my pleasure is entirely in diversion, in continual expression of joyous, gay features, ever ready to sing, dance, and joust; and I have my train borne by Jeunesse, who is never difficult about serving me.]

The ambiguity of Oiseuse derives from the ambiguity of love itself.

Otium as *oiseuse* seems to be a condition for love, one that love then dissipates, or should dissipate. The *Bestiaires d'amours* characterizes idle lovers as those who follow love because they have nothing better to do (p. 101, ll. 5-9), thus distinguishing them from seducers (p. 101, ll. 3-5) and faithful servants of love (p. 101, l. 9-p. 102, l. 1). In the *Epistolae duorum amantium,* the Vir objects that they have been idle in love (Letter XXII), but he does not make such idleness synonymous with *quies* or *requies* as the goal of love (Letter LXVII). The Mulier responds that excessive *alienatio* or distraction causes her apparent lethargy (*segnicies*) (Letter LXXXV), and the Vir allows that "Amor ociosus esse non potest" (Letter CIII).[52] This is because of constant physical and mental activity, a fact borne out in the *Rose* by the disappearance of Oiseuse after the carol and her absence during the lover's adventures. Hence, leisure as passage into the world suitable for Love is Oiseuse's role in the *Rose,* and it does not extend further semantically or contextually on either the literal or the allegorical level.

The other personifications fit easily into the aristocratic setting. The setting gives Oiseuse an aristocratic quality, a value not dissimilar to that accorded her by Gauvain in Wace's *Brut.* Hugh of Saint Victor found *otium* necessary to the contemplative life; in a different context, *oiseuse* has a positive value for the courtly life as conducive to *fin' amors.*[53]

Inside the garden most qualities have complementary companions: Deduit and Leece, Love and Beauty. Richesse, Largesse, Cortoisie, Franchise, and Jonece have exemplary companions. Oiseuse is unattended, although she has an obvious affinity for Guillaume. She opens the gate to admit him into the garden and is his partner in the carol (vv. 1251-52, 1257-58 [1249-50, 1255-56]). Outside the garden there are no pairs, each figure preserving sad isolation. There are, of course, artificial groupings in the arrangement of the wall. In the middle is Haine (v. 139 [ibid.]), with Felonie to the left (v. 153 [ibid.]) and Vilanie to the right (v. 157 [ibid.]). A second group begins next to Felonie (v. 169 [ibid.]) and includes Covoitise and Avarice (v. 196 [ibid.]). Then, in order, come Envie, Tristesse, Vieillesse, Papelardie; somewhat removed from all of them stands Pauvreté (v. 453 [451]). The pattern suggests affinities, as between Envie and Tristesse, with Vieillesse, Papelardie, and Pauvreté standing alone. But separation rather than unity is underscored. The similarities come down ultimately to the defects attributable to them all, and bring home the contrast between the orderly world of the carol and the distasteful, lifeless grouping outside.

There is no systematic pattern opposing the figures on either side of the wall. Guillaume has made a description, not a definition. However, a number of studies have suggested a rationale for the choice of figures inside and outside on the basis of their relation to each other.[54] Some oppositions are obvious: Amour—Haine, Richesse—Pauvreté, Leece—Tristesse, Jonece—Vieillesse, Largesse—Avarice. Others, plausible in the aristocratic context, suggest themselves: Oiseuse—Papelardie, Cortoisie and Franchise—Felonie and Vilanie, even Biautez—Envie and Deduit—Covoitise.

More suggestive of antitheses, however, is the relative length of each amplification. The greater the length, given the function of amplification, the greater the stress Guillaume presumably wishes to give to the abstraction described.[55] The following figures obtain for the garden of Deduit and the Images in the wall.

Garden	Wall
(1) god of Love, 120 lines (vv. 865-984 [863-984])	(1) Vieillesse, 68 lines (vv. 339-406 [339-404])
(2) Richesse, 110 lines (vv. 1017-1126 [1017-1124])	(2) Envie, 56 lines (vv. 235-90 [ibid.])
(3) Largesse, 64 lines (vv. 1127-90 [1125-88])	(3) Tristesse, 48 lines (vv. 291-338 [ibid.])
(4) Oiseuse, 58 lines (vv. 525-74 and 1251-58 [523-72 and 1249-56])	(4) Avarice, 40 lines (vv. 195-234 [ibid.])
(5) Cortoisie, 41 lines (vv. 777-95 and 1229-50 [775-93 and 1227-48])	(5) Papelardie, 34 lines (vv. 407-40 [405-38])
(6) Franchise, 38 lines (vv. 1191-228 [1189-226])	(6) Covoitise, 26 lines (vv. 169-94 [ibid.])
	(7) Pauvreté, 22 lines (vv. 441-62 [439-60])

(7) Leece, 34 lines
   (vv. 831–64 [829–62])
(8) Deduit, 30 lines
   (vv. 801–30 [799–828])
(9) Biautez, 28 lines
   (vv. 989–1016 [ibid.])
(10) Jonece, 20 lines
   (vv. 1259–78 [1257–76])

(8) Haine, 13 lines
   (vv. 139–51 [ibid.])
(9) Vilanie, 13 lines
   (vv. 156–68 [ibid.])
(10) Felonie, 4 lines
   (vv. 152–55 [ibid.])

The description of Love includes Douz Regarz (vv. 904–9 [ibid.]) and the two bows (vv. 910–20 [ibid.]) and ten arrows (vv. 921–77 [ibid.]), the latter illustrating not only the antithetical character of good and bad love, but also the various possibilities inherent in the polysemous word love itself. Vieillesse includes an extensive digression on Time built by anaphora—"Li Tens qui... " (vv. 361–88 [361–86]). A number of the figures in the garden have a companion.

The pairing of long and short descriptions is also suggestive. Love is opposed to Felonie, Richesse as nobility to Vilanie, Largesse to Haine, Oiseuse to Pauvreté (Pauvreté always anxious, dependent on others, preoccupied), Cortoisie to Covoitise, Franchise to Papelardie (contrasting openness with deceit), Leece to Avarice, Deduit to Tristesse, Beauty to Envy, and Jonece to Vieillesse. This is as far as one can go in searching for meaningful patterns or configurations founded on the contrasting figures inside and outside the garden.

In Guillaume de Lorris' description of the garden of Deduit, joy is achieved in noble love. The inclination of all the qualities (and, by antiphrasis, the disinclination of the defects) is towards love. Accordingly, at the conclusion of the carol all the participants except Guillaume and the god of Love retire to the solaces of love in secluded parts of the garden (vv. 1291–1300 [1289–98]).[56] Oiseuse having vanished, Guillaume is reduced to wandering through the garden curiously searching out whatever wonders he may find there.

The garden is thus neither narrative nor psychological analysis. The purpose of the amplification is entirely rhetorical: the evocation of joy through the qualities prerequisite to noble love. All the personifications, the natural and spiritual constituents of the garden, are there to that single end. The reader is not expected to analyze the joy or to appreciate a presumptive psychoanalysis of the author or anyone else. Rather he should open himself to the topical suggestiveness of the Image, by anticipation desire the joy and the qualities that are its essence, and, figuratively, seek out the source of the joy that animates the personifications during and after the carol.

A brief comparison with Alain de Lille will be instructive in conclusion. Like Alain's personifications, Guillaume's are determined by a rhetorical tradition that emphasizes description rather than definition; the complete description of the garden relies on integral coherence rather than systematization and universality. Ochsenbein has elucidated the distinction in his comparison of the technique used in the *Anticlaudianus* and Alain's treatise *De virtutibus et vitiis*.[57] Terminological precision gives way to semantic adaptibility in the literary work, what Ochsenbein calls the "circumstances" whereby, for example, Fama may appear among both the Virtues and the Vices. Such "inconsistencies" are so only when systematic, terminological precision is required, not when Fama may be good or bad depending on her function, and thus on the attributes chosen to qualify her and the complex of which she is a part. Careful attention to context and semantic range is what makes Guillaume's *Rose* an evocative Imagination and allows Jean de Meun to effect his own adaptation of it with relatively little difficulty. The pendant to the carol in the garden of Deduit is the psychomachia in Jalosie's castle. The addition of participating personifications and the change from garden with wall to castle with siege and combat as the organizing Image realize the possibilities for effective adaptation and, as it were, correction. In Guillaume, Franchise and Pitié prevail upon Dangier to become courteous; and Honte and Peur lead him back to the guardianship of the Rose. Jean preserves this opposition, but also elaborates upon the conflict by separating it into sequential confrontations. Since Male Bouche has been eliminated, Dangier, Honte, and Peur are left alone to defend the castle. And they do so against reinforcements on the other side from Deliz, Bien Celer, Hardement, and Seürté. Eventually a truce must be established and Venus called on the scene to direct operations. Her firebrand wins the day. Cortoisie, Pitié, and Franchise liberate Bel Acueil, while the army of Love routs the remaining figures in the crumbling castle. The decline of Guillaume's Amant from the idealism expressed in his dialogue with Reason, which is at least superficially in conformity with Guillaume's conception of *fin' amors,* leads to machinations and deception under the influence of a newly conceived Ami and Richesse. The intervention of Faus Semblant and Astinence Contrainte against Male Bouche turns the love service into a war between the sexes.[58] The adaptation is complete and credible. What for Guillaume was to be the capture of Jalosie's castle by Love becomes for Jean de Meun a victory of Venus.[59] Nature assures her success.

The *maneries rei,* the *sensus quo fiunt* for the figures in the garden of Deduit, as we are told in Guillaume's prologue, is Love's art. But in the garden Love's arrows are still in the quivers. Since Guillaume does not fall in love until after looking into the fountain of Narcissus, the description of the garden must refer to the predisposition to love rather than to love itself. As the preceding discussion shows, Guillaume intended no analysis of that state. Such an *effectus* was not his purpose. Rather he sought a particular rhetorical *affectus.* By evoking a predisposition to love in his reader through the description, he renders the reader attentive, receptive, well-disposed towards what is to follow. The ensuing noble love is the *affectus* Guillaume ultimately suggests to his reader. The nuances in the description are affective attributes deemed appropriate to a certain *joie de vivre* fully attainable in love itself. Our appreciation and anticipatory joy parallel Guillaume's wonder in examining and trying to know what the entire garden may be. The tendency to make the personifications in each group resemble each other makes each distinct personification one instance of an *interpretatio*. Taken together, they make base defect and courtly excellence *evidentissimae*, as Matthew puts it. Once Guillaume made his case credible, he could advance to the real subject of the *Rose*, love itself. But in the dream Guillaume is not yet in love, and the narrative as such is only beginning. The setting first undergoes a transformation by the introduction of another descriptive amplification.

THE ALLEGORICAL NARRATIVE: THE FOUNTAIN OF NARCISSUS AND THE ROSE

Matthew of Vendôme sees description as a means of controlling the thoughts and emotions of the reader. Something becomes visible from the angle and in the light desired by the author. A single abstraction suffices to designate and, in effect, to say everything that the author proposes to say by the amplification. That abstraction is a word, part of a vocabulary and a context represented by a type (*maneries*). The choice of words is material, contextual, and "class-conscious" in conformity with the demands of material style. The usage of the word may have more than one application, and its *potestas* may therefore be exploited to elicit now one, now another of the word's semantic possibilities. For example, the defects in the Image of the garden wall represent various manifestations of the abstract notion of defect within the contextual opposition nobility/villainy. The mind moves from the context to its heterogeneous content, the abstract words, and thence to the descriptive personification. The result is communication and understanding.[60] The same holds for the more intricate description of the inside garden. Here too the descriptive components derive from and refer back to the notion of nobility. As Matthew of Vendôme directs, superfluous elements have been suppressed or adapted to the single idea manifest in the descriptive variety. This is Imagination. For Imagination is visual representation of a unified whole in material diversity, a diversity that is formed by *interpretatio* to reveal the idea, and not just the literal parts of the representation. Thus the effect is not fragmentary, but synecdochic; each part expresses the whole.

In the narrative proper, the adventures of the lover after the description of the garden, Guillaume continues to discriminate among the lexicographical possibilities of his vocabulary. Static description turns to dynamic narrative after the lover sees the Rose. And a new, or at least augmented, cast of personifications appears. But the figures still have roles appropriate to the semantic possibilities of the abstractions they represent and the varying contexts that rise up in narrative sequence. Peur is frightened as Jalosie faults her inaction when Bel Acueil allowed the lover to kiss the Rose (vv. 3638-43 [3620-25]); but Peur also causes fear when she transfers the blame to Dangier (vv. 3713-30 [3695-3712]). Likewise, Honte has active and passive functions. Ashamed of her own laxity in the kiss episode, she first vindicates herself by discrediting Male Bouche (vv. 3561-70 [3543-52]), then confesses her own responsibility (vv. 3592-96 [3574-78]). Afterwards Honte shames Dangier (vv. 3678-3711 [3660-93]).

Male Bouche is slander personified. A "jangleor" (v. 2835 [2819]), she bruits about the kiss Bel Acueil accorded the lover; she surprises the secrets of lovers, then reports all the slander she can about them (vv. 3511-16 [3493-98]). Guillaume gives her lineage. Her mother was "une vieille iraise" (vv. 3517, 3520 [3499, 3502]) [an angry old woman]; her epithets are "punaise" [sharp], "poignant" [piercing], "amere" [bitter] (vv. 3518-19 [3500-3501]). Honte describes her as "losengier" (v. 3569 [3551])[61] and lying (vv. 3570-76 [3553-58]). We are again in the affective realm of the figures in the garden wall. Male Bouche's value remains uniformly negative. Since Male Bouche is an integral part of the Rose configuration, may we not (as with Jalosie below) see her as representing the lady's self-incriminations for falling so easily to Venus? This would parallel the lover's return to Reason. In any case, Male Bouche's principal function is clear: she discerns love and broadcasts it far and wide.

The description of most of the personifications in Guillaume's adventures is monovalent like that of Male Bouche;[62] their role is simple and semantically consistent—so much so that one has no difficulty identifying their function and connotations. It is therefore unnecessary to discuss in detail Ami, the Vieille, Franchise, or Pitié. Their actions are restricted to a single semantic value within the context of fin'amors, in accordance with the intention to praise or blame. Ami is the good counselor designated by the god of Love in his instruction; he demonstrates his friendship by advising the lover on ways to make his love more courteous and deferential. Reason is reasonable, in sententious reprimands appealing to Guillaume to turn away from unhappy love (vv. 3011-17 [2995-3001]).[63] Venus herself, as the personification of Love's folly, is depicted with the same economy. Reason is grouped with the lover, Venus with the Rose. Franchise and Pitié, characteristic of courtesy (Franchise was in the garden of Deduit, and is named alternately with Cortoisie as one of Love's good arrows), act upon Dangier, encouraging him to show franchise by taking pity on the disconsolate lover, a pity later withdrawn under the pressure of Honte and Peur. Thus there are two discrete configurations for Dangier that bring out distinct semantic possibilities in the word he

85

personifies. This requires some explanation, as a single sense for the abstraction *dangier* does not suffice to explain its function.

If all the figures encountered in the lover's adventures were as simple as Male Bouche, or even Honte and Peur, the narrative would be the largely static confrontation of opposites we find in works like Prudentius' *Psychomachia*. However, Guillaume takes advantage of the semantic possibilities of some Images for narrative elaboration and differentiation, and this results in sentimental and didactic nuances. The differentiation conforms broadly to the lover's evolution from an inferior to a superior love by the interaction of his complex of abstractions with that surrounding the Rose.

Words are susceptible of ambivalence, elaboration, and interpretation as their semantic field comes alive in abstract personifications. ''The single word, to recall Geoffrey of Vinsauf's terms, *sonat* or *verberat,* but it may also re-sound, re-verberate with some of its unactualized semantic potential.''[64] The arrows of the god of Love, for example, when used together, separately, or in different combinations, indicate different possible loves. Semantic reference is restricted only by the possibilities of the word's usage,[65] the rhetorical devices used to express them, authorial judgment (praise or blame), and context. Context brings the abstractions into various combinations—context is, in effect, the narrative equivalent for Geoffrey of Vinsauf's theory of determinations. Thus the fountain of Narcissus has various traditional meanings, each subject to praise or blame depending on authorial intention. One context, illustrated by Narcissus himself, Guillaume transfers to the *belles dames sans mercy.* But it also has meaning for those who, like Guillaume, are not haughty.

> Mais je me pensai qu'asseür,
> Senz peor de mauvais eür,
> A la fontaine aler pooie.
> (vv. 1519–21 [1517–19])

[But then I thought that I might be able to venture safely to the fountain, without fear of misfortune.]

Unlike Narcissus, Guillaume sees in the fountain not himself, but the roses reflected in the crystals. Like the garden of Deduit, the fountain of Narcissus has opposing values expressive of good and bad love (Guillaume/Narcissus). The narrative adventures preserve this opposition through divergent interpretations of the Images. The method is characteristic of the *integumentum* in moralizations of Ovid.

The auspicious beginnings at the fountain of Narcissus go quickly askew. Guillaume's first impulse is not to *fin' amors,* nor even to love as such, but to *rage.*[66] The refinement he undergoes is the substance of the ensuing narrative. For Love's arrows concentrate Guillaume's attention on the one Rose, and his passage through the garden has made it possible for him to assume a noble relationship to Love by swearing homage rather than submitting to servile domination. The steps are prefigured in the god of Love's instruction on the adventures of typical lovers (especially vv. 2465–90 [2452a–76]). They show a progression from the immediate, but "outrageous," possession of the love object (I) to the more refined contemplation of the person who, by her qualities (IV), inspires and ennobles the love.

Object of love	Quality of object	Quality of love
I. enterine joie [complete joy]	trop chier cheté [a possession too dear]	outrage [an outrageous request]
II. baisier [kiss]	Mout riche deserte [a rich reward]	fol [foolish]
III. de li uns regarz[67] [one look from her]		
IV. le veïst [I should like to see her]		

The progression from "outrage" towards contemplation of the beloved as sufficient to the needs of the lover elicits different responses from the lady, or rather the Rose complex, as the ensuing narrative shows.[68] The changes are evident in the comportment of Bel Acueil, Dangier, and Jalosie.

Bel Acueil is the son of Cortoisie. He therefore has an affinity for Guillaume, since Cortoisie both invited Guillaume to the carol in the garden and pierced his heart as one of Love's arrows. In addition, the first part of the god of Love's instruction deals with courteous social conduct in the lover. Like Oiseuse, Bel Acueil receives Guillaume courteously, offering him a leaf from the rose bush. And he is subsequently outraged by Guillaume's request for *le sorplus*. But *bel acueil* may also depict the relationship between lovers, particularly the way the lady receives an aspirant. In this context, Bel Acueil may grant or refuse a kiss when the request is made. Finally, Bel Acueil is restored by—and thus as a notion derives from—Franchise and Pitié, two other facets of courtesy active in the context of *fin' amors*.

Stress on the denotative and connotative range of words is fundamental to classroom instruction on composition: "Oportet versificatorem esse exercitatum in verborum significatione cognita et consignificatione, ex quibus duobus perpenditur vocis officium. Ignota enim verborum significatio ad nocendum est efficacior ceteris doctrinae offendiculis" (p. 186, § 25) [Hence on this point the poet ought to be practiced in the denotation and connotation of words, from which the function of a word is inferred. Ignorance of the meaning of words is more likely to do harm than are all the hindrances to learning (p. 88)]. The poet should heed usage (*usus*) as well as certain varieties of metonymy like synonyms, abstraction of attributes, and cause for effect. "Fit iterum multis aliis modis verborum permutatio, quando dictiones adjunctam vel affinem habent significationem, vel quando synodoche utimur vel methonomia'' (p. 187, § 31) [Variation of words is effected in many other ways, such as through words with a connected or related meaning, or through the use of synecdoche or metonymy (p. 89)]. The relation between the specific value of a word and its context is especially important.

Bel Acueil's opposite is Dangier. There has been considerable discussion of a suitable definition for this word. C. S. Lewis prepared a list of its possible meanings in the Middle Ages, and appended it to his *Allegory of Love.*[69] His preference went to refusal or difficulty in love,[70] although he acknowledged the problem of applying this meaning to all the actions of Dangier in the *Rose,* especially Dangier's slumber and his professed indifference to a "courteous love."

> Saches je n'ai vers toi point d'ire,
> E se tu aimes, moi que chaut?
> Ce ne me fait ne froit ne chaut.
> Adès aime, mais que tu soies
> Loing de mes roses toutesvoies.
>
> (vv. 3196–3200 [3180–84])

[Understand that I am not at all angry at you, and if you love, what does that matter to me? It leaves me neither warm nor cold. Love forever, as long as you are always far from my roses.]

Franchise and Pitié induce Dangier to liberate Bel Acueil and to retire into slumber. Lewis' description of Dangier is not entirely satisfactory either, although it is more nuanced than his general definition, and thus suggestive of Dangier's various activities: "the rebuff direct, the lady's 'snub' launched from the height of her ladyhood, her pride suddenly wrapped about her as a garment, and perhaps her anger and contempt.'"[71] Is it not then erroneous to strive to reduce *dangier* to a single, all-inclusive meaning? As Reason shows in Jean de Meun, a word may be defined or it may be clarified in its semantic variety, its various potentials. Thus one sense, one affective value may obtain in one episode or in one context, while another may be introduced in another scene—both *ex sensu quo fiunt.* Even in Lewis' description of the lady just cited, there is no place for the villainy of Dangier stressed in his initial appearance in the poem (v. 2825 [2809]). Jauss ascribes Dangier's ambiguity to the changeable sentiments of the lady. *La donna è mobile!*[72] Is Guillaume's lady villainous or fickle?

The text supplies an implicit answer to the question of Dangier's meaning. Honte exclaims to Dangier after the latter's failure to prevent the kiss: "Il n'afiert pas a vostre non / Que vos faciez se enui non" (v. 3695–96 [3677–78]) [It doesn't agree with your name for you to do anything but make trouble]. The emphasis on Dangier's name, and thus on the semantic aptness and utility of the word, takes us back to the dictionary. *Dangier* derives from *domniarium* as lordship or dominion. Hence *dangier* expresses aristocratic prerogatives. But the prerogatives may be rightly or wrongly exercised; and they may be usurped by those unfit to exercise them.[73] This occurs when Richesse falls under the influence of *losengeors* (vv. 1024-38 [ibid.]). C. S. Lewis' identification of the meanings of *dangier* in the Middle Ages includes both proper and improper practice: the power to act, and therefore to hurt; and the power to give, and therefore to withhold. There is for each act a corresponding excess. After setting forth the various denotations of the word, Lewis rightly puts them back together in the abstraction. "It must always be remembered . . . that the various senses we take out of an ancient word by analysis existed in it as a unity."[74] This insight could have alerted him to the divarication of Dangier in the *Rose,* but he ignored it in favor of an undifferentiated definition that in fact reduces *dangier* to one of its possible meanings. "There is therefore no question of deciding in which of the senses given above the word *danger* is used on each occasion: it is like asking a modern Frenchman to choose between English 'like' and English 'love' every time he uses the verb *aimer*. There are times when he could so decide; but on most occasions the question simply does not exist in the meaning-system of his language."[75] The comparison of "Frenchmen in the street" with Guillaume is unfortunate, and misleading. More cogent would have been a reference to the use of *aimer* and its cognates in Racine and Corneille, in Chrétien de Troyes—or to Shakespeare's use of "like" and "love"!

In Guillaume's *Rose,* Dangier is placed in a definite context by his company: Male Bouche, Honte, Peur, all decidedly unaristocratic notions. Thus he is frequently *vilains* among real villeins, in the service of an ignoble mistress, Jalosie. This deprives Dangier of his gentility. His authority over Bel Acueil and the lover, including the freedom to wield his club,[76] indicates a real danger or peril in the modern sense of the word (vv. 2943-50 [2927-34]). His villainy is apparent in the churlish way he protects the Rose and deals with Bel Acueil, the son of Courtesy. This is what Lewis calls "obstinacy, insubordination, lack of humility in an inferior." But the appeal of Franchise and Pitié is effective in the Rose complex precisely because Dangier, like Richesse, has a good side: he may grant as well as withhold, when he is moved to the service of nobility, when his lord—in this case the god of Love—is himself noble. This explains his change upon moving from the villainous companions serving Jalosie into contact with the complex including Love, Franchise, and Pitié. "A word standing alone has an element of undefinedness analogous to that of prime matter. It is, to be sure, a unit of meaning, but much of its meaning is held in suspension, in potency, until its position in discourse stabilizes its grammatical form and elicits the relevant areas of its meaning."[77] But in Guillaume's *Rose,* Honte is as stringent as C.

89

S. Lewis in circumscribing the word's semantic potential, and he thus brings Dangier back into the camp requiring that narrow meaning. Dangier shares the epithets of Vilanie in the garden wall: "Sembla bien estre outrageuse / E mesdisant e ramponeuse" (vv. 161–62 [ibid.]) [She seemed a creature of evil, an insolent and unbridled scandal-monger] and

> Bien sembloit estre d'afiz pleine,
> E fame qui petit seüst
> D'enorer ce qu'ele deüst.
> (vv. 166–68 (ibid.])[78]

[She seemed full of all sorts of defamation, a woman who knew little of how to honor what she should.]

The only recourse open to a villain become courtly is sleep. And that is the state Honte finds Dangier in after the kiss.

Jalosie's activation of Honte and Peur, and, through them, the awakening of Dangier, is a manifestation of the Rose complex. For there emanates from it concern for Guillaume's intentions in asking for the kiss. Thus the quality of his sentiments is subject to question. If his love is not courtly, Dangier asleep is a farce. When Honte alludes to the *potestas nominis* of Dangier, she ridicules the apparent courtesy of so villainous a personage presuming to play Bel Acueil's role. She imposes a context—that of *fole amour*—on him that excludes Franchise and Pitié by their very nobility. Dangier returns to his former task as guardian of the Rose.

> Se Bel Acueil est frans et douz,
> E vos seiez fel e estouz,
> Pleins de rampones e d'outrage:
> Vilains qui est cortois enrage,
> Ce oï dire en reprovier,
> Ne l'en ne puet faire esprevier
> En nule guise de busart.
> Tuit cil vos tienent por musart
> Qui vos ont trové debonaire.
> (vv. 3697–3705 [3679–87])

[If (Bel Acueil) is open and sweet, you are to be cruel and violent, full of offensive words that wound. I have heard it said in a proverb that a courtly boor talks nonsense, and that one can in no way make a sparrow hawk out of a buzzard. All those whom you have found agreeable consider you a simpleton.]

The very fact that Dangier may be responsive to Franchise and Pitié is an ironic response to Honte's allegation that Dangier can be only a villain. Lewis' various meanings show the limitations of Honte's view, which itself is the result of "jealous" derangement. Dangier may indeed have a function in the service of Franchise and the god of Love. That Dangier and Jalosie feel that Bel Acueil can go too far adumbrates an ignoble Bel Acueil that Jean de Meun will bring to the fore. The context, the "company one keeps," shows in Guillaume a courteous, or at least reasonable, Dangier together with Franchise and Pitié. Jean will elicit a different Bel Acueil under the influence of the Vieille. But Dangier's noble possibilities are scarcely developed in the *Rose*. He retains his fealty to Jalosie, who does not permit him to frequent courteous company for very long. Dangier's gruff authoritarianism and his villainy prevail in the service of an ignoble lord. His association with the guardians of the Rose and his subservience to Jalosie clarify all his actions. He can only sleep for Franchise and Pitié. Courtesy remains with her son Bel Acueil, and he is locked away in Jalosie's tower.[79]

Jalosie, in its simplest sense, is "fear." But as with *dangier,* translation does not explain adequately its significance in the romance, as far as we can judge Guillaume's intentions. In the narrative, Jalosie is fear that the Rose will be plucked. This is why she constructs the castle as a sure protection against intruding seducers.[80] Such fear embraces various kinds of jealousy. This is evident when Peur is sent by Jalosie (vv. 2859–62 [2843–46]) rather than Reason, who sent Honte, "li miauz vaillanz" of the four guardians (v. 2837 [2821]). Guillaume obviously does not read Jalosie as the lover's fear of rivals or simple fear of rejection by the lady.[81] Jalosie is linked to the Rose rather than to the lover. Guillaume's own fears regarding his lady's sentiments towards him are interiorized in scattered comments and reflections:

> je passasse la cloison
> Mout volentiers, per l'achoison
> Dou bouton qui iaut miauz de basme,
> Se je n'en crainsisse avoir blasme.
> (vv. 2781–84 [2765–68])

[I would very willingly have penetrated the enclosure for the sake of the rosebud, which was better than balm, if I had not feared to incur blame.]

He apostrophizes Bel Acueil locked in the tower.

> Je ne sai or coment il vait,
> Mais durement sui esmaiez
> Que entroblié ne m'aiez,
> Si en ai duel e desconfort.
> (vv. 4052–55 [4022–25])

[I do not know now how things are going, but I am terribly afraid that you may have forgotten me, and I am in sorrow and pain.]

Guillaume's jealousy is independent of Jalosie or Peur as guardians of the Rose.

Jalosie's conduct after the kiss reveals her signification in context: it is the lady's concern, after a moment of weakness, that the lover may not love her, that he may be only a *lecheor*. The prattle of Male Bouche aggravates her concern, turns it to panic. The arousal of Honte and Peur follows what appears not as love but as *rage*—even if it is her own *rage*. She first upbraids Bel Acueil for allowing "un garçon desreé" (v. 3550 [3532]) [a misguided wretch] near the Rose.

> Garz neienz, por quoi t'a failli
> Sens, que bien fusses d'un garçon
> Don j'ai mauvaise sospeçon?
> (vv. 3536–38 [3518–20])

[Worthless wretch, why have you taken leave of your senses to become the friend of a *knave* of whom I suspect evil?]

Bel Acueil has become *garz*, just as Dangier was momentarily courteous. Jalosie is also anxious about Chastity (see vv. 3548–52, 3602–9 [3530–34, 3584–91]). The possibility of lechery is underscored in

> garçons, qui, por lui [Bel Acueil] honir,
> De paroles le vont chuant.
> Trop l'ont trové icil truant
> Fol e bergier a decevoir.
> (vv. 3632–35 [3614–17])

[who, in order to bring him [Bel Acueil] to shame, go around flattering him with pretty speeches. These vagrants have too much found him a fool, a stupid shepherd easy to deceive.]

"Shepherds" (*bergier*) were not permitted in the garden of Deduit. Jalosie is thinking of the *pastourelles,* Andreas Capellanus' *rusticani* incapable of courtly love, and of the devastation wrought by the villein in the *locus amoenus* described in the *Lai de l'oiselet*. Her fear of duplicity mobilizes the guardians and brings Dangier back to his post and his club.

Jalosie is as much a part of the feminine qualities surrounding the Rose as Honte and Bel Acueil. It is of course possible to extend the word to include the jealousy of a husband[82] or the fear of parents concerned for their daughter's chastity before marriage.[83] But these possibilities, besides being prosaic and melodramatic in the context of the *Rose,* are unnecessary. It is much more interesting to depict the jealousy of the lady as suspicion of the lover's motives—and of herself, since it was Venus acting on Bel Acueil which led to the kiss, not any force actively employed by Guillaume himself, who is largely passive in that scene (see especially vv. 3409–23 [3391–3405]). Such suspicion makes feasible Guillaume's intended conclusion: the taking of the castle by Love. For once Love is manifest, suspicion is no longer appropriate, Jalosie may withdraw (or go to sleep?), and the castle no longer needs defending—"li chastiaus ... / Qu'Amors prist puis par ses esforz."

Guillaume de Lorris saw his poem as an art of love. He offers his reader exemplary instruction on suitable conduct leading up to and during love, as well as commentary on the nature of love and the actions and sentiments characteristic of it. But his *Rose* is no more a formal treatise than Jean de Meun's is a formal *Remedia amoris*. Of course, there is something of the treatise in the god of Love's expository discourse, as the *Echecs* Commentator suggests. But it is not systematic.[84] Rather Guillaume has recourse to *ymagination*. The personifications and accompanying descriptions and narrative add to the more formal instruction[85] the play of sentiment and ideas. This is as revealing, if not as didactic, as the second section of the god's discourse describing the suffering and "adventures" of the typical lover. We learn what may well happen as much as we find out what to do in Guillaume's *Rose* because the adventures are simple, typical, and topical. The simplicity is not cumbrous in the Images. The different meanings of the words personified may elicit variations and nuances. The differences are, however, less taxonomic than demonstrative. The given word's ambiguity within its semantic field allows for sharpness and variety in configuration with other discrete, simple qualities and objects, and contributes finally—and in Guillaume perhaps more than any of those to follow him—to the fascination, the ineffable that shimmers through the Image and constitutes its charm and appeal. There is in this respect a real fraternity between Guillaume de Lorris and Charles d'Orléans, the last great representative of courtly Imagination. "Pour le lecteur, il reste ainsi toujours quelque chose à deviner.... Grâce à ce mystère au cœur de l'affabulation allégorique ..., l'intention didactique ... se résout peu à peu et devient pur effet poétique."[86] This is so in the central Image of the poem, the Rose.

The Rose has been variously explained as the lady, love, joy, virginity. But on no occasion does Guillaume show the Rose other than as a rose, a rosebud growing in a garden. When Bel Acueil grants the kiss, it is a rose that Guillaume kisses (vv. 3357–73 [3339–55]). But in *somnia* a Rose is never just a rose, and the reader is led by the context to think from time to time on the possible significations the context permits. The Rose, like the grail, is a *mystère*—at once mystery and signification[87] blended in the mind's response to the Image. There is no escaping this inextricable blend of mystery and signification in the Rose Image, and whoever seeks one to the exclusion of the other has lost the Image. The various meanings of the Rose are elicited from its ambiguity and suggestiveness, the play between its appearance and the configurations in which it is placed, its possible discursive meaning in different settings. A number of readings are possible at different stages in the narrative, but no single one or group suffices to circumscribe the Rose. It is no longer merely an allegorical Image. It has the attraction and fascination, the numinous quality we attribute to archetypes.[88]

But here literary commentary reaches its limits as a discursive process, and we may do no more than contemplate the Rose in its various Imagined configurations, reassured perhaps in the knowledge that even a psychologist could do no more.[89] Then we pass on to complete this illustration of Imagination by considering Guillaume himself, at once the "I" and the eye, the lover, the dreamer, the narrator and author of the *Rose*. Here studies of the poem present us with a quandary. On the one hand, authors like Lewis and Gunn stress the individuality of the Guillaume persona, seeing in his allegorical adventures a kind of psychology, even an individual psychology, presented in medieval terms. This conforms to Guillaume's expressed intention of relating his own dream. Others, like Robertson and Fleming, seek to divorce the author Guillaume from the Guillaume persona in the narrative, in part because of the ironic character they perceive as fundamental to the work's allegory. The identification of Guillaume as author and Guillaume as persona is a historical problem relevant to the import of the author's own assertions in his prologue. There Guillaume as author affirms the veracity of his account and its relation through his own experience in the dream to an exemplary status relevant to all of us. Guillaume's alleged personal experience is thus expanded and abstracted in the exemplary and oniric mode suitable to the expression of *fin'amors* as an ideal. Like Helen and Caesar in Matthew of Vendôme's descriptions, Guillaume incorporates his *maneries*, his type as lover. Guillaume the author is the equation sign between the individual Guillaume referred to in the prologue and the topical Guillaume who serves as narrative persona. Abstraction and amplification of the individual ego and its thoughts, sentiments, and actions are the means provided in medieval poetics to demonstrate the 'manner' in Imagination.

The ambivalent world of allegory is thus evident in the ego's persona as well: the author of the prologue and several discursive interventions, the narrator of the dream, and the lover in the dream.[90] Furthermore, the narrative ego is subject to adaptation in conformity with context and authorial intention. The adaptation shifts the configurations complementing or contrasting with one another to fit the *Rose*'s didactic intent. They evolve through the various stages of the quest for the Rose: Love, submission to Love, to the Rose, and to that person

> qui tant a de pris
> E tant est dine d'estre amee
> Qu'el doit estre Rose clamee.
> (vv. 42–44 [ibid.])

[who is so precious and so worthy to be loved that she should be called Rose.]

There is no more need to individualize Guillaume than there is to define the personifications that group around him. He derives from the idea of love which makes him a lover. He may play as many roles, though he need not and

94

does not, as there are kinds of love, something that Jean de Meun knew and made use of in his adaptation of Guillaume's meaning. The real sense of a given setting depends ultimately on authorial intention. That intention is a matter of authorial finesse, and, no doubt, amatory finesse as well. By the same token, the topical Guillaume represented in the poem is allegedly the real Guillaume as author and lover. There is therefore no reason not to permit the same ambiguity to persist in referring to him. There is certainly no more justification for divorcing the once living Guillaume from his persona than there is for equating the persona with the individual.

Guillaume de Lorris' use of Imagination demonstrates the author's careful adherence to context—the art of courtly love—with meaningful variations in narrative and didactic elaboration and demonstration of the subject. Medieval notions of etymology and semantics explicit in the *Rose* accord with interpretive liberty evident in twelfth-century statements on mythological *integumenta,* as well as the methods of composition practiced by writers influenced by Chartrain poetics. The freedom they enjoyed to "Imagine," to derive significance from profane texts, was limited only by the obligation to conform to Scripture and dogma and to eschew heresy.[91] Similarly, Guillaume de Lorris' Images conform to literal or allegorical readings limited only by the subject of his romance: courtly love.

Guillaume de Lorris' fragment realizes the adaptation of Imagination to courtly literature. Raoul de Houdenc and Huon de Mery, as well as a handful of troubadours and trouvères, had made interesting experiments, and certainly Huon de Mery's *Tornoiement* is an impressive adaptation of personification and romance as an Imagination. But Huon's work is still largely the traditional psychomachia of vices and virtues, even if it introduces new, courtly figures into the army of Christ. *Bone amour* on Christ's side is not the principal subject of the poem. Guillaume's *Rose* is the first thoroughgoing representation of courtly love by poetic *imaginatio*.

5

Imagination and the Second Rhetoric

IMAGINATION AS A MENTAL FACULTY[1]

With the *Roman de la rose,* Guillaume de Lorris invented a new kind of poem,[2] the allegorical love poem, which was to survive and flourish down to the close of the French Middle Ages. Numerous *mutations brusques*[3] mark this tradition, and novel interpretations of love are readily apparent. Bestiaries were adapted to the subject of *fin' amors* by writers like Richart de Fornival, in the *Bestiaires d'amours,* and Nicole de Margival, who made the panther of the *Physiologus* the central Image of his lady in the late thirteenth-century *Panthère d'amours.* The hunt, falconry, the questing knight, siege warfare— such "noble" Images were readily adapted to ideal love. Innovations in thought appeared as each author strove to express more convincingly through Images the quality of courtly love. For example, in the *Roman de la poire* Reason encourages the lover to persevere in the service of Love and his lady,[4] in apparent opposition to Reason's role in Guillaume de Lorris, closer to the intentions of Huon de Mery. Still, Guillaume de Lorris, like Andreas Capellanus before him—Andreas' courtly love is an *amor sapiens*—favored a prudent love. The accommodation of love to reason prepared the way for Guillaume de Machaut, who, as D. W. Robertson, Jr., observes, encouraged "reasonable love."[5] Of course, not everyone conjoined love and reason. Richart de Fornival linked love and "boine volentés" because "amours a si grant francquise en soi k'ele ne daigne sivir raison, ains veut faire tout son fait purement de s'auctorité" (*Consaus,* p. 12, § 17) [love is of such high nobility in and by itself that it does not deign to follow reason; rather it wishes to do everything entirely on its own]. In the anonymous *Tresor amoureux* Love and Reason conflict, and Congnoissance must mediate between the two.

Machaut is a cornerstone in the adaptation of Imagination to courtly literature. Among his dits are allegorical writings akin to Guillaume de Lorris' *Rose.* The *Vergier* is closest to the *Rose* in using personifications to represent conventional love in an idealized setting.[6] Personification appears as well in the *Jugement dou roy de Behaingne* and the *Jugement dou roy de Navarre.* The *Dit de l'alerion* utilizes aristocratic birds of prey as bestiary figures to illustrate various features of courtly and other kinds of love. The *Dit dou lyon* combines personification and bestiary figures, notably in the lion as faithful lover. Other dits elaborate upon exemplary situations whose particular significance emerges from extensive disputation not unlike that in Boethius' *Consolation of Philosophy*, which inspired them: the *Remede de Fortune*, the *Confort d'ami* and the *Fonteinne amoureuse*. None of these dits uses elaborate narrative or extensive chronology. The *Voir-Dit* is the one exception, though even here the emphasis is on what transpires in the narrator's mind or in dream-vision settings, and there is no real conclusion to the narrative. Not even the septuagenarian poet seems conscious of the conventional ages of man that are decisive in Froissart's *Espinette amoureuse* and *Joli buisson de jonece*, and that will become common at the end of our period.

This writing is the product of Imagination. General usage corresponds to the rhetorical sense of *imago*. The rhetorical sense of Imagination includes the Image in the mind. Jehan le Bel provides a useful vernacular statement of the function of the mental Image. He distinguishes between *imagination* and *fantasie* by the usual attribution of, respectively, truth and falsehood. "Ymaginations est une poissance comprendans, en laquele les ymagenes des choses senties sont gardées. Ceste Vertus si soustrait plus le sanlance des choses de matères sensibles que ne font li sens. Car li sens ne rechoit le sanlant des choses, fors les choses présentes, et ceste si garde les sanlans et les ymagenes, encore soit la chose absens.'"[7] [Imagination is a cognitive power in which the Images of things perceived by the senses are retained. This force extracts the appearances of things from sensible objects more than do the senses. For the sense impression receives the appearance of things only from those things which are present, while the former retains the appearances and Images even when the things are withdrawn.] Related to this is the capacity to act upon an Image retained in the memory: "Li propres offices de ceste vertu est des ymagenes et figures ymagenées, ententions natureles estraire, ensi k'amour, haine, preut, damage, grevance u aidance" (p. 201) [The proper office of this power is to extract from the images and the imagined forms natural inclinations, such as love, hate, advantage, harm, grievance, or assistance]. *Fantasie* may invent valid or invalid Images, depending on experience, reason, madness, or simply the pleasure of constructing "un mont d'or u . . . castiaus en Espaigne" (p. 204) [a mountain of gold or . . . castles in Spain]. Both may operate when one is awake or asleep, and may or may not be allegorical. This is the traditional conception of Imagination descending from Boethius and Macrobius; in addition, there is a clear indication of the pertinence of Imagination to the expression of love and other emotions.

Interesting examples of the adaptation of the Imaginative faculty to love occur in two thirteenth-century romances, *Cassidorus,* which is a branch of the *Sept Sages de Rome* prose cycle, and *Cristal et Clarie*. In *Cassidorus,*

Imagination is unconscious memory. Cassidorus dreams of Helcana, whom he had seen and loved in Palestine and then forgotten upon returning to Constantinople. Imagination is related to the theory of memory widespread in classical and medieval rhetorical instruction.[8] "Se uns chevaliers voit dame ou damoisele, quele que ele soit, mais que ele li plaise, il la met en son sain, c'est a dire, l'ymagynation de lui, il la met en memoire, et iluecques prent en son cuer . . . et la met en memoire de ce qu'il li plaist a l'ueil. Autre chose dis je que amours n'est."[9] [If a knight sees a lady or a maid, whoever she may be, should she please him, he puts her in his heart, that is he puts her Image in his memory, and thereupon takes her to his heart . . . and places in his memory that which is pleasing to his eye. I say that love is nothing else than this]. The statement is part of a debate on different kinds of love which becomes narrative when Helcana inspires Cassidorus' dreams, urging him to search for her. The dreams are thus the effect of involuntary memory acting through a series of debates in the romance: "Et li souvint par une ymagination de la pucele qu'il ot veüe en son dormant" (§ 83) [and he remembered by imagination the maiden whom he had seen in his sleep]. Cassidorus sets out in quest of the forgotten maiden, going from land to land examining maidens whose famed beauty suggests that they may be the *ymage* of his dreams. His search is long and fruitless. Yet he remains sensitive only to the beauty that his Imagination reveals to him (§ 199). Finally, by chance recall, Cassidorus remembers who his dream maiden really is, and he hastens to Bethsaida. Helcana, who dwells there, emerges, as if from a dream.

Helcana estoit en une chambre, dont elle n'estoit issue des dont que Cassidorus s'estoit partis de li, et n'avoit veü clarté ne jour, se n'avoit esté de chandoiles ou de feu ardant. Les nouveles en sont venues que Cassidorus estoit venus la ainssi. Se ele ot joie, ce ne fait pas a demander. Elle a dit en haut: 'Viegne avant celui pour qui j'ai gardé prison, et me traie de ci, ou autrement je morrai.' (§ 201)

[Helcana was in a room which she had not left since Cassidorus had taken leave of her, nor had she seen any light except of candle or fire. News reached her that Cassidorus had arrived there. There was no need to ask whether she was joyful. She cried out: "Let him come forward for whom I have stayed in prison, and draw me from here, or else I shall die."]

The final transition is into a dream world of *senefiance* akin to Guillaume's entrance into the garden of Deduit. There is even instruction provided by a wondrous child who is to become the hero of the *Helcanus* continuation of *Cassidorus* (§§ 346–74). This fairy-tale world is later linked, in the *Kanor* branch of the *Sept sages* cycle, to the forest of Broceliande, which was also allegorized by Huon de Mery. A tournament in the Forest Perilous uses Huon's technique in turning the Evil Knights into abstract personifications.[10]

The motif of the quest for a dream maiden, an episode in *Cassidorus,* is expanded into a complete narrative and an exemplary art of love in *Cristal et Clarie*. Memory is not involved as in *Cassidorus,* but rather the emergence in dream of an unknown maiden who inspires Cristal's quest. Clarie is unaware of Cristal and her effect on him (vv. 7589–91).[11] The figure of Clarie moves through successive visual transformations from Cristal's dream that awakens his *pensers* and an impulse to set out on what becomes a ten-year quest for the most beautiful maiden in the world. Clarie, like Melior in *Partonopeu de Blois,* appears as a *sovenir* (v. 1922), a *samblance* (v. 3120), and, after Cristal sees her for the first time (v. 6795), an *examplaire* (v. 7165) of her idealized qualities.

> Clere est de male teche et pure,
> En lui a gentil creature,
> Sage est, cortoise et debonaire,
> De totes valors est samplaire.
> (vv. 7757–60)

[She is clear of any bad quality and undefiled, she is noble, prudent, courteous, and proper, exemplary in all worthy qualities.]

The narrative imposes topical developments characteristic of courtly love onto a fairy-tale quest pattern. Extensive authorial digressions, interior monologues and dialogues, and debates are combined with the portrayal of dangerous forests, mysterious fountains, beasts natural and supernatural, a witch at once malevolent and benevolent, devils, an evil hand. Prototypes of Clarie are encountered on Cristal's quest: thirty beautiful maidens (v. 1179), then Narde (v. 2429) and Olinpa (v. 2616), two maidens almost as beautiful as Clarie. The three beautiful maidens are contrasted with three malevolent fays (v. 5993). The affinity of Cristal to Clarie permits an "etymological" analysis of their names.

> Ja est plus clere
> C'onques ne fu voire ne glace,
> Mirer se poet on en sa face
> Et si est plus blans de cristal.
> (vv. 7200–7203)

[She is indeed more clear than glass or window ever was; one can see one's reflection in her face, and she is whiter than crystal.]

Clarie's mirrorlike appearance figures her emergence as an exemplar of what is good and valuable and thus worthy of admiration in love, just as Cristal's quest for his lady becomes exemplary of the lover's progress towards a good love (vv. 1–9). The extensive prologue on love, Cristal's conduct and sentiments, Clarie's responses to his declaration, their success in bringing their love to consummation and marriage provide, like Guillaume's *Rose,* a combination of explicit didacticism and marvellous adventure. The union of Nature and Love (vv. 4568, 7395–97) harks back to material we have observed in the twelfth century, and forward to Machaut's use of them in the *Prologue*. The narrative and didactic elaboration of an unconscious Image that becomes a memory even before it is actually perceived suggests the "archetypal" sources of courtly Imagination.

The trend was away from pseudohistorical romance towards abstraction and didacticism. The *ymage* thus tended to obliterate narrative: romance was moribund in France as a mode for the expression of courtly idealism. The dit took its place. The transformation is perceptible if one compares *Cristal et Clarie* to Richart de Fornival's *Bestiaires d'amours*. The Fornival *Bestiaires,* like *Cristal,* is a *salut d'amour,* or semiepistolary appeal to his lady in the mode of a didactic Imagination.[12] The *Bestiaires* analyzes *fin'amors* as an oscillation between life and death, the birth of love and the refusal by the lady. The bestiary Images, the didactic subject, and the appeal to the lady[13] combine much as the anonymous author of *Cristal et Clarie* arranges *aventures merveilleuses* to fit the sequence of the birth, growth, and consummation of Cristal's love. The difference between the two—a fundamental one for the integrity of the dit as distinct from romance—is that the romance grows from a *matière* onto which a *surplus de sens* is grafted, as Marie de France pointed out, while in the dit *matière* is the *surplus* worked into a given *sens* discursively set forth. Hence the possibility for the lady, in her *Response,* to turn the Images to a new meaning and reject the lover's proffered service. The adaptation of *matière* to a given *sens,* characteristic of the dit, will become firmly established in Machaut. Although the *sens* may be commonplace, the suggestive force of Images intelligently and sometimes profoundly adapted to it provides the interest and fascination of the late medieval dit. It illustrates the prismatic effect of ideas seen through their material manifestations.

IMAGINATION IN MACHAUT'S *REMEDE DE FORTUNE*

Frequentatio patterns the description of Machaut's lady in the *Remede de Fortune*. Description traditionally establishes a coherent configuration of abstract qualities deemed worthy of admiration and emulation.[14] In the *Remede* description, however, the literal lady has entirely dissolved into—in effect sublimated as—her abstractions. The description (vv. 167–352) is a classification under twelve headings.[15] Each heading has two parts: first, an assertion that the lady evinces the given quality; second, the lover's determination to reflect and thus realize the given quality in himself by imitation.[16] For example:

> Et sa maniere asseürée,
> De tous et de toutes loée,
> Son biau port, son gentil maintieng

> Qui pareil n'ont, si com je tieng,
> Tout aussi com l'enfant le mestre
> Aprent, m'aprenoient a estre.
> Car, sans plus, de leur ramembrance
> Maintieng, maniere et contenance
> Loing de li souvent me venoit
> Milleur, quant il m'en souvenoit.
>
> (vv. 197–206)

[And her confident manner praised by all, her fine gait, her noble bearing, unparalleled in my estimation, taught me, as the master teaches the child, how I should be. For merely by calling them to mind, my bearing, manner, and contenance often improved, even when she was far away, when I remembered her qualities.]

The description converts the real lady into an Imagination. The lady *bone et bele*, fragmented into qualities that emanate prismatically from her essential *bonté* (v. 177), becomes a "miroir et exemplaire / De tous biens desirer et faire" (vv. 171–72)[17] [mirror and examplar for desiring and doing all things that are good].

Machaut's catalogue of specific *biens* expressive of his lady's *bonté* is a configuration of qualities inherent in the lady he loves, as her literal conduct in the dit makes apparent. The imitation of abstractions is the same process as that described by de Ghellinck in his article on imitation of a mental Image, or—in Geoffrey of Vinsauf's words—an archetypal Image. Machaut's use of the Image is also characteristic of Imagination as a function of memory. Reflection on his lady's qualities increases his own *bonté*.

> Et pour le bien qu'en li vëoie,
> De tout bien faire me penoie
> Et me gardoie de mesprendre,
> Si qu'on ne me peüst reprendre,
> A mon pooir, car sa bonté
> M'en donnoit cuer et volenté.
>
> (vv. 173–78)

[And for the good I saw in her, I strove to do everything that is good and avoided doing wrong, so that I might not be found blameworthy; and I did so to the best of my ability, for her goodness gave me the desire and will to do so.]

Bonté is transferred from the lady to the lover through the mirror Image. Even conventional rhetorical description is set aside in favor of clearly differentiated qualities. The physical lady is abstracted, fragmented, and unified in the idea of *bonté* that emanates through her various attributes. The abstraction of the lady as her qualities is a sublimation anticipating the sublimation of courtly love argued in the lai that follows almost immediately on the description.

The lai occupies a prominent position in the structure and argument of the *Remede*. In it Machaut puts the fundamental idea of the dit: the primacy and sufficiency of hope in love. This idea anticipates the appearance of Hope personified in the main didactic section of the *Remede*, where she develops systematically the ideas set forth schematically in the lai. The lai is discursive, argumentative, and informative; its impact is rhetorical, since it is meant to sway and therefore convince the reader.

The theme of the lai is set down in its opening sentence: the sufficiency of *dous Penser, Souvenir,* and *Espoir de joïr* in love (vv. 433–35). The argument is supported by repetitive and incremental assertions of the theme (*interpretatio* as amplification), each introduced by a word or phrase underscoring the demonstrative intention: "Car pour un cuer saouler" (v. 440) or "Encor y a maint resort" (v. 445). The weightier side of argumentation is dissipated by the light and rapid movement of the short lines and the rhyme play, by the very repetition that makes fewer demands on concentrated attention, that persuades by restatement. The style is thus appropriately middle.[18] This is typical for Machaut's poetry. It is Dante's *gradus sapidus et venustus* "qui est quorundam superficietenus rhetoricam aurientium" (II.vi.4) [which is the style of those who hold to rhetorical devices on the literal level of the poem]. The elegant figural ornamentation common to classical Middle Style and much Old French verse corresponds as well to Geoffrey of Vinsauf's *ornatus facilis*[19]—the language of Horace's *prodesse* and *delectare*.

Stanza 2 of the *Remede* lai continues to elaborate on the "souffisance" (v. 463) of *dous Penser, Souvenir,* and *Espoir*. In the first part, the presumptive desire for other *biens* is branded irrational ("fol cuidier," v. 461) and deceptive ("il vuet trichier," v. 464). In the second part, Machaut develops figuratively the beneficial effects of merely contemplating the three *biens* of ideal love, rehearsing thereby his own contemplation of the lady in the description preceding the lai. Thus he is able to realize in stanza 3 a "Douce Pensée" (v. 480) in *Souvenir* ("adès me souvient / De la desirée," vv. 482–83) and *Esperance* (v. 485). Images being a feature of memory, they assure the constant presence of the descriptive Image of the lady and make permanent its beneficial influence on the lover's character and disposition. The combination spurs the lover on to service and acknowledgement of the lady's right to accept or reject his service (vv. 487–94), that is, of her *dangier*.

The succeeding stanzas analyze in an abstract, admonitory manner different courtly topics, adapting each to Machaut's conception of love characterized by *dous Penser, Souvenir,* and *Espoir* as supreme rewards: vision of the lady (stanza 4), desire (stanza 5), silence in the lady's presence (stanza 6), and fear (stanza 7). These subjects, traditionally a source of pain and grief in unrequited love, lose their bitterness because the three consolations are the real ends in love. They leave nothing more to be desired, focused as they are on

Images in the memory. Still, the lover would let his lady know his sentiments, without of course being so presumptuous as to express them outright and face to face (stanza 8). The dilemma is resolved in stanza 9 by a projection in Imagination as a prayer to Love, who "Li porra bien dire / Que pour s'amour fri" (vv. 599–600) [can indeed tell her that I burn for her love]. The prayer as poem, a *vocis imago,* satisfies the need for self-expression to the lady. There will be delay, and fidelity and long suffering are still necessary (stanza 10). Suffering, however, can have only the sense of bearing delay with patience supported by hope: "Aligement / N'en vueil, fors souffrir humblement / Ma douce maladie" (vv. 624–26) [I wish for no assuagement other than to bear humbly my gentle malady]. Stanza 11 supports the interpretation by describing how the lady's *dous regard* may nullify the pain of desire.

> Car s'il [desire] fait mon cuer trambler,
> Taindre et palir
> Et fremir,
> A bien souffrir
> Dou tout m'acort.
>
> (vv. 662–66)

[For if it (desire) makes my heart quake, blush, pale, and tremble, I agree to bear it all well.]

This is possible because serving his lady is a pleasant task in itself (vv. 672–75). "La me confort" (v. 680): the lover agrees to wait patiently—with fear and trembling (vv. 662–64).

The conclusion subverts the thrust of the preceding argument by denying the efficacy of *dous Penser, Souvenir,* and *Espoir,* that is of Imagination, in assuaging fear and anxiety. It brings the lai back to the narrative. For the poet knows what good love is, but lacks the understanding necessary for inner accommodation to that knowledge. Hence the need to introduce Hope in the subsequent didactic elaboration. She, in fact, gives meaning to the *Remede's* title.

Like the god of Love's instruction in the *Roman de la rose,* the lai provides a discursive framework, a conceptual structure from which Machaut draws the ensuing Imagination of Esperance's consolation and reinforcement of the lover's understanding of his love and his lady. This alters his conduct towards her to fit the ideal expressed in the lai, as shown at the end of the dit. The lai is thus a preamble; it brings to the fore the essential self-sufficiency of good love. Machaut's conception of the relation between *souffisance* and good love is original in courtly writing.[20]

In a number of places Machaut states that the sole subject worthy of his verse is love. This is explicit in the *Prologue.* The art of love is one of the two arts stressed in the *Remede de Fortune,* and it is pervasive in his fixed forms.

It therefore is incumbant upon us to inquire into Machaut's conception of love: what meanings he assigned to the word, what experiences he commonly associated with it, what conduct he saw as appropriate to the person in love. The examination will lead us back to his use of Imagination, and clarify his poetics as well.

For Machaut, love has certain limits. This had always been acknowledged. Jean de Meun had distinguished between the prerogatives of Venus and Amour. In Machaut's time, Jean Froissart stressed the ages suitable to love in the *Espinette amoureuse* and the *Joli buisson de jonece*. At the end of the *Joli buisson,* Froissart turns to another lady, the Virgin Mary, as a more suitable object in later life for prayer and supplication. But Machaut was not inclined to view matters in this way.

> Or vueille Amours qu'en juenesse durer
> Puist ceste amour toudis, sans envieillir
> Et sans morir; si serons sans finer
> En paradis d'amours.
>
> (Balade CCXXV, vv. 17–20).

[May Love grant that this love always remain young, without aging and without death; and we shall then live forever in love's paradise.]

Even allowing for the hyperbole typical of courtly exclamations, there is more to Machaut's words than foolishness in love. Indeed, his notion of *jeunesse* does not seem far removed, as an ideal, from the troubadours' *jovens* as the sum and acme of noble qualities.[21] This is apparent in the *Voir-Dit*. There stress is not on age, personal allusions are discreet or deliberately vague, and the personages, as in the *Rose,* are typical, representative Images showing forth the poet's ideas and convictions. Youth is traditionally essential to love. To wish to love always is to wish for eternal youth, but this connotes eternal possession of the qualities aligned with courtly love. From another perspective, the end of youth in the literal sense may mean the end of courtly love, as in Froissart's *Joli buisson.* Or the love may in effect transcend time to acquire an almost religious character. Both possibilities are typical and topical. But in only one poem, an isolated balade,[22] does Machaut follow Froissart from courtly love to a specifically religious sentiment.

Machaut's attitude towards love raises a large problem: the reconciliation of inherently divergent, indeed contradictory attitudes to love, public life, and Christian morals in medieval thought. The standard illustration of the problem for students of courtly literature has been Andreas Capellanus and some romancers like Chrétien de Troyes. Certain gradualistic features of Andreas' thought help to explain the divergent views in his treatise, as well as to account for different kinds of love.[23] Similarly, Machaut is careful to scale obligations to different imperatives. For example, in the *Confort d'ami* he avoids conflict in man's duties to God, the lady, and himself and his family by appeal to traditional hierarchy. More explicitly in the *Lyon*, he qualifies different men and ladies by the kind of love they practice. Men may be false (vv. 939–88), faithful (vv. 989–1118), deceitful (vv. 1119–1212), recreants or "Frere aisié" (vv. 1213–1344), chivalrous knights (vv. 1345–1504), braggarts (vv. 1505–22), or peasants (vv. 1523–86). Ladies may be deceitful (vv. 1593–1606), perspicacious or lacking in finesse (vv. 1607–20), "playgirls" (vv. 1621–34), devoted to chivalrous knights (vv. 1635–56), seductresses (vv. 1657–66), or *belles dames sans mercy* who are haughty for fear of being deceived (vv. 1667–98). As used by Machaut and Andreas the distinctions, like those made on the principle of material style, are qualitative differences among conventional types.

There were, however, inevitable difficulties with such gradualism, which varied according to the quality of love depicted and the worthiness of the lover and the loved one. Such difficulties are especially remarkable in the misunderstanding between the poet and his lady in the latter part of the *Voir-Dit*, where different interpretations (including one given by the king of France) of the lady's conduct and Machaut's reaction to it are set forth. But before taking up Machaut's treatment of the problem of courtly love and moral imperatives, let us first sketch in the near background to the problem by examining in some detail certain of his contemporaries who also dealt with the irreconcilable imperatives of Christian and public morals and of courtly love.

COURTLY LOVE AND CHRISTIAN MORALITY: TENSION AND GRADATION

Perhaps the best illustrations of the ambivalent, often ambiguous, approach to *fin' amors* may be found in three authors who wrote in the thirteenth and fourteenth centuries: Watriquet de Couvin and Jean and Baudouin de Condé. They wrote both for and against love in a manner that may well seem contradictory. Or they treated subjects seemingly inconsonant with any kind of courtly love, such as charity, the duties of princes,[24] the education and moral betterment of young gentlemen, and "dirty" stories. This variety encouraged D. W. Robertson, Jr. to consign all conceptions of love in the Middle Ages not sanctioned by the Church to the same low class. "Just as medieval art developed certain conventional ways of indicating the identity of a saint, the character of a vice, or the ramifications of an idea represented by a pagan deity, medieval literature developed a conventional language of narrative or descriptive motifs which were designed to communicate ideas." So far so good. Robertson has not set the contexts which may provide conventional motifs. The motifs remain topics adaptable to any context and thus any intention the author finds suitable. But Robertson goes on to equate the motif with given religious themes. "The theme may be treated with some seriousness, as it is in *Troilus,* or comically, as it is in the Miller's Tale, but it [is] a theme devised to stimulate thought rather than emotion. When the young man in Guido Faba's *Dictamina rhetorica* writes to his beloved, 'non possum aliud nisi de vestra pulcritudine cogitare,' we recognize a symptom, or a feigned symptom, of the lover's malady; and when he adds that he must have her grace 'sine qua mea mors vita creditur et vita mortua reputatur,' we know exactly what he wants and why he wants it.''[25]

Do we? The *artes dictaminis* included the love letter in illustrations, and those letters were meant to serve a purpose.[26] The possibility of widespread epistolary deception is incredible, but even more incredible is the argument that such letters were merely idle entertainment for students or a broad male attempt to seduce women ignorant of epistolary techniques and therefore presumably blind to "what he wants and why he wants it." Moreover, there are extant the *Epistolae duorum amantium,* whose editor argues convincingly for their authenticity. Like them, Andreas Capellanus puts honor and virtue ahead of delight, as do the Commentator on the *Echecs amoureux* and Christine de Pisan. What assurance do we have that Guido Faba's lover is doing or thinking otherwise, that his love is not *fine* but *fole?*

Beyond the naiveté of a lover who would make, and a lady who would listen to, such a bald-faced request to fornicate as Robertson makes the letter out to be (but why teach the writing of such letters in a serious treatise on the art of letter writing?), he raises questions pertinent to an understanding of Imagination and the usage of the expression *fin'amors* among poets traditionally classed as courtly. First, does a given Image in fact always carry with it a specific context, and thus impose a concomitant and essentially unchanging nucleus of truth or signification?[27] And, corollary to this question, was there only one way—the so-called Christian, rigorist way—to view human love when not sanctioned by sacrament?

No one denies that a given Image is amenable to various interpretations. For example, John Fleming in his reading of Oiseuse as Lechery in Guillaume's *Rose* on the basis of the mirror she looks into while combing her hair admits that there were other traditional ways in the Middle Ages to understand maidens looking into a mirror.[28] The context, he insists, makes the intent of the Image clear. But he excludes categorically the context of courtly love. The fact that Oiseuse is combing her hair equates her with lechery, and this clinches the argument to Fleming's way of thinking: fair love is foul. There is something of the *petitio principii* in this argument, stemming from Robertson's contention that all medieval literature not explicitly designated otherwise is conducive to charity, a conclusion he bases on recognized authorities. But he does not acknowledge the authority of those who designate some literature as a literature of courtly love.

The evidence examined earlier in this study shows some variety of thought on the subject of love. The Commentary on the *Echecs amoureux* allows three specific contexts: carnal love, conjugal love, and courtly love. For the last, the Commentator advises reading the god of Love's instruction in Guillaume's part of the *Rose* for a straightforward statement on the subject and the conduct appropriate to the good lover. "Il doit tous les commandemens d'amours a son pouoir garder et acomplir ansi qu'ilz sont escript ou *Rommant de la rose* et es aultres livres aussi d'amours. Le livre meismes dont nous parlons en parle en briefves parolles assez souffissamment et par subtille maniere, se y poelt on regarder qui vouldra. Car par ceste maniere polra ly amoureux acquerre lotz et pris et bonne renommee" (fol. 300 r-v). [He must keep and follow to the best of his ability all the commandments of love as they are set down in the *Roman de la rose* and in the other books about love. The very book we are treating discusses it briefly and quite satisfactorily and with subtlety, and whoever wishes may see it there. For in this way the lover may acquire renown and esteem and a good reputation.] That Guillaume de Lorris and poets like him could envisage a love neither foul nor explicitly sanctified, but still courtly because it leads to "lotz et pris et bonne renommee," emerges clearly from the Commentator's analysis. And the passage suggests that he did not see Guillaume's Oiseuse as opening the door to lechery, but rather to what was to become a *fin' amors*.

Fleming's extensive use of the *Echecs amoureux* Commentary to corroborate his reading of the *Rose* ignores the fact that the verse *Echecs* is an *adaptation* of material much of which is indeed derived from the *Roman de la rose,* but not always with the same intention as that of either Guillaume de Lorris or Jean de Meun. Reinterpretation of earlier material was traditional in medieval adaptation. We saw it used in the *Response* to Fornival's *Bestiaires.* Deletions, additions, and extensive amplifications demonstrate that we may not simply view the *Echecs* Commentary as a commentary on the *Roman de la rose*. Yet a great many of the passages adduced by Fleming are freely, even tendentiously, set forth as firm evidence for his reading of the *Rose.* The Commentator does frequently allude to the *Rose*. But most explicit references are to literal or material features of the romance. They concern, for example, the use of personification in dream visions (fol. 13 v), dreams as a means to avoid accusations of falsehood (fol. 14 r), the value of octosyllabic verse (fol. 93 v), or purely material similarities like the description of Haine in the garden wall (fol. 242 v). But the two poems do not coincide in context, and the differences are important. Fleming ignores significant alterations in the verse *Echecs,* like the encounter with Diane outside the garden of Deduit, the noble quality of love in Arthurian romance, and details like Venus' sending the would-be lover to the garden of Deduit (fols. 197 r–199r).

The Commentator was not blind to the differences between the two poems. He referred to the god of Love's instruction on *fin' amors* for a more complete discussion of the subject than his own work offered, as was shown above. For interpretation of fables is open to authorial determination, "scelon ce que on voelt les fables des poettes et les narrations diversement entendre et ramener a diverses sentences" (fol. 288 r) [insofar as one wishes to interpret in various ways the fables and narrations of the poets, and provide them with variant readings]. This is in fact the freedom of the *involucrum*.[29] There in fact are passages where Fleming's interpretation of the *Rose* contradicts the Commentator's. Fleming describes the fountain of Narcissus as an Image for "the folly of self-love" that will lead to "fornication of the heart."[30] The Commentator, however, asserts that Guillaume de Lorris "dit . . . moult de choses de ceste fontaine a sa recommendation" (fol. 322 r)! [relates . . . many things about that fountain that redound to its credit]. And he perceives the love between Narcissus and Echo as a "vraye amour loyal" (fol. 328 r). A proper understanding of the relation between the *Rose* and the verse *Echecs amoureux,* and between the two poems and the *Echecs* Commentary, will be possible when there is a critical edition for the latter two. Until then extreme caution must be taken to verify and substantiate both similarities and differences among them. Distinctions will need to be made between the literal and diverse allegorical levels upon which the poems may be read, between Guillaume de Lorris' poem by itself and as incorporated into Jean de Meun's vaster design as well as into the verse *Echecs* and its Commentary. These distinctions are crucial for the Commentator. Thus his understanding of the two-part *Rose* and its hierarchical conception of love is more discriminating than Robertson's and Fleming's monumental view of the romance; in this the Commentator resembles his contemporary Christine de Pisan. We must remember that the verse *Echecs* is modelled on the *Rose* as the Charrette section of the *Lancelot* Proper is an adaptation of Chrétien de Troyes' romance; but the two texts are not the same in either content or signification.

WATRIQUET DE COUVIN

The perspective on love may vary between texts by the same author. Robertson correctly reads Watriquet de Couvin's *Tournois des dames* as a castigation of female domination over men, or rather of the senses over reason.[31] But it is simply wrong that all Watriquet's writings, and those of his contemporaries, furnish "abundant materials for the exemplification of moral and theological ideas," and thus that "the same underlying attitude, transferred to the somewhat less theological but no less moral realm of courtly entertainment, is responsible for the prevailing conception of poetry."[32] The use of exemplification as Imagination is indeed obvious in Watriquet. That it was confined to moral and theological subjects is not. Robertson cites Watriquet's *Tournois des dames, Dis de la nois, Dis de l'iraigne et du crapot,* and *Mireoirs as princes* because they counsel wisdom and prudence and explicitly or implicitly condemn love (without separating out conjugal love or love between the betrothed). The cards are stacked! Watriquet also wrote works in praise of good love. His *Mireoirs as dames* unites Beauté and Bonté as the goal of thirteen steps into a palace containing the "ymage" (v. 923) of his lady. The steps to her love are Nature, Sapience, Maniere, Raison, Mesure, Pourveance, Charité, Humilité, Pitié, Debonnaireté, Courtoisie, Largesce, and Souffisance. In the palace the lover encounters Plaisance, Bontez, Simplesce, Maniere, Verité, and Droiture, Entendement, Leesce, Biautes, Honnour, and Loiautez. The description passes to a psychomachia in which the aforementioned qualities overcome their opposing vices and defects (vv. 758–839). Watriquet's Imagination is "uns fins paradis terrestre / Vuis de courous et plains de joie" (vv. 942–43) [a refined earthly paradise, free of vexation and filled with joy]. The whole Image is a lesson for ladies (vv. 1158–70) which combines the form and intention of the garden of Deduit and the fountain of Narcissus in Guillaume de Lorris' *Rose*.

The *Dis des quatre sieges* recounts a dream the poet had while lying in the arms of his *amie* (vv. 13–17). It singles out four admirable qualities worthy of imitation, including arms and love, which are both essential to the attainment of honor (vv. 133–59).[33] The same argument is in the *Dis du preu chevalier* (vv. 290–91). The union of "Vraie amour" and Loiauté and Science in this dit adds significance to the *cuer fin* referred to in the conclusion.

> Et pour ce qu'ensi fu parez
> Preus chevaliers et comparez,
> Loiaus, sages et de cuer fin
> Vrais amis, ci vous ferai fin.
> (vv. 321–24)

[And since the courtly knight was thus adorned and set forth—a faithful, prudent, and true lover of perceptive heart—I shall here make an end.]

Similar praise of love appears in the *Dis de l'escole d'amours*.

Robertson's broad assertion that all literature of this time was dominated by traditional moral or didactic concerns is undercut by Watriquet's own words in the *Dis des trois chanoinesses de Coulogne,* in which he denies any deep sense in favor of a story patently designed, as Christine de Pisan says,[34] to make us laugh for the pleasure of laughing.

> Il n'a homme desi à Sens,
> S'adès vouloit parler de sens,
> C'on ne prisast mains son savoir
> Qu'on fait sotie et sens-savoir;
> Qui set aucunes truffes dire
> Où parlé n'ait de duel ne d'ire,
> Puis que de mesdit n'i a point,

> Maintes foiz vient aussi à point
> A l'oïr que fait uns sarmons.
>
> (vv. 1–9)

[There is no one from here to Sens, were he always eager to speak sensibly, whose knowledge people would not esteem beneath foolishness or stupidity. If you can tell a few jokes that contain neither grief nor ire, and providing they are not slanderous, they are often as worth listening to as a sermon.]

Chaucer knew this when he wrote the *Canterbury Tales*. Watriquet's poem is merely an account of "risées pour esbatre / Les roys, les princes et les contes" (vv. 256—57) [jokes for the entertainment of kings, princes, and counts]. In fact Watriquet makes very clear: (1) the distinction between the love described in poems like the *Escole d'amours,* which are "choses de pris" (v. 142) [estimable], and the kind found in fabliaux; and (2) the purpose of the latter to provoke laughter.[35] *Fin'amors* for Watriquet is a stabilizing influence on human conduct. With Maniere and Souffisance, it stands guard against Fortune in *Li dis de l'escharbote.* He thus rehearses the qualities and distinctions in love discernible in courtly writing from Andreas Capellanus to Christine de Pisan and the Commentary on the *Echecs amoureux.*

JEAN DE CONDÉ AND BAUDOUIN DE CONDÉ

Watriquet's near contemporaries Jean and Baudouin de Condé also offer useful illustrations of good love, useful because of their extensive writings and the range of subjects taken up in their dits. An ambivalent attitude towards love emerges from all their writings taken together. But within any given poem they are consistent in praise or blame. Jacques Ribard has put it very well: "On aborde ici un domaine où les genres littéraires conditionnent dans une large mesure leur sujet même."[36] The context is primary and determinant. There are love poems representing carnal love, courtly love, conjugal love.[37] Moreover, praise or blame is not massive. Jean de Condé exemplifies the deleterious effects of bad love on a good knight in the *Blans Chevaliers* and the beneficial results of good love on a villainous lord in the *Chevalier a la mance.* We shall confine ourselves here to the writings that are explicitly courtly in their presentation of love.

In the *Dis de la pelote* Jean de Condé sets forth the three kinds of love designated by Andreas Capellanus as *amor simplex, amor venalis,* and *amor sapiens,* that is, love for carnal pleasure, love for gain, and love which is "honnieste" (v. 89). These descriptions fix contexts encompassing various shadings and colorings.

> Mès pluiseurs guises sont d'amours,
> N'ont c'un non, mès grant differense
> A ès fais.
>
> (vv. 14–16)

[There are several varieties of love; they have but one name, but their effects are very different.]

Courtly love is the one that interests Jean de Condé.

> Boine amours est viertus si finne
> Qu'elle ne cange ne ne finne
> En cuer d'amant; tant est poissans
> K'adiès est ses pooirs croissans;[38]
> Mès li pluisour n'ont cognissance
> De connoistre sa grant poissance.
> (vv. 1–6)

[Good love is a quality so fine that it neither changes nor ends in the lover's heart; so powerful is it that its force ever grows. But most have not the capacity to comprehend its power.]

Fine connaissance makes such love accessible only to a happy few. For them Jean de Condé sets forth the qualities of the *fin' amors* they strive to achieve. Much of what he says recalls Andreas Capellanus. Good love must be faithful; this is what Jean de Condé finds so rare in the world. Where fidelity is upheld, the lovers achieve an equality lacking in what often passes for love, but is so in name only.

> Et est leur amours si ivielle
> C'on ne poroit savoir li quelle
> Est menre; si bien est partie
> Qu'elle est en cascunne partie
> Si ferme et si enrachinnée,
> Si conjointe et si affinnée,
> Sans ordure et sans villonnie,
> Qu'elle est si ivielle et hounie
> Com est la mers quant est sans onde.
> (vv. 99–107)

[And their love is so equal that one could not find out which is the lesser. And it is so well divided that it exists in each party as something so firm and so fixed, so united and so refined, free of foul or villainous traits, that it is as smooth and as calm as the waveless sea.]

This corresponds to what we have observed in some poems representing exchanges between the man and the woman, especially in the *chansons féminines*.

Love arises not from beauty, as in Andreas' *amor simplex*, but from *bonté* (v. 148), as in Andreas' *amor sapiens* and Machaut's *fin' amors*.[39] Besides evincing *hounesté*, good love is "delitable" and "pourfitable" (vv. 153–54). It thus has all the good qualities and none of the defects of the two other kinds of love—adapting, of course, the sense of *delit* and *proufit* to the new context.

> Car l'amant fait à bien entendre
> Et ne li lait penser n'entendre
> A mal faire, ansçois l'en reprent,
> Et ensi ceste amours comprent
> Les autres poins cangiés em bien.
> (vv. 155–59)

[For it causes the lover to strive after that which is good, while preventing him from thinking of or seeking after wrongdoing; rather it corrects his conduct. Thus this love embraces the traits of the two other kinds of love, but changes them into goods.]

Hence the elevated quality of courtly love, which only the wisdom of science and letters may comprehend.

> Car en lui a viertu hautisme.
> De ses biens ne di pas le disme,
> Et qui plus avant en vorra
> Enquerre, trouver le poura
> Ès livres de philosophie,[40]
> Si m'en tairai à ceste fie.
> (vv. 167–72)

[For in it resides the highest virtue. I do not express the tenth part of its goods. If anyone wishes to investigate the subject further, he may find it set forth in the books on "philosophy." For this reason, I shall have no more to say about it for now.]

There remains only to call down the benediction of God on good lovers (vv. 173–76). The idealism of courtly poetry was not without its romanticism! Machaut would soon be appealing in one breath to God, Venus, and Love, and Chartier lamenting the way falsity had undermined the fine ideal of courtly love. And Jean de Condé himself is merely continuing the praise of courtly love that we find in his father. Baudouin de Condé asserts in his *Conte d'amours:*

> Or i soit raisons regardée:
> S'amours n'est francement gardée
> Par ciaus qui sont franc et jentil,
> Coment le garderoient il,
> Li vilain qui n'ont connissance
> Ne foi?
> (vv. 169–74)[41]

[Let's be reasonable about it. If love is not upheld courteously by those who are courteous and noble, how could those villains maintain it who are neither understanding nor faithful?]

Only by such *connissance,* or finesse, does the lover eschew infidelity and attain an understanding of love turned towards God and blending with charity

(vv. 319–46). Scheler summarizes the thought in these lines: "L'amour véritable n'abandonne d'ailleurs jamais ses adeptes, car il est un reflet de la divinité."[42] There is no way to construe this love as charity alone, or as devotion to God, Christ, the Virgin Mary, or the saints and martyrs. The love evoked by Baudouin is so equal that one cannot discern which of the two lovers loves less. Only death can separate them. Neither is true of love between man and the deity or His elect.

Jean de Condé develops these ideas in two other poems devoted to *boine amour*, the *Lais de l'ourse* and the *Confors d'amours*. In the former he emphasizes love's origin in God.

> De Dieu vient, de Dieu fu donnée,
> Qui sa poissance a ordenée;
> Dieux et amours sont d'un acort;
> Ce nous tesmoigne en son recort
> Jehans de Condé par raison:
> Nus ne puet la haute maison
> De paradis pour nul avoir
> Ne pour eil sans amour avoir.
> Diex as vrais amans le pramet
> Et chiaus en sa grant gloire met
> Qui de cuer l'aiment finement.
>
> (vv. 143–53)

[It derives from God, by God was it given and its power established. God and Love are of one mind. Jean de Condé bears witness to this fact by the use of reason in his writing. No one can gain the high dwelling of paradise through possessions or anything other than love. God promises it to true lovers, and places those in his great glory who love him truly and nobly.]

There is no mistaking Jean's intention. The love he speaks of is between man and woman, whatever their station or circumstances. Class and status are less important than nobility of heart and susceptibility to the educative process the lover undergoes as part of his service.

> Qui li fait lige hommage,[43]
> Preu y peut avoir, nient damage,
> Tant a en li de biens planté.
>
> (vv. 99–101)

[He who does him liege homage may derive real profit, but no harm, from doing so, so plentiful are the goods he contains.]

Just as the vile man becomes courteous through love (vv. 31–39), so even a woman of low birth may inspire noble sentiments if the love for her is *boine et vraie* (vv. 62–73). Evidently the marital, theological, and class distinctions evident even in Andreas Capellanus do not disturb Jean de Condé. In any case they are set aside. But he does retain one essential factor: the ennobling and egalitarian impulse of courtly love.

In the *Confors d'amours,* Jean de Condé pursues the notion of "refinement" in *fin'amors.* He takes up the suffering the lover endures for the sake of the hoped-for reward. This suffering is conducive to the self-improvement that makes him worthy of his lady's esteem (vv. 85–88). The source of his perseverence is hope (vv. 41–48). As Baudouin de Condé states in the *Prisons d'amours, entendemens* and *connissance* are essential to love well and with sufficient hope.

> Par ce set de cascun l'afaire,
> C'on doit laisier ne c'on doit faire,
> Ne coi furnir ne quoi eslire.
> (vv. 343–45)

[Thus he understands in everything what to avoid and what to do, what to accomplish and what to choose.]

Individual differences provide the variety against which the author sets his generalizations (vv. 350–80). This suggests that love may take many forms and adapt itself to various social contexts and circumstances. But love's essential quality, its quintessence, is whole and simple; it may be refined upon, but not changed.

THE *TRESOR AMOUREUX*

The *Tresor amoureux,* a dit tentatively attributed to Froissart,[44] takes up in debate form the relation of *fin'amors* to religion, of prowess and morality to love, of the different kinds of love to one another, and of *congnoissance* to *fin'amors.* The manner of presentation is principally the balade cycle, the mode Imagination.

The prologue identifies Imagination as the means whereby a dream acquires meaning and thus becomes allegorical.

> Ceste belle vision,
> Il me vint en advision
> Que je l'escrisoie en un livre
> Pour en avoir mieulx à delivre
> Remenissance ou retentive
> Par memoire ymaginative.
> (vv. 89–94)

[That beautiful vision inspired me to write it out in a book, in order better to recall or retain it through Imaginative memory.]

Imagination permits the realization of love in thought.

> Que vie d'amours substantive
> Puet bien un vray amant avoir
> Par pensée ymaginative.
> (p. 91: XV, vv. 8–10)

[For a true lover may indeed have a substantial love life through Imagination.]

Here is the reality and primacy of the poet's archetypal representation. But such Imagination requires understanding, and understanding comes from discrimination, the ability to choose consciously and intelligently. There are steps in such a choice. The first is between the religious and the secular life.[45]

Outside the palace of life containing the principal goods in human existence (vv. 283–92) stand two tents. The first is for those who choose to devote their life to God (vv. 153–58). Religion is a refuge for disconsolate lovers, a harbor similar to reason in Guillaume de Lorris.[46] But the narrator is now paying his "passage" (v. 208) through Love's realm, and this tent does not suit his purposes any more than do Reason's admonitions in Guillaume's *Rose*. He therefore expresses his preference for Love's tent, and passes on to the palace, where his lady is guardian of the treasury of mercy, with Grace as her treasurer (vv. 293–305).

This second step brings to the fore the person and role of Congnoissance. Congnoissance conducts the poet to the palace and explains its meaning to him (vv. 208–19). She is the source of knowledge and understanding in love. By her explanation of what the lover sees in the palace, the dit becomes a *vera imaginatio*.

Congnoissance is assisted by her three sisters, Reason, Souffissance, and Loyauté. She praises the life of reason, setting a standard for conduct in love.

> Car Congnoissance nous aprent
> Par doulceur et par courtoisie,
> Qu'on puet bien amer sagement
> D'amour loyal et renvoisie.
> (p. 179: XXXIII, vv. 11–14)

[For Congnoissance teaches us gently and courteously that one may love wisely with a love that is faithful and joyous.]

Careful attention to proper conduct requires finesse—the *fin' amors* of a *cuer fin*[47]—which in turn allows for individual understanding. The idea conforms to the notion that there are as many kinds of love in the world as there are men and women (p. 165: XX, vv. 12–16). This does not preclude a hierarchy of loves. One should aspire to the most honorable love one can conceive of (vv. 17–18). Andreas Capellanus did not ask otherwise. That Congnoissance makes this possible is afterwards illustrated when she comes to the author's assistance.

> Congnoissance fait concevoir
> Qu'est amours de loyal amy;
> Congnoissance fait parcevoir
> Fiere haïne d'ennemy;
> Congnoissance à homme endormi
> Fait esveillier son sentement;[48]
> Congnoissance fait clerement
> Congnoistre tous oscurcis fais,
> Tant que par bon entendement
> Congnoissance met tout à pais.
>
> (pp. 240–41: XXIX, vv. 11–20)

[Congnoissance makes one conceive what the love of a faithful lover is; Congnoissance causes one to perceive the fierce hatred of an enemy; Congnoissance causes the senses of a person asleep to awaken; Congnoissance makes one perceive clearly all obscure deeds—to such an extent that through proper understanding Congnoissance brings all things to repose.]

Congnoissance attends the poet while he is writing, weighing and judging sentiments, thoughts, and actions (pp. 241–42:XXX). This is possible because the poet's love is reasonable and moderate; otherwise, she would be unable to intervene (pp. 243–44: XXXII, vv. 11–16).

The third step is a mythological Imagination. To explain her estimation of the poet's love, Congnoissance interprets a tale of Io, Jupiter, and Argos (pp. 244–51: XXXIII–XL). This mode of inner reflection brings self-knowledge and an awareness of how one should pursue the life one has chosen.

> Pour mieulz savoir et mieulz sentir
> Quel tu es, ymagine en toi
> Où ton cuer se veult assentir,
> Ainsi qu'un homme sans chastoy.
>
> (p. 248: XXXVII, vv. 1–4)

[To know and perceive better what you are, determine in your Imagination where your heart is drawn, and do so like a man, without need of chastening.]

The possibilities range from the religious life to the life of folly. Congnoissance's lesson is to adapt to one's time of life and station in the world, in effect achieving a kind of "humilité" (p. 249: XXXVIII, vv. 10–12).[49] And the poet appreciates the fact that

> Congnoissance la discrée
> Par moralité et hystore
> M'ot la doctrine administrée
> Et rafreschie ma memoire
> De verité toute notoire.
>
> (p. 251: XLI, vv. 1–5)

[Discreet Congnoissance had, by moralization and tale, provided me with the instruction and refreshed my memory with well-known truth.]

The fourth step in the lover's progress is the debate between Amour and Congnoissance. Congnoissance's service to Reason as well as to the lover is prominent. Congnoissance is active in moral and religious decisions. But she also effects a compromise with Love whereby it becomes meritorious and beneficial in the world.

Amour charges that the lover is guilty of hypocrisy for listening to Congnoissance when she speaks of arms and love. As with most debates in courtly literature, the import of the question goes beyond the immediate case. When the lover obtained assistance from Congnoissance, he broke his vow of total fealty to Love (vv. 2582–86). For Congnoissance is not ultimately subject to Love, but to Reason, and regularly takes directions from her (vv. 2675–84). And Reason is frequently Love's enemy.

Congnoissance's defense, supported in some ways by other personifications and eventually by the narrator himself, stresses her adaptability to the context in which she appears. She is indeed Reason's sister. But she also introduced the lover to love outside the palace of life. Both the religious and the amorous life fall within her purview. Congnoissance's introduction of the lover to love is corroborated by Beau Parler.

> s'elle ne fust
> Neant qu'un ymage de fust,[50]
> Il ne congnust vous ne vos gens,
> Qui tant sont preux, courtois et gens,
> Ne les biens qu'on puet parcevoir
> En vous servant et recevoir.
> (vv. 2667–72)

[if she were no more than a wooden image, he would have known neither you nor your followers, who are so worthy, courteous, and noble, nor the goods that one may know and receive in your service.]

Love acknowledges this, but still insists that Congnoissance's counsel is a two-edged sword (vv. 2675–79). For she at first tried to dissuade the lover from choosing the amorous life. However, Congnoissance points out that her efforts were to no avail (vv. 2761–68), and that she therefore confined herself to making his love honorable. Finally the lover himself admits that what Congnoissance says is true (vv. 2842–44). Then he rehearses the traditional hierarchy of worldly goods.

> elle [Congnoissance] prise
> Entre les haulz biens terriens

117

> Vo [Love's] noble estat sur toute riens,
> Excepté de sa seur Raison.
>
> (vv. 2852-55)

[She (Congnoissance) prizes among the high earthly goods your (Love's) noble state above all things, with the exception of that of her sister Reason.]

This is love as Andreas Capellanus wished it: one of the great goods here on earth, above which however one may rise to higher moral and religious perfection under the aegis of Reason. That way led to the first tent the lover inspected. But the lover sees himself as neither perfectly good nor reprehensible, despite his awareness of the extremes.

> Se je savoie tout le bien
> Du monde et n'en feïsse rien,
> En devroie je estre prisiez?
> Je croy que non; ne deprisiez
> Aussy, se tout le mal savoie
> De ce monde, se je n'avoie
> Vouloir de le mettre à effet.
>
> (vv. 2871-77)

[If I knew all the good in the world and made no use of it, should I be esteemed on that account? I think not; nor should I be blamed if I knew all the evil in the world, if I had no intention of making something of it.]

Since Congnoissance is unable to lead the lover to "pure reason," she assumes her function on the less exalted, but in no way reprehensible level of *fin' amors*. And where finesse is required, *congnoissance* is essential.

Thus Congnoissance brings reason into the moral context of *fin' amors*. The disagreement between them concerns priorities. In Love's view of matters,

> Vous avez assez de renom
> De mes gens et estes nommée
> Bonne et sage, mais bien amée
> Seriés de moy, se essaucier
> Me volsissiés et avancier
> Autant que vous faites Raison,
> Vo seur, et ceulz de sa maison.
>
> (vv. 2730-36)

[You have a good reputation among my followers, and are considered good and prudent. Yet I would like you if you were willing to exalt and advance me as much as you do Reason your sister and those in her retinue.]

But Congnoissance refuses to tamper with a hierarchy established by God. Her gloss of the story of Io shows how the victims of vain, unreasonable passions are brought by Reason to know their Creator and are thus "born again'' (vv. 2793–2828). But what may be best in God's eyes is rarely perceived or understood perfectly by men. The poet was untouched by the sense of the Io fable, but rather preferred even to do without Reason, if necessary, for his love (vv. 2766–2768). But this is not categorical condemnation of love. Reason is the highest terrestrial good, but love remains estimable (vv. 2852–63). Even when Love rejects the lover's service and expels him from her palace he remains faithful (v. 2965), principally through the good offices of Congnoissance, who keeps him from folly and endeavors to reinstate him in Love's favor (vv. 2989–96). She does so by seeking first a satisfactory compromise regarding the answers to some questions raised earlier in the debate about prowess and love (vv. 3000–3003). No answers are imposed by decree or fiat; Love and Congnoissance leave them up to the reader. There are seven questions that pertain to love and prowess. Understanding (''entendement,'' v. 3039) will provide answers suitable to each individual reader.

1. Is it preferable to attain honor and fame in arms or in love? (vv. 3064–69)
2. To live in constant joy (''deduit''), is it preferable to serve love faithfully or follow arms with honor? (vv. 3070–74)
3. Is it preferable to have knowledge together with a good conscience or good fortune in the uncertain life at court? (vv. 3075–80)
4. Can there be anyone so well born that he could honorably follow both arms and love? (vv. 3081–86)[51]
5. Why is Love more successful in pursuing one person than a hundred others under his domination? (vv. 3087–90)
6. How can Nature allow a child of noble character to become ill bred? (vv. 3091–96)
7. Why, of all the children born of the same father and mother, does one child excel? (vv. 3097–3104)

Love is content with the questions, and feels confident that most answers will favor him. The conclusion of the *Tresor amoureux* shows him shaking hands with Congnoissance.

It would be difficult to offer clear and forthright answers to these questions. To those who would argue that the exercise of arms raises it above love and makes the responses a foregone conclusion, one may point out that the examples of feats of arms in Froissart's *Chronicles* are hardly uniformly glorious, however he may praise *prouesse* in his prologues. And *Li Jouvenciaus,* Chartier's *Quadrilogue invectif,* and the *Journal d'un bourgeois de Paris* show that the example of *Jehan de Saintré* was not universal. In Froissart's time one could be either honorable or dishonorable in arms, as one could in love. An illustration of both is the representation in *Jehan de Saintré* of arms and love as good to excess followed by decline. The lady is unfaithful in love, but the hero himself exceeds what is honorable by organizing an *emprise d'armes* without the king's permission. Both love and prowess demand self-control, and that is precisely what Congnoissance seeks in the *Tresor amoureux*. The third question makes this explicit, as it is applicable to the way one fights or loves. And the fourth question suggests that the combination of love and prowess would be the acme of noble self-realization. The remaining three questions touch on natural degress of nobility, particularly *noblesse de cœur* as distinguished from *noblesse de sang*. The distinctions apply as much to different kinds of love as to different degrees of prowess deriving from the intrinsic nobility of the lover or knight. Congnoissance is after the same distinction as the god of Love in Guillaume de Lorris when he recognized the nobility of the lover's sentiments and treated him as a vassal rather than a serf.

6

Guillaume de Machaut and the Sublimation of Courtly Love in Imagination

and yet thei spake hem so,
And spedde as wel in love as men now do;
Ek for to wynnen love in sondry ages,
In sondry londes, sondry ben usages
—Chaucer[1]

Ici a commencé pour moi ce que j'appellerai l'épanchement du
songe dans la vie réelle
—Nerval, *Aurélia*

THE *REMEDE DE FORTUNE* AND THE *ROMAN DE LA ROSE*
There are some incidental similarities between the *Remede de Fortune* and
Guillaume de Lorris' *Rose,* similarities in structure and pattern characteristic
of many dream visions in the late Middle Ages.[2] The poems are not entirely
dissimilar in context, despite the episodic character of Machaut's dit. Inno-
cence, youth, and *oiseuse (Remede,* v. 48) keep the *Remede*'s lover occupied
with various whims and pastimes; he is disturbed only by a persistent attraction to the "fleur souvereinne" (v. 59) that is his lady. Struck, as if by Love's
arrows, with her beauty, he is badly in need of instruction (vv. 87–93).
Instruction is given by the abstract perfections, the *bonté* (v. 177) he sees in
his lady. She becomes the mirror and exemplar of all desirable good (vv.
171–72). This description of the lady's virtues and graces leads to *congnoissance* in the sense used in the *Tresor amoureux.* This in turn permits the
analysis of love in the lai. But a misunderstanding separates the lady from the
lover, and he retires, "com se fust songe / Ravis en parfonde pensée" (vv.
748–49) [as if in a dream, borne off by profound thought] into the Parc de
Hedin (v. 786), a park

enclos
De haus murs et environnez,
Ne li chemins abandonnez
N'estoit pas a tous et a toutes.
(vv. 790–93)

[enclosed and surrounded by high walls. Nor was the way open to all.]

No *bergiers* allowed![3] Nor is any *deduit* (v. 819) lacking. But the lover, overcome by melancholy and despair, is long oblivious to the charms around him (vv. 2971–3012). The same inner alienation from the loveliness surrounding the disconsolate lover was used in Machaut's earlier *Vergier,* itself heavily marked by the influence of Guillaume de Lorris.

> Et comment que li lieus fust gens,
> Assis en sus de toutes gens,
> Delitables et pleins de joie,
> Certes, nul solas n'i avoie;
> Car a ma gracieuse dame,
> Qui a mon cuer, mon corps et m'ame,
> Me fist Amours adès penser
> Loyaument, sans vilein penser.
>
> *(Vergier,* vv. 67–74)

[And even though the place was pleasant, located far from all people, delightful and abounding in joy, surely I took no pleasure in it. For Love made me ever think faithfully, and with no villainy, on my gracious lady who possesses my heart, my body, and my soul.]

The fountain (vv. 825, 836) and the "haiette" (v. 829) recall Guillaume de Lorris' advancement through the garden of Deduit towards the fountain of Narcissus. Other brief passages scattered through the *Remede* recall Guillaume de Lorris and even Jean de Meun: the *meffet* (v. 1210),[4] idolatry (vv. 3190–3354),[5] the placing of the lady, like the Rose, "outre une haiette" (v. 3378) [beyond a hedge], the *mesdisans* (v. 4204).

But the similarities are details. The differences are more striking. Machaut's conception of love is far more idealized than Guillaume de Lorris', or even than his own in the *Vergier.* Machaut retires to the garden because of disconsolate love, while the *Rose* lover goes there by chance, and falls in love after his arrival. The long discourse of Esperance is unlike anything in Guillaume de Lorris in length and utterly unlike him and Jean de Meun in content. The park itself is a place of solitary escape rather than proximity to the lady. The *mesdisans* are circumvented successfully. Reason and God are Love's allies (vv. 4250–56). The conclusion is happy.

In the *Remede de Fortune* Machaut gives ideal love a preeminence that is meant to capture its purity and realize its essential nobility. Walter Benjamin has suggested that the extreme in conceptualization comes closest to the idea's expression.[6] It is in this sense that we may say that Machaut comes closer than any other courtly poet to the expression of *fin'amors* as idea. His love is in fact a sublimation. Machaut's attempt to effect such a sublimation is historically significant and intellectually original.

To understand what may have impelled Machaut to propose so extreme a kind of love, one must recall that a certain reaction to the vogue of erotic allegorical literature—however restrained the eroticism may have been— occurred in thirteenth- and fourteenth-century France. Personification allegory continued to serve as an agent for moral satire. The fourteenth-century *Roman de Fauvel* castigates ecclesiastical abuses and moral turpitude. More pertinent to our subject, Gace de la Buigne's *Roman des deduis* relates a siege in the form of a psychomachia in which the forces of vice are routed by those of Chastity, who sally forth from the castle to the battle cry "Viellece, Viellece, Viellece!"[7] Jean de Meun himself ridiculed some forms of romantic and sexual love in his continuation of the *Rose*. And the *Queste del saint graal* is a powerful condemnation of the love idealized in Lancelot du Lac.

A counterreaction is apparent in courtly literature. The prologue to Jakames' *Roman du Castelain de Couci* contains a vigorous defense of love, with special emphasis on its beneficial and worthwhile features. This is an obvious response to those striving to undermine "Amours, qui est principaument / Voie de vivre honnestement."[8] These examples indicate the continuing crisis of credibility in courtly idealism into the later Middle Ages, by which Erich Köhler explains the attacks on courtly idealism and love in Jean de Meun and the *Queste del saint graal*,[9] and to which the dit and the allegorical love poetry were a partial response.[10]

Machaut's contributions to dit literature and to the controversy about courtly love are significant: the love garden and the personifications of the *Dit dou vergier;* the allegory built on falconry Images in the *Dit de l'alerion;* the singular affair with Péronne d'Armentières dissolving into abstract, semilearned discussions in the *Voir-Dit;* figures from the Bestiaries on the enchanted river island in the *Dit dou lyon,* peopled only by those whose love is sincere and their ever-present enemies the *médisants.* The most influential of these writings, the *Remede de Fortune,* freely adapts not only material from the *Roman de la rose,* but, more substantively, certain ideas from Boethius' *Consolation of Philosophy* to the subject of *Fin'amors.*

Machaut took very seriously the instruction set forth in the *Remede.* He saw in it not only a love poem, but also a guide to the good life in all spheres of human activity. The example of Boethius' famous work must have deeply impressed him, since so many of his dits are consolatory in purpose. The debate in the *Jugement dou roy de Behaingne* offers intellectual consolation in a conclusion which permits two persons to understand and appreciate their sorrow. Consolation allows Esperance to encourage and instruct the disconsolate lover in the *Remede.* The *Dit dou lyon* is consolatory as well, as are the *Alerion,* the *Fonteinne amoureuse,* and the conclusion to the *Voir-Dit.*

THE *CONFORT D'AMI*: THE UNION OF HOPE AND IMAGINATION

The *Confort d'ami* is the broadest and most nearly systematic treatment of Machaut's thought on hope and consolation. Charles the Bad's imprisonment by the English[11] is the occasion for consolation, and Machaut himself plays the role of Boethius' Philosophia in offering consolation in the contexts of love for God, the lady, and honor. The foundation for love is hope in all three cases. Machaut's analysis in the *Confort* relies on the *Remede de Fortune*. In fact it expands the scope of the *Remede* beyond the courtly context at the same time that it integrates courtly love into an explicitly gradualistic worldview. Against despair caused by the loss of worldly possessions and loved ones, the result of inimical Fortune, Machaut recommends the reading of Boethius *(Confort,* vv. 1904–8).[12] Job (vv. 1707–20), Christ (vv. 1723–25), and Socrates (vv. 1758–67) provide Images of resistance to the melancholy (v. 1769) and despair (v. 1779) that may follow Fortune's bad turns. Hope provided them with consolation and a means to escape the power of Fortune. The same is possible in love. Charles' desire for the lady he is separated from is exacerbated by the fear of losing her (vv. 2057–2102). Charles needs to use his *entendement*[13] (v. 2106), which can provide him with Douce Pensée, Souvenir, Desir, and Bon Espoir during the forced separation (vv. 2113–21). Bon Espoir is especially important.

> Combien qu'il soit de tele sorte
> Que tu es si mal entendans
> Que tu n'iès mie ad ce tendans
> Qu'i te servent de leur mestier,
> Quant tu en as plus grant mestier,
> Eins reputes a desconfort
> Leur bien, leur douceur, leur confort.
> (vv. 2122–28)

[So that matters have come to such a pass that your great lack of understanding prevents you from striving to win their assistance when you need it most; rather you find disagreeable their goodness, their gentleness, and their consolation.]

Hope frees Souvenir and Douce Pensée (vv. 2133–2208) as well as Desir (vv. 2209–36) from the grief and sorrow of despair. In turn, they give consolation. Imagination is part and parcel of the consolation.

> Je t'ai dit que Douce Pensee
> Est de Souvenir engendree,
> Dont toutes les fois qu'il avient
> Que de ta dame te souvient,
> Se tu n'as pas en temps passé
> Son commandement trespassé,
> Eins l'as servi sans decevoir,
> Tu dois en ton cuer concevoir,
> Ymaginer, penser, pourtraire
> La biauté de son dous viaire.
> (vv. 2153–62)

[I have told you that Douce Pensee is born of Souvenir. Thus every time you happen to recall your lady, providing you have not earlier failed to follow her commands but have rather served her faithfully, you must conceive, imagine, think about, and portray in your heart the beauty of her sweet face.]

Machaut does not demonstrate this contention in the *Confort,* but refers Charles to the *Remede* and one of his lais for a more thorough argument.

> Et se son pooir [Hope's] vues savoir,
> Sans oublier chose nesune,
> Quier en "Remede de Fortune"
> Et en mon "Lay de Bon Espoir"
> Ou je l'aimme, et hé desespoir.
>
> (vv. 2246-50)

[And if you wish to know her (Hope's) power, with nothing left unsaid that is pertinent to the subject, look into the *Remede de Fortune* and my "Lay de Bon Espoir," in which I express my love for her, and my hatred of despair.]

In the *Confort* Machaut introduces examples showing the pattern of hope and despair in love: Orpheus and Eurydice (vv. 2277-2352, 2517-2640), Pluto and Proserpina (vv. 2353-2516), Paris and Helen (vv. 2645-82), and Hercules and Deianira (vv. 2683-2716). The choice is curious, since all the examples prove the unfortunate effects of desire despite the initial benefits of hope. But in each case Machaut ignores the misfortune to stress the immediate advantages of hope (much as Guillaume de Lorris turned the fountain of Narcissus from a mirror of self-love to a source of *fin' amors*). This is mythographic adaptation to context and meaning. Yet the tragic conclusion to each example suggests the misfortunes of immoderation in love or despair. For instance, Paris and Helen do not illustrate the ravages of desire leading to the fall of Troy.

> Cuides tu, se Paris pensast
> Que dame Heleinne le tençast
> Ne qu'a s'amour deüst faillir,
> Qu'il la fust alee assaillir?
> Nennil, mais quant pas ne failli,
> Je di qu'espoirs moult li vali,
> Qu'espoir, ymagination
> Font le cas, c'est m'entention,
> Et les besongnes mieus en viennent
> A tous ceaus qui en bien les tiennent.
>
> (vv. 2673-82)

[Do you think that Paris would have gone against Helen if he thought that she would hold it against him or betray his love? No indeed. But since he did not fail, I maintain that hope was of great help to him, that hope and imagination make the argument valid, as I understand it. And matters turn out better to those who uphold them.]

The union of hope and Imagination in this passage is the foundation for good love and consolation.

Charles' contemplation of the lady's Image is therefore the source of Douce Pensee and Souvenir. And it serves to satisfy Desir through hope of recovering the real lady, much as Paris foresaw gaining the person and love of Helen.[14] The conclusion of the Hercules Image shows not his death, but the benefits of hope.

> Et aussi estoit la presente
> La douce ymage cointe et gente
> De la bele Deyamire
> Ou Herculès souvent se mire.
> Aussi bien te pues tu mirer
> En ton ymage et remirer
> Sa grant biauté, son cointe atour
> Et son gentil corps fait a tour,
> Et esperer qu'encor sera
> Li bons jours qu'elle te fera
> Joie par parole et par fait
> De cuer fin, loial et parfait.
>   (vv. 2751–62)

[And also present was the sweet image, at once attractive and noble, of the beautiful Deianira, in whom Hercules often mirrors himself. Just so, you may mirror yourself in your image and consider its great beauty, its attractive attire, its gentle person perfectly fashioned, and hope that the fine day will yet come when she rewards you with joy, in words and deeds and through a fine, true, and perfect heart.]

"Idolatry" would seem to be an essential element in Machaut's notion of ideal love! He returns to it towards the end of the *Remede* in a prayer to Love and Hope, as well as in the idealized Image of the lady he adores.

> Et quant riens plus ne ressongnay,
> A deus genous m'agelongnay
> Emmi la sentelette estroite,
> Les mains jointes, la face droite
> Vers le lieu precieus et digne
> Qui m'estoit apparence et signe
> A l'esperence que j'avoie
> Que la ma dame trouveroie.
>   (*Remede*, vv. 3189–96)

[And when I no longer feared anything, I knelt down on my knees in the middle of the narrow path and, with clasped hands, my face turned directly towards the precious, worthy place which gave form and substance to my hope of finding my lady there.]

Yet such idolatry is merely an Image conceived in the mind to express a sincere love, much as mythographic figures exist only as unreal shapes until they acquire a truth through Imagination.

en amours n'a si bonne chose
Ne qu'amant doient amer si
Comme esperence, après merci.
Si te lo que tu la repreingnes
Et que dedens ton cuer la teingnes
Avec l'ymage gracieuse:
S'aras compaingnie amoureuse,
Aussi comme une trinité,
Car ce sera une unité
De toy, d'espoir et de l'image.
                    (*Confort,* vv. 2254–63)

[In love there is nothing so good, nor which lovers should love more than hope, except for mercy. I advise you to return to it, and to hold it in your heart together with the graceful image. Thus you will have a loving companionship, like a trinity, for it will be a unity of you, hope, and the image.]

The example of Boethius provides the pattern for right thought and right conduct (*Confort,* vv. 3749–58).[15] Thus the central section on love and hope in the *Confort* parallels the instruction in the beginning and concluding sections on God and honor. The Biblical examples provide hope in and comfort from God, just as mythological figures encourage hope for the lady's love. Similarly, in the third part of the treatise honor and the good life reward perseverance in following the examples of illustrious and honorable forebears (vv. 3903–28). The Imagination of the lover's devotion corresponds to service to God and the family name. There are, of course, dangers in all three areas. In love, we have seen them adumbrated in the very examples Machaut uses to provide comfort, which serve as both promise and warning.[16] For example, despair should not make Charles break his marriage; not only is a broken marriage socially wrong, it also angers God (vv. 3619–22). And ladies are among the sources of knightly honor, and should be upheld, like arms and religious devotion, with "science," for "N'autre honneur n'as, n'autre science / Qu'armes, dames et conscience" (vv. 3251–22)[17] [You have no other honor or science but arms, ladies, and good conscience]. There is good reason to suppose that Machaut is speaking of Charles' wife, whom he, like Paris and Pluto, abducted. The threat of Orpheus' and Hercules' fates is therefore very real. Transcending their faults by an ideal love would permit Charles to escape the loss and sorrows he must otherwise fear. The dissipation of fear is possible by hope.

But how did Machaut unite *fin' amors* and *conscience?* Part of the answer lies in the sublimation of desire and the consequent virtuous character of love. Of course, Charles' lady is his wife, so that sublimation is not quite so imperative as it may have been for Machaut in the *Remede.* But the problem goes beyond the conjugal-courtly dichotomy. In fact, Machaut's thoughts on the subject have a place alongside those of Watriquet de Couvin and the Condés.

The distinction between conjugal and extraconjugal love suggested by the case of Charles the Bad is in fact no solution. There are enough difficulties with love in marriage to preclude our settling for the superiority of marital affection over extramarital courtly love. Charles loved his wife and feared to lose her—with good reason: she had been abducted and forced to marry him. However, the example of Paris and Helen suggests that their love was real. Charles is not a counterpart to Galoain or Count Limors in Chrétien's *Erec*, who tried to force marriage and love on Enide. Rather Machaut disposes of the distinction between love and marriage simply and disarmingly. Like Andreas Capellanus, he postulates a polarity, arguing both that marriage be preserved and that love have its own, separate rights. One of his balades expresses this clearly (without the *Confort*, one might be inclined to view it as preposterous or merely humorous):

> Et si devés amer, j'en suis tous fis,
> > Vo mari com vo mari
> Et vostre amy com vostre doulz ami;
> Et quant tout ce poez par honneur faire,
> Vous ne devez vo cuer de moy retraire.
> > (Balade CCXXXI, vv. 12–16)

[And you must surely love your husband as your husband, and your beloved as your sweet love. And since you may accomplish all this honorably, it is wrong of you to take your heart back from me.]

Here as elsewhere we must beware of reading our scholarly sense of irony and propriety into an aristocratic spirit widespread in French literature of the Middle Ages—at least not before we are clear in our own minds regarding the terms of the quarrel of the *Roman de la rose!*

> Ne fai pas clers tes consaus d'armes,
> Qui doivent prier pour les ames
> Et doivent compter et escrire
> Et chanter leur messes ou lire
> Et consillier les jugemens
> Aus consaus et aus parlemens.
> Si que tien chascun en son ordre
> Si bien qu'il n'i ait que remordre.
> > (*Confort*, vv. 3105–12)

[Do not make your military counsel of clerics, who are supposed to pray for souls, keep accounts, write, sing or read mass, and give counsel on judgments handed down in conference and court. Let each person keep to his assigned place so that there may be nothing to criticize.]

This method of keeping tidy books, with every person and idea in place, is not only a horizontal classification, it is also a vertical evaluation based on generic distinctions in material style.

The *Confort d'ami* concludes with an admonition to love and serve God above all else, even one's own honor. For honor is

> la perfection
> Ou toute humeinne creature
> Doit plus tendre et mettre sa cure,
> Après la joie qui ne fine
> Qui seur tout est plaisant et fine.
>
> (vv. 3920–24)

[the perfection towards which every human being must strive and apply himself, second only to the joy without end that is above all else pleasing and fine.]

Similarly, after discussing the *ymage* of the lady cultivated, served, and adored in the lover's heart, Machaut puts everything into proper perspective. He establishes in this way a hierarchy of "idols," giving precedence, but not exclusivity, to God.

> Mais, pour chose que je te die,
> Garde toy bien que t'estudie
> Soit adès tout premierement
> En servir Dieu devotement,
> Qu'il n'est amour qui se compere
> A s'amour, foy que doy saint Pere,
> Ne chose, tant soit pure, eu monde,
> Ne que riens contre tout le monde,
> Ou comme une ymage en pointure
> Contre une vive creature.
>
> (vv. 2763–72)[18]

[But, whatever I may say to you, see that you apply yourself ever and foremost to serving God devoutly. For no love is comparable to His love, by the faith owed Saint Peter, nor is there anything on earth so pure, like a speck in comparison to the whole world, or a painted Image compared to a living creature.]

The idolatry of Pygmalion that Jean de Meun castigates with such wit in the *Roman de la Rose* becomes, in Machaut's conception of love, an acceptable idolatry.[19]

> Pymalion fist l'image d'ivoire
> Que moult pria et ama sans recroire,
> Mais il n'ot pas si tres noble victoire
> Ne tel eür
> Comme j'aray, se Morpheüs avoire
> Ce que je tieng qui sera chose voire.
>
> (*Fonteinne amoureuse*, vv. 963–68)[20]

[Pygmalion made the ivory image to which he prayed often and which he loved constantly. But he gained no victory so noble, nor fortune so good as I shall have if Morpheus makes true that which I believe to be true.]

Pygmalion *in bono,* and in love, reflects Machaut's tendency to rationalize and idealize love. The lady is now an Image to adore and imitate rather than an object to desire and possess. The Image sets forth a truth, and thus escapes the folly and fantasy read into it by Jean de Meun. The technique is still Macrobian. In the last analysis, Machaut's truth is the primacy of hope through the Imagination.

THE *REMEDE DE FORTUNE:* MACHAUT'S MATURE CONCEPTION OF *FIN'AMORS*

We may now follow Machaut's advice in the *Confort d'ami* and turn to the *Remede de Fortune* for his justification of the synthesis of *fin'amors* and Boethius as hope in love. The principal episode in the dit represents the poet visited by Esperance personified. She offers consolation to the lover "sick unto death," a sad victim of Fortune and Love, as he describes his state in a long complainte. She is the most obvious adaptation from Boethius, the Philosophia of the *Consolation.*[21] But the change of name points to two obvious differences between Machaut and Boethius. First, the context is different; Boethius had no use for love not directed towards God, His creation, or humanity.[22] Second, the controversy over the value of idealized love must have become very acute for Machaut to have had to resort to the unlikely resources of Boethius to support his idealization. Yet like Guillaume de Lorris, who adapted Ovid to a new context, Machaut succeeded in accommodating certain elements from Boethius' *Consolation* to his own understanding of courtly love. The replacement of desire by hope effected a real sublimation of love.

In courtly literature before Machaut and in a good number of his own fixed forms and in the dits preceding the *Remede* and the *Jugement dou roy de Navarre,* love is linked to both desire and hope. The general definition of love in Andreas Capellanus implies them both. Sight and reflection on the object of sight (*visio* and *cogitatio*) lead to desire—"Aliquis super omnia cupit alterius potiri amplexibus" [Each one wishes above all things the embraces of the other]—and to hope—"omnia de utriusque voluntate in ipsius amplexu amoris praecepta compleri"[23] [by common desire to carry out all of love's precepts in the other's embraces]. I understand willingness to serve and obey as predicated on hoped-for rewards. Andreas' ensuing differentiation among kinds of love is based on the extent to which desire gives way to hope. It also implies shifting emphasis from direct *visio* to *cogitatio,* that is, in the Boethian hierarchy of cognitive faculties, from *sensus* to *imaginatio.* The immediate sensual satisfaction of desire (*amor rusticanorum,* venality) is condemned. Andreas prefers the qualities and virtues one may acquire in service of the loved one and in contemplation of his or her Image in the mind's eye as the sum and total of those qualities. At the extreme, *amor purus* is a form of love that excludes the satisfaction of physical desire.

Nonetheless, desire is still present, even in *amor purus*.[24] Guillaume de Lorris has the god of Love combine both hope and desire in the instruction given the lover. Hope is a temporary consolation for unsatisfied desire.

> Beneoite soit Esperance,
> Qui les amanz ensi avance!
> Mout est Esperance cortoise:
> El ne laira ja une toise
> Nul vaillant ome jusqu'au chief,
> Ne por perill ne por meschief.
>
> *(Rose,* vv. 2629-34 [2615-20])[25]

[Blessed be Hope, who thus furthers the cause of lovers! Hope is very courteous: right up to the end, she will never leave any valiant man, in any peril or distress.]

In Machaut's two earliest dits, the *Vergier* and the *Jugement dou roy de Behaingne,* desire and hope still unite in *fin' amors.* Most difficulties arise from their incompatibility.

In the dits antedating the *Remede,* the lover's unhappiness and grief are caused by the turns of Fortune's wheel. The ups and downs of Fortune in courtly love are implicit in Andreas Capellanus' maxim "Semper amorem crescere vel minui constat" (p. 310) [It is well known that love is always increasing or decreasing (p. 184)]. This fact is fundamental to the maintenance of love as set forth in book 2. It is to assure that love will continue to grow, and thus escape the turns of Fortune, that Andreas insists on an *amor sapiens. Amor sapiens* is less subject to the fluctuations and vicissitudes common in other kinds of human love. "Qui enim probus invenitur et prudens, nunquam facile posset in amoris semita deviare vel suum coamantem afficere turbatione. Sapiens igitur, si sapientem suo connectit amori, suum amorem in perpetuum facillime poterit occultare et sapientem coamantem sapientiorem sua solet exhibere doctrina et minus sapientem sua consvevit moderatione reddere cautiorem" (p. 17). [A man who proves to be honorable and prudent cannot easily go astray in love's path or cause distress to his beloved. If a wise woman selects as her lover a wise man, she can very easily keep her love hidden forever; she can teach a wise lover to be even wiser, and if he isn't so wise she can restrain him and make him careful (p. 35).] Guillaume de Lorris also alludes to the place of Fortune's wheel in love (*Rose,* vv. 3981-91 [3953-63]). The Image is frequent in love poetry after Guillaume.[26] Machaut uses it in the first half of the complainte in the *Remede,* where Fortune and Love appear as allies against the lover, destroying his happiness.

Is it not, then, astonishing to hear Esperance assert that

> amy vray ne sont pas en compte
> Des biens Fortune, qui bien compte,

Mais entre les biens de vertu.

(Remede, vv. 2801-3)

[true lovers are not reckoned among the rewards of Fortune, if one reckons rightly, but among the rewards of virtue.]

To her way of thinking, the remedy to Fortune's wheel is love itself. In the complainte Machaut presents the traditional view of the relationship between love as desire and love as hope. As we have seen, love conventionally subsumes both desire and hope. But Esperance, and we may confidently assume Machaut himself, does not equate them. Desire is subject to Fortune because desire may be satisfied or denied by someone or something not subject to the will of the person who desires. The possibility of denial of the object of desire causes fear, suffering, despair, death. All this is exemplified in the first part of the *Remede,* where the lover, afraid to speak and convinced he has lost the esteem of his lady, retires in solitude to die a lover's death. This is certainly a conventional representation. In what seem to be his last moments, the lover sings his complainte to Fortune and Love, whom he holds equally responsible for his plight. Then Esperance appears, like Philosophia in the *Consolation,* in the quiet splendor of sunlight shining through clouds on a dark, melancholy day (vv. 1481-1505).[27]

Conventions apparent in chansons and in the *Roman de la rose* justify the appearance of Esperance at this moment as a turn of Fortune's wheel for the better. But her appearance is also foreshadowed in the lai which the lover recites to his lady near the beginning of the *Remede.* The lai pleases the lady so much that she wishes to know the author's name. The lover, fearful lest by revealing his name he incite her anger or displeasure, falls dumb and withdraws from her presence. Clearly, he fails to comprehend the import of his own composition. For the lai argues that douce Pensée, Souvenir, and Espoir suffice for the happiness of the lover because they bring him contentment (vv. 431-44). The "port d'autre confort," the "Plus querir" of desire are the cause of the lover's melancholy when Esperance appears to him. Esperance supplants desire and liberates the lover from the very Fortune blamed for his ills in the complainte. The separation of hope and desire makes possible the cleavage between love and fortune. The stress in the lai on mollification of the pain caused by desire becomes the burden of Esperance's instruction. Yet all Esperance really does, like her counterpart in Boethius,[28] is to recall to the lover, and make him understand and appreciate, what he said in the lai, what he knows but does not yet understand.

Briefly, there are two kinds of *biens* enjoyed by the person possessing self-mastery ("de toy la signorie," *Remede* v. 2485): *Patience* and *Souffissance,* which together are conducive to *Bonneürtez,* or *beatitudo* (vv. 2487-89). They are "bien de Nature" (v. 2469) in the Boethian sense of gifts natural to man and thus not subject to change or loss.[29] They are not among the *biens de Fortune,* which may be granted or withdrawn at the turn of her wheel. To achieve *Bonneürtez* a proper understanding of Fortune is essential, for from that understanding men may draw hope (vv. 2505-2742). To understand Fortune is to be able to live with, rather than subject to, Fortune. Fortune's turns can be explained very simply: whatever goes up must come down. But also, whatever comes down must go up (vv. 2689-2734). The ineluctable rotation is regular and thus predictable. Hope is not only possible, it is assured to him who understands Fortune. He need merely await the upward turn of the wheel after it brings him low. The fear, hilarity, grief, and desire that afflict those subject to Fortune give way through understanding to *Bonneürtez* (part of man's nature) founded on patience and contentment. This thought was already familiar to the lover from his lai. It also preserves the lineaments of Boethius' thought, despite a rather exuberant optimism (vv. 2717-21). But what does it all have to do with love?

As Machaut declares in the lai, love, rightly understood, is not a manifestation of desire. Nor can it be construed as a *bien de Nature,* since love is not given to man as part of his nature. It is rather a *bien de vertu* (v. 2803), founded on virtue because of the fidelity of the lover. The constant heart is not subject to Fortune (vv. 2804-10). This does not exclude hope for love, at least love of a Platonic sort. All good men and women admire virtue, as Boethius taught.[30] Thus the lady whose foremost quality is *bonté* (v. 177) cannot fail to recognize the faithful aspirant to her love (vv. 1796-1808, 1827-58). The lover himself may rest content in the awareness of the *bonté* he gains from love for his lady; he too becomes virtuous, and virtue, as Boethius said, is its own reward.[31] What more could he "desire"—or rather, hope for? In this conception of love the virtuous lady will inevitably reward the virtuous lover by returning his love. No doubt this is what impressed the lady when she heard Machaut's lai, for she later remarks:

> Mais quant Esperence s'en mesle,
> Je ne doy pas estre rebelle
> A son voloir, eins vous ottroy
> Loiaument de m'amour l'ottroy;
> Qu'elle m'a dit que vous m'amez
> Et vuet qu'amis soiez clamez.
> (vv. 3841-46)

[But when Esperance intervenes, I must not revolt against her will. Rather I grant you faithfully the gift of my love. For she told me that you love me and wish to be called my beloved.]

Thus the lady's love is also confirmed by hope. Hope for love (but no more!) is not subject to Fortune, for the lady as well as for the gentleman. All of this

133

conforms to the *Remede*'s description of the lady as the source of the lover's virtue. What differences may we then perceive between the object of desire and the object of hope? The lai provides a succinct answer to this question. The lover consoles himself with "l'Espoir de joïr" [the hope of enjoyment]. Enjoyment of what? The sight of his lady, including conversation and reflection on her Image as expressive of beauty and worth. This is douce Pensée and Souvenir.

> Mais quant je voy
> Le trés bel arroy
> Simple et coy,
> Sans desroy
> De son corps, le gai,
> Et que je l'oy
> Parler sans effroy,
> Par ma foy
> Si m'esjoy
> Que toute joie ay.
> (vv. 495–504)

[But when I see the very beautiful adornment, neat and pleasing and without blemish in her gay self, and when I hear her speak calmly, indeed I am so joyful that I possess every joy there is.]

To see his lady is always possible, and to a certain extent it is a condition a virtuous lady can readily accede to (vv. 3343–48) and even feel honored by. Not only the conduct of the lady in the *Remede,* but also that of Bel Acueil in the *Rose* when he first comes forth to greet the lover (*Rose,* vv. 2787–2822 [2771–2806]), make that much obvious. The lady would simply be manifesting her courtesy. But to seek further rewards is to desire, and therefore to ask too much.[32] Then she may feel compelled, like Dangier in the *Rose,* to dismiss the lover abruptly and angrily. The lover who desires is subject to Fortune and change, may lack sincerity or become insincere,[33] and is perforce unhappy.

> Qui vorroit plus souhaidier,
> Je n'os cuidier
> Si fol cuidier
> Que cils aimme de cuer entier
> Qui de tels biens n'a souffisance;
> Car qui plus quiert, il vuet trichier.
> (*Remede,* vv. 459–64)

[Were someone to ask for more, I dare not go so far as to presume that he loves wholly and sincerely when he is not content with such rewards. For he who seeks more wishes to deceive.]

The lover should make his lady's beauty not an object of desire, but an object lesson (vv. 339–42). Contemplation of her Image makes him aware of the inner worth it represents, and thus encourages him to conform his own character to the lady's example.

Machaut's description of the lady makes this apparent (vv. 167–326). She possesses *bonté* (v. 177), understood as the sum and source of her virtue and qualities: she possesses both physical and spiritual perfection. Abstractions are transferable attributes. "Le poème est donc comme un miroir flatteur que le prince ou le chevalier consulte avec anxiété ou complaisance pour y retrouver l'image de ses amours.... Pour répondre à cette interrogation, le poète de cour lui propose normalement le regard de sa dame où, nouveau Narcisse, il contemple son image."[34] The transfer is dependent only on the lover's capacity to perceive and willingness to emulate. The lady's Image shows him what he must attain in order to equal her[35] and thus show himself worthy of her love.

The lady's perfection is also a source of hope for the lover, since the realization of that hope depends entirely on his own willingness to conform to her example (v. 338). And that possibility is very real, since we know from the beginning of the *Remede* that the lover's special talent—Machaut as narrator identifies himself with the lover throughout the dit—is to be a lover (vv. 45–70). Esperance herself reminds him of this fact in the course of her instruction (vv. 2618–27).

There are other sources of happiness allied to hope. Dous Regard softens the pain of desire as soon as it appears, and renders the lover immune to the sickness and grief associated with desire in most courtly literature.

> Car comment que Desirs m'assaille...
> Certes bien en vain se travaille,
> Car tout garist son dous regart
> Qui paist d'amoureuse vitaille
> Mon cuer et dedens li entaille
>   Sa biauté fine.
>
> (vv. 639, 644–48)

[For however Desire may assail me... he assuredly struggles in vain. For her gentle look heals everything, and nourishes my heart with the nourishment of love and engraves in it her exquisite beauty.]

To possess the lady's Image is to possess her qualities, that is what makes her desirable. But their realization is inner possession. This is meaningful as hope (vv. 3337–48). Therefore Esperance proclaims that he who desires errs, while he who is content with Dous Regard really loves (vv. 1994–2002). This fits neatly into Boethius' conception of happiness.[36] The lover may now exercise the *Patience* and *Souffissance* essential to the good and happy life. He is virtuous, and love is the reward for that virtue.

The fact that Esperance envisages a lover unmolested by desire, and therefore content with less than might satisfy desire, makes it clear that Machaut is proposing sublimation when he replaces desire with hope.[37] Only in this manner is it possible for him to describe love—*vraie amour*—as a *bien de vertu*. Machaut means no glossing or halfway measure similar to that often found in courtly writing, where the lady and the lover are more chaste, or more nearly chaste, because they are faithful to one love and exclude all others.[38] Machaut's words do mean what they say. Love is to rise above desire if the lover is to be happy and virtuous. To wish for more is immoderate. Moderation is essential to the reasonable, happy, virtuous life in the *Remede de Fortune*, as in Boethius. Again we are brought back to hope as the remedy for misfortune born of desire, and to *vraie amour* as the remedy to Fortune.

Machaut goes no further. The distinct categories of God, love, and honor set up in the *Confort* obtain in the *Remede*. Human love does not become a stepping stone to higher forms of love. The idea of using it in this way could have occurred to him from reading the *Consolation,* or by analogy: he relates the music of love poetry to angelic music in the *Prologue* (V, vv. 105–46). His lady remains very much in this world, as does the love itself. In the concluding section of the *Remede* the lover, revitalized as it were by Esperance, returns to his lady to apologize for his silence after reading the lai, and to declare his hope. The two go on to participate in an active social life of dances, feasts, mass, promenades, parties, concerts, and carols. The conventional description of these activities exemplifies the preceding instruction: to see one's lady, speak with her and share a common understanding, to grow inwardly by her example, are sufficient to the lover who realizes all his hope in the Image, the sight, and the *bel acueil* of his lady.

Sight, the *dous regard,* is allied to hope and a sense of security in the lover. It is also important to the lady. She is able to perceive her suitor's sincerity even when he is mute in her presence. For no false lover can counterfeit the colors of sincere emotion. (vv. 1780–85). White, red, dark, and blue in the lover's face form the heraldic shield of faithful love. Here Machaut uses the popular device of the heraldic emblem to describe the lover's changing colors and the sentiments associated with them (vv. 1863–78).[39] The effectiveness of the shield depends on the arm bands of hope, broken when the lover despairs of his love and is dying of unrequited desire (vv. 1941–46). For hope to be possible, the shield must be held up and shown to the lady (vv. 3420–28). This takes place in the *Remede* when the lover comes out of retreat.

Thus Machaut's lover is content in the realization of hope. Just before meeting his lady again he offers a prayer to the god of Love, asking only to see and speak to her (vv. 3343–48). The extensive description of the entertainment and pastimes suggests mutual contentment and exemplary happiness. There are no activities, secret or otherwise, to imagine beyond what

Machaut shows, contrary to what some readers have argued from the examples of other dits and of the romances.[40] Machaut's representation of the foolish lover, both in the *Remede* and later in the *Voir-Dit,* shows how the danger of excessive melancholy (Chaucer's "sorwful ymagynacioun") is overcome, replaced by a splendid vision of light and harmony within oneself and in the world. This is a "plaisant ymagination" (*Prologue* V, v. 61). The same concerns return in Machaut's instruction as the *ami* in the *Confort d' ami* and the *Fonteinne amoureuse.* Devotion to the highest kind of love releases the lover from the dreadful sickness which befell those whose sorrow vanquished their rational faculty and drove them to despair in mad *pensers.*[41]

A few sentences from Balzac's *Peau de chagrin* seem to sum up the instruction contained in the *Remede de Fortune.* The author of *Le Lys dans la vallée* would certainly have had no difficulty appreciating the conception of love espoused in the *Remede.* "L'homme s'épuise par deux actes instinctivement accomplis qui tarissent les sources de son existence. Deux verbes expriment toutes les formes que prennent ces deux causes de mort: VOULOIR et POUVOIR. Entre ces deux termes de l'action humaine, il est une autre formule dont s'emparent les sages, et je lui dois le bonheur.... *Vouloir* nous brûle, et *Pouvoir* nous détruit; mais SAVOIR laisse notre faible organisation dans un perpétuel état de calme. Ainsi le désir ou le vouloir est mort en moi, tué par la pensée; le mouvement ou le pouvoir s'est résolu par le jeu naturel de mes organes. En deux mots, j'ai placé ma vie, non dans le cœur qui se brise, non dans les sens qui s'émoussent; mais dans le cerveau qui ne s'use pas et qui survit à tout."[42] And a little further on: "Ma seule ambition a été de voir. Voir n'est-ce pas savoir?" Transposed into the world of the *Remede de Fortune,* Balzac's words retain their full significance. Hope gives the lover a life free from consuming desire in the knowledge and vision of his lady's perfection. And it holds the promise of happiness in imitation of her virtue. Imagination makes that knowledge attainable.

THE TRANSITION FROM THE *JUGEMENT DOU ROY DE BEHAINGNE* TO THE *JUGEMENT DOU ROY DE NAVARRE*

The conception of *vraie amour* founded on hope is set forth by Machaut for the first time in the *Remede.* The two earlier dits, the *Vergier* and the *Jugement Behaingne,* make nothing of the idea; they know only the problem created by unsatisfied desire, and see hope only as a temporary consolation. In the *Vergier* hope is uncertain, as the lover swings between desire and hope. There is no more than the possibility of pity sometime in the future, after loyal, secret, but also long service to the lady (*Vergier,* vv. 1290–93). The same is true in the *Jugement Behaingne.* The wavering between hope and desire is an effect of Fortune (vv. 684–700, 725–45), much as it is in the *Remede*'s complainte. Noteworthy by contrast is the role of sight in the two dits. Sight is a source of grievous desire, indeed of a kind of impotence. In Macrobian terms, the Image is an *insomnium*.

> Quant je vueil faire ma clamour
> A ma dame de ma dolour,
> Je ne la puis araisonner
> Ne je ne puis un mot sonner,
> Einsois pers toute contenance,
> Scens, vigour, maniere et puissance,
> Tant sui dou vëoir esperdus.
>
> *(Vergier, vv. 1095–1101)*

[When I wish to remonstrate with my lady because of my pain, I cannot speak to her nor can I utter a single word. Rather I lose all self-control, wit, strength, manner, and force, so overwhelmed am I when I see her.]

In the *Jugement Behaingne* sight is decisive in the debate as to whether the lady or the gentleman suffers more in love. The lady's loved one has died, the man's has been unfaithful. He is judged the greater sufferer. The lady no longer sees her loved one and thus has no object for either hope or desire, whereas the unfaithful lady is still alive and thus condemns the man to hopeless desire for what once was (*Jugement Behaingne*, vv. 1005–8).[43] Before the *Remede* then, Machaut followed tradition in fusing desire and hope in *fin' amors*.[44] He was still very close to Guillaume de Lorris: hope is a conventional consolation, and there is no escape from suffering caused by unrequited desire, especially when the lover despairs of satisfying it. Fortune still holds sway, as at the end of the first part of the *Rose*.

It is therefore particularly significant that the *Jugement dou roy de Navarre* reverses the decision handed down in the *Jugement Behaingne*. The reversal has been ascribed to bemused, ironic condescension to the wishes of ladies offended by the decision favoring the man in the earlier poem.[45] But it was Machaut's new conception of love that made the revision necessary. Since the second *Jugement* and the *Remede* are virtually contemporary,[46] Machaut must have been anxious to correct his earlier conception of love as desire. In the *Jugement Navarre*, Desire is no longer among the counsellors who hand down the decision. In its place stands Souffissance,

> Qui de trés humble pacience
> Estoit richement äournée
> Et abondanment säoulée
> Et pleinne de tous biens terriens.
> Elle n'avoit besoing de riens,
> Ne li failloit chose nesune;
> Hors estoit des mains de Fortune
> Et de son perilleus dangier.
>
> *(Jugement Navarre, vv. 1288–95)*

[who was richly adorned with and liberally abounding in most humble patience, and was full of all mundane goods. She required nothing, nor did she lack anything at all. She was outside Fortune's reach and her perilous domination.]

Only the real death of the loved one can deprive the lover of hope, and this is precisely the cause of the lady's loss in the *Jugement Behaingne* as well as here (*Jugement Navarre*, vv. 1842–56). But the man may still derive consolation and satisfaction from the knowledge that his lady is unworthy of him, the memory through *dous penser* and *souvenir* of past joy, and the hope that she may yet improve. And finally—a rather astonishing addition to the circumstances in the *Jugement Behaingne*—the lady left him for a good marriage! (*Jugement Navarre*, vv. 2517–30). This stress not only on *souffissance* and *espoir*, but also on *mesure* and *bonneürtez*, shows how profound a change occurred in Machaut's conception of love in the *Remede*, and underscores the extent to which love has now become a sublimation.

Each of the two *Jugement* poems debates an amatory problem, as in the dialogues of Andreas Capellanus and in numerous *jeux-partis*. The question seems trivial, even silly: Who suffers more, the lady whose lover has died or the man whose lady has abandoned him for another?[47] However, as so often in such debates, the immediate question is a convenient pretext for exemplifying important ideas and sentiments that determine the arguments and the final judgment. The later *Jugement Navarre* replaces love by desire with love by hope.

The change is apparent in the respective catalogues of abstractions accompanying the judge in each poem. As personifications, they make up his counsel. In the *Jugement Behaingne* appear Hardiesse, Prouesse, Largesse, Richesse, Amour, Biauté, Loiauté, Leesse, Desirs, Pensers, Volenté, Noblesse, Franchise, Honneur, Courtoisie, Jeunesse, and Raison (vv. 1476–91).[48] In the *Jugement Navarre* only two personifications survive from the earlier poem, Raison (vv. 1163–92) and Largesse (vv. 1265–78); the others are Congnoissance and Avis (vv. 1155–62), Attemprance (vv. 1193–1200), Pais and Concorde (vv. 1201–18), Foy and Constance (vv. 1219–26), Charité (vv. 1227–32), Honnestez (vv. 1233–38), Prudence and Sapience (vv. 1239–64), Doubtance de meffaire, with Honte and Paour (vv. 1279–86), Souffissance (vv. 1287–1304), and Mesure[49]. Just as the first *Jugement* harks back to the *Rose* in its choice of personifications, so the new *Jugement* shows the striking influence of the *Remede*.

In the *Jugement Behaingne,* Raison expounds on the dangers of love.

> Il n'est ame,
> N'homme vivant qui aimme si sans blame,
> S'il est tapez de l'amoureuse flame,
> Qu'il n'aimme mieus assez le corps que l'ame.
> Pour quel raison?

Amour vient de charnel affection,[50]
Et si desir et sa condition
Sont tuit enclin a delectation.
        Si ne se puet
Nuls, ne nulle garder qui amer vuet
Qu'il n'i ait vice ou pechié; il l'estuet;
Et c'est contraire a l'ame qui s'en duet.
        Et d'autre part,
Tout aussi tost com l'ame se depart
Dou corps, l'amour s'en eslonge et espart.
Einsi le voy partout, se Dieus me gart.[51]

                    (*Jugement Behaingne,* vv. 1704–19)

[There is no one alive whose love is so blameless—once he has been scorched by the flames of love—who does not love the body more than the soul. Why? Love comes of carnal desire, and its desires and its states are all inclined to delight. And no man nor woman who is willing to love can exclude vice or sin from it; it's unavoidable. And it is contrary to the soul, which is grieved by this state of affairs. And on the other hand, just as swiftly as the soul departs from the body, love quits it and is dissolved. I see it happen everywhere, so help me God.]

The decision is a foregone conclusion. Since the object of the lady's desire is dead, the desire itself must die with her just as it did in the deceased lover. But the gentleman's lady is unfaithful. He therefore is subject to jealousy and the suffering of unrequited desire. This is Reason's conclusion, and the judge accedes to her authority (*Jugement Behaingne,* vv. 1931–56).

Interesting in this debate is the conflict between Reason and Love. Reason insists that she never approved the gentleman's love (*Jugement Behaingne,* vv. 1725–26). Her words recall Reason in the *Roman de la rose.*

        Les maus d'amer
    Sont en son cuer qui li sont trop amer;
    Qu'Amours le fait nuit et jour enflamer,
    N'il ne vorroit, ne porroit oublier
        Son anemie.
    Savez pourquoy? Pour ce que Compaingnie,
    Amour, Biauté et Juenesse la lie,
    Et Loiauté, qu'oublier ne vueil mie,
        En grant folie,
    En rage, en dueil et en forcenerie
    Le font languir, et en grant jalousie,
    Et en peril de l'ame et de la vie.

                    (*Jugement Behaingne,* vv. 1728–39)

[The pains of love are in his heart, and they are very bitter for it. For Love makes him burn night and day, so that he would not, nor could he forget his fair enemy. Do you know why? Because Company, Love, Beauty, joyful Youth, and Fidelity cause him to languish in great folly, rage, grief, and madness, and in great jealousy, to the peril of his soul and his life.]

However different matters may have appeared while there still was the possibility that the lady would return his love, Reason insists that he ought to have given up Love and returned to Reason when she did finally abandon him for another (*Jugement Behaingne*, vv. 1746–51). This is consistent with Reason in Guillaume de Lorris' part of the *Rose*.

Of course, her opinion is not to the liking of Love and his followers. They attribute the gentleman's plight to his failure to allow Love to assuage his suffering by finding him a new, worthier love (vv. 1808–11). The solution is reasonable, and credible in Machaut even after the *Remede de Fortune*. In the later *Dit de l'alerion*, the lover loses an unworthy lady because she is unfaithful. Love intervenes to comfort him and find him a better lady (*Alerion*, vv. 3813–21). Even Reason encourages him to persevere in his good intentions while awaiting a more worthy love. And Reason leads the lover back to the garden of Deduit! (*Alerion*, vv. 4675–96) Essential in all these cases is adherence to the right kind of love rather than abandonment to desire, sadness, melancholy, a more or less figurative death like that after the complainte in the *Remede*. What does change, along with Reason's attitude to love, is the nature of love itself.

> Or couvient que chascuns s'apuie
> A bonne Amour secretement,
> Se viveront discretement
> A la soubreté de souffrance.
> La trouveront il Esperance
> De cui il seront pourveü,
> Quant a ce point seront veü.
> (*Alerion*, vv. 4668–74)

[It then behooves each person to rely secretly on good love, if they will live cautiously by the sobriety of long suffering. There they will discover Hope, with which they will be provided when they find themselves thus far advanced.]

These lines bespeak the profound change that accounts for the composition of a second *Jugement* with its new dramatis personae and new debate. Machaut is not striving to assuage women offended by the pronouncement against the lady in the *Jugement Behaingne*. He is presenting a retrial because his new conception of *bonne amour* in the *Remede* requires it.

In the *Jugement Navarre*, Machaut acknowledges the divergence and variety of forms and subjects he has written about (vv. 884–87). This is apparent despite superficial resemblances, in the divergent judgments handed down in the two dits. And there are other significant adaptations. Machaut separates Love and Nature in the *Jugement Navarre*.

> Car Bonne Amour en sa part tient
> Un cuer d'amant tant seulement
> Sans naturel commandement.
>
> (vv. 2174–76)

[For Good Love retains on his side a lover's heart alone, without the incitements of Nature.]

This conforms to Esperance's argument in the *Remede*. Love is not a *bien de Nature* but a *bien de vertu*. In both poems Machaut liberates love from external determination, dependence on another's will, and the misfortune of deceit. The bond between good love and virtue is implicit in the *Jugement Navarre*. Nature has no part in it.

> Nature donne bien couleur
> A ami d'un plaisant cuidier
> Qui li fait folement cuidier
> Acomplir ce qu'Amours desprise.
> Et par si faite fole emprise
> Sont fait maint incouvenient
> Qui valent trop meins que niënt.
> Plus desclairier ne m'en couvient
> Pour ce que point d'onneur n'en vient.
>
> (vv. 2186–94)

[Nature does give to the beloved the appearance of a pleasant thought which makes him foolishly presume to accomplish what Love scorns. And from such a foolish undertaking spring many improprieties which are worth much less than nothing. It is not proper for me to say more about it, for it redounds to no one's honor.]

These words are uttered by Pais.

In the trial Machaut plays the advocatus diaboli against his own ideas. He bases his case on feminine frailty, specifically woman's changeableness. The subterfuge is worthy of Jean de Meun, who founded his mysogynist bias on well-known and time-honored authority (*Rose,* vv. 15195–242 [15165–212]). Machaut uses *la donna è mobile* commonplace to demonstrate the unstable, fickle nature of woman. The argument has a certain cogency in a debate between a man and a woman, and Machaut, still playing the advocatus diaboli, interjects into the argument the erroneous opinion that the trial has to do with the two sexes. But the issues at stake go beyond the participants in the Imaginative trial. As Daniel Poirion has stated, ''la vraie poésie n'est pas le simple reflet de la vie superficielle. Bien souvent, elle cherche à rejoindre l'essentiel, au-delà de la circonstance.''[52] Whatever its appeal to those of Jean de Meun's persuasion, the diatribe against women raises serious questions that the counselors are quick to recognize and take umbrage at.

Most immediately, it contradicts Machaut's own protestations of service to ladies, and indeed the import of his entire œuvre. But beyond this (medieval writers are not necessarily consistent from work to work), the very universality of Machaut's condemnation undermines one of the cornerstones of the *Remede*'s teaching.

> Il est certain—et je l'afferme—
> Qu'en cuer de femme n'a riens ferme,
> Rien seür, rien d'estableté,
> Fors toute variableté.
>
> *(Jugement Navarre, vv. 3019–22)*

[It is certain, and I affirm it, that there is nothing solid in a woman's heart, nothing sure, nothing stable, but only absolute changeableness.]

If this is so, the goodness of the lady essential to the argument of the *Remede* is universally untenable, and the description of her qualities an *insomnium*. The whole foundation of *fin'amors* collapses before eternal feminine wiles.[53] The *médisance* is roundly condemned by the counselors.

Of course Machaut never argued that all women, or men, are perfect. The hierarchical distinction among the birds in the *Alerion* shows his awareness of realities and possibilities, and suggests the options left to the male lover in the *Jugement Navarre*. In the *Alerion,* the loss or betrayal by a loved one brings the lover back to Love and Reason so that he may await a new, worthier love. The two *Jugements* show, by topical adaptation, the same possibilities. The unfaithful lady in the *Jugement Behaingne* takes a lover "nouvellement, sans cause, autre que mi" (v. 705) [out of fickleness, for no reason, other than me]. She excuses herself on the grounds that Love, to whom she is ultimately subject, changed her inclination (vv. 746–63). In the *Jugement Navarre,* she leaves her lover for a good marriage. But marriage is no impediment to love. The pronouncement Andreas Capellanus ascribes to Marie de Champagne reverberates in Charité's words when she advises Machaut that, if the lady marries by necessity or through the counsel of her family,

> ce n'est pas fais
> Dont cils doie enchargier tel fais
> Comme de lui desesperer;
> Eins doit penser et esperer
> Qu'elle y a profit et honneur,
> Quant en la grace d'un signeur
> Seroit de droit nommée dame.
> Ceste raison bon cuer enflame
> D'amer mieus assez que devant.
>
> *(Jugement Navarre, vv. 2517–25)*

[this is nothing such that he ought to take on the burden of despair. Rather he ought to think and hope that she has profit and honor from it, when, by the grace of a lord, she should by rights be called a lady. This reason does enflame a heart to love much better than before.]

The idea is important to Machaut and is implicit in the understanding achieved in the conclusion to the *Voir-Dit*. For precisely the fact that the gentleman can hope for love despite his lady's marriage while the lady cannot because her lover has died necessitates the change in the second *Jugement* (vv. 1842–56). The *Jugement Behaingne,* where love is a manifestation of desire, may conclude that death removes the object of desire and thus releases the desire. But in the *Jugement Navarre,* the death of the loved one destroys all hope, and therefore the sorrow remains. This is not so if the loved one marries another person, since the lover may still hope in the virtuous sense of the *Remede de Fortune.*

Machaut concludes the *Jugement Navarre* with a recapitulation of the ideas found in the *Remede.* Reason pronounces the verdict, as she did in the *Jugement Behaingne.* Bonneurtez and those favored by him are not subject to Fortune, nor are they dependent on persons or circumstances. Self-sufficient love provides hope, and hope in love effects the realization of love.

> La est Bonneürtez assise
> Entre ami et loial amie
> Qui ne vuelent que courtoisie.
>
> (*Jugement Navarre,* vv. 3900–902)

[Happiness is there established between a lover and his faithful beloved who wish only courtesy.]

This new "courtly" love necessitated a reconsideration of the thesis propounded in the earlier *Jugement Behaingne.* The new conception is set forth and argued in the *Jugement Navarre* in an exemplary case, and in the *Remede.* The change is psychologically sound. The love of the *Jugement Behaingne* seeks to project the Image of the lady onto the real lady, and love is thus either an imposition or is dependent on that lady's acquiescence. The *Jugement Navarre* internalizes the Image as a pattern for virtue and excellence. Even the lady's marriage to another man cannot forestall such Imagination, nor deprive it of efficacy.

MACHAUT'S LATER DITS:
THE CONTINUED UNION OF IMAGINATION AND HOPE

After the *Remede de Fortune,* all Machaut's dits adhere more or less explicitly to the new conception of *fin' amors.* In the *Dit dou lyon:*

> Et se Dieus me doint nom d'ami
> De li que j'aim trop mieus que mi,
> Que s'il estoit a ma devise

Qu'en lui de mon petit servise
Deüsse avoir aucune joie,
Riens plus ne li demanderoie
Fors tant qu'a son trés dous viaire
Peüst bien mes services plaire
Et qu'elle sceüst que siens sui,
Si que mieus l'aim que mi n'autrui,
De cuer, sans pensée villeinne.
(vv. 249-59)[54]

[And if God were to grant that I be beloved of her whom I love more than myself, and it depended on me that my small service should bring me some joy, I would ask no more of her than that my service should provide her pleasure and that she would know I am hers such that I love her more than myself or any other, sincerely, with no villainous thought.]

The passage is entirely consistent with the opening lines of the lai in the *Remede,* as well as with the life of the lover after he returns to his Lady at the end of that dit. In the *Alerion:*

Et cil qui a destre se tiennent,
Si qu'amant loial se maintiennent,
N'ont chose qui bien ne leur plaise.
S'il ont merci, il sont moult aise;
S'il ne l'ont, il prennent substance
De par moy [i.e. Amour] et bonne Esperence,
De quoy il sont si bien chevi
Qu'il sont tout adès assevi
(vv. 2897-2904)

[And those holding to the right so that they remain faithful lovers, have nothing that does not please them. If they have mercy, they are very happy about it. If they do not, they draw sustenance from me [i.e. Love] and from good Hope, with which they are so well provided that they are ever content.]

This contrasts with the "Faus prians" (v. 2860) who require their lady's *merci* (v. 2878) to satisfy desire.

S'il l'ont, il n'en scevent que faire,
N'il leur desplaist, n'il leur puet plaire,
N'il ne scevent de quoy il vivent.
Adont dedens leurs cuers s'avivent
Foles pensées couvoiteuses,
De bien pointes et souffraiteuses.
La ont il planté de deffaut
Et si ne scevent qu'il leur faut.
Et s'on les sert de brief refus,
Estre n'en puelent que confus,

145

Car parmi le refus s'aïrent,
Pour ce qu'a senestre se tirent.
(vv. 2879-90)

[If they have it, they don't know what to do with it; it doesn't displease them, nor can it please them, nor do they know what sustains them. Whereupon in their hearts revive foolish, possessive thoughts, at once goaded by and lacking good. There they have an abundance of lack, and yet don't know what they lack. And if they are given a quick refusal, it can only mix them up; for in the very act of receiving the refusal they grow angry, wherefore they pull to the left side]

There is no more qualitative distinction in Machaut's mind between possession or lack of *merci* than there is in Andreas Capellanus between *amor purus* and *amor mixtus*. But for Machaut, *merci* is a secondary consideration, and *fin'amors* may offer just as much contentment without it. Christine de Pisan expresses similar views in the *Rose* debate, and the Commentator on the *Echecs amoureux* makes such a distinction characteristic of *fin'amors*. In these works, as in the *Alerion* (vv. 4341-48), the union of Reason and Love accounts for the division between the good and bad lover. The *Fonteinne amoureuse* expresses the same ideas,[55] stressing the domination of hope over melancholy. despite the long complainte in which hope seems to surrender to desire, melancholy, and despair. Hope is possible because of the lady's Image.

Car d'Esperance la seüre
Par ton ymage nette et pure
Contre Desir et sa pointure
Me garniray.
(*Fonteinne amoureuse*, vv. 2267-70)

[For I shall arm myself with sure Hope against Desire and his sting by means of your clear and pure Image].

Hence Imagination restores Esperance. Venus herself loses her inflammatory character (vv. 1307-24) and becomes consolation distinct from Desire (vv. 2351-66).

Machaut's new conception of love is bound up with his attempt to fit good love into traditional ideals, and in particular into a Boethian framework. This is implicit in the *Remede* and the *Confort*. But it is also evident in the *Jugement Navarre*. In Reason's decision, the implications of Machaut's conception of *Bonneurtez* are set forth not only for love (vv. 3893-3908), but also for Nature (vv. 3857-76),[56] prosperity (vv. 3887-88), friendship (vv. 3889-92), knighthood (vv. 3909-27), and learning both public and private (vv. 3928-56). Nor are these the only domains within which the principle of *Bonneurtez* is operative (vv. 3881-83). Here again we encounter the emana-

146

tion of an abstract principle into the frequent and varied realms of human activity and experience. The technique is *frequentatio*.

> Mais je n'en diray hui le tiers,
> Non mie, par Dieu, le centisme.
> Car dès le ciel jusques en bisme
> Ses puissances par tout s'espandent,
> Et de ses puissances descendent
> Circonstances trop mervilleuses,
> Et sont a dire perilleuses,
> Qui s'apruevent par leur contraire.
>
> (*Jugement Navarre*, vv. 3840–47)

[But I shall not express now even a third, nay, in faith, the hundredth part of its power. For its power extends everywhere from heaven even into the very depths, and there descend from its power very marvellous circumstances, ones which are perilous to say, but which are proven by their opposite.]

Reason, who is speaking, thus extends by Imagination the scope and instruction beyond love itself in order to situate and support her analysis of love. Machaut does much the same thing in his presentation of Art at the outset of the *Remede*. The use of proof by contraries is a device familiar from Scholastic logic.[57] At the beginning of the *Jugement Navarre* Machaut opposes the grief from the plague of 1348–49 to the joy and good fortune that follow,[58] when a reasonable love is possible, one that guarantees the lover's happiness because of the sublimation of desire in hope (*Jugement Navarre*, vv. 2919–21). This too is common, traditional wisdom (*Jugement Navarre*, vv. 2122–24). Similar thought appears at the beginning to the *Alerion* (vv. 1–129). And it is, as we have seen, systematically and gradualistically elaborated in the *Confort d'ami*.

In the *Voir-Dit* Machaut suggests *merci* along with the sublimation. Yet even here he leaves the curious in doubt, as Venus causes a cloud to descend upon Péronne d'Armentières in bed with her septuagenarian lover. We never learn whether Machaut suffered the disappointments of a Goethe or the successes of a Hugo with young women (*Voir-Dit*, pp. 157–60). This is because it does not matter whether he obtains *merci* or not, since love is self-sufficient and not dependent on desire. Elsewhere in the *Voir-Dit* Machaut argues for hope as a palliative to desire, an escape from the wheel of Fortune, and a source of security and integrity in love.[59]

In Machaut's fixed forms we find the new conception of love in some poems, while others still advance the more conventional courtly love described in the *Vergier* and the *Jugement Behaingne*. Perhaps most of them were written in Machaut's earlier, less settled years. The longer dits fall principally after his fortieth year. Only among the lais does the new concep-

147

tion appear especially prominent. One has the impression that Machaut deemed the new love suitable to the most difficult and consequently most excellent fixed form. The emphasis on hope in the lais is striking, given the importance assigned to both the subject and the form of the lai in the *Remede* and the *Voir-Dit*.[60] The one other prominent subject in the lais is the Virgin Mary.

Machaut's idealism is obviously impracticable in most times and places. The quarrel in Jean le Seneschal's composite *Cent Ballades* concerning the relative advantages of fidelity and infidelity,[61] the whole tricky question of sincerity that will suddenly loom large in courtly writing at the turn of the century, and the superhuman demands of virtuous hope as Machaut envisages it—all these considerations were to bring crashing down the whole elevated structure of the *Remede,* like the nave at Beauvais a century earlier, almost as soon as it was raised. The Image was too abstract for *matière.* Yet it is still curious to observe this final, outwardly effortless extension of the courtly spirit to the limit of a love both virtuous and mundane, before skepticism and cynicism, or realism, discarded it once and for all. The debate in the *Belle dame sans mercy* and the conclusion to *Jehan de Saintré* are telling arguments against Machaut's conception of *fin' amors* as a viable ideal, despite the rigor and authority of his argument.

The characteristics peculiar to Machaut's conception of courtly love have significant implications for the notion of love as an art and for Imagination in the art of poetry. Certainly the stress on hope and the resulting sublimation of desire had repercussions on otherwise conventional commonplaces, embroidered upon and varied in expression, but largely the same for most courtly poets since the twelfth century. In particular the sublimation raises anew the question of the relation of the love Machaut describes to Christian morals, especially in the light of his amalgamation in the *Voir-Dit* of reasonable love and an "idolatrous" representation of the god of Love and the Image of the lady.

SUBLIMATION, MORALITY, AND IMAGINATION

Sublimation represents a movement away from the concrete apprehension of a person or object by means of a transpersonal, idealized projection. The Image which realizes that projection reacts upon the individual realizing the sublimation by Imagination so as to depersonalize him or her. Thus the type tends to supplant the individual, as the arts of poetry foresaw in the instruction on *descriptio* as representation.

> Davumque a pectore tolle,
> Nec vultu mentire Numam. Concordia vultum
> Affectumque liget.[62]

148

[Take Davus out of your heart, and do not feign Numa in your face. Let Concord bind together your expression and your sentiments.]

In Machaut's case, the movement from desire to hope entailed the idealization and sublimation in the Imagination of love. For time has no power to cause the Rose of such a love to fade and die.

> Mais vraiement ymaginer ne puis
> Que la vertus, où ma rose est enclose,
> Viengne par toy [Fortune] et par tes faus conduis,
> Ains est drois dons naturex; si suppose
> Que tu n'avras ja vigour
> D'amanrir son pris et sa valour.
> (Balade notée XXXI, vv. 9–14)

[But truly, I can not Imagine that the virtue wherein my rose is enclosed comes from you (Fortune) and your false conduct. Rather it is a true natural endowment. And it presumes that you will never have the power to lessen her renown and worth.]

Accordingly, a more impersonal, abstract Image becomes appropriate to the representation of the lady. She becomes, in keeping with Machaut's conception of Art expressed in the *Remede*, a "master" to imitate and to love. Imagined only as the abstractions representing her qualities—*ex sensu quo fiunt*—the qualities exist in a realm outside any materiality save their representation in the lover himself. But, ideally, to equal the lady in love the lover must divest himself of his materiality as well, that is, his desire must sublimate as hope. Only in this way can the Rose never fade and the aging poet experience the love described in the *Voir-Dit*. Machaut is coming close to Intellection, the incommunicable direct contemplation of abstractions that precludes poetry because it would pass beyond the *vocis imago*, the verbal representation of the idea as an Image formed in the mind and projected onto paper. In the *Remede*, we have observed the progressive abstraction from the description of the lady to the description of love. Machaut could go no further. He thus returned to a real world bathed indeed in the splendor of a sublimated love, but actualized in mundane activities in the final description of life with his lady.

The principal Image in the *Remede* is the extended dialogue—at points, the debate—between the poet and Esperance personified. The second Image is in two parts that are circumjacent to the dialogue. It contains the lai, and exemplifies the good and bad love elucidated by Esperance. The plan is thus as follows:

Poet and Lady: Fearful love (vv. 357–1495)—1139 lines
Poet and Esperance (vv. 1496–2964)—1469 lines.
Poet and Lady: hopeful love (vv. 2965–4256)—1292 lines.

The first meeting between the poet and the lady illustrates the wrong kind of love, based on fear, uncertainty as to the lady's feelings towards him, and the possibility of the lover's failure to realize his desire. The second meeting illustrates the right kind of love. It rests on the certainty that the lady knows his sentiments and cannot but respond to a love purified and sublimated as hope.

But most significant is the appearance of Esperance herself. Besides the formal discussion of love and hope, Esperance realizes metaphorically her qualities by the Boethian Image of light penetrating clouds. This Image, at the beginning and the middle of her section,[63] recalls the splendor and revitalizing influence of Boethius' Philosophia, of whom she is an obvious parody.

Finally, the *Remede* is interspersed with various emblematic Images, the most interesting of which are the shield of love described by Esperance[64] and inspired by the features of the lover himself that, in Machaut's estimation, are "la vraie et loyal enseingne / Que nuls faus amoureus ne porte" (vv. 1854–55)[65] [the true and faithful emblem that no false lover bears]; the statue of Nebuchadnezzar's dream from Daniel 2.32–33 (vv. 1001–1096); and the ring of Esperance (vv. 2094–2109, 4053–96). But because of its more discursive character, the *Remede* is not Machaut's best example of an elaborate Imagination.

As personification began to recede as a viable trope for Imagination, a new source of Images already latent in personification assumed prominence: Ovidian mythography. The greatest immediate influence upon the choice of figures were the mythographies, above all the *Ovide moralisé*.[66] The *Ovide moralisé*, like the later Commentary on the *Echecs amoureux*, allows for three kinds of allegorical readings for the Images of the gods and goddesses borrowed from Ovid: historical, astrological, and moral. Historically, the figures of classical mythology were considered euhemerizations, and became patterns for conduct in later historical events and persons; this is broadly a kind of typology, or allegorical figuration not so much in the sense of prefiguration as of exemplification.[67] Both Machaut and Froissart use it extensively. It functions as proof in argumentation in Machaut's debate poems because of the alleged historicity of the mythological personages.[68] The astrological sense construes the gods and goddesses as planets that influence the lives of men. It is reflected in Froissart's treatment of the commonplace ages of man. The scheme is worked out in the *Joli buisson de jonece,* which, together with the *Espinette amoureuse,* describes the young man's progress during the age of Venus, from that of Mercury to that of the Sun, that is, from childhood playmates through a *fin'amors* to the time when the grizzly poet turns to the Virgin Mary in prayer.[69] The chronological progression prefigures Charles d'Orléans' *Retenue d'amours* and *Songe en complainte,* except that in the latter dit Nonchaloir supplants the Virgin Mary. Astrological figures also encompass natural phenomena and bestiary figures, both of which are invented and allegorized with some originality in Machaut's and Froissart's love poems.[70] Finally, the moral allegory of mythological figures is paramount in the *Ovide moralisé* in imitation of which both poets expressed their views on the morals of courtly love through both personifications and mythological figures.

The moralizations of Ovid thus established an awareness of the allegorical possibilities of mythology and illustrated a methodology useful for Imagination. A few gods and goddesses had already intruded into vernacular literature, making their presence acceptable and assimilable, by extension, to non-religious contexts. Furthermore the standard medieval source of religious allegory, the bestiary, had been successfully mined for Images amenable to the context of courtly love by Marie de France, Richart de Fornival, Nicole de Margival, and others.[71] But the bestiary did not prove durable. Only Machaut used it extensively and with originality, in the *Dit de l'alerion*.

The *Alerion* is an elaborate, although structurally simple, allegorical disquisition on good and bad love. A discursive framework describes, classifies, and ranks the various loves of the poet in conformity with an aristocratic hierarchy of birds of prey. Its simplicity is apparent by comparison with Fornival's *Bestiaires,* in which there is elaborate interplay between argument and bestiary illustration. The *Alerion* is limited to one kind of animal, ravenous birds of prey differentiated according to their relative nobility determined in the sport of bird hunting.[72] The technique is alternation of letter and gloss. There are five sections in the *Alerion* distinguishable by one of four birds as "beast":

1. The sparrow hawk (vv. 130–1557).
2. The alerion, part 1 (vv. 1558–3028).
3. The eagle (vv. 3029–3812).
4. The gerfalc (vv. 3813–4524).
5. The alerion, part 2 (vv. 4525–4784).

Different kinds of ladies are identified with the different birds, and their actions are interpreted autobiographically by Machaut in chronological sequence within the context of *fin'amors*. The relative mobility of the different ladies' love corresponds to the bird with which each is assimilated. The gloss is itself continuous, insofar as the lover's quest of his lady, his errors and fortune, provide a view of love typical in Machaut. There is emphasis on excellence and hope in order to "vivre seculerement" (v. 2; cf. vv 4668–90) and virtuously.

But despite its ingeniosity and the interest of much of Machaut's interpretations, indeed despite its originality the consistent glossing of detail moves the *Alerion* dangerously close to the "one-to-one" relation that Rosemond Tuve has shown to be inimical to the best allegory.[73] When all *mystère* is *significa-tion*, little or no *merveille* remains for the nondiscursive play between letter and sense that distinguishes Guillaume de Lorris. The *Dit dou lyon*, chronologically prior to the *Alerion*, avoids this pitfall by a more ambivalent representation of the Lion on the Island of Loyal Lovers. Like Guillaume's Rose, the Lion is not glossed. Yet his fidelity in an amorous context illustrates meaningfully the trials and rewards of noble love.

But Machaut's didacticism in the *Alerion* is deliberate. Detailed interpreta-tion of each episode in the bird section is his constant concern.

> Or poons nous ci regarder,
> Pour aucuns poins de droit garder,
> En faisant en po d'argument,
> Pour moustrer plus evidemment
> De ce que j'ay ci devant dit
> Les entencions de mon dit,
> Dont je moustre par exemplaire.[74]
>
> (vv. 1633–38)

[Now we may consider this matter, in order to keep certain facts straight, by means of a topical elaboration so as to demonstrate more convincingly, on the basis of what I said before, the intention of my dit; this I shall show by exemplification.]

Imagination should express the Image in the heart of the lover. In the *Lyon*, Machaut represents the lady as the Image in his heart that inspires thought, the *immoderata cogitatio* of Andreas Capellanus.

> Car la trés douce imprecion
> De son ymagination
> Est en mon cuer si fort empreinte
> Qu'encor y est et yert l'empreinte.[75]
>
> (*Lyon*, vv. 207–10)

[For the most gentle impression of her Imagination is so firmly impressed in my heart that the impression is still there and ever will be.]

These *pensers* provide the substance of the various Images, particularly the bes-tiary figures, that people the *Lyon* and the *Alerion*. As in Raoul de Houdenc's *Roman des eles*, the alerion is an Image of the ever rising virtue and quality of the lady.

> Lors par ymagination
> Perçoit dedens s'entention
> Sa dame monter par humblesse
> Tout au plus haut air de noblesse.
>
> (*Alerion*, vv. 2589–92)

[Then by Imagination he perceived with his understanding his lady rise in humility to the very heights of nobility.]

The Imagined flight transpires entirely in the Imagination of the poet.

> Quant monter la voit telement
> Des yeus de son entendement
> Et bien parfaitement y pense.
>
> (*Alerion*, vv. 2593–95)

[When he sees and considers thoroughly with the eyes of understanding her great upward flight.]

A psychomachia ensues wherein the poet is torn between an awareness of his own circumscribed qualities and his will to rise with the lady. One is as if transposed into the sentiment inspiring Bernart de Ventadorn's Image of the rising and falling lark. The Image reverts, however, to its source, the unified perfection of the lady contrasted with the uncertain inner dichotomy of the lover.

> Il la voit par voie ordonnée
> Comme alerion eslevée
> En haut air de grace et d'onneur
> Avec Amours, son droit signeur,
> Si haut que li entendemens
> De l'amant en ses jugemens
> Ne scet desclairier verité,
> Tant y a haute quantité
> De noblesses et de vertus.
>
> (*Alerion*, vv. 2651–59)

[He sees her rise like the alerion in ordered flight into the upper reaches of grace[76] and honor with Love, her proper lord; so high was she that the lover's understanding could not by his estimation of it express its truth, so great is its nobility and virtue.]

The lady's inimitable virtues nonetheless require imitation in the lover in order for him to be worthy of her. She is so far above him that he can scarcely comprehend, let alone overcome, the distance. The Image is an adequate rendering of the descriptive problem in Imagination.

The *Jugement Behaingne* and *Navarre* and the *Confort d'ami* stress allegorical personification and mythological figures. Remarkable in the three dits is Machaut's use of examples as proof. These are taken not only from Ovidian mythology but also from recent French history. Their significance derives from the context, from the careful delineation of truth in the form of sensible Images.

The sublimation of *fin' amors*, its separation from Nature and desire, was effected by showing its subordination to and derivation from Bonneurtez and virtue, as well as its complementary relationship with Souffissance and Esperance. The attempt in the *Remede* to elicit a more refined love distinguishable from other kinds, whether courtly or not, corresponds to an artistic intention

153

going back to Andreas Capellanus and Guillaume de Lorris, and typical of the troubadours and trouvères as well. But Machaut, like Andreas Capellanus, is concerned with questions that transcend poetic evocation, questions which concerned scientific and moral writers in the twelfth century. *Frequentatio* in example, personification, and bestiary figures, leads to a *fin'amors* that was unique to and died with Machaut. But it had parallels which are meaningful and explicit in other realms of man's moral, scientific, and political life.

7

Imagination in the Writings of Jean Froissart

Denn wir sind Allegorien,
und so solltest du uns kennen.
Herold:
Wüßte nicht, dich zu benennen,
eher könnt' ich dich beschreiben.
—Goethe[1]

THE *PRISON AMOUREUSE:* INTERLACE AND IMAGINATION

Froissart understood the place of Imagination in composition.

Car a savoir forment desire
Tout ce dont il me poet escrire,
Tant pour la matere nouvelle
Que pour ce qu'il me renouvelle
Pluiseurs ymaginations
Que j'ai sur tels intentions;
Et disoient sus ceste entente
Les lettres dont je me contente.
(*Prison amoureuse*, vv. 3437–44)[2]

[For I very much wish to know all that he may write to me about, as much for the new subject matter as for the fact that his writing revivifies several of my imaginations on such contexts. And the letters spoke to that context, whereof I am pleased.]

Froissart's subject is *fin' amors;* his art is the invention of significant Images.

Froissart's elaboration in the *Prison amoureuse* of his courtly "matere nouvelle" through myth (the Phaeton story), a pseudo-Ovidian narrative (the love of Neptisphelé and Pynoteus), and a dream vision describing a psychomachia with courtly personifications, is a striking illustration of thought represented by Images complementary and coherent on both the literal and allegorical levels. The structure resembles to an extraordinary degree the fine interlocking of adventure, vision, and exposition in the *Queste del saint graal*. It is significant that in explaining the stories and dream Froissart asserts

155

that they are not nightmares. The Images in themselves are empty and unreal things, "toutes coses vainnes et nulles" (IX, 1. 158); what matters is their substance, their meaning. Like Guillaume de Lorris, Froissart uses conventional Images to represent by subtle linking and interpretation the "matire . . . bone e nueve" of courtly love.

No work on courtly love, except perhaps Richart de Fornival's *Bestiaires d'amours*, so finely interlaces Image and interpretation as does Froissart's *Prison amoureuse*. Even in Machaut's *Alerion* didacticism frequently overwhelms the Image, destroying the careful blending of *signification* and *merveille* essential to allegorical *mystère*. Like the *Queste del saint graal*, the *Prison amoureuse* is structured by three separate but interrelated modes: the literal narrative relating conventional adventures of two lovers, Rose and Flos; the dream or vision containing the psychomachia with personifications, the invented story of Neptisphelé and Pynoteus, and the ride of Phaeton; and the exposition, including the inserted fixed forms.

The literal level is simple and clear. Rose and Flos exchange letters about their adventures as courtly lovers. The focus is alternately on the beginnings of Rose's love and the permanence of Flos' (the *Moi* of the poem). The suite of adventures constitutes no complete, broadly coherent narrative like those in the *Espinette amoureuse* and the *Joli buisson de jonece,* nor does it concentrate on a single important episode as in the *Remede de Fortune* and the *Fonteinne amoureuse*. There is not even the unity of the exemplary episodes in the final section of the *Remede* describing in detail typical activities in the life of a happily united courtly couple. There are of course felicitous details that give great freshness to Froissart's dits, like the poet's struggle with his lady for the purse she stole from him.[3] But the coherence of the work is based principally on Flos' advice; it is this advice, in Images and exposition, that Froissart stresses in the *Prison amoureuse*.

INVENTION OF IMAGES

Froissart drew from well-known Ovidian tales like the Judgment of Paris and Apollo's chase of Daphne (in the *Espinette amoureuse*) and Venus and Adonis (in the *Joli buisson de jonece*). But he also invented his own "Ovidian" material: Papirus and Ydoree (in the *Espinette*), Ydrophus and Neptisphoras (in the *Joli buisson*), and Neptisphelé and Pynoteus (in the *Prison amoureuse*).[4] He does indeed "renouvelle pluiseurs ymaginations."

Neptisphelé and Pynoteus (vv. 1316–1988) resemble Pyramus and Thisbe as well as Phaeton, as Scheler pointed out.[5] However, Froissart stresses their originality: "un petit dittié amoureus, qui se traitast sus aucune nouvelle matere qu'on n'aroit onques veü ne oÿ mise en rime, tele com, par figure, fu jadis de Piramus et de Tysbé, ou de Eneas et de Dido, ou de Tristran et de Yseus" (V, ll. 44–48) [a little poem about love which would treat some new subject matter unseen and unheard before in rhyme, such as figuratively were Pyramus and Thisbe, Aeneas and Dido, Tristan and Yseult]. This shows that Froissart was using previous material for a new figure, a new *matière* more suitable for the allegorical sense he intended. His reflections recall Ovidian mythographies, and make one think of the Pygmalion story as well. His words are ambiguous, but clearly amenable to such a reading.

> Adont tournai sus une glose
> Qui nous approeve et nous acorde,
> Si com Ovides le recorde,
> Les oeuvres de Pynoteüs,
> Qui par grant art et non par us
> Fist l'ymage parlans et vive,
> D'aige et de terre.
>
> (*Prison amoureuse*, vv. 1295–1301)

[Therefore I sought a gloss that would validate and fit for us the works of Pynoteus, as Ovid records them. He, by great art and in no ordinary way, made the talking, living Image from water and earth.]

In what amounts to a narrative gloss of Ovid, Froissart puts together a new tale in conformity with the medieval practice of adapting new *matière* from old. From the purely formal point of view, this is similar in Imagination to Guillaume de Lorris' adaptation of excerpts from Ovid's *Ars amatoria* to the instruction given by the god of Love. Similarly, Machaut had adapted *poetries* to his intention, in one place realizing Dido's wish for a "parvulus Aeneas" in Vergil by making her "enceinte" (*Jugement Navarre*, v. 2121), elsewhere removing the conclusions to the Ovidian mythologies (*Confort d'ami*).

The adaptation of *matière* to *sens* demonstrates effective use of the Images. Thus Machaut counters one example by advancing another in the *Jugement Navarre* (vv. 2830–35). This is good rhetoric, provided one's own example is unimpeachable and cannot be countered by a better one. Prudence, whose domain includes memory, turns one example to a new truth by rereading:

> Guillaume, maintenant
> Voy je bien vostre entention;
> Mais j'ay contraire opinion
> Qui de la vostre est trop lonteinne.
>
> (vv. 2928–31)

[Guillaume, now I see your intention. But I have a contrary opinion that is far removed from yours.]

In effect, this is the rhetorical trick of turning an opponent's argument against him. In literature it is adaptation. We have observed Jean de Meun's use of it, as well as that found in the *Response* to Richart de Fornival's *Bestiaires*.

Froissart's adaptations employ the same technique.

Such adaptation was justified as an improvement on the original version or versions. Froissart saw Neptisphelé and Pynoteus in this way:

> Se j'avoie tous mes escrips,
> Nouvellement et viés escrips,
> Quis et cerchiet de cief en cor,
> Et plus que je n'en ai encor,
> Se ne peuïsse je trouver
> Nulle matere pour ouvrer
> Si amoureuse ne si belle,
> Si jolie ne si nouvelle,
> Comme ceste est.
>
> (*Prison amoureuse*, vv. 1304–12)

[If I had sought and looked through all my writings from beginning to end, those recently composed and the old ones, and more of them than I still possess, I could not find any subject matter to work on that was so lovely and beautiful, so joyful and original as this one is.].

By combining material from several of Ovid's best tales, Froissart achieves a more successful, truer rendering of ideal love apposite both for himself and for Rose (vv. 1989–95).

The veracity is the truth of *mystère* inherent in any significant Image.

> Et pour ce que ceste matere
> Me sambla de tres grant mystere
> Et moult tres amoureuse ossi,
> En le maniere l'escripsi
> Que devant moi le vi en lettre,
> Ensi que me sceus entremettre
> Dou ditter et del ordonner.
>
> (vv. 1996–2002)

[And because this subject matter seemed to me to possess mysterious significance and was quite suitable for the expression of love as well, I put it into writing just as I saw it written; thus I did my best to put it into verse and into good order.]

Similarly, in the *Espinette amoureuse* the magic mirror that shows Froissart his lady while they are separated is verified by analogy with the invention of the Roman lovers Papyrus and Ydoree, a story allegedly derived from Ovid (*Espinette*, v. 2672).[6] Its truth is figural. It is true because the formal elaboration of the Image manifests a truth about love. The mirror Image is a reflection of truth, and thus a representation of it. Love makes it visible in the mirror. It thus makes the representation of the loved one meaningful and true.

> Dont se lors pooie veoir
> Ma dame ens ou mien mireoir,

Croire le doi et a moi plaire,
Car j'ai figure et exemplaire
Qui est toute cose certainne.
(Espinette, vv. 2725-29)

[Therefore if I could perceive my lady in my mirror, I must believe it and be pleased by it; for I have a figure and example as evidence of its absolute certainty.]

The magic of mirrors would not bother Froissart even on the literal level. In his *Chroniques,* he argues that a particularly large bear killed in the forests of Gaston de Foix must have been a metamorphosed human because a similar change befell Acteon in Ovid.

Nous trouvons en l'escripture que anciennement les dieux et les deesses, a leur plaisance, muoient les hommes en bestes et en oyseaux, et aussi bien faisoient les femmes. Aussi peut estre que cel ours avoit esté un chevalier chaçant es forests de Bisquaie. Si courrouça ou dieu ou deesse en son temps, pourquoy il fu müez en fourme d'ours, et faisoit la sa penitence, si comme Acteon fu müez en cerf.[7]

[We find written record that in former times the gods and goddesses changed men at their pleasure into beasts and birds, and they did so as well to women. Thus it may be that that bear had been a knight hunting in the woods of Biscay, and that he angered a god or goddess in his time, on account of which he was metamorphosed into the shape of a bear, and did his penance in that way, just as Acteon was once metamorphosed into a stag.]

The *Chroniques* contain ample evidence of Froissart's superstitious nature. He would certainly have had little difficulty in regarding Ovidian Imaginations as both literally and figuratively true. The tendency to euhemerize mythology and give it a historical sense would have encouraged his inclination to accord historical and figural sense to his inventions.

In summary, the story of Neptisphelé and Pynoteus is as follows. Pynoteus—hunter, poet, master of the seven arts and of necromancy—loves Neptisphelé, sister of Cybele; their love is realized in joyful encounters in the garden of Neptisphelé's home (vv. 1316—80). Neptisphelé is devoured by a lion; Pynoteus discovers her girdle, and lamenting his loss, promises vengeance (vv. 1381—1517). By magic, Pynoteus summons all the wild animals, and they deliver up the guilty lion, then devour it (vv. 1518—88). A statue (*ymage*) of Neptisphelé is made by Pynoteus. In a complainte, he contrasts the sufferings of Hades (Pynoteus' death) and the decision to "restore" Neptisphelé to life as a statue (resurrection of Neptisphelé). The statue is not made of the usual materials, but of a moist combination of earth and water. Pynoteus then prays to Phebus to impart his *vertu* to a laurel leaf that will bring the *ymage* to life; the prayer includes a long digression, like a *credo,* summarizing the ride of Phaeton (vv. 1589-1918). Light descends into the laurel leaf and through it into the statue. Neptisphelé returns to life from a distant, dark realm of travail. She desires to return to her family, to the visits in the garden (vv. 1919–88). Pynoteus marvels:

> C'est m'amie ne plus ne mains.
> Et ne l'ai je ouvré a mes mains
> Et, telle qu'elle est, donné fourme?
> Et elle maintenant m'enfourme
> Que c'est Neptisphelé m'amie,
> Qui droit chi s'estoit endormie!
> Se je puis parler par congié,
> Ne sçai ossi se j'ai songié.
>
> (vv. 1960–67)

[It is my beloved for sure. And did I not fashion her with my hands and give her the shape she has? And now she informs me that she is my beloved Neptisphelé who had gone to sleep on this very spot! If I may have leave to speak, I don't know myself whether or not I have dreamed.]

The blending of various sources in the literal story raises the kinds of questions many medieval authors could not resist answering by exposition. A dream, reality, truth? These superficially contrasting modes of experience require a common foundation to hold them together in a meaningful system. But before proceeding to the exposition, like the knights in the *Queste del saint graal* to the hermits, Froissart links his Ovidian invention to other Imaginations. The prayer to Phebus includes a lengthy summary of Phaeton's ride. This narrative thus moves into relationship to the principal story of Neptisphelé and Pynoteus. Pynoteus' descent into Hades parallels Phaeton's fall from the chariot of the sun; Phebus' restoration of Neptisphelé to life corresponds to the restoration of the sun to its rightful place in the heavens.

But Froissart also prepares for the expository mode with Rose's dream. In allegorical poetry kaleidoscopic experience shifts and reforms into new patterns, all ultimately illuminating the truth which the exposition will help to clarify. "The curious inner revolution experienced, as *gestalt* replaced *gestalt,* came from moving out of the area of imitated literal life into an area where universals rather than particulars seem to be met, into an area where ideas themselves confront one or interact."[8]

MULTIPLE EXPOSITION AND COHERENCE IN NARRATIVE

Rose's dream is inspired by the reading of Froissart's Ovidian invention of Neptisphelé and Pynoteus.

Et ce qui m'a ensonniiet ce terme, ch'a esté une ymagination que j'ai pris sus un songe qui m'avint assés tost apriés les lettres que darrainnement m'envoiastes; de la quele ymagination je n'en sçai qui encouper fors vostre livret de Pynoteüs et de Neptisphelé. Et croi ensi que la plaisance que j'ai eü, et par pluiseurs fois, au lire, m'a aresté ou songe et ou pourpos que j'ai eü, sus le quel avis j'ai ditté et ordonné un petit dittié.

(VII, ll. 19–27)

[And what has preoccupied me during this time has been an Imagination that came to me, based on a dream I had rather soon after the letter you recently sent me. I don't know where to place blame for that Imagination except on your book about Pynoteus and Neptisphelé. And therefore I believe that the pleasure I took in reading it several times fixed me on the dream and the intention I have had. In accordance with that intention, I have drafted and arranged a little poem.]

Rose asks Froissart's opinion of his composition (VII, l. 33), which requires the poet's careful attention. He reads the poem for two reasons, pleasure and understanding. Indeed, once he has discovered the double sense of the poem, he returns to the beginning to read it again to the end.

> Et lors qu'au lire je me pris,
> Je me solachai en lisant,
> Car li ver furent moult plaisant,
> Bien ordonné et bien assis.
> Des foelles lisi jusqu'a sis
> Et puis recommenchai mon tour
> A la premiere page, pour
> Mieuls concevoir et cler entendre
> A quoi la matere poet tendre.
>
> (vv. 2237–45)

[And when I began to read it I delighted in the reading, for the verses were very pleasing, well arranged, and well set. I read up to six pages, then began again on the first page in order better to comprehend and clearly to understand what the subject intended.]

The movement from narrative to idea is achieved by the replacement of Ovidian figures with personifications. The Imagination is approaching the ideas themselves as metonymy supersedes allegory; the metaphorical transfer is now effected directly rather than indirectly.

Nonetheless, the personifications still act in given settings: first a psychomachia, second an imprisonment. The outline is as follows:

Frame: conventional springtime setting in which Rose falls asleep and dreams (*penser,* v. 2316).

I. Psychomachia (vv. 2318–2846).
   a. Complaint by the three ladies Justice, Pity, and Reason, overcome by Orgueil[9] because the noble lords no longer support them; Rose promises help (vv. 2318–2423).

b. War counsel, composed of Honor, Prowess, Hardement, Desir, Jonece, Loyauté, Avis, and Emprise. All counsel instant action, except Avis, who advises calling in his mother Atemprance beforehand; his advice rejected as "le consel d'une fame" (v. 2495) (vv. 2424-2527).

c. Preparations for battle; Avis defects to other side to join Atemprance (vv. 2528-2677).

d. Battle: near victory turned to rout by the forces of Avis and Atemprance; the absence of Desir in the combat (vv. 2678-2846).

II. Imprisonment (vv. 2847-3396).

a. Rose's lamentations in prison of Atemprance (vv. 2847-97).

b. Atemprance provides, besides herself, her two sons, Souvenir and Avis, and two daughters, Congnissance and Esperance, to console Rose and relieve his melancholy (vv. 2898-2960).

c. Communication between Rose and his lady, using Souvenir as messenger; in particular, a complainte "figuré sus le bestiaire" (v. 3157) with allusions to contemporary historical events and personages (vv. 2961-3314).

d. Deliverance of Rose by the Eagle (vv. 3315-96).

Frame: Awakening of Rose (vv. 3397-3420).

There are two distinct contexts for the dream vision. The first, identified by Scheler, deals with political and military events about 1369: "Toute la narration allégorique qui fait l'objet du dittier adressé par Rose à son ami Flos, a été inspirée par le souvenir de la bataille de Bastweiler perdue par le duc de Brabant et de ses conséquences."[10] The Lion and the Eagle in the complainte are to encourage the Holy Roman Emperor (Eagle), brother of the Duke of Brabant (Lion), to intervene in support of the latter. The liberation at the end corresponds to the freedom gained by the Duke after almost a year of captivity.

But the political context is not paramount in the *Prison amoureuse,* nor does it offer the richest allegorical reading.[11] The representative love story has more significance than the particular historical events. An episode in the *Espinette amoureuse* will help clarify this point.

Froissart must leave his lady at one point for England. The voyage has the topographical imprecision of most allegorical love poetry, although some allusions permit a broad identification of Froissart's itinerary from somewhere in France to Dover by way of Calais in 1400.[12] The ostensible purpose of the voyage is health (vv. 2382-88). While in England Froissart visits Philippa de Hainaut, wife of Richard II, and presents her with a virelai (vv. 3128-33).[13] Then the queen gives him leave to return to France. These barely discernible realia are buried in a long narrative including Froissart's love sickness and his conversation with his lady, who appears in the mirror she gave him to take along to England. The Image centers on the Ovidian invention of Papyrus and

Ydoree. Now, we know this voyage to England had not only amorous but also political reasons.[14] In a similarly elusive way, the political is interwoven with the amorous dream of Rose in the *Prison amoureuse*.

Rose professes not to understand the meaning of his dream (vv. 3393–3417). He sends it to Flos for an interpretation. "Et pour ce que vostres sens est grans et ymaginatis et abuvrés en tels oevres, je vous pri que vous voelliés sus mon songe mettre aucune exposition nouvelle, ensi que la matere le requiert" (VIII, ll. 22–25) [And since your mind is great, imaginative, well versed in such writings, would you be so good as to give an original interpretation to my dream, in harmony with the demands of the subject matter]. The reverse of Imagination is exegesis. We have seen that Froissart began almost immediately to "expose" Rose's poem in his own mind, going back to the beginning in order to read it correctly once he had fixed its context and intention (vv. 3437–42).

The original inspiration for Rose's dream, the Neptisphelé and Pynoteus story, gave the two Imaginations an affinity demanding elucidation satisfactory to both. There are common literal ties, such as the lions, loss and deliverance, the love context. More importantly, however, Pynoteus' thoughts on the sufferings in Hades and Rose's apprehension before entering prison deprived of his "deduit" converge on a common truth, as do Phebus' miracle and the arrival of the imperial Eagle in the dream. But the Eagle's appearance is justified as well by an older and more profound *mystère,* and as such is eminently suited to exposition when contemplated by Flos. The appeal for the Eagle's assistance—the Eagle is the real Duke's brother—expresses the brotherhood of all kings.

> On dist que jadis par mystere
> Li roi si s'appelloient frere,
> Ja ne fuissent net d'une mere.
> (vv. 3138–40)

[It is said that in former times, by some mysterious significance, the kings addressed one another as brothers, even though they were not born of the same mother.]

The same mystery brings together Flos and Rose as lovers, and it subsumes the union of Flos' Ovidian invention and Rose's dream, as it does the exposition that illuminates their affinities.

One must regard Flos' exposition as one does the hermits' interpretations in the *Queste del saint graal.* Flos is as much a persona as they are. In both cases there is an attempt to express the ineffable—the mystery of the grail, the mystery of royalty, the mystery of love. In the final analysis, the exposition is simply another means, like narrative or dream vision, of converging on the ineffable that forms the Images and concatenations of discursive explanations. "Expositors within the work tell us the meanings of what we have seen, an

163

incomparably trustworthy check upon our fancies and errors. But we do not wait for these assistances, to take in significances; we are able very soon to take what must have been the mediaeval reader's own pleasure in the . . . expositions: corroboration of what we thought, a second and unassailable confirmation of meanings, suggestions, connections, that we had felt and seen already through the action.''[15] The tale, dream, or vision, together with the exposition, ''represent two of the ways we have developed to refer to things too complex to state in full, though experienced by all of us.''[16] The exposition is enmeshed in the narrative like another, perhaps brighter, thread in Froissart's tapestry. It serves to make the total representation greater than any of its parts; context gives meaning to Images which, through their form, express more than the discursive context can express.

Two epistles set forth the exposition. The first (IX) links the Neptisphelé-Pynoteus story to Rose's dream; the second (XII) appends a Phaeton exposition, since the latter is prominent in Pynoteus' prayer to Phebus but neglected in the first exposition. The strands of expository material in the expositions hold the three literal sequences together.

First Flos elucidates Rose's dream by itself. The gloss is an amplification of the *matière* provided by Rose, ''pour . . . la matere dou dit songe acroistre'' (IX, ll. 9–11) [in order to amplify the subject matter of the aforementioned dream]. It is not an imposed *surplus de sens,* but part of the dream as its discursive amplification. Since the dream is composed of personified abstractions, the interpretation becomes only the clarification of the concepts. It is essential to Rose's *mystère*. Imagination makes the interpretation possible. ''Chiers amis, apriés la teneur de vostres lettres, je vous envoie une exposition faite et arestee sus cesti songe parmi l'aÿde de Dieu et d'une ymagination que j'ai eü'' (IX, ll. 14–17). [Dear friend, according to the tenor of your letter I am sending you an interpretation composed and founded on that dream, with the help of God and an Imagination I have had.] The theme of the poem is the life of love, ''par la quele guerre et bataille j'entens la vie amoureuse'' (IX, ll. 52–53) [by which war and battle I understand the life of love], especially that of Rose and his lady as exemplary lovers. Defeat and imprisonment are therefore the effect of the lady's qualities on the lover. The methodical glossing is essentially equational: the bed and room Rose sleep in are the ''douce pensee, gaie et amoureuse'' (IX, l. 20) that absorbs the lover; the three personifications that appear to him, Justice, Pity, and Reason, acquire second meanings in harmony with the context: ''bonté, biauté et maniere bien arree'' (IX, l. 24) [goodness, beauty, and proper comportment]. These are the subject of amorous thoughts and the source of the poem's Imagination. The war counsel results from the lover's desire properly to serve, love, fear, and obey his lady. Avis, inspired by Atemprance, cautions him against the perils lying in his path if he follows open attack, especially through the great effort and the danger of jealousy. But courage and desire prevent him from following Avis' reasonable counsel, and he loses self-control, or "maniere et contenance" (IX, l. 32), like Guillaume de Lorris when he first approaches the Rose. Thus when Avis abandons him in battle the lover falls silent, *esbahi*, into that mutism typical of lovers before their lady. Nevertheless his other qualities inspire the lover to act, and the battle takes place. This is the "vie amoureuse de vous et de vostre dame, les priieres, les responses, les refus et les escondis" (IX, ll. 53–54) [your and your lady's life of love, the prayers, responses, refusals, excuses] familiar from the adventures of the lover in the *Roman de la rose*. But the qualities of the lady overwhelm him, particularly with Avis and Atemprance united under the banner of noble Orgueil. Desir abandons the lover to impotence, and he finds himself in prison under the guardianship of Atemprance, there to suffer trials and tribulations "quant vous estes escondis et refusés de vostre dame, ou que vous en avés responses ou samblans qui ne vous sont pas bien agreable, ou que vous estes batus des verges et des assaus de jalousie" (IX, ll. 63–67) [when you are dismissed or rejected by your lady, or you receive from her answers or glances that are not very agreeable, or you are beaten by the rods and assaults of jealousy]. We recognize again the turn of Fortune to which the lover's foolishness makes him vulnerable. But there are consolations in adversity, and they soon appear as Atemprance's children Espoir, Souvenir, Avis, and Congnissance. Finally, the Eagle itself arrives, equated in this context with "francise, qui amainne avoec li humilité, pité, misericorde et debonnaireté" (IX, ll. 78–79) [franchise, who brings with her humility, pity, mercy, and nobility]. In fact, the lady's *franchise* is the dominant virtue, bringing in its train all the others, and promising the most hope. The lover returns to the Image of the lady's qualities whence the dream sprang, "ravis en parfaite joie, en pensant et ymaginant la bonté et biauté de vostre dame souverainne" (IX, ll. 93–94) [delighted by complete joy, while thinking on and imagining the goodness and beauty of your sovereign lady].

Flos is not content with the exposition. In reconsidering Rose's poem and letter, Imagination suggests another significant reading (IX, ll. 105–7). Flos means the link between his Ovidian invention and Rose's dream, "car les pensees et ymaginations que on a as coses enclinent les corages en diverses mervelles" (IX, ll. 112–13) [for the thoughts and imaginations that one has about things incline our hearts to diverse wonders]. And Flos concludes:

dont, en lisant ces lettres, je me repris et jettai ailleurs mon avis et ymagination sus aultre fourme et bien propisce a ceste matere et selonc le teneur des lettres que dou tamps passé m'avés envoiies et par les queles je m'avisai que ceste aultre exposition j'escriroie et le vous envoieroie, ensi que j'ai fait, a fin que vous aiiés avis sus l'un et l'autre pourpos, et le plus agreable retenés pour vous ou tous deus. (IX, ll. 114–21)

[Thus, while reading your letter, I had second thoughts and cast my thought and imagination onto another form quite suitable to the subject; and one in accordance with

165

the tenor of the letters you sent me in the past, and through which I came to my decision to write this second exposition and send it to you, as I have done, so that you may apply yourself to the one interpretation or the other, and retain the one that pleases you, or both of them.]

The exposition centers on the desire prominent in the dream. Desire is the initial undoing and final salvation of the lover. Pynoteus and Neptisphelé are equated, respectively, with *desir* and *plaisance,* the cause and effect of amorous attraction. This state continues until the intervention of the Lion, or the *envie* of the *médisants.*[17] But love prevails, as Pynoteus (*desir*) appeals to Phebus (the god of Love) and the latter, inclined to pity, restores the lady by reviving Neptisphelé (*plaisance*). Flos presents both sides of the equations to make the link between Rose's dream and his Ovidian invention obvious. Both offer hope and encouragement to persevere, in expectation of the favor of the god of Love, and the lady. Without this interpretation the dream and tale are incomplete, substantially empty marvels, less to be feared than explained (IX, ll. 155–58). Explanation restores their integrity. Their *mystère* aroused Rose's curiosity, and Flos offered the *matière* necessary as substance and exposition to make them significant.

However, Flos' exposition is incomplete. Not all loves end happily, and the Phaeton story has not been elucidated or fit into the second exposition. Rose points out that his lady examined the "doctrines" set forth by Flos "et sus ymaginé une nouvelle matere, qu'elle dist qui y faut, selonc l'ordenance dou livret de Pynoteüs et de Neptisphelé . . . ; et est li ymaginations de li tele qu'il li samble que li exposition de mon songe ne fet nulle mention de Phebus, de Pheton, ne de la grant poëtrie qui dedens est contenue" (XI, ll. 25–28, 31–34) [and had imagined a new subject matter on it, which she said it lacked, one in harmony with the composition of the book on Pynoteus and Neptisphelé. . . . and her imagination is such that it seems to her that the interpretation of my dream makes no mention of Phebus, Phaeton, or the narrative about them]. Once such an exposition "selonc l'ordenance de l'orison que Pynoteüs fist a Phebus, dieu dou Solel" (XI, ll. 39–40) [in conformity with the composition of the prayer Pynoteus made to Phebus, god of the Sun] has been added, "s'en sera de tant li livres creüs et la matere augmentee" (XI, ll. 41–42) [the book will be that much larger and the subject amplified]. Flos acknowledges the lacuna and provides the requested exposition in Letter XII.

Phaeton's ride provides the most extensive and complex exposition, despite its relative brevity and subordinate position in the Neptisphelé and Pynoteus story. It mirrors both Rose's dream and the pseudo-Ovidian story in representing the "vie amoureuse" by antiphrasis. Phaeton is the victim of *fole amour.* Phebus (Amour) engenders Phaeton (*desirs*) in Climene (the "imagination d'un amant") (XII, l. 70). An inquiry by Mercurius (*dous regart*) regarding Phaeton's father is the *visio* leading to *cogitatio* (Imagination here) in An-

dreas, and precedes Phaeton's question to his mother in Froissart. *Dous regart*
and *ymagination* lead to *amour,* that is, Phebus, "et s'en vient Desirs, par
l'esmouvement de Douls Regart et le consel d'Ymagination, en la presence
dou dieu d'Amours" (XII, ll. 81–83) [and Desire came, at the instigation of
Dous Regart and the counsel of Imagination, into the presence of the god of
Love]. There Phaeton confronts Phebus with the request to pilot the chariot of
the sun. The paradigm conforms to Andreas Capellanus' general definition of
love: "Amor [Phebus] est passio quaedam innata [Phaeton] procedens ex
visione [Mercurius] et immoderata cogitatione formae alterius sexus [Cli-
mene]"[18] [Love (Phebus) is a certain inborn suffering (Phaeton) derived from
the sight (Mercurius) of and excessive meditation upon the beauty of the opposite sex (Climene)]. Essential however to Andreas' conception of good love
are the *praecepta* "ob quam aliquis super omnia cupit alterius potiri amplexibus
et omnia de utriusque voluntate in ipsius amplexu amoris praecepta compleri"
[which causes each one to wish above all things the embraces of the other and
by common desire to carry out all of love's precepts in the other's embrace].
Properly used, *praecepta* control passion and desire, and prevent immoderate
fear of disclosure or the loss of love. Opposed to such control is the impulse of
desire: "Postquam vero ad hanc cogitationem plenariam devenerit, sua frena
nescit continere amor, sed statim procedit ad actum"[19] [Then after he has
come to this complete meditation, love cannot hold the reins, but he proceeds
at once to action]. Phebus as love strives to put Phaeton into the way of reason
so that he will not be borne away and destroyed by *fole plaisance,* like those
Andreas describes in Book 3 of the *De amore.* But Phaeton pays him no heed,
and rides off giving free rein to his horses.

In Rose's dream Desir impells the lover to do battle against Orgueil, despite
the warnings of Avis, who therefore goes over to the other side to join
Atemprance. In the context of the Phaeton story, this means Desir seeks to
lead a "vie amoureuse" without the assistance of Love. The separation is as
radical as that between Love and Venus in Guillaume de Lorris' *Roman de la
rose.* Particularly to be feared if Desir acts alone is the intervention of
"jalousie" (cf. XII, l. 91). But Phaeton heeds no counsel, and overcomes his
father's objections. He advances to the chariot. Here a supplementary allegorical equation is added. The chariot (*fole plaisance*) is hitched to four horses,
Jonece, Lie Pensee, Uiseuse, and *Fole Emprise.* This is not the company in
Guillaume de Lorris' garden of Deduit. The horses need a firm hand to
"gouvrener et sieuir la vie amoureuse bellement et sagement" (XII, ll.
103–4) [direct and follow the life of love with grace and prudence]. Phebus
(as Love) advises Phaeton, as Andreas did Walter and the god of Love did
Guillaume, "qu'il mainne les chevaus rieuleement et sagement" (XII, l. 106)
[to guide the horses according to the rules and with prudence]. Love's advice
Flos glosses as *avis,* which, in Rose's dream, "conselle l'amant de li sage-

167

ment gouvrener et maintenir en l'estat amoureus" (XII, ll. 109–10) [advises the lover to conduct himself and maintain himself prudently in the amorous condition]. Specifically, Phebus enjoins Phaeton "qu'il tiegne le voie et le chemin de Raison et tire tous jours sus frain, c'est a dire que il s'avise" (XII, ll. 112–14) [to keep to the way and path of Reason, and always to hold in his reins, that is to pay attention to what he is doing]. Froissart is in the mainstream of courtly writers who seek an accommodation between reason and love in *fin'amors*. Accordingly, and again in conformity with Rose's dream, Phaeton is fitted out with a whip (Atemprance) and a bridle (Congnissance) (XII, ll. 115–17). All to no avail, as the lover, ignoring such *avis* (what else may one expect from desire alone?), rides off from Love as fast as possible with the spurs of Outrequidance (XII, l. 120). All that Love and Phaeton's mother Imagination have counselled is forgotten. The horses, further glossed as "Diviers Meurs, contraires a Bonnes Virtus" (XII, ll. 126–27) [various ways of life opposed to good virtues], take advantage of Phaeton's ignorance and lack of control to bear him away from Reason's path "ensi que li amans fort enamourés, espris et enflamés des brandons amoureus, pert souvent maniere, avis et contenance, et oublie au ferir et au cachier les chevaus de l'escorgie d'Atemprance, mes chemine tous jours avant, sans rieule et sans mesure" (XII, ll. 130–35) [as the lover very much in love, inflamed by and burning from the firebrands of love, often loses moderation, self-control, and comportment, and forgets to strike and drive on his horses with the whip of Temperance, but pushes ever on without control and without measure]. The horses lead on desire, as Love no longer holds them to their right path. The disaster parallels that of the lover in the psychomachia of Rose's dream and recalls Venus' firebrand in the *Rose*. Phaeton's is a *fole amour*.

There are also links with the primary events in the Neptisphelé-Pynoteus story: the lion killing Neptisphelé and Pynoteus' prayer to Phebus. As in the *Roman de la rose*, where the firebrand of Venus leads to discovery of the lover and the intervention of Male Bouche and Jealousy, the lion makes Neptisphelé the victim of *envie* (IX, ll. 130–38).[20] The intervention of the *médisants* in Phaeton's case is more serious, because Phaeton lacks discretion. So far his case parallels the events leading up to the construction of Jalosie's castle in the *Rose*. But *pité* and *franchise* intervene, as in Guillaume de Lorris, when Jupiter and Nothus extinguish the fires started by Phaeton's wild ride. *Fole amour* must return to the *voie de raison* and submit to the tutelage of the god of Love.

Mes souvent, quant Pité et Francise voient l'amant en che parti et amorti de toute joie, il li pourcachent sa pais enviers sa dame et estaindent les gengles et les envies des mesdisans et li renluminent sa joie [return to Phebus of the chariot of the Sun]; et se ceste grasce li revient, lors se poet il tenir pour euwireus et, de che jour en avant, lui aviser et atemprer par quoi il se gouverne plus sagement en la vie amoureuse qu'il n'ait fait. (XII, ll. 150–57)

[But often, when Pity and Franchise see the lover in this situation and deprived of all joy, they reconcile him with his lady and silence the prattling and envious chatter of the slanderers, and brighten his joy anew; and if that grace is returned to him, he may then consider himself fortunate, and henceforth take stock and moderate his conduct, whereby he conducts himself more prudently than before in the life of love.]

The pattern is the same as at the beginning of the courtly tradition, and as Guillaume de Lorris revitalized it.

visio   + cogitatio   > passio   > amor
dous regard + ymagination > desir   > amour
Mercurius   + Climene   > Phaeton > Phebus

The alternative to following Phebus, that is the *praecepta* indicated by *avis* and *atemprance,* is the wild chariot ride and the ultimate destruction of *fole amour.* But Froissart, like Andreas Capellanus, Guillaume de Lorris, and especially Machaut before him, leaves the lover with consolatory hope, provided he correct his *fole amour* and found his love life on prudence and good order, as reason would dictate.[21]

TITLE IN NARRATIVE AND EXPOSITORY EMANATION

The title of the *Prison amoureuse* is significant for Froissart's conception of Imagination. As a rule, medieval commentaries and accessus took the title seriously in treating literature. Together with *materia* and *intentio,* it was an important and constant desideratum in the formulae for interpretation. Conrad of Hirsau describes the title thus: *"Titulus . . .* est brevis ostensio sequentis operis"[22] [The title . . . is a brief presentation of the ensuing work]. An accessus to Prudentius' *Psychomachia* reads: "Titulus uero a nomine Titan dicitur, quia sicut hinc uniuersa illuminantur, sic per titulum subsequens opus manifestatur"[23] [Title comes in fact from the name Titan; for just as the latter illuminates the world, so the title makes known what the ensuing work is]. The accessus use various devices: simple summary statement of the contents,[24] translation,[25] names of principal personages.[26]

The significance of the dit's title is usually obvious: *Roman de la rose; Panthère d'amours; Dit dou vergier, dou Lyon, de l'Alerion, de la Fonteinne amoureuse.* It singles out a striking Image from which derive the fascination and discursive elaboration of the dit. For example, Baudouin de Condé says of his dit, the *Prison d'amours:*

Ceste prizons dont ci parolle
Iceste cançon de carolle,
C'est la prizons d'amors sans doute

> Et mult set poi qui de çou doute.
> Car cil ki premerains le dist
> Par amors le canta et fist,
> Ne onques n'eut entention
> Se de la prizon d'amors non.
>
> (vv. 128–35)

[The prison spoken about in the preceding carol is of course the prison of love; he who doubts it shows his ignorance. For the one who first said so sang and wrote about it out of love; nor did he intend any other meaning than that of prison of love.]

Baudouin justifies the Image and interpretive title on the "auctorité / D'un rondet" (vv. 124–25). Similarly, the title *Alerion* refers to the most noble of the predatory birds represented, and thus is identifiable with the lady and the best love. It is the source of the most important interpretation in the dit. Froissart also uses a central Image as the title and core of his dits: *Joli buisson de jonece, Orloge amoureus, Paradis d'amour.* But a title may be enigmatic. We learn only about halfway through Machaut's *Remede de Fortune* that the remedy does not spring from Fortune but rather is used against Fortune, and that the remedy is Hope (*Remede,* v. 2286). On the other hand, the bush that inspires the title to Froissart's *Espinette amoureuse* at first glance hardly seems worthy of such prominence. As sometimes happens in medieval poems, the title seems to give undue weight to a minor subject. The title to the romance *Palamède* has been recently changed, despite its prologues, to *Guiron le courtois.*[27] However, the title *Espinette amoureuse* is significant.

The *Espinette* is a variety of hawthorn known elsewhere in Froissart's time as "blanche espine."[28] It appears nine times in the poem, in verses 385, 619, 986, 1017, 1393–95, 1922, 1947, 3659–60, and 4198. Most are passing references, hence the apparent insignificance of the hawthorn rose in the poem. The first and most important reference coincides with the beginning of the poet's love.

> Je me tenoie en un moment
> Et pensoie au chant des oisiaus,
> En regardant les arbrissiaus
> Dont il y avoit grant fuison,
> Et estoie sous un buisson[29]
> Que nous appellons aube espine,
> Qui devant et puis l'aube espine.
> Mais la flour est de tel noblece
> Que la pointure petit blece.
> Non pour quant .I. peu me poindi,
> Mais m'aventure a boin point di.
>
> (vv. 380–90)

[I paused a moment to think on the song of the birds while looking at the bushes found there in great profusion. And I was standing under a bush we call *hawthorn* which blooms before and after dawn. But its flower is so noble that its prick causes only a small wound. Nevertheless it did prick me a little—but I'll relate my adventure in due course.]

The *pensée* of Froissart (also v. 378) is expanded in what follows to include the Judgment of Paris. Paris, who represents Froissart, receives from Venus the promise of a fair lady's love. When the vision vanishes, Froissart is still alone, but now perplexed, under the *espinette* that inspired it (vv. 619–21). A first *aventure* (v. 684) soon takes place. He meets a maiden and falls in love while reading together with her Adenet le roi's *Cleomades* (vv. 696–787). Thus the single, briefly described Image of the hawthorn rose, like Rose's reflections on Neptisphelé and Pynoteus in the *Prison amoureuse*, gives rise to both the dream vision of the Judgment of Paris and the actual encounter with the maiden Venus promises him in the dream.

A similar encounter later inspires the composition of a virelai. He presents a rose to his lady in the third adventure (vv. 981–1007), then retires to compose the virelai "desous le rosier" (v. 1017) [under the rosebush]. In the seventh adventure, Froissart alludes to the beginning of his love under the hawthorn (vv. 1393–96). Similar allusions occur in his lengthy complainte (vv. 1922, 1947):

> quant je dors et quant je velle,
> Tous jours m'est presente en l'orelle
> Ma dame, qui blance et vermelle[30]
> Est com la rose.
> (vv. 1944–47)

[Whenever I sleep and whenever I wake, always present to me is the voice of my lady, who is white and red like the rose.]

This clarifies the juxtaposition of the lady's qualities and the "pointure" (thorn prick) in verse 1922. And it prefigures their narrative and expository amplification. "Et lors aparmoi je propose / Les grans biens de li et les glose" (vv. 1948–49) [And then by myself I consider her great qualities and I comment on them]. In verse 3659 he shares the midday meal with his lady while seated under the hawthorn. The final allusion occurs in the last line of the dit, where the title is given: "Ains languis en vie ewireuse / Dedens l'Espinete amoureuse" (vv. 4197–98) [Rather I languish in a happy life in the *Espinette amoureuse*]. The Image in the title is indeed significant. It is a bush under which one lunches and reads books; and it is the book or dit itself. Finally, its flower may be glossed as the qualities of the lady. "Froissart joue sur le mot," remarks Fourrier.[31] And he enriches the significance of the

Image by inventive amplifications, glosses, and narrative developments. From the single finger prick in verse 389 arises a poem of varying modes and levels, which includes the sequence of Images and figures, the comparisons more or less amplified, that Froissart uses to elucidate his narrative: the Judgment of Paris, Phebus' chase of Daphne, the pseudo-Ovidian mirrors of Papirus and Ydorée. It includes as well the rhetorical, abstract developments of thought and emotion contained in the fixed forms. And finally, it underscores a suite of eighteen adventures alternating, as in the *Roman de la rose,* with solitary reflections, lamentations, expressions of joy and hope. It transcends the single *Espinette amoureuse* to include the *Joli buisson de jonece,* its conclusion both in plot, Imagination (he leaves the hawthorn at the end), and thought (he abandons the life of love at the end).

The *Espinette* has a prologue which is meaningful only when taken together with the *Joli buisson.*

> Pluiseur enfant de jone eage
> Desirent forment le peage
> D'amours paiier, mais s'il savoient
> Ou se la congnisance avoient
> Quel cose leur faut pour paiier,
> Ne s'i vodroient assaiier,
> Car li paiemens est si fes
> Que c'est uns trop perilleus fes.
> Non pour quant gratieus et gens
> Samble il a toutes jones gens.
> Je m'i acord, bien ont raison,
> Mais qu'il le paient de saison,
> En temps, en lieu, de point et d'eure!
> Et se c'est desous ne deseure
> L'eage qu'il leur apertient,
> Folie plus que sens les tient.
> Mais tant qu'au fait, j'escuse mieux
> Assés les jones que les vieux,
> Car jonece ne voelt qu'esbas,
> Et Amours, en tous ses esbas,
> Quiert cheuls trouver et soi embatre
> Entre euls, pour soi et ceuls esbatre.
>
> (vv. 1–22)

[A number of young people are eager to pay love's passage. But if they knew or realized what they have to pay, they would not want to make the attempt. For such payment is very dangerous to assume. Nonetheless it appears pleasant and fine to all young people. I agree with them, they are quite right—provided they pay in season, and at the right time, place, moment, and hour! If they are too early or late, they have more folly than good sense. But as far as the deed itself is concerned, I would more easily excuse the young than the old. For youth seeks only to play, and Love in all his games seeks them out and joins company with them in order to amuse himself and them.]

The cycle begun in youth is complete at the end of the *Joli buisson,* where the aging lover, sensing the folly of continuing to act as if he were still young,[32] turns in prayer to the Virgin Mary.

In the *Joli buisson* the ages of man are assimilated to the seven planets (vv. 1598–1707), for "leurs saisons ont toutes choses" (v. 1735) [their seasons contain all things]. Particularly significant is the passage from Mercury (ages four to fourteen) through Venus (ages fourteen to twenty-four) to Mars and Jupiter. The first transition is represented by the Judgment of Paris in the *Espinette.* The poet approves Paris' judgment and thereby passes from the tutelage of Mercury to that of Venus (vv. 522–36).[33] One cannot always remain a child. With Venus he enters into Jonece. Jonece personified sets forth the "astrological" description of the ages of man in the *Joli buisson* as suggested in the reference to the "saison" of the "enfant" and the "jones gens" in the *Espinette* prologue.

Venus' words to her new ward in the *Espinette* fit into this context.

> .X. ans tous entiers
> Seras mes drois servans rentiers,
> Et en apriés, sans penser visce,
> Tout ten vivant en mon servisce.
> (vv. 605–8)

[for ten full years you will serve me and be maintained by me; and afterwards, with no vile thoughts, you will spend the rest of your life in my service.]

Froissart is first the young lover, then the poet of love. For, like Charles d'Orléans later, Froissart continued to write love poetry after love itself passed away. The period as *servans rentiers* corresponds to the training of a young knight before he assumes his adult obligations. Froissart does not describe the full ten years of service, but breaks off in the *Espinette* shortly after the lady's formal acceptance of his service under the hawthorn (vv. 3659, 3696–98). In the *Joli buisson* we are at the end of the ten years (v. 2005). Taking leave of Venus is now "in season." The "joli buisson de jonece" in the aging man's dream fades, as Mercury did earlier, and with it Venus and the hawthorn disappear. "Teles vuiseuses" (v. 5156) [such idle occupations] seem sinful now (cf. *Joli buisson,* vv. 5152–86).

In the *Prison amoureuse,* Flos himself raises the question of a suitable title. Froissart elaborates extensively on the "proprieté de la signification que g'i regarde et pour quoy tel nom je li baille" (XII, ll. 11–13) [suitability of the signification I see in it and why I give it such a name]. The title is determined by two considerations. First, the contents of the work he and Rose have compiled:

nos deus afaires presens et passés en regardant et ymaginant lettres, epitles, escriptions, traitiés amoureus, balades, virelais, complaintes et toutes manieres de devises, dont nous avons l'un l'autre ensonniiet par pluiseurs fois, ensi com il est contenu et ordonné rieuleement dedens che livre. (XII, 11. 16–21).

[both our affairs past and present, while considering and imagining letters, epistles, inscriptions, writing on love, balades, virelais, complaintes, and all kinds of writings which oft we both have concerned ourselves with, as they are contained and arranged in order in this book.]

Second, and more to the point, is the nature of the *vie amoureuse* itself. That life is a prison, but a "prison jolie et amoureuse" (XII, l. 29). This prison, inhabited by Rose and his lady as by Flos and his, is agreeable when the lovers are "assés en unité parfete" (XII, l. 31) [in quite complete harmony], that is, in a state of equality.[34] Thus the Image inspires the Imagination of the entire poem. The *vie amoureuse* is a *prison amoureuse,* and that is precisely what we see in the *Prison amoureuse.* Though more elaborate, the principle of amplification is the same as in Raoul de Houdenc's relatively simple *Roman des eles.*

IMAGINATION IN FROISSART'S OTHER WRITINGS

Froissart's other writings sustain the importance of Imagination in his poetics. There are examples of its action in *Meliador.*[35] Imagination provides the allegory of the clock in the *Orloge amoureus* (vv. 19–25). Exposition in a didactic mode of an object of everyday experience does not destroy the initial fascination, the *mystère* the poet perceives in the object.

> Et se n'est pas seulement ordonnés
> Tant pour proufit et pour grant efficace,
> Qu'il est garnis de mistere et de grasce,
> Et la façon de li, selon m'entente,
> D'un vrai amant tout le fait represente
> Et de loyal amour les circonstansces.
>
> (vv. 26–31)

[And it is not composed only for profit and efficiency; for it is adorned with mystery and grace. And its form, to my understanding, represents all the features of a true lover, and the characteristics of a faithful love.]

The emanation of mystery into the poet's life enhances contemplation and wonder before the object. The method is similar to Froissart's derivation of Rose's dream from the story of Neptisphelé and Pynoteus. In both cases, two modes of reality meet in common signification.

In the *Paradis d'amours,* Froissart explicitly cites Pygmalion to distinguish between substantial and vain Imagination. Pygmalion derives nothing but empty Imagination from his statue, whereas Froissart has the consolation of his poetry,

> ma querelle gaie
> Qui à la fois me resgaie.
> Ju sui enclos en la haie
> Là où Melampus abaie
> Après son mestre Acteon.
> (vv. 1134–38)

[my happy complaint, which at the same time makes me happy again. I am enclosed in the brush where Melampus bays after his master Acteon.]

In the *Paradis d'amours* Imagination is a source both of despair, where it is without substance like an *insomnium,* and of joy, where it is nourished with hope, the substance of future happiness. These are Radolphe of Longchamps' *confusa* and *vera imaginatio.* The validity of Imagination is its substantiality rather than its empty vanity.

> Dont, quant j'ai bien conceü les substances
> Et la vertu qu'il moustre et segnefie,
> Et j'ai aussi consideré ma vie,
> A son devoir est justement parée
> Quant je l'ai à l'orloge comparée.
> (*Orloge,* vv. 32–36)

[Thus when I have clearly conceived the substance and the quality it represents and signifies, and I have also considered my life, the latter is fitted to do its duty when I have compared it to the clock.]

The timepiece that delineates a good love also marks its end in the *Espinette amoureuse* and *Joli buisson de jonece.* Froissart's diversified Imagination is founded on a firm and consistent reading of his material. This will hold even after his ten years of love service are complete and he retires to verbal allegiance to Venus. The fixed forms continue to express an idealized love in Imagination. Despite the conclusion to the *Joli buisson,* Imagination preserves an undying Image in the heart.

> Et puis en moi imaginai
> La beauté ma dame et le pris;
> A la rose je le compris,
> Et saciés qu'en riens ne mespris.
> En ce doulc pourpos demorai
> Et demorrai voir à toutdis,
> Et quant j'irai en paradys
> Avecques moi l'emporterai.
> (*Joli mois de may,* vv. 197–204)

[And then I imagined the beauty of my lady and her renown; I compared her to the rose, and you may rest assured that I did not err in doing so. I persevered in this sweet intention, and shall do so in truth all my life; and when I go on to Paradise, I shall take it with me.]

In this way Froissart can internalize his love as a rose that never fades, not even with death (vv. 289-97). His fate is not that of Troilus.

8

Verisimilitude and Imagination:
The Crisis in Late Courtly Poetry

Ausi di jou de moi, bele tredouce amie, ke jou croi ke aucune
medicine est par quoi vous me poés resusciter, mais jou ne sai
quele la medicine est, fors tant ke par la nature d'une beste saice on
le nature d'une autre.
                                   —Richart de Fornival

Et que savez vous, damoiselle?—En non Dieu, sire, il me moustra
bien hier quant il a force m'en faisoit porter. Car bien sachiez que
se il m'amast si comme il dit, ja telle chose n'eüst faite envers moi.
                                   —*Laurin*[1]

IN THE SECOND RHETORIC, poetry as invention relies on imitation, which in
turn looks inwards to the Imagination. At the end of the medieval period the
Second Rhetoric was to die out, but not without producing a number of
remarkable works illustrating the failure of Imagination as Guillaume de
Lorris, Machaut, and Froissart had used it to express courtly love and chivalric ideals.

The crisis in courtly literature that began at the end of the twelfth century
reached a climax in the *Queste del saint graal*. Transportation of Arthurian
history into the allegorical mode permitted the condemnation of the courtliness exemplified by the Arthurian romances, particularly by Chrétien de
Troyes. Jean de Meun's continuation of the *Roman de la rose* follows on the
devastation of the Arthurian ideal in the Lancelot-Grail cycle of the Vulgate
romances. The post-Vulgate *Roman du graal* expands on the theme of the
corruption of courtly values by human sinfulness. The knights of the Round
Table are blind to their own error in the *Queste;* like Amant in Jean's *Rose,*
they sink into clumsy foolishness and sensuality, murder and rape. The
courtly ideal as associated with courtly love persisted less, however, in romance than in the fixed forms and dream visions of the Second Rhetoric. Its
final demise came at the beginning of the fifteenth century. But it came less
from rigorist morality than from social and political problems that emerged in
the courtly tradition as frailty. Death, infidelity, war, old age—these are the
discordant themes that loom so large in Christine de Pisan, Chartier, and

Charles d'Orléans. Only in Chaucer and Gower do we perceive any serious questioning of courtly love as such in a context like Jean de Meun's. But even they are not adamant in their criticism. They only seem no longer to take the subject very seriously.

DEATH AND LOVE

> She replied: "Ulalume—Ulalume—
> 'Tis the vault of thy lost Ulalume!"
> —Poe

Robertson and Fleming identify the change in the late Middle Ages from abstract personification to example. "As a general statement . . . , the history of medieval allegorical poetry is one of an increasing degree of literary exemplification. There is in the history of this poetry . . . a movement from broad intellectual abstraction to concrete example and, hence, to verisimilitude."[2] Imagination thus moved gradually from the abstractions characteristic of earlier periods (personifications, bestiary figures) through mythological figures to exemplary personages in settings outside the dream. In a real, even contemporary, world of time and space personal problems or diversity may impinge. The shift reflects a new mentality and sensibility, and new topics arose to modify and replace the old ones.[3] The earlier preference for personification in garden and by fountain and for favorite mythological subjects like the Judgment of Paris, Pygmalion, Piramus and Thisbe, had given way by 1400 to poems about the end of love, and especially the death of the loved one. The poems are "realistic" in the sense that they are set in a given time and place and show forth limitations and finality. The prevailing mood is one of resignation, even despair, as Genius' prediction of the garden of Deduit's impending end received historical confirmation.

The theme of death was not unknown before 1400. The death of the lover is a frequent threat in the verse of the troubadours and trouvères.[4] Machaut used it in the two *Jugement* poems. But for him the death of the loved one was a pretext for defining two kinds of love and setting forth a particular conception of love. Even the *Voir-Dit* is oblivious to the eventual death of the narrator or the loved one, despite allusions to Machaut's age and infirmities. Love brings back youth and increases worth; the affections seem to enjoy an eternal springtime safe from the outside world. Some of Machaut's fixed forms propose similar idealistic dream worlds. Imagination is a metaphorical world where roses do not die, dreams become reality, and good love soars beyond the snares of Fortune. In Froissart the emphasis passes from the beginnings of love to its prosecution. The passage of time is perceptible; the dreams are episodic mirrors of day-to-day activities. Venus herself acknowledges chronological change and human limitations in the *Espinette amoureuse,* and the ages of man's life are weighed in the balance of love. A cleavage begins to become apparent between the possibilities of the dream world and the realities in the waking world of age, care, and sin. The *Joli Buisson de jonece* illustrates the rude awakening under the "planet" of the Sun, as the poet sees his own aging face in the mirror.

Christine de Pisan, in several cycles of balades and rondeaux, carries Machaut's and Froissart's conception of love to a conclusion reflective of experience not possible in the world of ideas, but perfectly comprehensible outside any dream world that is not a nightmare. Thus Christine subscribes to Genius' condemnation of the Garden of Deduit in Jean de Meun. Either by the death of her husband or by the unfaithfulness of one lover or the other (sex is no guarantee of legitimacy or victimization, as Jean de Meun made clear), the earlier idealism is violently, painfully amputated. The grief of the lady whose lover has died in Machaut's *Jugement* poems, or that of the lover whose lady has been unfaithful or married another, is poignant. But each still exemplifies an idea. Christine's lovers are not speculations on the quality and character of the best love. Rather they illustrate how she came to despair of the ideal, both in her private loss and in what she perceived around her. Imagination for Christine loses *senefiance* and love becomes false or confused.

What becomes of the exemplary lover under these circumstances? Oton de Grandson, the *Cent balades,* and Alain Chartier offer various answers. But in one way or another they all sound the knell for medieval courtly Imagination.

THE INVENTION OF ARGUMENTS:
NEW THEMES IN OTON DE GRANDSON

Chaucer's praise of Oton de Grandson—"flour of hem that make in Fraunce"—suggests the effect he had on his contemporaries. His invention of new topics makes Oton a forerunner of the last courtly poets, and puts the crisis of courtly idealism in sharp focus. He emphasizes the misfortunes that befall love and actually bring it to an end. Three possibilities are prominent in his writings: the death of the loved one, followed by a new love; infidelity; death of love and despair.

Oton's "Complainte de Saint Valentin"[5] begins with the lover's lamentations on Saint Valentine's Day because of the death of his lady (v. 38). The loss is said to be irreparable. Where could one find such perfection again?

> Car mon cuer vouldroit, a par soy,
> Choisir selon le temps passé,
> Ne jamaiz ne seroie amé
> De nulle qui approuchast celle,

179

Se trop grant debonnaireté
Ne se mesloit en la querelle.
(vv. 75-80)

[For my heart would, of its own accord, chose in conformity with its past experience. Nor would I ever be loved by anyone like her, if very high gentility did not intervene.]

This is no longer the dream world of Rose and Flos, where the mythology of Neptisphelé and Pynoteus illustrates the resuscitation and ongoing vitality of courtly love. Oton is speaking about a death in the real world. Mutability accounts for the conditional *se* in verse 79, which becomes prominent in what follows. Saint Valentine and Love intervene in fact (note the "trop grant debonnaireté" of verse 79) to encourage the distraught lover to seek a new love, permitted by Loyalty because Love would again be the source of the affection (vv. 105-12).

Love's argument is not unusual, but is to a certain extent topical. In the *Alerion* Machaut counsels the lover to forget an unfaithful lady. In the *Jugement Behaingne* he makes a similar recommendation to the lady whose lover has died, and practices what he preaches after the death of his first lady by loving Péronne d'Armentières in the *Voir-Dit*. The same is true in the *Songe vert*, nearly contemporary with the *Jugement* poems, whose theme is the rejuvenation and replacement of love after the beloved has died. Oton's dependency, his determination never to love again, conforms to the lady's decision in Machaut's *Jugement* poems. Christine de Pisan will express the same sentiments after the death of her husband.[6] But Machaut's lady was an Imagination, Christine's husband was real.

The Image of the lady can be transferred from one love to another without infidelity. Fidelity is to the love that unites the two lovers. The beloved hardly exists apart from her ideal Image, the abstract qualities that inspire her lover and determine his choice. She is the imitation of an idea, the mirror and projection of the Image in his heart. Thus the lover's reservation in the stanza cited above—"Se trop grant debonnaireté / Ne se mesloit en la querelle"—is taken up by Love and amplified in praise of a new lady:

Maiz vien t'en rendre,
En *tresgrant debonnaireté,*
A la non pareille beauté
Qu'on puist en ce monde veoir.
(vv. 123-26; emphasis mine)

[But come surrender yourself, out of a spirit of very high gentility, to the unparalleled beauty that is visible in this world.]

And indeed the resemblance between the former lady and the new one is striking—and effective.

J'entray en trop forte pensee,
Car aucunement ressembloit
A la belle qu'avoye amee.
(vv. 205-7)

[I fell into profound thought, for she rather resembled the beauty I had loved.]

The movement from *visio* by way of *cogitatio* cuts the thread binding the literal to the metaphorical, the real to the ideal world: Nominalism has triumphed over Realism. Imagination is infidelity, and loves are replaceable parts! The choice of "la merveille de ce monde" (v. 226) is easy. The former lady is not reincarnated in the new, she is replaced. The authority of Love seems irrefragable.

Et pour ce, sans nul penser faint,
La serviray toute ma vie,
Priant pour celle dont j'ay plaint
Si longuement la departie.
(vv. 245-48)

[And for this reason, with no false intention, I shall serve her all my life, while praying for her whose passing away I have lamented for so long a time.]

Love continues to be the same ineffable, abstract Image sought in the lady, an Image which can be projected onto another, providing a constant source of renewed wonder and revivified love. Even Machaut had known a revitalization through Péronne.

Yet the inadequacies of such projection could not escape detection. For Machaut in the *Voir-Dit,* a tension arises when Péronne's Image ceases to fit reality. Matthew of Vendôme had taught that description as Imagination should suppress all attributes not suitable to the mental conception one has of the object of description, or to the abstract type figured in the particular description. Part of the art of love is the approximation of the lovers to that ideal Image. It is part of the projection and the trials. But the discrepancy between Péronne and her Image shows that the divergent attributes suppressed in the Image were not necessarily absent in the individual. Death, rejection, or other circumstances incompatible with the *imaginaria visio* tend more and more to make the realization of the Image impossible, or rather incredible. The corollary and antithesis of Machaut's sublimation is Oton de Grandson's new love.

Oton himself does not fail to recognize human imperfection; his poetry lays heavy stress on the unfaithful and haughty in love, those *belles dames sans mercy* who ought to fear the fountain of Narcissus:

Encores ce de quoy plus me merveil,
C'est quë Amours n'a nul pouoir sur elle.

Seulle veult estre sans choisir nul pareil.
Nul oncques maiz n'y ot parler de telle.
(*Livre messire Ode,* vv. 2069–72)

[Moreover, what makes me marvel even more is Love's lack of power over her. She wishes to be alone, without choosing a partner like her; no one ever heard speak of anyone like her.]

The lady in a balade turns the tables on the "Complainte de Saint Valentin" by arguing that her infidelity is the effect of Love—a new love! "Je n'ay riens fait qu'Amours ne m'ait fait faire" (RN XLIX, v. 10) [I did nothing which Love has not caused me to do]. The cynical refrain announces the crisis in courtly literature. Machaut's defense in the *Jugement Navarre* of the unfaithful lady of the *Behaingne* is that she married and found a new, worthy love. Who is to say the lady in Oton de Grandson's balade has done otherwise? Imagination supposes universal applicability. Machaut urges in one of his balades: "Aimez vostre mari comme vostre mary, / Et vostre amy com vostre doulx amy". However, the finality of the Image of the unattainable lady as the unfaithful lady is unmistakable in Oton. The "Complainte amoureuse de Sainct Valentin Gransson" that concludes Piaget's edition is an insistent appeal to the lady to cease her infidelities and return to her lover. The Image of the unfaithful and unattainable lady was to give Oton de Grandson a popularity and influence far beyond what his talents as a poet would lead one to expect. Her Image, together with those of Saint Valentine's Day and other "metaphorical-realistic"settings, exercised a pervasive influence on Chartier, Chaucer, and Charles d'Orléans. Curiously, there is something Ovidian about his ladies, and his lovers are left only to recite complaintes.

FROM DIT TO COMPLAINTE

Another curious novelty is evident in Oton: the movement from the dit to the complainte. The dit itself was never a well-defined form, nor was its length or subject explicit in the beginning. Rutebeuf's major writings are dits. Nicole de Margival's *Panthère d'amours* is a dit of over 2600 lines, but it contains short dits interspersed among the balades, chansons, and rondeaux incorporated into the dream vision the large dit relates.[7] The complainte, usually a long poem, is regularly a part of the dit. Both Machaut and Froissart balance the lai and complainte in their dits containing fixed forms.[8] The complainte has its place at the moment of the poet's greatest despair, when it appears that the lady is irrevocably lost. In Froissart's *Espinette* this occurs when the lover hears of his lady's impending marriage. The *Fonteinne amoureuse* begins with a complainte because the lover feels himself permanently separated from his lady. Froissart's *Bleu Chevalier* is one long complainte thematically akin to Machaut's *Fonteinne amoureuse* through the use of the imprisonment motif. Oton de Grandson, in his one composition long and complex enough to be called a dit, the *Livre messire Ode,* uses a complainte to express a hopeless love.

But more striking are the discrete complaintes in Oton's work.[9] When the lady is in fact irrevocably lost, there is no recourse but to lamentation—or so it seems to be henceforth, unless one finds a new love, as Oton does in one poem. Earlier it had been the lovers' delay or mistakes in attaining equality with their ladies that prolonged their grief. This is still true in the *Livre messire Ode* (vv. 2265–69). But otherwise Oton takes a different tack from Machaut's. For Machaut the unfaithful loved one reveals the lover's error in judgment, and hence releases him to seek another more worthy of his sentiments. Corneille's heroes and heroines like Horace, Nicomède, Chimène, would not act otherwise. Machaut responds to the ignobility of the gerfalc in the *Alerion* by waiting for a new object for his affection (vv. 4019–60). But there is also the Eagle the lover loses through his own error (*Alerion,* vv. 3779–81). A parallel in Oton's *Livre messire Ode* is also one of the few examples of *poetrie* as *ymagination* in his writings.

The *Livre* is interspersed with mysterious figures who appear episodically to represent a certain state of love having some bearing on Oton's, then disappear. They are, as it were, potential adventures in the lover's quest for his lady. One of these lovers expatiates on his attachment to a falcon and a sparrow hawk; he lost the hawk through too much attention to the falcon:

> J'ay debatu par poetrie
> Et ainsi que par rimerie
> La douleur que mon cueur sentoit,
> Feignant que par deduit c'estoit.
>
> (vv. 1478–81)

[I have expounded by *poetrie* as well as in rhyme the pain my heart felt, feigning that what I did was pleasing.]

He goes on to equate the bird Images with his love. Oton acknowledges the validity of the comparison. But here the lover is unfaithful, while in Machaut's *Alerion* the lady had been unworthy. The alerion itself, the most noble of birds, brings to a satisfactory conclusion the period of trial and error. Its return to the poet is the return of a good love believed to have been lost. Oton de Grandson and the lovers he represents have recourse only to the complainte.

The complainte tended to replace the dit, as did the rondeau and balade cycle. In both, the reality of infidelity comes more and more to the fore. The *Cent Balades* of Jean le Seneschal set the debate, Christine de Pisan's balade and rondeau cycles illustrate its convolutions, and Chartier's *Belle dame sans mercy* caps it as the lover's very perfection seals his doom. The stanzaic arrangement of the *Belle Dame,* with its hundred regular strophes, is typical of the complainte.

The attack on the ideal of courtly love would seem to reflect simply greater awareness of the realities of love. Yet it is not possible to argue that men's and women's eyes suddenly opened to what preachers, moralists, humanists, and even a good number of courtly poets themselves had been teaching since the times of Marcabru and Bernart de Ventadorn. "Ne ce n'est pas, ne d'ier, ne d'uy / Que les meschans vont celle voie" (Christine de Pisan, *Cent Balades*, XXXI, vv. 11–12) [The discourteous didn't start down that path just yesterday or today]. Men and women could be, and are said to have been, perfidious. But never had the topics of change and imperfection enjoyed such prominence in the very subject Dante lauded for its excellence.

The demise of the courtly ideal came not from outside, to which it seems to have remained largely impervious, but from within, and at the very moment authors like Machaut and Froissart were striving to extend and thus to elevate the traditional idealism. It came by way of a breakdown in Imagination itself as the aesthetic of courtly poetry. Excessive abstraction and the dissolution of distinction, as in Oton's Saint Valentine's Day poem on the death of his lady, eliminated an essential trait of courtly Imagination, its recognition of unique excellence.

> A la douçor de la bele seson,
> Que tote riens se reprent en verdor,
> Que sunt biau pré et vergier et buison,
> Et li oisel chantent desor la flor,
> Lors sui joianz quant tuit lessent amor,
> Qu'ami loial ne voi més se moi non;
> Seus vueil amer, et seus woil ceste honor.[10]

[With the sweetness of the new season when all things grow green again, when the meadows, orchards, and bushes are beautiful and the birds sing on the flower, then am I joyful when everyone ceases to love. For I see no faithful lover except myself. I want to love alone, and I wish to be the only one to have that honor.]

In Machaut's *Remede* the description of the lady is a mirror in which the lover seeks his own reflection, in order to be like his lady and thus an equal worthy of her love. Machaut's idealism does not alter this traditional notion of the lady as mirror.[11] What had existed before was the possibility of representing esential distinctions in the qualities of the lady and lover, and especially in the configuration or at least combination and hierarchy of those qualities.

Erich Köhler's description of the different qualities of knights of the Round Table is valid for all courtly figures and the Images that represent them. "Die Tatsache, daß es sich hier nicht mehr bloß um den Einzelnen schlechthin, sondern um seine Individualität handelt, bekundet sich darin, daß der *aventure*-Träger nicht ein beliebiger Ritter der Tafelrunde, sondern immer ein bestimmter, auserwählter ist, an dessen Taten sich erst die Gemeinschaft bestätigt findet. Die Artusrunde bildet einen erlesenen Kreis von *Gleich-*

Gestellten, aber nicht *Gleich-Gearteten.* Sie alle sind zum Abenteuer, d. h. zu jedem Abenteuer *aufgerufen,* aber *erwählt* ist jeweils nur einer."[12] [It is no longer merely a question of the individual; his individuality is also at stake. This is apparent from the fact that the knight who achieves the adventure is not just any knight of the Round Table; rather, it is always a particular knight elected to vouchsafe the group's integrity by his achievements. The Arthurian knights form an elite circle of equals; but they are not all alike. Each and every one is summoned by the call to adventure—that is, to each adventure. But only one is destined to achieve it.] There is evident in early Arthurian romance a movement away from purely historical chronicle and its insistence on literal factuality. Geffrei Gaimar exclaimed at the moment romance was to emerge from chronicle history (his *Engleis* contains a version of the Havelock lai):

> N'est pas cest livre ne fable ne sunge,
> Ainz est de veire estoire estrait
> Des anciens reis e de els fait.
> (Shorter Epilogue, vv. 16–18)[13]

[This book is neither fable nor idle dreaming. Rather it is taken from true history about the former kings, and they are the subject of it.]

Chrétien's romance world apparently possessed for him no historical basis. Arthur does not figure in the *translatio studii et imperi* in the *Cligès* prologue. Rather the Arthurian world is a suitable escape for those weary of the world's falsity and baseness, as he argues in *Yvain.* Not that the ideals of subsequent courtly literature are lacking in historical writing. Geoffrey of Monmouth had extolled courtesy, chivalry, and love at Arthur's court, and the *Echecs amoureux* and its Commentary were still repeating and elaborating on his words at the end of the Middle Ages in France. Gaimar himself had criticized a certain contemporary named David for leaving love out of English history.

> Ore dit Gaimar k'il tressailli,
> Mes s'il uncore s'en volt pener,
> Des plus bels fais pot vers trover:
> Ço est d'amur e dosnaier,
> De boscheier e del gaber
> E de festes e des noblesces,
> Des largetez e des richesces
> E del barnage k'il mena,
> Des larges dons k'il dona;
> D'iço devereit hom bien chanter,
> Nient leissir ne trespasser.
> (vv. 6502–12)

[Now, Gaimar says he erred. But if he still wants to make the effort, he can write verse of the finest subjects: that is, about love and lovemaking, kissing and teasing, festivals and noble undertakings, largesses and high possessions, the knighthood he practiced

185

and the generous gifts he gave. These are the subjects one should sing about, without leaving out or passing over anything.]

Gaimar is speaking of Henry Cortmantel. But his conception of the subject is that of Wace and Chrétien, his abstractions those of Guillaume de Lorris. The transfer from historical personage to romance Imagination permits the invention of the varied exemplary types Köhler suggests. The abstract qualities and deeds in Gaimar's court are thus preserved by Chrétien for use in the Imagination of Guillaume de Lorris. Variation of the abstract attributes and exploitation of their semantic range permit adaptation, refinement, and originality. The didactic intention of historical romance permits the transfer of distinct, exemplary types to the particular mode of allegorical romance based on personification, and eventually to the late medieval dit with its exemplary mythologies.[14]

Andreas Capellanus recognized the same distinctions in the kinds and quality of love. They lie behind his implicit refusal to set forth a systematic code of love for all times and places. And they are fundamental to his division of lovers into a hierarchy consistent with his own society, but with due regard for essential differences in quality, character, and worthiness by the possibility of crossing class lines (see for example "Plebeius nobiliori feminae," etc.) because of inherent nobility. Each lover has a unique, though typical or stylized, potential capable of being realized, not in knightly adventures as in Arthurian romance, but through the adventures described in the *Roman de la rose:* encounters with the lady leading to the formation and education of the lover.

When, however, the death of the first lady in Machaut's *Voir-Dit* is literally followed by a return to poetry for the sake of Péronne d'Armentières, we may well recognize that a courtly principle takes precedence over individual inclination, as if by some *hoc agat*. But it is also obvious that unique excellence is coming close to interchangeability.[15] Oton de Grandson goes the full distance. Thereupon the discrimination of Imagination is lost, and the poetry will follow soon enough. Uniqueness is henceforth interesting only as the decline from the ideal.[16] We have a sudden flourish of unfaithful, harsh, cruel ladies and cynical, deceptive lovers. The old man rather than the young lady defends courtly love in the *Cent Ballades* compiled by Jean le Sénéschal. Jean de Garencières admits that love may turn to hate.[17] In the *Belle Dame sans mercy* the perfect lover dies because perfection and love have temporal limits. Various attempts to retain the old ideal by the composition of dits for another lover, a practice regularly followed by Chaucer, gains for the "other" our commiseration. Machaut's *Fonteinne amoureuse* and Froissart's *Bleu Chevalier* are attempts in this direction. But they do not succeed in rejuvenating courtly Imagination sufficiently to preserve it as a viable mode. More successful was the interlace of various loves of the author, friends, or patrons in Froissart's *Prison amoureuse* and, to a certain extent, Chartier's *Livre des quatre dames*. Oton used this technique as well in his *Livre messire Ode,* bringing in a number of episodic, anonymous cases of varied interest. So too did Chartier in the *Belle dame sans mercy,* linking the sorrowful lover before an intransigent lady to the death of his own mistress in a situation not unlike that in Machaut's *Jugement* poems. But no solution would finally hold but that of Charles d'Orléans. In the sequel to his youthful *Retenue d'amours,* he takes leave of Love without so much as trying to determine what Love may have to offer to replace his dead lady. This poem, with the significant title *Songe en complainte,* picks up Froissart's acknowledgement of the ages of man. The approach of Vieillesse is imminent, and the poet lapses into Nonchaloir. No wonder dreamless sleep is characteristic of Charles d'Orléans' later verse. In him, Imagination gives way to bemused contemplation of "chasteaulz en Espaingne et en France."

RENÉ D'ANJOU

There were writers who continued the courtly tradition into the French Renaissance: the Burgundian poets, the Grands Rhétoriqueurs,[18] the circle linked to the Marots, and the Lyon poets like Scève and Louise Labé. Italian influence began to make itself felt beginning with René d'Anjou. And Imagination continued as a method and a mode. Dante's writings treat it prominently. And Pico della Mirandola's treatise *De imaginatione* bears witness to continuing concern with the subject. However, love when treated by these writers is by and large something new. Dante's Beatrice is not the lady of medieval French literature, not because her attributes change, but because her essence does. Machaut's sublimation of courtly love remained secular, subject still to the incriminations of Male Bouche. Male Bouche is possible because of the jaunty indifference to good love professed by the Maiden in the *Cent Ballades.* But that indifference is predicated on infidelity, which leads in turn to suspicion and refusal by the beloved, and the complainte and death or old age of the lover. All these factors come together in the writings of René d'Anjou, king of Sicily.

René's two principal works are the *Mortifiement de vaine plaisance* and the *Livre du cuer d'amours espris.* In both Cuer is the central figure, and both stress the failure of courtly love.[19] The *Cuer d'amours espris* concludes with the failure of the lover's suit before Reffus and his abandonment of hope in the Ospital d'Amours. René's praise of Alain Chartier in this work shows that the lesson of the *Belle dame sans mercy* is paradigmatic in Cuer's defeat.

René's vision encompasses a wide range of loves: courtly, conjugal, faithless, adulterous, playful. The variety is suggested in the catalogue of famous lovers buried in the cemetery outside Love's palace. For René responded to the dichotomy suggested by the two parts of the *Roman de la rose* not by a sharp choice between the two authors, as in the quarrel of the *Roman de la rose*, nor by a *Rose moralisée* in the manner of Jean Molinet. Rather, like Andreas Capellanus, René is aware of many possible kinds and degrees of love. He knows that Love's arrows are more than Guillaume's five good ones and five bad ones, and that they may be mixed or fewer than those used by the god of Love in capturing the lover.[20] The cemetery for lovers ranges far and wide: Roman emperors, Greek heroes, Arthurian knights, kings and grandees of France, and love poets. Wives (their own or those of others), mistresses, courtesans, and ladies define by their situations the style and decorum of different loves. The height of the banners of those interred in the cemetery bears witness to the nobility of their loves. The whole is a veritable *poetrie* of typical loves. Nero's love for "la belle Romaine . . . Cristine" (§ 157, v. 8) is not of the quality of Marc Anthoyne's (i.e. Marcus Aurelius') for his wife Faustina (§ 159), so Nero's banner hangs below the others (§ 156, ll. 2–3). Caesar Augustus' love for his wife Livia stands high, for he was to her "mary et vray pasteur" (§ 155, v. 11) [husband and true shepherd]. The same distinctions apply to the poets Ovid, Machaut, Boccaccio, Jean de Meun, Petrarch, and Chartier.[21] Ovid, whose work is associated with "tout l'art de rethorique, fait per personnages" (§ 207, l. 25), shows

> comment
> Se pourra gouverner vers sa dame ung amant
> Tresbien, saigement, proprement et a point.
>
> (§ 208, vv. 10–12)[22]

[how a lover may conduct himself towards his lady very well, prudently, properly, and correctly.]

This conforms to Guillaume de Lorris' adaptation of Ovid in the discourse of the god of Love. The gravestone representation of Jean de Meun's rosebush shows only one rose (§ 213, ll. 6–8), and suggests the end of love Genius sees in the passing away of the garden of Deduit:

> Jehan Choppinel je suis, aussi dit de Mehun,
> Qui, entre autres amans, puis dire que fuz l'un
> Des poetes regnans qui plus parla d'amer.
> Au Dieu d'amours me suis voulu serf[23] reclamer,
> Celuy qui les amans en bien amer conforte.
>
> . . . .
>
> Si a l'on mis aussi, au dessus de mon corps,
> Cest escript, pour monstrer et donner a entendre
> Que des amoureux fault chascun soy venir rendre
> Gesir a l'ospital, en ce point que je y gis.
> Tous amoureux n'avront en fin autre logis.
>
> (§ 214, vv. 2–6, 9–13)

[I am Jean Chopinal, also called de Meun, who together with other lovers can say that I was one of the reigning poets of love. I agreed to be called serf to the god of Love, who comforts lovers who love well. . . . And the inscription has been placed over my body to show and make known that each lover must come to the hospital here where I lie. No lover will have any other lodging in the end.]

Alain Chartier is René's exemplar of poets. He stopped writing at his lady's death, and his Amant endured the harsh rejection of Reffus—as will Cuer in René's work. No doubt Péronne d'Armentières read the *Rose*, as did René, for she refers to it in one of the letters in the *Voir-Dit:* "Par ma foi se ce que vous m'escrisiés tenoit autant comme li rommans de la Rose ou de Lancelot, il ne m'en anuieroit mie à lire" (p. 28) [If what you wrote were as long as the *Roman de la rose* or *Lancelot*, I would most assuredly not mind reading it]. Neither saw falsehood in Jean's Amant. Otherwise René would have placed Jean's tomb outside Love's cemetery, in the unconsecrated ground reserved for false lovers (§ 220).

But René does not leave the literal conclusion to the *Cuer* in doubt. Cuer's fate is that of Troilus, and of Lancelot in the grail romances upon which the *Livre du cuer d'amours espris* is modelled. Cuer's quest fails because of the *médisants*. "Mais ce ne fut pas sans coup ferir, car il donna tel coup a Reffus, sur ung viel bacinet qu'il avoit, qu'il le fist tout embruncher sur les ioeulx; et l'un, qui estoit gros, villain et bossu, quant il le sentit ferir, luy ramena ung coup de toute sa force sur la teste, tellement que la coiffe de fer ne le garantist qu'il ne luy abbatist une des machoueres, et si cruellement l'ataindit que la cervelle de la teste luy paroissoit. Si cheut de celuy coup comme mort, et les mesdisans commencerent a chargier sur luy tellement qu'il n'estoit pas filz de bonne mere qui ne luy donnoit son coup" (§ 313, ll. 35–43). [But he didn't give in without a fight. For he gave Reffus such a blow on an old basinet that he caused it to fall down over his opponent's eyes. And one of the *médisants,* a big, villainous, hunchback fellow, upon seeing Cuer's blow, dealt a blow himself with all his might on Cuer's head, so that the latter's iron coif didn't prevent one side of his jawbone from being severed; and the blow was so cruel that the brain in his head was laid open. And he fell from that blow like a dead man, and the *médisants* began to rain blows on him—not one good mother's son spared him.] A description worthy of Prudentius! The exemplary dream is the menace, the nightmare of all good lovers who may fail. It is a complainte against treachery and treacherous loves, as René's epilogue brings out at the conclusion of the dream (§§ 314–15). Like Guillaume de Lorris, René d'Anjou thought his dream might be true: "Cueur, on peult tel songe songier / Qui n'est pas trouvé mensongier" (§ 31, vv. 2–3) [Cuer, one may dream a dream that does not turn out to have been false]. But the truth of René's *paraboles* (§ 1, l. 35) is twofold: the total vision of love's diversity and the specific threat of its failure. Guillaume de Lorris' promise of victory in the siege of Jalosie's castle becomes, under Chartier's influence, a defeat. René does not envisage a new love, nor even a new attack.

LA BELLE DAME SANS MERCY

C. S. Shapley has argued that Chartier's poem is a powerful and compelling indictment of the notion of courtly love as an ideal.[24] For him, the lady's realistic assessment of the lover's suit undermines every traditional argument in favor of courtly love, especially the rhetoric of that argument. Even when pushed into a corner, the lady can appeal to experience and thus demonstrate the probability that she will be deceived. She underscores the frailty of sincerity because of the passage of time: even a guileless lover may cease to love.

> Ung douleureux pense tousdis
> Des plus joyeux le droit revers,
> Et le penser des maladis
> Est entre les sains tout divers.
>
> (vv. 569–72)

[A person in grief always thinks the exact opposite of someone happy; and the thoughts of the ill are totally different from those of the healthy.]

The lady has read her *Cent Ballades*. She has taken to heart Christine de Pisan's balade and rondeau cycles describing frustrated and betrayed love. Obviously, the hell of haughty ladies depicted in Andreas Capellanus does not frighten her. Alain Chartier has finally undone courtly love in France.

Or has he? One of the lover's appeals to the lady is that he may die if she continues to spurn him (vv. 263–64). Her rebuff:

> Si gracieuse maladie
> Ne met gaires de gens a mort,
> Mais il chiet bien que l'en le die
> Pour plus tost attraire confort.
>
> (vv. 265–68)

[So gracious a malady rarely slays. But it behooves one to say so in order sooner to win consolation.]

And yet Chartier has the lover die (vv. 783–84). This outcome presents more problems than Shapley resolves.

It is typical of Chartier to pose dilemmas whose solution is clear, but whose realization depends on the determination of his public to uphold seriously the ideal which they profess and which is the subject of the given work. The last two stanzas of the *Belle Dame* are not a peroration on the death of a language whose words have lost their sincerity, but an appeal to keep that language alive by the realization of the ideal it expresses.

Sy vous pry, amoureux, fuyez
Ces vanteurs et ces mesdisans
Et comme infames les huyez.
Car ilz sont a voz fais nuisans.
Pour non faire les voir disans,
Reffus a ses chasteaulx bastis,
Car ilz ont trop mis, puis dix ans,
Le pais d'amours a pastis.
   Et vous, dames et damoiselles,
En qui honneur naist et s'assemble,
Ne soiez mie si cruelles
Chascune ne toutes ensemble.
Que ja nulle de vous resemble
Celle que m'oyez nommer cy
Qu'on appelera, ce me semble,
La belle dame sans mercy.

(vv. 785–800)

[And I appeal to you, lovers, to flee those boasters and slanderers, and to decry them for the infamous people they are. For they impede your progress. In order to give them the lie, Reffus has built his castles; for they have devastated the country of love for the past ten years. And may you, ladies and maidens in whom honor is born and collected, not be so cruel, either individually or collectively. May none of you resemble her whom you hear me name here, and who will be called, it seems to me, the *belle dame sans mercy*.]

Chartier's *Excusacion* bears out this conclusion. Accused in a literary quarrel of having decried love, defamed the good name of ladies, and made men afraid to love, Chartier denies all. He has merely related the complainte of a sad lover (*Excusacion*, vv. 209–16), without implying any more (vv. 177–84). Ultimately, the truth or falsehood of the debate in the *Belle Dame* depends on what happens in the real world. Accordingly, Love's anger subsides, and the decision on the validity of the *Belle Dame* is left to the ladies (vv. 225–32).

Chartier's *Quadrilogue invectif, Le Curial, Livre des quatre dames,* and *Livre de l'esperance* parallel the development of the debate in the *Belle Dame*. In each of the five works an ideal Image is held up for acceptance or rejection: France, the courtier, knighthood, the moral man, the courtly lover. The reader is confronted inexorably with the choice between the ideal and its corruption in practice. Just as the *Quadrilogue invectif* is a reaction to the losses of the Hundred Years War, so the *Belle Dame* is to those ensuing from the *Cent Ballades*.[25]

Shapley's study raises another problem. Are the traditional language and Images of the lover credible in Chartier's time? An answer may be found in Christine de Pisan's poems.

Christine vigorously defended courtly love in the quarrel of the *Roman de la rose*. In that quarrel, as in the *Rose* itself, no real distinction is made between marital and extramarital love. The problem is familiar to scholarship in the contrasting views expressed by Andreas Capellanus and Chrétien de Troyes on the feasibility of love in marriage. Andreas presents arguments for fundamental differences deriving from traditional, institutional conceptions of Christian marriage: the subordination of wife to husband, the error of jealousy in marriage, etc. Chrétien rode roughshod over such differences, representing essentially the same *fin'amors* within, without, and before marriage in *Erec, the Charrette,* and *Cligès.* And even in Andreas the opinion attributed to Marie de Champagne on the incompatibility of love and marriage is not taken to be universally true.[26] In any case, the literature does not suggest that it was a crucial problem in romance or chanson. The *Rose* quarrel ranges indiscriminately over the Ovidian extramarital examples and the truly conjugal examples like the Jealous Husband in Jean de Meun.

Christine de Pisan was a widow who wrote love poems about her husband and his death. The language of the poems is indistinguishable from usual courtly verse. "Ces mots et ces motifs, quoique mille fois répétés, gardaient un pouvoir d'expression que risquent de faire oublier nos statistiques et nos inventaires."[27] Hers is the language of the lover in the *Belle dame.* This is the only language Christine knew to express sincere, and conjugal, love. The language of courtly love was very close to that of conjugal love, according to the *Echecs amoureux* Commentator. Christine herself would surely not have wished to see the expressive language of the only suitable love she knew disappear beneath the canvas painted with a heavy hand that Jean de Meun throws up for our inspection. Even the excesses of ideal love seem appropriate to the representation of love for her dead husband. In the Image of Hero and Leander Christine sees all lovers.

> Ainsi pery furent d'un seul courage.
> Mirez vous cy, sanz que je plus sermone,
> Tous amoureux pris d'amoureuse rage.
> Voyez comment amours amans ordonne!
> *(Cent Ballades* III, vv. 21–24)

[Thus they died joined by a single heart. Mirror yourself in them, without my having to discuss further, all you lovers caught in the vexations of love. See how Love disposes of lovers.]

Her grief at the loss of her husband is a "rage desmesurée" (*Cent Ballades* VI, v. 1). She can no longer write, so great is the despair, so empty is she of "sentement" (*Cent Ballades* I, vv. 9–12). The Image of the deceased loved one, here historically and biographically verifiable, evokes the same language of grief used by Machaut, Oton de Grandson, and Chartier himself in the preliminary section in the *Belle Dame* where he speaks of his lady's death.

Qui voudroit mon vouloir contraindre
A joyeuses choses escrire,
Ma plume n'y saroit attaindre,
Non feroit ma langue a les dire.

(*Belle Dame,* vv. 17-20)

[If someone would compel me to write of joyous subjects, my pen would be unable to express them, my tongue could not utter them.]

Just so, Christine in a complainte to Death:

Quant tu m'ostas le bel et bon et sage,
Laquelle mort a tel tourment me livre
Que moult souvent souhait, pleine de rage,
Que mes griefs maulx soyent par toy delivre.

(*Cent Ballades* IX, vv. 13-16)

[When you took from me him who was handsome, good, and prudent, that death delivers me over to such torment that I quite often wish—when filled with vexation—that my grievous suffering be relieved through your intervention.]

Christine's personal grief seems to find adequate and meaningful expression in the traditional abstractions, Images, and conventions of courtly love. That many of the poems on her deceased husband were composed as long as ten years after his death detracts in no way from what for her was a viable, expressive language about love. It had been no different in the brief time of joy before his death.[28] Clearly, the language of courtly conventions was the only one she knew to communicate the reality and the depth of her feelings. Diane, the guide in the *Echecs amoureux* to the good love exemplified in Arthurian literature, speaks in Christine's *Dit de la rose* of "les roses jolies, / Qui en nul temps ne sont palies" (vv. 306-7) [the joyful roses that are never faded]. Christine herself asserts that there she is speaking of good love.

J'entens de l'amour ou n'a vice,
Mal, villenie, ne malice,
Car quiconques le die ou non
En bonne amour n'a se bien non.

(vv. 614-17)

[I mean that love that contains no vice, evil, villainy, or malice; for whatever anyone may say, in good love there is only good.]

This is uttered in condemnation of Jean de Meun's representation of love. Christine's ideal was still akin to that of Machaut, Guillaume de Lorris, and Chrétien de Troyes. But the roses did fade, and Genius' condemnation of the garden of Deduit prevailed.

Around the turn of the fourteenth century there appeared a plethora of books and debates alternately defending courtly love or attacking it by a largely cynical appeal to faithlessness, either as an advantage or as a danger.

No doubt the pleasure of debate was behind this. In Christine's cycles, and even to a certain extent in the *Belle Dame*, an interest in sentimentality for its own sake is also manifest. The sorrows of lovers are no longer the necessary *épreuves* on the way to happiness. They rather bear witness to the lover's growing awareness of how hopeless his or her suit is, and they finally decline into despair and silence.

> A Dieu, Amours; aprouchiée
> Suis de mort par toy; j'en sue
> Ja la sueur, et fichiée
> Suis ou pas, m'ame perdue
> Ne soit pas mais de Dieu eue.
>
> *(Cent Balades d'amant et de dame,* C, vv.
> 17–21)

[Farewell, Love. I have come near to death because of you. I am sweating the sweat of death, and am on the path on which my soul will not be lost, but received by God.]

The distorted syntax in the French is not inappropriate, after the smooth and polished rhetoric of over four hundred years. The lover has consigned herself to a lover's death. The silence is as final as Chartier's at the end of the *Belle Dame sans mercy*.

But the sense of devastation, the manifold attempt to heal the wounds caused by ideals wrenched from souls whose secular faith endured through crisis and criticism, was the effect of diversity. Chartier would try to uphold the various spheres of noble activity by the same Imagination that he used to speak of love. But since success depended on the practitioners, the link between Idea and individual that earlier had been productive of the *laetus horror* evoked in the *Epistolae duorum amantium* now found only horror before devastation and diversity. The age-old conflict, apparent in the first troubadours, between inner and outer worlds, Imagination and the senses, joy in winter, sorrow in summer, becomes universal by the end of the Hundred Years War.

In May, when every harte floryshyth and burgeneth (for, as the season is lusty to beholde and comfortable, so man and woman rejoysyth and gladith of somer commynge with his freyshe floures, for wynter wyth his rowghe wyndis and blastis causyth lusty men and women to cowre and to syt by fyres), so thys season hit befelle in the moneth of May a grete angur and unhappe that stynted nat tylle the floure of chyvalry of alle the worlde was destroyed and slayne.[29]

For Chartier, the desolation had spread from Agincourt, and was to overwhelm the mind (*Esperance*), the nation (*Quadrilogue*), the court (*Le Curial*), and love (*Belle Dame*). The world stood before the dilemma of the *Livre des quatre dames,* with no more resources in Imagination to praise or blame in an orderly, satisfying manner. The diversity of the world was of concern in

England, where it had an effect on Imagination and Imagination's literary inventions.

THE ENGLISH RHETORICIANS: GOWER AND CHAUCER

In England, some of the troubles with idealized love that Christine de Pisan and Chartier pointed to received thorough, wide-ranging examination. Like Christine, Chaucer seems to have been impressed by the frailty of love, the deleterious effect on the mind of continual sorrow, the world's hostility towards happy love. He struggles to adapt various perspectives in a meaningful whole. The attempt had to take into account not only ethic and ethos, as Professor Payne has suggested,[30] but also the various kinds of love that should be reducible to an orderly system and hierarchy. Chaucer portrays himself as no lover, just as he pretends to be a poor poet in *The Canterbury Tales*. The ostensible removal of the poet/narrator from sentimental involvement suggests his inability to resolve dilemmas and conflicts in a manner suitable to himself. Payne's contention that Chaucer was dissatisfied[31] with his work is certainly credible: no other medieval poet has left so many incomplete or reworked writings. The failure seems to lie in the implications of the Retraction, which reminds one of Chartier's abandonment of love, as it anticipates that of Charles d'Orléans. Unlike Troilus, who smiles at his earthly folly, Chaucer trembles before the judgment of his poetry on the Last Day.

Gower's *Confessio amantis* offers a more balanced, nearly systematic treatment of the problems of courtly love in the Genius-Amans dialogue. Gower's study of the subject correlates the errors of bad love with examples that show good love. Amans' uncertain way through this blend of instruction and exemplification suggests the mystification of the individual—even an Everyman lover like Amans—before abstractions and precepts that no longer seem to obtain universally, or even in closed contexts. Uncertainty as to right conduct in Andreas' dialogues becomes critical in the *Confessio*. Amans is not so firmly convinced—so decisive and authoritative—as the interlocuters in the *De amore*. The emphasis on perplexity is indicative of the doubts and problems that beset Gower's French contemporaries. Both Gower and Chaucer are familiar with Latin and French poetics and rhetorical tradition.[32] This lodges them—whatever their "English" traits[33]—well within the final stages of French courtly literature.

Chaucer's use of Imagination and its cognates conforms to the practice of the French poets. An Image as memory may be recalled, and projected onto reality. The projection in words is thus a transferred Image.[34]

> Whan any speche ycomen ys
> Up to the paleys, anon-ryght
> Hyt wexeth lyk the same wight
> Which that the word in erthe spak,

Be hyt clothed red or blak;
And hath so verray hys lyknesse
That spak the word, that thou wilt gesse
That it the same body be,
Man or woman, he or she.
And ys not this a wonder thyng?
(HF 1074-83)

This contrived or "Imagined" scene presents the lineaments of Imagination in personification. Another passage describes the entire process succinctly in the traditional manner: "For mannes hed ymagynen ne kan / N'entendement considere, ne tonge telle" (*Troilus* 4.1695-96).[35] Chaucer's Imagination extends to the various kinds of love described in the *Echecs amoureux* Commentary. The scope of Chaucer's exemplary illustrations is much broader than that of any other writer in our period. Nevertheless, courtly love falls within his purview.

Chaucer's conception of courtly love conforms to French usage in the expression *fyn lovynge* (LGW F544, G534). He delimits it in a gradualistic manner, fitting his judgment to context and character. The defense of *fyn lovynge* in the *Legend of Good Women* presupposes sincerity in the lovers (cf. F. 69). This is the problem of the *Cent Ballades* and the *Belle Dame sans mercy*. But Chaucer holds to Machaut's stress on *souffissance,* the loss of which (BD 703) plunges the lover into the *rage* of a Dido (BD 731-734) or a Troilus, of Arcite and Palamon (KnT 1804-10). The end of such love is despair or death (BD 1309-10), and indeed the reappraisal from a new level of observation, as in *Troilus'* "comic" conclusion. The examples in courtly literature forced the same reexamination by the reader. The relativity of gradualism is also apparent in the cleavage between love and "foul delyt, which that thow callest love" (LGW 1380) which we know from the *Echecs* Commentary and the *Tornoiement Antecrist*. Chaucer's tendency to emphasize the decline of *fyn lovyng* into a worse state is symptomatic of his generation's questioning of the reality or possibility of courtly love as an ideal.[36] In his case, the inversion of Guillaume de Lorris' progress from rage to love involves a concomitant lowering of the quality of Imagination to the farce, of the quality of courtly love to Jean de Meun's vision.

The lowering or sinking of Imagination is represented as idle fantasy or melancholy disturbance. Hence the allusions to "sorwful ymagynacioun" (BD 14), the "cloude of errour" which "lat hem nat discerne / What best is" (Tr 4.200-201), as desire turns to paranoic egocentricity (Tr 5.617-30). "Evyl ymagynacyoun" (LGW 1523), "veyn ymaginacioun" (KnT 1094) and "derke ymaginyng" (KnT 1995), "derke fantasye" (FrT 844) consume the mind like Racine's *flamme noire*. The domination of such affections is detailed by the Parson. "Now comth wanhope, that is despeir of the mercy of

196

God, that comth somtyme of to muche outrageous sorwe, and somtyme of to muche drede, ymaginynge that he hath doon so muche synne that it wol nat availlen hym, though he wolde repenten hym and forsake synne" (ParT 693). Replace "mercy of God" with the beloved's *mercy*, and the parallel with Chaucer's despairing lovers is obvious.[37] The opposite is the bright vision of fair beauty, corresponding in *poetries* to the valid depiction of abstract truth in the form of concrete analogy—a *vera imago*.

> trewly she
> Was hir [Nature's] chef patron of beaute
> And chef ensample of al hir werk,
> And moustre; for be hyt never so derk,
> Me thynketh I se hir ever moo.
>
> (BD 909-13)

The transposition into the domain of Imagination entails the abandonment of the gross and material, when Chaucer, in imitation of Boethius, leaves the world in its clouds and mists for the clear realm of thought visible in dream vision (HF 523-28, 973-78).

Chaucer did not confine his examples to those offered by social or religious categories. *Fyn lovyng* was as germane to good conjugal love as to extra-, pre-, or postconjugal love.

> he shal maken, as ye wol devyse,
> Of wommen trewe in lovynge al hire lyve,
> Wherso ye wol, of mayden or of wyve,
> And forthren yow, as muche as he mysseyde
> Or in the Rose or elles in Creseyde.
>
> (LGW F437-41, G427-31)

The emphasis is on fidelity because fidelity distinguishes *fyn lovyng* from other kinds of love.

Infidelity is a nightmare theme in Chaucer's vision of love, as in Christine de Pisan and Chartier. *Anelida and Arcite* rehearses the theme in a manner foreshadowing the *Belle dame sans mercy*. Anelida was "thirled with the poynt of remembraunce" (Anel 350). The Images, as is traditional in rhetorical instruction, are "of remembraunce the keye" (LGW F, G 26),[38] and thus the inspiration for the composition of the dream visions. Troilus' fate recalls that of the lover in the *Jugement Behaingne,* both in his rage because of Criseyde's infidelity (cf. the *Jugement Behaingne,* vv. 1724-39) and in the postmortem solution.

> Tout aussi tost com l'ame se depart
> Dou corps, l'amour s'en eslonge et espart.
> Einsi le voy partout, se Dieus me gart.
>
> (*Jugement Behaingne,* vv. 1717-19)

[Just as soon as the soul leaves the body, love withdraws and flees away. I see it happen so everywhere, so help me God.]

Thus Theseus is condemned for not loving faithfully.

> O, often swore thow that thow woldest dye
> For love, whan thow ne feltest maladye
> Save foul delyt, which that thow callest love!
> (LGW 1378–80)

The distinction implied between the loves of Alceste and Theseus is the same as that made in the *Echecs* Commentary between *fin' amors* and *amour commune*. Indeed, the elevation of women in the *Legend* parallels that of Troilus, and their common fate is indicative of human disintegration following betrayed love. The sin is not in the Good Women or in Troilus, but in those who betrayed their fidelity and made their own love into *foul delyt*. Chaucer's heroes and heroines rarely have the capacity to overcome past sorrow that Machaut suggests in the *Alerion* and the *Voir-Dit,* or that Chaucer may have perceived in Oton de Grandson. The betrayers are false-seeming liars, and Theseus is their exemplar. Or they are victims of circumstances but lack the will and *souffissance* necessary to dominate those circumstances, as we may observe by contrasting Constance and Criseyde. Betrayal was a fascinating subject for Chaucer's time, indicative of the intrusion of time and corruption into love subject to change and decline. The opposites of Alceste and Troilus are thus Theseus and Criseyde. The corruption of aristocratic ideals in reality, reflected here in love, was the subject of Chartier's virulent indictment. Among those who betray the courtly ideal or mouth it about hypocritically for private advantage, fidelity is but an imposition, elevated sentiment and trust—fine words on the descent into delight and mutability. The Manciple could see behind such antics, and his depiction is cogent.

> Ther nys no difference, trewely,
> Bitwixe a wyf that is of heigh degree,
> If of hir body dishonest she bee,
> And a povre wenche, oother than this—
> If it so be they werke bothe amys—
> But that the gentile, in estaat above,
> She shal be cleped his lady, as in love;
> And for that oother is a povre womman,
> She shal be cleped his wenche or his lemman.
> And, God it woot, myn owene deere brother,
> Men leyn that oon as lowe as lith that oother.
> (MancT 212–22)

The Manciple is speaking of "lust volage" (v. 239), as traditionally eschewed in *fin' amors* and roundly condemned in the *Legend of Good Women.*

It is noteworthy that the figures Chaucer adopts from *poetrie* are put to rhetorical service. That is, they have in themselves no application until he assigns them one. In this way they may represent diverse ideas, in conformity with the suitability of their character and traditional actions to the author's intentions.[39] Here Chaucer's usage corresponds to that envisaged in the treatises of the Second Rhetoric. And his elevation of types fits the notion of material style, or the adaptation of representation to class and station in life. The Manciple's view of the world and love is that of a Manciple. It differs from those of Alceste, the Knight, and the Wife of Bath. The lady the Manciple sees lie so low would arouse Alceste's curiosity as to how she arrived there and by whom, and perhaps an inquiry as to why she is "brought" there rather than going there of her own accord. Despite Chaucer's discretion in judging *fin'amors,* however, like his contemporaries he appears to be more interested in derogation from the ideal than in its successful realization. The *complainte* is a frequent device in his courtly pieces.

Chaucer's Imagination suggests a quandary, a "dissatisfaction" that Payne deduces from the number of incomplete works he has left, notably the *House of Fame, Anelide and Arcite,* the *Legend of Good Women,* and the *Canterbury Tales.* Reliance on book-learning, experience, and the Imaginary vision in search for truth did not lead, as in Machaut or the *Queste del saint graal,* to a clear elucidation of that truth, but rather to the discovery that commonplace arguments, when assembled from diverse contexts, do not unify. They produce only contradictions. The courtly love of Machaut and Froissart did not measure up against the experience of Christine de Pisan, the *Cent Ballades,* or the *Belle Dame sans mercy.* How was the poet to invent a suitable representation of that ideal? The *Parlement of Fowls* may contrast the law of Venus and the law of *kinde;* but the latter is itself not clear from the birds' debate, and the resolution of the poem lacks finality, even if it does preserve a certain courtliness in the delay accorded the tercel in making her choice.[40] The problem is the "key," the "keye of remembraunce" that Chaucer could not find. Like Marie de France long before him, Chaucer was still seeking "ceo k'i ert" in his *matière.* Such topical invention was always directed by a governing intention. But topical invention is a means to discover truth as verisimilitude. What if experience and the past suggest various, indeed contradictory truths? The only solution at the end of the quest is the unfinished book, followed by silence and retraction.

Chaucer's contemporaries who came under French influence evince both his use of Imagination, and the general breakup of courtly values inspired by Jean de Meun's criticism. Lydgate adapted the *Echecs amoureux* in *Reson and Sensuallyte.*[41] Gower made abundant use of Imaginary examples as evidence in the *Confessio amantis* (cf. 2.1897–1901).[42] Imagination can be "fals" or "fol" (1.958, 2269), but also apposite (1.386–88). It is the *ingenium* or *skil* of the author that makes it so.

ye have told me such a skile
Of this ensample now tofore,
That I schal evermo therfore
Hierafterward myn observance
To love and to his obeissance
The betre kepe.
                              (1.1866–71)

The process is evident in Gower's "Tale of Three Questions," especially in
the description of the king's adept use of Imagination:

Of depe ymaginaciouns
And strange interpretaciouns,
Problemes and demandes eke,
His wisdom was to finde and seke.
                              (1.3069–72)

The sense of such "strange matiere" (1.3092) was reached by "avisement"
and "entendement" (1.3121–22). Indeed, the composition of the *Confessio* is
dependent on Genius' desire to hinder Amant's excesses, to keep his love safe
from the Seven Deadly Sins and their corollary vices, and to direct him, by
examples of admirable and reprehensible conduct taken from history and
legend, towards a good love. The pitfalls are many, and lie on both sides of
the Middle Way suitable to a prudent love.[43] Permanence as fidelity and
happiness are hard to come by in love. In the end, Old Age catches up with all
human beings, to resolve the struggle as it did for Froissart and perhaps for
Machaut, and as it would for Charles d'Orléans.[44] But before allowing Amans
to outgrow love, Gower sets forth one of the most interesting medieval dis-
quisitions on the subject. The structure and argument are based on the use of
Imagination in all its usual senses. The purpose is to convince by descriptive
exemplification. The principle of Imagination thus relies on memory as a
source of exemplary Images suitable to argument. The examples are fashioned
to provide simple, clear morals apposite in love. The amplification elaborates
on the Seven Deadly Sins in the context of love. That is, the Sins are
specialized.[45] Each abstraction or abstract personification falls into configurations with other abstractions, then expands through exemplary figures into the
frame narrative and the examples that enforce the sense of the particular
configuration.

To hem that ben lovers aboute
Fro point to point I wol declare
And wryten of my woful care,
Mi wofull day, my wofull chance,
That men mowe take remembrance
Of that thei schall hierafter rede:
For in good feith this wolde I rede,

That every man ensample take
Of wisdom which him is betake,
And that he wot of good aprise
To teche it forth.
(1.72–82)

Wisdom, as revealed by Reason and not by Will, is crucial to cogent Imagination, and thus to correct use of *skil* in invention.

Gower nuances love's different manifestations in accordance with context and moral value. His configurations juxtapose by similitude or opposition various abstractions elicited from and illustrated by the examples. In this way, love as a preservation of *kinde* or species expands by analysis into different kinds of love that are in turn variously praised or blamed. The capacity to love well is dependent on the domination of Reason over Will.

For love is of a wonder kinde,
And hath hise wittes ofte blinde,
That thei fro mannes reson falle;
Bot whan that it is so befalle
That will schal the corage lede,
In loves cause it is to drede.
(3.1323–28)[46]

Thereby vision becomes confusion, and unity tends to division (cf. the prologue 849–55, 967–1001).

Gower is aware of "gentil love" (8.2345) governed by Reason. This is "love in good manere" (8.2010), where fidelity is preserved (8.2015) and there is accord with Reason (8.2020–26). All other kinds partake of lust, and "such lust is noght to loves kinde" (8.2028). Gower envisages a love akin to *fin'amors*, based on "juggement" (5.2491) or discrimination. Such "pure love" (5.2623) is acceptable—and rare (5.2625–36). In a fitting amplification of this problem, Genius embarks on a discussion of wisdom and love, in Book 8 under the general subject of Lust. The subject is pertinent to the proper exercise of Reason, for which Imagination provides examples in need of interpretation. By then the lover finds his Middle Way, eschews excesses, and in the end can turn from Youth to Old Age with the equanimity of a Charles d'Orléans. The reasonableness of Genius' lesson and the lover's change is vouchsafed by Cupid's withdrawing his arrowhead from Amans' heart and Venus' return of his letters of retention.

Most examples of good love in Gower lead to marriage and offspring. "Lex docet auctorum quod iter carnale bonorum / Tucius est, quorum sunt federa coniugiorum"[47] [Authority teaches 'that the fleshly pilgrimage is more secure for those who have the bands of wedlock upon them']. This is the essence of Guenevere's advice to two lovers in Chrétien's *Cligès*. Gower even extends the illustration to Pygmalion, thus turning Jean de Meun's Image into something akin to Machaut's in the *Fonteinne amoureuse* (4.371–436). The wife does not preclude the paramours. However, marriage is calmer and more peaceful, if there is love and reason in it (4.1467–84).[48] For some, of course, marriage was impossible.

> Ther was Tristram, which was believed
> With bele Ysolde, and Lancelot
> Stod with Gunnore, and Galahot
> With his ladi. . . .
> (8.2500–03)

Gower's "gentil love" is their only recourse, sad and often unsatisfactory as circumstances may make it. Yet it was a permissable, even worthy, option in his eyes. In this he shared the opinion of the *Echecs* Commentator. Thus the *Confessio amantis* serves as a guide through love and out of it, an *Ars* and *Remedia* beginning with youth and extending to Elde. The discriminating reader will perceive how apposite examples are to his or her particular demonstration, and direct the will reasonably so as to avoid the sins of lust and realize the virtues of courtly love. As in warfare and the governance of the state—human activities Gower most frequently compares to love—there are virtues and excesses. The *Tresor amoureux* raised the question of the relative worth of prowess in arms and love, and it was to reappear at the end of our period in *Jehan de Saintré*.

> Mi Sone, it is wel resonable,
> In place which is honorable
> If that a man his herte sette,
> That thanne he for no Slowthe lette
> To do what longeth to manhede.
> For if thou wolt the bokes rede
> Of Lancelot and othre mo,
> Ther miht thou sen hou it was tho
> Of armes, for thei wolde atteigne
> To love, which withoute peine
> Mai noght be gete of ydelnesse.
> (4.2029–39)

The correlation between love and prowess, or chivalry, is an old topic, especially in Arthurian romance. Chaucer also used it in Book 3 of the *Troilus*. Gower, like the *Echecs* Commentator, recognizes this fact, but criticizes arguments like Geoffrey of Monmouth's linking the two. The example of Hercule following directly on the preceding citation in the *Confessio* confirms this fact. The old and venerable examples contrast in Gower's mind with "amour commune au monde," or with Tereus' which "Nou regneth comunliche aboute" (5.6034). Prowess in arms is suitable for love, provided that like love it is honorable prowess (3.2241–2360, 4.1596–1710).

In the last analysis, Old Age resolves all love's problems, and thus it effects in Amans something like Death in Troilus. Removed from youth, he emerges from his dismay with only a keen interest—an objective, "scientific" interest—in the phenomenon love as set forth in its diversity in the *Confessio*. The mirror of self in which John Gower finds his own Image is the same mirror Froissart looks into at the end of the *Joli buisson de jonece*. Gower's way to *reposer* (8.2907) is Charles d'Orléans' way to Nonchaloir.

9

Imagination in the Poetry
of Charles d'Orléans and René d'Anjou

Novus tropus in figura,
Nova fit translatio,
Novus color in junctura,
Nova fit constructio.
In hac Verbi copula
Stupet omnis regula.
—Alain de Lille[1]

AGE AND LOVE: SHIFTING CONTEXTS IN IMAGINATION

One or two voices did go on past the time when the ideal of courtly love could still be considered viable. A major demarcation was brought about in Charles d'Orléans' middle years, however, by the death of his lady. His two longest love poems, the *Retenue d'amours* and the *Songe en complainte,* encompass the two stages in his life, much like Froissart's *Espinette amoureuse* and *Joli buisson de jonece.* Henceforth, Charles' attitude to conventional Imagination and idealism is that referred to in the refrain to Rondeau IV: "J'ay esté poursuivant d'Amours, / Mais maintenant je suis herault" [I have been a follower of Love, but now I am his herald-of-arms].

The *Retenue,* the first poem in Charles' autograph, is conventional, already dated at the time of its composition. It depicts the poet's initiation into the service of his lady, including a reading of the rules of Love. Peopled with personifications, it recalls Guillaume de Lorris' *Rose.* There are two significant differences, however: the unity of Venus and Love, and the intervention of Aage. Like her counterpart in Froissart's *Espinette,* Venus is here quite different from the source of burning *rage* in Guillaume de Lorris, and she has none of the rollicking cynicism of the goddess in Jean de Meun. Beauté and Jeunesse are given greater prominence than in the *Rose,* and are brought into close conjunction with Venus. But they are too well brought up to be wanton or unmindful of what is fitting and proper. Jeunesse is no mere child; she is "Dame Jennesse" (v. 17), who encourages the lover to love for the honor and worthy endowments that Love bestows on his servants (vv. 61–69); "Contre vouloir nul n'est contraint d'amer" (v. 70) [No one is compelled to love against his will]. Beauté intervenes in favor of the poet, seeking solace and mercy for him from Love (vv. 281–90). She oversees the contractual agreement made between the lover and Love, a conceit reflecting the use of homage in Guillaume de Lorris and the *trouvères* (vv. 311–14). In fact Beauté reads the rules of Love. The letters of retention given at the end confirm the agreement. Although Venus is not active in the *Retenue*, she is regularly associated with Love. Jeunesse leads Charles in the beginning "vers Venus et Cupido" (vv. 118–19). Venus is named with Love in the retention as a retainer (v. 401).

The intervention of Aage signals the transition to Jeunesse:

> quant je fu enforcy,
> Ung messagier, qui Aage s'appella,
> Une lettre de creance bailla
> A Enfance, de par Dame Nature,
> Et si lui dist que plus la nourriture
> De moy n'auroit et que Dame Jennesse
> Me nourriroit et seroit ma maistresse.
> Ainsi du tout Enfance delaissay
> Et avecques Jennesse m'en alay.
>
> (vv. 12–20)

[When I had grown, a messenger named Age gave letters of credence to Childhood, in the name of Lady Nature, and told her that she would no longer take charge of my upbringing, and that Youth would raise me and be my mistress. Thus I left Childhood and went on my way with Youth.]

Aage's presence is ominous, introducing the passage of time into the timeless world of Guillaume de Lorris. This comes home to Charles in the *Songe en complainte*, written after the death of his lady and at the end of Youth. The death confronts him with grief and the obligation to bear the loss; Love suggests that he make matters right by a new love. The *Songe* is linked to the *Retenue* by the reappearance of Aage at the outset as "Ung vieil homme" (v. 12) who reminds Charles of his appearance in the *Retenue* (vv. 19–24). He returns to lead Charles from Youth to Old Age.[2]

> Or est ainsi que Raison, qui sus tous
> Doit gouverner, a fait tresgrant complainte
> A Nature de Jeunesse et de vous,
> Disant qu'avez tous deux fait faulte mainte.
> Avisez vous, ce n'est pas chose fainte;
> Car Vieillesse, la mere de courrous,
> Qui tout abat et amaine au dessoubz,
> Vous donnera dedens brief une ataint.
>
> (vv. 25–32)

[Now resoun which that doth eche wrong redresse / And passith them hath made a gret compleynt / Vnto nature on thee and on thi maystres / Of wrong doon y drede thou, wolt be taynt / Avise thee now for yowthe y se hir faynt / For yelde the modir of vnweldynes / That alle downe betith in hir crewelnes / Not for thi good caste with thee to aqueynt (vv. 2564–71).]

With the death of Charles' lady (v. 55 [2594–95]), therefore, Love returns the letters of retention, and he moves, in the company of Comfort, towards the land of Passe temps in Nonchaloir to await Vieillesse. Although the time for loving has passed, the poet's interest in the subject does not flag (v. 495 [2990]). His later poems represent a remarkable revitalization of poetic Imagination.

THE BALADES: AN INAPPROPRIATE FORM

Charles' balades are for the most part conventional in their use of Imagination and in their subject matter, especially before the composition of the *Songe en complainte*. The poet laments his love through abstractions, sometimes personified. The personifications rarely go beyond simple metonymy, a single personification of an explicitly named abstraction. Even when several are grouped into a configuration, the sense is clearly literal. The exact equivalencies allow for little play on or between the literal and allegorical levels. The metaphors are clearly tagged. The appeal lies in elegant phrasing rather than in the metaphorical play of meanings that gives a fascinating lustre to the best allegory.

> Desploiez vostre banniere,
> Loyauté, je vous en prie,
> Et assailliez la fróntiere
> Ou Deuil et Merencolie,
> A tort et par felonnie,
> Tiennent Joye prisonniere.
> De moy la font estrangiere;
> Je pri Dieu qu'il les maudie!
> (Balade XXV, vv. 1–8)

[O stedfast trouth displaye thi baner / Support my right y pray the hertily / And fresshe assayle this newe and strong fronter / Of thought and woo that this on why / O welaway hath holde felonsly / The litille ioy y had for prisonere / So that to me they make him a straungere / I biseche god a-cursid mote they dey (vv. 944–51).]

Occasionally a flourish on the literal level loosens the bonds between letter and meaning, suggesting something more than what a discursive reading of the letter offers. For example, the fair wind in Balade XXVIII:

> En la nef de Bonne Nouvelle
> Espoir a chargié Reconfort,

Pour l'amener, de par la belle,
Vers mon cueur qui l'ayme si fort.
A joye puist venir au port
De Desir, et pour tost passer
La mer de Fortune, trouver
Un plaisant vent venant de France,
Ou est a present ma maistresse,
Qui est ma doulce souvenance
Et le tresor de ma lyesse.
(vv. 1–11; emphasis mine)[3]

[Hoffe howe for in þe shuppe of fresshen glad tidyng / Hope hath a-fresht with lusty recomfort / To cary to the fayrist borne lyvyng / Which is myn hertis lady and cheef resort / And if he may attayne the ioyfulle port / In self passage y mene to his desere / The see of fortune playn to his plesere / *A ioly wynd* als blowyng *into* fraunce / Where now abidyng is my sovl maystres / Which is the swete of alle my remembraunce / And hool tresoure of my worldly gladnes (vv. 1037–47).]

Operative entirely within the literal sense of the Image, the "plaisant vent" nonetheless resounds on the allegorical level with a freshness consonant with the poet's hope. An ironic hope, no doubt: when does the wind blow from France to England? (Note the correction in the English.)

Yet there are balades of striking Imaginative quality whose technique foreshadows the wonderful efflorescence in the rondeaux. Balade VIII effectively blends the literal and the allegorical to such an extent that, as in the earlier dits, they unite in a dream vision that is Imagination.

Quant je suis couschié en mon lit,
Je ne puis en paix reposer;
Car toute la nuit mon cueur lit
Ou rommant de Plaisant Penser,
Et me prie de l'escouter;
Si ne l'ose desobeir
Pour doubte de le courroucer:
Ainsi je laisse le dormir.
(vv. 1–8)

[When y am leyd to slepe as for a stound / To haue my rest y kan in no manere / For alle the nyght myn hert aredith round / As in the romaunce et of plesaunt pancer / Me praiyng so as him to hark and here / And y ne dar his loue disobay / In dowtyng so to do him displesere / This is my slepe y-falle into decay (vv. 412–419).]

The fragmentation of the literal ego of the first two lines into *cueur* and ego (cf. v. 5) thoughtfully engrossed in a romance makes the separation between literal and figurative vanish entirely. The fragmentation and subsequent constellation of elements is sustained in the second stanza.

> Ce livre si est tout escript
> Des fais de ma Dame sans per;
> Souvent mon cueur de joye rit,
> Quand il les list ou oyt compter;
> Car certes tant sont a louer
> Qu'il y prent souverain plaisir;
> Moy mesmes ne m'en puis lasser:
> Ainsi je laisse le dormir.
>
> (vv. 9–16)

[In this book which he redde is write & bound / As alle dedis of my lady dere / Which doth myn hert in laughter oft abound / When he hit rett or tellith the matere / Which gretly is to prayse without were / For y my silf delite it here mafay / Which if thei herde so wolde eche straungere / This is my slepe y-falle into decay (vv. 420–27)].

The concentration on the *livre* in these lines is an effort to evoke the qualities and actions of the lady, here not made explicit, by the affective reaction of the two "readers," *cueur* and *moy*. Greater fragmentation takes place in the third stanza: since the heart and the ego are reading, the eyes become a third, unwilling, participant; a duality in the reconstellated Image results in harmony with the heart and eyes of stanza 1. The "eyes of the heart" are commonplace in Charles' time, but here the Image shows the real eyes turned inward and thus rendered metaphorical by the introspective thrust of the whole stanza.

> Se mes yeulx demandent respit
> Par Sommeil qui les vient grever,
> Il les tense par grant despit,
> Et si ne les peut surmonter:
> Il ne cesse de soupirer
> A part soy; j'ay lors, sans mentir,
> Grant paine de le rapaiser:
> Ainsi je laisse le dormir.
>
> (vv. 17–24)

[As with myn eyen a respit to be found / As for an howre y axe not for a yere / For which dispite welnygh he doth confounde / That they ne kan fulfille my desere / For which to rage and sighe as in a gere / He farith so that even as welle y may / As make him stynt likke out a cole of fyre / This is my slepe y-falle into decay (vv. 428–35).]

In the envoi an antithetical element appears as the personification of love, a notion which had not been explicit before. It is another fragmentation of the ego insofar as the love is the poet's just as are the heart and eyes. It is merely refracted into a distinct entity, as is Plaisant Penser with the romance.

> Amour, je ne puis gouverner
> Mon cueur; car tant vous veult servir

> Qu'il ne scet jour ne nuit cesser:
> Ainsi je laisse le dormir.
>
> (vv. 25–28)

[Thus may y loo more souner wyn my bere / Then make my froward hert to me obay / For with myn hurt he doth him silf achere / This is my slepe y-falle as in decay (vv. 436–439).]

The retarded apostrophe to Love (lacking in the English) delays the establishment of context and sustains the poem by increasing expectancy. This device recalls the romances read by the poet's heart, where retarded identification holds in balance the appreciation of the adventure of the incognito knight. The naming, here the designation of context, classifies the kaleidoscopic Image which, until the apostrophe in the envoi, was universally referential and non-particular. As in the romances, Charles is making effective use of what Geoffrey of Vinsauf calls *ordo artificialis,* the representation of the beginning in the middle or at the end of the work.

Balade VIII is a tour de force. As a form, the balade tends toward static Images because of its relatively limited confines. But it is nonetheless a long form for the easy elaboration of the compact union of sense and letter characteristic of Charles' rondeaux. The fragmentation which renews the Image cannot always be sustained in the same mode, and there is a tendency to slip back into simple personification or mere abstract didacticism. In Balade XXXV, the Image is fully elaborated in the first stanza:

> J'ay ou tresor de ma pensee
> Un mirouer qu'ay acheté.
> Amour, en l'annee passee,
> Le me vendy, de sa bonté.
> Ou quel voy tousjours la beauté
> De celle que l'en doit nommer,
> Par droit, la plus belle de France.
> Grant bien me fait a m'y mirer,
> En attendant Bonne Esperance.
>
> (vv. 1–9)

[Within the tresoure haue y of my thought / A myrroure which y bought but late perde / Of god of loue as when forgete y nought / This yere a-past which solde it of bounte / To me / wherin ay se y the bewte / Of hir that ought ben callid wel trewly / The most fayrist bitwene this and Europe / Gret good god wott hit doth me in to prye / In abidyng my gladsom in good hope (vv. 1250–58).]

The notion of *pensée* as the mirror of the heart linking the ego and the lady, sold by Love from his bounty, is set against the Bonne Esperance expected but not yet forthcoming. The remaining stanzas add little to the complex Image beyond static repetitions—*interpretationes* only on the level of sense. The "yeulx de Joyeuse Plaisance" in stanza 2 are the only incremental element in the Image, and they have been introduced, though of course not so suggestively, in verse 5:

> Je n'ay chose qui tant m'agree,
> Ne dont tiengne si grant chierté,
> Car, en ma dure destinee,
> Maintesfoiz m'a reconforté;
> Ne mon cueur n'a jamais santé,
> Fors quant il y peut regarder
> Des yeulx de Joyeuse Plaisance;
> Il s'y esbat pour temps passer,
> En attendant Bonne Esperance.
>
> (vv. 10–18)

[Ther nys likyng sett me so hye a-loft / Nor which y ought to take in such cherte / For in the paynfulle destene was me wrought / Ful often tyme hit recomfortid me / That in myn hert nys ioy in no degre / More then biholde how she is in-goodly / With gladsom eyen levting no poynt a-slope / This is the bayte y bayte on wot ye whi / In abidyng my gladsom in good hope (vv. 1259–67).]

The final stanza reinterprets *pensée,* but still adds nothing to the Image in the first stanza, apparently complete for Charles.

> Advis m'est, chascune journee
> Que m'y mire, qu'en verité
> Toute doleur si m'est ostee;
> Pour ce, de bonne voulenté,
> Par le conseil de Leauté,
> Mettre le vueil et enfermer
> Ou coffre de ma souvenance,
> Pour plus seurement le garder,
> En attendant Bonne Esperance.
>
> (vv. 19–27)

[Me thenkith eche day syn y my myrrour bought / As in hit to biholde where-so y be / That euery woo therwith is fro me brought / Wherfore in my good weele this am y he / Bi trouthis counselle and my fantase / Shall rolle it vp to kepe it more clenly / To eft sone that me lust as for hit grope / In tresoure of my thought to kepe it drye / In abidyng my gladsom in good hope (vv. 1268–76).][4]

The "coffre de ma souvenance" is a restatement of the "tresor de ma pensee" in verse 1. The allusion to the passage of life in stanza 2 is taken up again by the "chascune journee." The prevailing structure is the accumulation of abstractions held together loosely by the initial "mirror of the heart" Image. The thinness of this Image extended through three stanzas contrasts remarkably with the dense Image that develops incrementally from stanza to stanza in Balade VIII. Balade XXXV, not VIII, is representative of Charles' balades, whose subject tends to conventional court poetry. However, some interesting changes can be seen in the balades following the death of the lady that inspires the *Songe en complainte*.

Most remarkable is the enhanced expressive ability of the Imagery, and its greater substance. The affective value of the Images grows at times so intense and deep that the love poems themselves, dealing at least implicitly with the lady's death, acquire a greater persuasiveness (or at least the modern temper accedes to a tragic courtly love more readily than to other kinds).

> En la forest d'Ennuyeuse Tristesse,
> Un jour m'avint qu'a par moy cheminoye,
> Si rencontray l'Amoureuse Deesse
> Qui m'appella, demandant ou j'aloye.
> Je respondy que, par Fortune, estoye
> Mis en exil en ce bois, long temps a,
> Si qu'a bon droit appeller me povoye
> L'omme esgaré qui ne scet ou il va.
> (Balade LXIII, vv. 1–8)

[In the forest of noyous hevynes / As y went wandryng in the moneth of may / I mette of loue the myghti gret goddes / Which axid me whithir y was away / I hir answerid as fortune doth convey / As oon exylid from ioy al be me loth / That passyng welle alle folke me clepyn may / The man forlost that wot not where he goth (vv. 2395-2402).]

The rest of the balade sets forth the lover's complainte before "l'Amoureuse Deesse." Still, the most telling line is the refrain. And the refrain leaves the poem open to broader signification in accord with the literal, but virtually archetypal statement of loss and state of being lost in the lover. In other poems the Imagination dominates the literal context and setting and deepens its straightforward meaning—all the more so because of Charles' subtle, seemingly effortless interpenetration of letter and sense, his blurring of frontiers between adjacent levels.[5] Saint Valentine's Day finds him "Sur le dur lit d'Ennuieuse Pensee" (Balade LXVI); Death destroys the urge to write: "Tout enroillié de Nonchaloir" (Balade LXXII). Whole series of suggestive, often repeated Images abound in the first lines and refrains: "Par les fenestres de mes yeulx" (Balades XCV, XCVI); "Des amoureux de l'observance" (Balade CII); "En la forest de Longue Actente" and "L'ostellerie de Pensee" (Balade CV); "Escollier de Merencolie" (Balade CXVII); "En la chambre de ma pensee" (Balade CXIX). It is fitting that the balades in Charles' autograph end with the series from the *concours de Blois,* with "Je meurs de soif auprés de la fontaine" and its variations, where theme and Image merge in an integral whole. In these poems Charles' Images, so enigmatic and mysterious, are still significant. Mystery and significance never completely obliterate or obscure one another, but rather blend finely into a higher suggestiveness transcending sheer mystery. The Images play themselves out divorced from all particular reference, yet filled with the universality of an idea immanent in well-arranged proverbs.[6] No wonder Villon was among the participants!

> Hor du propos si baille gaige,
> Ce n'est que du jeu la maniere,
> Nulle excusacion n'y quiere,
> Quoyque soit prouffit ou domage.
> (Rondeau CCCXXXV)

[If he places his challenge out of turn, that's only the nature of the game. He needn't look for an excuse, whether it was profitable or harmful.]

Yet even in these balades the amplification of the Image reveals the difficulties of the form. Accumulation replaces magnification. To compensate for the difficulties of static elaboration in the balade, Charles turned more and more towards the Rondeau. His Imagination gained in richness and intensity in the shorter form, while drawing nearer to the pure *jeu* alluded to in the preceding citation.

THE QUEST IN IMAGINATION:
BALADE EXPANSION AS NARRATIVE IN RENÉ D'ANJOU

The expansion of Charles d'Orléans' chivalric Images suggests the narrative movement of the quest.

> En la forest de Longue Actente,
> Chevauchant par divers sentiers
> M'en voys, ceste annee presente,
> Ou voyage de Desiriers.
> Devant sont allez mes fourriers
> Pour appareiller mon logeis
> En la cité de Destinee;
> Et pour mon cueur et moy ont pris
> L'ostellerie de Pensee.
> (Balade CV, vv. 1–9)

[In the forest of Long Expectation I go riding this year on various pathways in the voyage of Desire. My foragers have gone ahead to ready my lodging in the city of Destiny; and for my Heart and myself they have reserved Thought's hostelry.]

This is the dramatis personae of a potential allegorical romance transposed into the sphere of Imagination. Charles himself went no further in this direction than the *Retenue d'amours* and the *Songe en complainte*. But his contemporary René d'Anjou, a poet whose work Charles admired, did go further in the *Cuer d'amours espris,* in which the balade stations of Charles d'Orléans become adventures in an Imagined quest for Doulce Mercy. The work is thus conceived in the context of love, and its mode is Imagination, as René himself makes clear in the description of Love's palace.[7]

The entrance to Love's palace—a splendid piece of late medieval description—is surmounted by two statues "d'ambre jaulne, aornees d'or d'alquimye fait de la quinte essence et de pierres precieuses moult richement entaillees et eslevees, qui tenoient ung mirouer d'une table de dyamant grande et large" (§ 236, ll. 20–23) [of yellow amber, adorned with alchemist gold made of quintessence and precious stones very richly carved in high relief; they held a mirror made of a large, broad diamond table]. The two statues or *ymaiges* represent Ymaginacion and Fantasie. The mirror reveals the falsity of treacherous lovers. The subtlety of the mirror becomes the hope or despair of love, as suggested by the names of the two statues understood as *somnium* and *insomnium*. It will be the latter for René's Cuer.

René's Imagination confirms the hypothesis that a larger canvas might develop the balade Images of Charles d'Orléans. René followed the example of the *Roman de la rose*, which he knew and recommended. But like Péronne d'Armentières in the *Voir-Dit*, he linked it to the structural principle of the Arthurian prose romances in order to compose an allegorical questing romance. This gave his vision greater sweep and complexity.[8]

Comme jadis des haulx faiz et prouesses, des grans conquestes et vaillances en guerre et des merveilleux cas et tresaventureux perilz qui furent en fin menez, faiz et acomplis par les chevaliers preux et hardiz Lancelot, Gauvain, Galhot, Tristan et aussi Palamides et aultres chevaliers, pers de la table ronde, ou temps du roy Artur et pour le sang greal conquerir—ainsi que les antiques histoires le racontent au long—aient esté faiz et dittez pluseurs romans pour perpetuel memoire: aussi et pareillement, pour vous mieulx donner a entendre ceste mienne euvre, qui est de la maniere de la queste de Tresdoulce Mercy au Cuer d'amours espris, ensuyvray les termes du parler du livre de la conqueste du sang greal. (§ 3, ll. 1–10)

[As in former times several romances were composed and put into words for the sake of preserving the memory of the high deeds and acts of prowess, the great conquests and courage in war, the wondrous accomplishments and most adventurous perils that were brought to an end, achieved, and accomplished by the worthy and courageous knights Lancelot, Gauvain, Galahad, Tristan, as well as Palamedes and other knights who were peers of the Round Table—all this the old stories relate at some length—just so, in order to facilitate your understanding of this my composition, which describes the quest of Tresdoulce Mercy by the Cuer d'amours espris, I shall keep to the language of the book on the achievement of the quest for the Holy Grail.]

Just as the author of the *Queste del saint graal* imposed an ascetic judgment on the actions of the knights of the Round Table, so René adapted the grail quest to a love quest. In so doing he had the Images of the *Roman de la rose* and Charles d'Orléans' later balades and rondeaux to draw upon. His adaptation is threefold: first, the incorporation of a conception of love that comprehends both parts of the *Roman de la rose;* second, a redistribution of the fundamental male and female poles of the *Rose* into a more complex interrelationship of configurational foci; and third, the adaptation of Charles d'Orléans' Image with tagged name to narrative, thematic, and moral or affective progression.

The principal motif borrowed is the quest. Cuer, accompanied by Desir and occasional other companions, moves from Esperance to the final attack on the Manoir de Rebellion where Doulce Mercy is held by Reffus. But since René imitates the prose romances, the "termes de parler" include the structural principle of interlace. We not only observe what transpires in and about Cuer himself, but also are transferred on occasion to Honneur's preparations for open battle with Male Bouche and reminded of the varied activities of Esperance, observe the parts of the castle of Love, follow the efforts of Desir while Cuer is imprisoned in the castle of Tristesse and Courroux, and finally perceive the machinations of Reffus and Male Bouche in preparation for the ambush and final undoing of Cuer which separates him permanently from Doulce Mercy. Thus does René adapt the fragmentation of the ego observed in Charles' Ballade VIII to narrative elaboration.

René's Imagination includes several possible loves. But a fundamental structural and thematic adaptation accounts for René's use of prose romance structure: the multiplication and diversification of Imaginative foci, including the invention of contraries within the configuration about a given focus. Guilliame's *Rose* is posited on only two foci: the male pole (Amant) and the female pole (Rose). The narrative derives from their interaction. Guillaume does suggest diversity within a given focal complex: the intervention of Reason in Amant's configuration, the temptation of Dangier to be courteous, and the domination of Love and Venus. And it appears that Guillaume may have intended to finish with Love finding a place in the Rose's configuration: "Qu'Amors prist puis par ses esforz" (v. 3504 [3486]). But such internal adaptations are only hinted at, not followed through, by Guillaume de Lorris. That was to be the task of René d'Anjou in the courtly dit.

Desir is the origin of Cuer's quest, and his goal is Doulce Mercy. This suggests the bipolar Amant and Rose. But Doulce Mercy, being at the quest's goal, has little prominence along the way except by her absence. This shifts the emphasis to the obstacles Cuer encounters. Just as Reason opposes Amour in the *Rose,* various notions like Jealousy, Envie, Tristesse and Courroux, and Melancolie rise up in Cuer's path. They represent possibilities for interior conflict, the oxymoronic character of Love's progress through the adventures in the quest. They lead to the ultimate opposition—not within Cuer himself but, as Amour points out, between Doulce Mercy and Reffus. Love is defeated, as Reffus' victory depends on Male Bouche, not Love. This is a betrayal, for, as Amour also states, Reffus is "de notre mesgnye" (§ 248, v. 8) [part of our following], as are his assistants Honte and Crainte (§ 263, v. 26). Cuer must take pains not to kill Reffus or his assistants, who are stationed

214

with Doulce Mercy to guard her against overzealous, unworthy suitors (§ 263, vv. 27–33). The description of Love's palace constantly emphasizes the divergent, oxymoronic possibilities of any love. But other foci are also present, notably Honneur as enemy of Mesdisance, and Esperance with her various roles in human conduct. Thus Renon may achieve the liberation of Cuer from Tristesse's castle while Honneur his lord pursues independently his struggle against Male Bouche (§ 102). At the same time, Cuer goes on a separate quest of Doulce Mercy. All these distant activities combine as it were in a galaxy of constellations and gravitate in the same direction. Cuer's failure at the Manoir de Rebellion is his alone, however. The god of Love does not appear in his defense as in the *Rose*. And Honneur's activities continue in spite of the defeat. Both Love and Honneur would have been advanced by Cuer's success; but they are not dependent on it.

The choice and arrangement of personifications is linked to careful delineation of place. René adapted Charles d'Orléans' Imagination to describe Cuer's encounters, transferring to his real quest Charles' discontinuous Images of forests, woods, and meadows in balade sequence. The adventures are largely the same: the Forest de Longue Actente, the Fontaine de Fortune, the Val de Parfond Penser, the Fleuve de Lermes, the Tertre deveé de Liesce, the Pre de Dure Responce, the Pas Perilleux. After them come the crossroads of the Chemin de Forcennerie and of Joyeux Pencer (§ 10). The latter leads by the "fortunes de la mer" to the Isle d'Amours, and finally to the Manoir de Rebellion (cf. § 46). Many of these adventures are expanded according to Cuer's specific role and the personages encountered, like Jalosie, Desespoir, Melancolie, Soucy, and Tristesse, who oppose Cuer and his Desir. Even Desir and Cuer themselves may fall out, when the former's occasional mockery incites the latter's anger (§§ 108–15, 140–44). In the Plain de Pensee Ennuyeuse, Desir concludes the first such quarrel by reminding Cuer that "si plus ne voulons farser, / Nostre ennuy ne savrons passer" (§ 114, vv. 2–3) [if we no longer wish to joke, we'll not be able to pass through our distress]. The contention has overtones of the quarrel between Amant and Reason over the latter's language in Jean de Meun's *Rose*.

But to overcome *ennuy* in René's dit one must gain Doulce Mercy. In a quest, success is achieved by combat. The combat becomes a psychomachia in Imagination, a psychomachia structured on oxymoron. The context facilitates the deployment of abstractions in a conflicting configuration, and thereby assigns to each personification its office and appropriate attributes and actions within the epideictic intention. The result may be as clear and obvious as in Prudentius, where the Seven Sins and the Seven Virtues fight for Man's soul. The designation of Faith as captain of the virtues shows the context, and the details of the specific combats as well as their outcome are determined by that intention. The result is description, although there is more action represented than, for example, in Raoul de Houdenc's *Roman des eles*. Alain de Lille used the psychomachia in the *Anticlaudianus,* but with a greatly augmented cast of combatants. Where Prudentius sought to illustrate the various possibilities for morality and sin, Alain chose to envisage the possibility of human perfection. His New Man is a Galahad seen in a vision. Jean de Meun in turn adapted the psychomachia to his own context, in which Love gravitates between Reason and Nature, and the personifications fight a battle of the sexes in which duplicity and personal advantage ultimately serve Venus, who is active on both sides, like Amour in the *Cuer d'amours espris*. As in Prudentius, victory suggests defeat; both, in the last analysis, illustrate the same problem: "Spiritibus pugnant variis lux atque tenebrae, distantesque animat duplex substantia vires" (*Psychomachia,* vv. 908–9) [Light and darkness with their opposing spirits are at war, and our two-fold being inspires powers at variance with each other]. Similarly, in the conclusion to René's *Cuer,* Cuer gravitates between the possibility of Mercy and the onslaughts of Reffus, both dependent upon the authority of the god of Love.

But the soul from which Imagination draws and orders its descriptions is not so easily explained as our mind, bent on conceptual understanding, may presume. Prudentius: "Novimus ancipites nebuloso in pectore sensus sudare alternis conflictibus" (vv. 893–94) [We know that in the darkness of our heart conflicting affections fight hard in successive combats]. There are thus ambiguities in no way belied by Prudentius' obvious dichotomy. The splendid palace of Love in René has its hospital, which Love's protector Reffus fills with his victims. The antinomies that seem to have given Chaucer so much anguish are here interwoven like the human and animal in the Renart legend. Reffus may be won over by courtesy (Humble Requeste) or payment (Promesse). He may be haughty, but his haughtiness is that of a villain like Dangier. He certainly shows no courtesy. Thus Pitié in Reffus' eyes is a "vielle" (§ 229, v. 2; § 230, l. 13). Reffus may be beaten with a club, but not killed, in Love's service; such treatment suits villainous servants who are insensible to courteous treatment. He thus functions in René's text like Dangier in Guil-laume de Lorris.

In René's Imagination, a courteous refusal is no more incoherent than good *dangier* in an aristocratic setting.[9] But his conception of love makes sadness and vexation unbearable, a source of "sorwful ymagynacioun" leading to death. Thus an anomaly appears after Cuer has defeated Courroux and seized Tristesse in the Château du tertre deveé d'Amours, when Tristesse offers her service to Love at Cuer's instigation: "serviray sans mandement / Amours a son commandement" (§ 70, vv. 14–15) [I shall, without need for specific instructions, serve Love at his command]. It turns out to be a deceitful, indeed impossible offer. Sadness in the service of Love is as impossible as a happy marriage in the *Quinze joies de mariage* or *fin'amors* in Jean de Meun. Tristesse's deceit is unworthy of nobility. René adapts Jean de Meun's conception of deceit in love to the character of Tristesse, demanding courtesy for the courteous, deceit against the deceitful. Pitié herself exclaims:

> Maiz gardez vous, sur toute rien,
> De faillir a homme de bien!
> Puisque une fois l'avez promis,
> A le tenir estes soubzmis.
> Mais Reffuz et telle merdaille,
> Decepvez les, ne vous en chaille!
>
> (§ 226, vv. 74–79)

[But avoid above all betraying a worthy man! Once you have made a promise, you are bound to keep it. But as for Reffus and such crap—cheat 'em and don't worry about it.]

Pitié's characterization of Reffus and his kind is as appropriate as the cruelty of the Virtues in Prudentius.

Like Charles d'Orléans, René achieved a revitalization of Imagination by exploiting semantic range and diversified settings. Guillaume de Lorris had profited from such Imagination by careful choice and semantic adaptation in the invention of personifications and their actions. Charles d'Orléans, impelled by the mystery of his own Images, was raising them above contextual specificity to leave them shimmering in their own mysterious illumination. René retained context in the *Cuer,* but his amorous setting does not preclude love's diversity. The specific tale of Cuer ends in failure. But the conclusion is the same as Chartier's in the *Belle Dame.* It is not absolute, but rather in keeping with the awareness of uncertainty in love that dominates fifteenth-century courtly literature. René's "piteux cas" and "griefve paine" (§ 315, l. 3) culminate in Charles' decision to love no more—"sicque si fort ne souvent je ne puisse estre tempté ne ainsi tourmenté de ce subtil esperit au vouloir impossible, nommé le Dieu d'amours, qui embrase les cuers de tresimportun desir, lequel fait gens tant amer qu'ilz en meurent ou si treffort languissent qu'ilz n'ont ung seul bon jour" (§ 315, ll. 8–12) [so that I may not be so greatly or frequently tempted or tormented by this subtle spirit of impossible will named the god of Love, who inflames hearts with a most importunate desire, which in turn causes people to love so much that they either die of it, or languish so grievously that they have not a single good day in their life]. René retains only that idle curiosity about the love of others evident in Chartier and Charles d'Orléans. René concludes his epilogue to Jean de Bourbon, who also appears as one of the victims of Love in *Cuer,* "priant a Dieu qu'il vous doint ce que vostre cuer desire, et autant de bien et, en amours, de joye comme pour moy vouldroye" (§ 315, ll. 17–19) [praying God that he grant

217

you your heart's desire, and as much good and joy in love as I would wish for myself]. René would treat his own and Charles d'Orléans love in the same way, and Charles saw fit to record it in his autograph (Rondeaux X and XI).

THE RONDEAUX: QUINTESSENTIAL GLOSS

Charles' rondeaux derive from the cliché or proverbial phrase susceptible of verbal or Imagistic elaboration. The blending of literal and abstract in the Image, whatever its ultimate source in human consciousness, constitutes the material of his Imagination. This is particularly evident in the rondeaux which begin with the same first line, whether they are all by Charles or also by others. Almost invariably the rondeaux of others contain a suggestive Image with affinities to Charles' Imagination. Some even go beyond him, looking, however distantly, towards sixteenth-century metaphoric language.[10] Some of the Images appear in the balades composed after the *Songe en complainte*. The rondeau groups with a common first line are miniature sequences like the *concours de Blois* series.

A list of their first lines will demonstrate the preceding comments.

1. *Tant sont les yeulx de mon cuer endormis:* XXVI, XXVII.
2. *Mais que mon mal si ne s'empire:* XCVII; *Mais que mon propos ne m'empire:* XCVIII.
3. *Des amoureux de l'observance:* CV–CVII, CXI, CCXXXV.
4. *L'abit le moine ne fait pas:* CXXV–CXXVI, CXXIX–CXXX.
5. *De fol juge, briefve sentence:* CXXVII–CXXVIII.
6. *En la forest de Longue Actente:* CXXXI–CXXXIV, CXXXVIII, CCXXV–CCXXVIII.
7. *Dedans l'abisme de douleur:* CXXXIX–CXLI; cf. CCCCXXII–CCCCXXIII: *Dedens la maison de doleur.*
8. *Le trucheman de ma pensee:* CXV, CCX–CCXII.
9. *Las! le faut il? esse ton vueil?* CCXVI–CCXVII.
10. *Au plus fort de ma maladie:* CCL–CCLI.
11. *Ou millieu d'espoir et de doubte:* CCLXXVII–CCLXXVIII, CCXCII.
12. *Hola! hola! Soupir, on vous hoit bien:* CCCVIII–CCCIX; cf. also CCCX using the *caÿment* of CCCVIII–CCCIX, and CCCXL–CCCXLI: *Et ou vas tu, petit soupir?*
13. *Jaulier des prisons de Pensee:* CCCLXXXIII–CCCLXXXVI, CCCLXXXIX; cf. also CCCLXXXVII–CCCLXXXVIII on the *prisonnier* motif.
14. *Comme monnoye descriee:* CCCXCII–CCCXCIII.
15. *Escollier de Merencolye:* CCCXCVII–CCCXCVIII.
16. *Chose qui plaist est a demi vendue:* CXXIII–CXXIV, CCCXLV.
17. *Quant Pleur ne pleut, Souspir ne vente:* CCLXXX–CCLXXXI, CCCL.

218

The first line is important not only in the poems Charles wrote to accompany poems of others using the same Image or phrase, but also in sets entirely by him.

1. *Et de cela, quoy?* CLXXXII–CLXXXIII.
2. *A ce jour de Saint Valentin:* III, LXI, CX, CCXLVII–CCXLIX, CCLIV; cf. CCLXXVI, CCCLV.
3. *M'apelez vous cela jeu:* CXCIX, CCCCXXXIII.
4. *Mort de moy! vous y jouez vous:* CXCIV, CXCVIII.
5. *En faictes vous doubte?* CCXXII–CCXXIII.
6. *Pourquoy moy:* CCLXXI–CCLXXII.
7. *Petit mercier* poems: CCCXXIX–CCCXXX.

There are also many poems that do not share a common opening line but that have in common a word or motif: recipes (CXVI–CXIX), confession (CCCLX–CCCLXII), the *fenoches* and *nox buze* poems (CCLVI, CCCLXXI–CCCLXXII), those attached to a feast day like Saint Valentine's, May Day, or New Year's. In them the suggestive Image is the focus for elaboration and discursive context. Perusal of the index to the first lines in Champion's edition of Charles d'Orléans makes this readily apparent.

The rondeaux contain many of the conventional abstractions of amorous French poetry before Charles, as Norma Goodrich's study of his major themes shows.[11] Even the subjects treated while Charles is in Nonchaloir or Vieillesse are conventional: Death, Old age, Melancholy. One need only add an explicit religious context, as in his Latin poem *Canticum amoris,* to see that this is so.

> A torporis ocio iam, mens, excitare,
> Ipsius delicias miras contemplare,
> Et ut Sponsum dulcius discas adamare,
> Bellatorum agminum cetus speculare.
>
> (vv. 341–44)[12]

[From idle torper rise up, o mind, and consider His wondrous delights; and, that you may learn to love more sweetly the Spouse, consider his hosts in warlike array.]

Charles splits the ego off from the *anima* apostrophized throughout the *Canticum* as the sentient, commiserating agent and the personal will, and from the *mens* capable of perceiving divine Images that contribute to the betterment and salvation of the *anima.*

> Attende memoriam tanquam vas preclarum
> Quo thesaurus conditur tot materiarum,
> Rerumque scaturiunt facies tantarum
> Quod excedunt numerum pluvie guttarum.
>   Per hanc reminiscitur mens preteritorum,
> Auditorum facies servat ac visorum,

> Concipit ymagines multas futurorum,
> Retinet misteria mira secretorum.
> (vv. 113–20)

[Consider memory to be like a clear receptacle in which is contained the treasure of so many things; and the features of so many things splash about in it that their number surpasses that of raindrops. Through it the mind recalls the past, it preserves the lineaments of things heard and seen, and it conceives many images of the future and holds the wondrous mysteries of what is hidden.]

The vast panorama of earthly, human, and heavenly worlds that Charles spreads out before our mental eye is a conventional evocation of the universe typical of the Franciscan poetry that inspired the *Canticum*.[13] It also harks back to earlier Chartrain conceptions of Imagination as a means to understand God and His world and to achieve the moral betterment of the individual. Visual representations abound as the mind and soul (*mens* and *anima*) sweep from the animals and plants subject to man upwards towards God through the orders of angels and hosts of the Saved on whom hope of salvation depends. Each Image perceived by the *mens* reverberates as truth in the *anima*,[14] the truth of knowledge, submission, love. "Temetipsam intuens, anima, mirare / Numquid tibi tanta tu poteras prestare" (vv. 153–54) [Consider thyself, soul, and marvel that you alone could never present so much for consideration]. The reprimand to the soul is carried over into Charles' profane poetry, where love and personal concerns are objects of contemplation and reflection in the Imagination: "Ibi semper, anima mente conversare, / Non cessas" (vv. 617–18) [May the soul never cease to converse there with the mind].

We may observe this in rondeau CCCXXV. The refrain, an incomplete sentence, sets the static Image of the well and the poet's mood.

> Ou puis parfont de ma merencolie
> L'eaue d'Espoir que ne cesse tirer,
> Soif de Confort la me fait desirer,
> Quoy que souvent je la treuve tarie.

[From the deep well of my melancholy I do not cease drawing the water of hope. Thirst for Consolation makes me desire it, although I often find the well dry.]

The Image is founded on the tension between Merencolie and Confort, each related to Hope in an alternately negative or positive way. Hope is construed as the transition from Melancholy to Consolation, a movement rendered in Imagination as drawing the water of Hope from the well. This is Hope for Consolation, assuagement of the Melancholy. But to draw from the well the water of Hope is frequently a vain endeavor, since the well may be dry—that is, the Melancholy is without any redeeming quality. Yet the source of Hope is seen only in Melancholy, only the well can contain the refreshing waters.

One must lower to the very bottom of Melancholy—the depths rise up as it were to the surface when the poet draws—to discover whether Hope is present: only in the depths of Melancholy may it, on occasion, be found. The refrain is a remarkably dense commingling of Images and abstractions. But the result is order and signification, a configuration of interdependent and mutually illuminating components. The separation of abstract and concrete in the Image disappears as parallel, indeed overlapping sequences tag or identify the concrete *matière* with the abstractions: well of Melancholy, water of Hope, thirst for Consolation.

The first development effects an abrupt recomposition of the refrain Image.

> Necte la voy ung temps et esclercie,
> Et puis aprés troubler et empirer
> Ou puis. . . .

[For a time I see it to be clean and clear; then afterwards grow troubled and bad in the well. . . .]

The water's changes from clear to troubled and obscure figure the changeability of Hope even when present. The attributes *Necte* and *esclercie*—the refreshing suggestion of unadulterated Hope—recede before uncertainty and confusion. For *troubler* and *empirer* do not suggest so much that the water becomes impure as that it is obscure, impenetrable, uncertain, in a dark and troubled state, "grown worse." Hope is not an absolute. Even present it may be troubled.

Another recomposition of the Image takes place in the second development.

> D'elle trempe mon ancre d'estudie,
> Quant j'en escrips, mais pour mon cueur irer,
> Fortune vient mon pappier dessirer,
> Et tout gecte par sa grant felonnie
> Ou puis. . . .

[In it I dip my ink of study when I write about it. But, in order to vex me, Fortune comes to tear up my paper and feloniously throw everything back in the well. . . .]

The change effects a complete rereading of the refrain. It is a kaleidoscopic effect: the literal terms of the Image are transferred as the well of water becomes an ink well, whence the matter of the poem is drawn. The Image reverberates in turn against the previous readings of the well by the return of the *puis* in the refrain. This evokes anew the cliché that the courtly poet may write only when love provides some hope, some consolation. The intellectual cliché contrasts Hope and Fortune, and the paper and ink are thrown back into the well of Melancholy whence the ink came. The circle is complete. The significance of the poem, carefully kept free of specific context—love, life, religion, art—expands into a universal statement through an Image whose variations leave the mind to think on, dream on, apply, and return to the well of Melancholy for new sustenance, new inspiration. The rondeau moves from careful tagging in the refrain to more concrete Images in each development. However, the refrain context sustains the imposition of meaning and contributes to enhanced expectancy in ever more concrete incremental Images.[15]

The compactness and suggestiveness of this rondeau, its literal and allegorical density in Imagination, are not confined by explicit contextual walls. This is the charm of Charles' best poetry, and helps to explain why the rondeau became his preferred form. Rondeau CCCXXV is not unique. The "petit mercier, petit pannier" of Charles' rondeau contains, among its "mirlifiques," its "menues oberliques," the sudden discovery of "quelques bagues plus autentiques." This is the evocatory charm—the *carmen*—of "Je meurs de soif auprés de la fontaine."

The original Imagery in Rondeau CCCXXV sets a standard for Charles' later balades and rondeaux. He adapted some Images from Oton de Grandson and Chartier, and invented a whole new set for his own purposes, bringing about a brief revitalization of courtly Imagination. Unfortunately, the times were not with him, his impact was not great, a new taste was already on the way. The French Renaissance was to learn a different metaphorical language from Italy and from a new attention to the classics. Italian poetry was already in full bloom in Charles' lifetime, but it seems to have had no effect on his poetry: Italy provided him with "fenoches" and "nox buze," but no "bagues plus autentiques."[16]

The reason for Charles' Imagistic innovations can be understood and appreciated. Conventional abstraction was overworked, and by the fifteenth century had paled to gray meaninglessness.[17] Also, Charles tended to blend the literal and the abstract by "tagging." The new Images were not immediately connotative. Therefore the tag by a conventional abstraction gave that abstraction more meaning because of the object it designated, and at the same time furnished a familiar context. The Image itself opened the abstraction to greater suggestiveness, and the total configuration provided understanding, a combination of knowledge and insight into *mystère* that Charles' predecessors had always sought and that he realized masterfully in his best rondeaux.

VANISHING CONTEXT AND FADING IMAGINATION

Some of Charles' rondeaux, like the Blois balade sequence, lack any immediate context. Although the vocabulary is typical of amorous poetry, it is not explicitly confined to that context. Rondeau CCCCXXXII depends on the universality of proverbial knowledge.

Prenons congié du plaisir de noz yeulx,
Puis qu'a present ne povons mieulx avoir,
De revenir faisons nostre devoir,
Quant Dieu plaira, et sera pour le mieulx.

[Let's take leave of our eyes' pleasure, since we cannot now have it any better. Let's make it our duty to return when it pleases God, and that will be best.]

The contexts of *fin' amors* and advancing old age are obvious applications for these lines. But so is the more abstract, but nonetheless significant sequence of things askew, of the very Images of poetry fading from the mind.

Il faut changer aucunefoiz les lieux,
Et essayer, pour plus ou moins savoir:
Prenons congié....

[One must occasionally change places, and make an effort to know more or less....]

The final development makes explicit the universally applicable proverbial mode of the poem, as if to undermine the notion of Imaginative expression by bringing together the two ages of youth and old age kept separate in the *Retenue* and the *Songe en complainte*. Love's frequently antithetic, even oxymoron combinations recur as the Imagination of *choses vues*. Thus does Charles express the universal validity of proverbial statements, even when they are contradictory and precede specific application. Unlike Chaucer, Charles does not plague himself with contradictions and applications.

Ainsi parlent les jennes et les vieulx;
Pour ce, chascun en face son povoir....

[Thus speak young and old; therefore, let each do the best he can....]

This apparently youthful call is immediately undermined by age's hopelessness. Or is it youth's?

Nul ne mecte sa seurté en Espoir,
Car au jour d'uy courent les eurs tieulx quieulx.

[Let no one put his trust in Hope, for today fortunes are so-so.]

In any case, Machaut's idealism is gone. And Imagination itself is sinking into a soft, melancholy sunset.

Salués moy toute la compaignie
Ou a present estez a chiere lye,
Et leur dites que voulentiés seroye
Avecques eulx, mais estre n'y pourroye,
Pour Viellesse qui m'a en sa ballie.

(Rondeau CCCCXXXV)

223

[Greet everyone from me, there where you are with happy faces; and tell them that I would gladly join them, but I would not be able to because of Old Age which has dominion over me.]

Little more remains, and this is the last poem in Charles d'Orléans' autograph. Sleep, ever more deep, closes out the dreams.

The universality of many of Charles' rondeaux actually preludes his silence. There is a gradual separation of poetry from rhetoric as the poem divests itself of specific context and retreats into dream. The dream is comprehensible as glossing, game, or silence.

Glossing is essential to allegory. Charles often provides it by the abstractions that tag the Images. But much of the gloss is that *mystère* wherein lies the fascination of Imagination. Such *mystère* lies far deeper in the mind, further back in dreams, than a gloss as such could penetrate. Only the Image itself can reach it.

> Ma plus chier tenue richesse
> Ou parfont tresor de Pensee
> Est soubz clef, seurement gardee,
> Par Esperance, ma Deesse.
> (Rondeau CCCXXIV)

[My dearest wealth, in the deep treasure of Thought, is kept under key, safely guarded by Hope, my Goddess.]

For Charles, in a very real sense, where there is hope there is life. And where life is, Imagination is meaningful. Experience remains a source of the same revitalization of Images that Froissart spoke of in the *Prison amoureuse*. Like Flos and Rose, we too would pry into the poet's meaning, attempt to extricate sense by careful glossing, exact translation. But something is always lost in translation: "Se vous me demandez: et qu'esse? / N'enquerez plus, elle est mussee" (Rondeau CCCXXIV) [If you ask me: what is it? Ask no more, it's hidden]. And indeed, the Images reflect no more than the passage of life, of hope for "chasteaulz en Espaigne et en France" (Rondeau LIV). Life becomes a pastime, in all the lightness and profundity of the word.

> Avecques elle, seul, sans presse,
> Je m'esbas soir et matinee;
> Ainsi passe temps et journee.
> Au partir dy: "Adieu, maistresse."

[With her, while I am alone and unencumbered, I amuse myself morning and evening. Thus I pass time and the day. On leaving, I exclaim: "Farewell, my mistress."]

What more is there to say? "Que voulez vous que plus vous die, / Jeunes assotez amoureux?" (Rondeau LX) [What more do you want me to say, young, silly lovers?] With age, Hope cedes to Passe temps, and the gloss gives way to poetic games.

The realm of Nonchaloir in the *Songe en complainte* leaves room for play and the poetic game, before Care and Worry descend and games are no longer fun. This setting has its origin in courtly convention.

> De balader j'ay beau loisir,
> Autres deduis me sont cassez;
> Prisonnier suis, d'Amour martir.
> (Balade XL, vv. 31–33)

[To balade now y haue a fayre leysere / Alle othir sport is me biraught as now / Martir am y for loue and prisonere (vv. 1440–42).]

The courtly imperative to write derives from the lady herself, the traditional fount and *matière* of poetry.

> Jeune, gente, plaisant et debonnaire,
> Par un prier, qui vault commandement,
> Chargié m'avez d'une balade faire.
> (Balade XIX, vv. 1–3)

[Most goodly yong o plesaunt debonayre / Yowre sendyng which me gaf comaundement / A balad forto make ye speke so fayre (vv. 762–64).]

The game doesn't lose its attraction as amusement, even when the "poursuivant d'Amours" matures into the herald-judge of Rondeau IV.

> Souper ou baing et disner ou bateau,
> En ce monde n'a telle compaignie,
> L'un parle ou dort, et l'autre chante ou crie,
> Les autres font balades ou rondeau.
> (Rondeau CCCXLVII)

[Supper at the baths or dinner on the boat—there is nothing on earth like it. One talks or sleeps, and another sings or shouts; the others write balades or a rondeau.]

The conventional scenes of courtly life seem to perpetuate themselves much as the heavy traditions in late medieval literature are said to do; the sense and substance gone, they are little more than idle pastimes. Charles obviously saw something of this.

> Quant tout est fait, il fault passer sa vie
> Le plus aise qu'on peut, en chiere lie.
> A mon advis, c'est mestier bon et beau.

[When all is said and done, one must pass one's life as comfortably as possible, while putting on a good face. In my opinion, that's a fine, attractive occupation.]

225

The *bon et beau* have become quite empty. Yet Charles was very much an aristocrat, maintaining conventions it may never have occurred to him to doubt because, as pastimes, they are the *bon et beau* of past times. The difficulty is that the Image would not persist. Folly may intrude into Pastime as much as into Love. Excess is now the danger. "Tousjours parle plus fol que sage, / C'est une chose coustumiere" (Rondeau CCCXXXV) [A fool customarily talks more than a wise man. It's a common occurrence]. Reticence, even taciturnity impose themselves as the only alternative when the game becomes too frivolous, and sense evaporates.

> Se l'en me dit: "Vous contez rage,"
> Blasmez ma langue trop legere;
> Raison, de Secret tresoriere,
> La tance, quant despent lengage.

[If someone says to me: "You're talking crazy," blame my tongue for being too easy. Reason, treasurer of Secret, reprimands her when she squanders speech.]

Even the best may become too much: "Beau chanter si ennuye bien!" (Rondeau LVIII).

These proverbial condemnations of loquacity are not infrequent in the rondeaux.

> D'espoir, et que vous en diroye?
> C'est ung beau bailleur de parolles,
> Il ne parle qu'en parabolles,
> Dont ung grant livre j'escriroye.
> (Rondeau CCCXXII)

[About hope?—What should I tell you about it? It's a fine talker, and speaks only in parables, about which I could write a big book.]

René d'Anjou did write that book of *paraboles* and Espoir. Charles wrote a rondeau. A nagging sense of futility dominates these reflections, as time passes and the meaning of life's Images slowly recedes from them—as it did for earlier poets, and now for Charles himself at the death of the beloved or the announcement of old age, separation from country and long waiting.

> Et pour ce, de vostre partie,
> Se voulez croire mes conseulx,
> D'abregier conseiller vous veulx
> Voz faiz, en sens ou en folie.
> (Rondeau LX)

[And therefore, as far as you are concerned, if you want to follow my advice, I would advise you to abbreviate what you write, whether it's sensible or foolish writing.]

Write rondeaux, not balades—the lyric lai is long forgotten. The example of Charles' own experience is conclusive. "En le lisant, je me riroye, / Tant auroit de choses frivolles" (Rondeau CCCXXII) [While reading, I would laugh to myself, so much frivolity was there in it]. The resultant melancholy teaches a mournful, though not really bitter lesson.

> Par tout ung an ne le liroye,
> Ce ne sont que promesses folles
> Dont il tient chascun jour escolles;
> Telles estudes n'esliroye.
>   (Rondeau CCCXXII)

[I wouldn't read it for a whole year. They are only silly promises with which he daily holds forth; I wouldn't choose such studies.]

This is the material to which the "Escollier de Merencolie" applies himself.

> Quant tu es courcé d'autres choses,
> Cueur, mieulx te vault en paix laisser,
> Car s'on te vient araisonner,
> Tost y treuves d'estranges gloses.
>   (Rondeau LXIV)

[When you are distressed by other things, it's better for you to leave it be; for if someone comes to talk, you'll find odd interpretations in it.]

The "estranges gloses" that provide the *merveille* of earlier allegory are now only irritants to conversation.

As meaning becomes too grievous or distressing for words, silence remains the only suitable theme. Was not poetry meant to express joy, or the consolation of hope? The loss of hope condemned the amorous poet to silence in Machaut, Christine de Pisan, Chartier.

> De tes levres les portes closes
> Penses de saigement garder,
> Que dehors n'eschappe Parler
> Qui descuevre le pot aux roses.
>   (Rondeau LXIV)

[Strive to keep the doors of your mouth prudently closed, lest Speech escape and betray the roses' pot.]

Mystère seems to dominate more and more the signification which is deeply buried in an inscrutable Image.

> Quelque chose derriere
> Couvient tousjours garder,

> On ne peut pas monstrer
> Sa voulenté entiere.
> (Rondeau LXVII)

[One must always keep something back. One cannot show all one's will.]

But *mystère* without Imagination is darkness and silence.

> Plus penser que dire
> Me convient souvent,
> Sans moustrer comment
> N'a quoy mon cueur tire.
> (Rondeau XLVI)

[It behooves me often to think more than to speak, without revealing in what direction nor towards what my heart inclines.]

These lines effectively eliminate context from the Image.

Like Chaucer, Charles seems to have discovered how difficult it is to reconcile contexts. Life is after all a "merveilleuse brouee" [strange kettle of fish] with "Mainte chose demenee / Estrangement, ça et la" (Rondeau LXVIII) [many things pulled about in strange ways, hither and thither]. It seems better to ignore such confusion than to try to comprehend it.

> Ce qui m'entre par une oreille,
> Par l'autre sault, com est venu,
> Quant d'y penser n'y suis tenu;
> Ainsi Raison le me conseille.
> (Rondeau LXVI)

[Let what enters through one ear go out through the other, just as it came in, as long as I don't have to think about it. That's the advice Reason gives me.]

Reason is above Imagination, as the philosophers taught, and does not require its help to arrive at truth; nonetheless, he who sees nothing thinks nothing, and writes no poetry. "Comme ung chat, suis viel et chenu, / Legierement pas ne m'esveille" (Rondeau LXVI) [Like a cat, I'm old and wizened; I don't wake up easily]. Thus all Charles' glosses and games, his pastimes and worries, converge on silence. "D'en tant parler, ce m'est follie, / Il vault trop mieulx que je me taise" (Rondeau CCLXXXIX) [To talk so much about it is foolish of me; I do better to keep still]. Charles does not withdraw amid the vivid Images of death and corruption so widespread in his age. There is only the gradual diminution of sight and sound, as all the faculties, including Imagination, cease. All light, music, words, and thought end. Imagination is dead, the dreams are blind, sleep is absolute: "Plus je n'en dy, / N'escry . . . (Rondeau XLI) [I neither say nor write any more about it].

To the end Charles persisted in showing the Belle Heaumiere as *belle*. The later half of her life is lost in darkness. In so doing he completed a circle taking him back to the times when courtly poetry began. We have seen how the dit inverted romance, replacing a *matière* with a *surplus de sens, a sens* elaborated through a *surplus de matière* in Guillaume de Lorris and Richart de Fornival. With Charles there is a return to *matière,* the topics of that long tradition. But the topics are more and more divorced by Age and Vieillesse from specific application. It is a curious phenomenon, this poetry no longer narrative romance nor didactic dit nor even rhetorical balade, but rather a simple rondeau almost devoid of *matière* and *sens* in the old sense, subsisting by Images disappearing into the mind from which they arose—a well of Melancholy that may flow from the pen or run back into the well. It is pure Imagination. For as the earlier commentator stated, cognition by Imagination "non est in istis sed secundum ista."

Conclusion

"Do you still think then that Love is beautiful, if this is so?"
"It looks, Socrates, as if I didn't know what I was talking about
   when I said that."
"Still, it was a beautiful speech, Agathon. . . . "
                                          —Plato[1]

THE INTEGUMENTUM permitted any doctrinally acceptable reading of the given text. The author of the *Queste del saint graal* could adapt an apocryphal or invented Adam and Eve to his subject, just as the author of Branch XXIV of the *Renart* did for his. The Images themselves have no fixed significations (although an author might choose to use them in traditional ways). This could lead to error, as when, without thinking, Lancelot identified black with evil and white with good in the *Queste*. The principle of the *integumentum* was amenable to interpretation in secular, nonreligious literature. The traditional correspondence between the Panther and Christ in the bestiaries is adapted to the Panther and the lady in Nicole de Margival's *Panthère d'amours*. In each instance we have to do with Images. But as *matière* the Images are meaningless without a context to determine the character of semantic reference. This helps explain what seemed to the editor Scheler an indecorous comparison between Marguerite de Flandres and an elephant in Baudouin de Condé's *Conte de l'oliphant*. Marguerite and the Elephant are both Images, and become meaningful along the lines of their mutual intersection. Elephants are not ridiculous on coats-of-arms. But they are meaningful. We must likewise be wary of misrepresenting the Panther in Nicole de Margival's dit. "Pour Nicole de Margival la femme ne ressemble pas à la panthère, elle *est* panthère."[2] The lady and the Panther are Images: she is what a Panther is, or more precisely, she represents what a Panther represents. As in most allegories of this type, "Some statable concept or nameable abstraction is generally a key and an indication; but so is the literal 'thing'."[3] The result is understanding.

   Imagination is the configuration of concrete and abstract *matière*. The discrete components of the configuration express through their relationships an idea that gives them form and meaning; that is, the idea provides for the

230

integrity of the configuration. Each Image is potentially metaphorical, and thus not terminologically fixed or taxonomically categorized. Even literal components can be seen as abstractions. The grail is a vase, the Rose in Guillaume de Lorris a flower. But the vase and flower are closer to what an *Urpflanze* would be than to the real objects.[4] As synecdoche, the significance of the configuration derives not from substantial properties peculiar to discrete components, but rather from the relation of those components to one another, and their separate contribution to the whole. Thus the sense of any episode in the *Roman de la rose* derives from the configurations of abstractions that form and reform about the Rose. The semantic range of the abstract components allows for shifting meanings and affective developments on different levels and in different contexts. The adaptation of the conceptual components or abstractions may be metonymic or allegorical in mode. Modification occurs in three ways: (1) replacement of one or more components in a configuration by one or more others; (2) addition or deletion of components; (3) adaptation of the semantic value of components.

The components in configuration form a *registre* in Zumthor's sense of ''un complexe de motifs et d'expressions formulaires,''[5] that is, of topical material adapted to a specific intention at a given place in the author's *matière*. The realization of such topical amplifications is the invention of ''argumenta, quae transferri in multas causas possunt'' (*De inventione,* II.15.48) [arguments which may be transferred into a great number of cases]. For medieval writers Imagination derives its validity from the emanation of an idea through the configuration the author invents to convey the idea to the observer or reader. As Zumthor argues, ''la structuration ainsi opérée . . . a accusé, 'isolé', éternisé [nota bene!] la situation originelle, réelle ou fictive, l'a fixée, soustraite aux fluctuations de l'expérience, l'a saturée ainsi de puissance significative, d'autant plus universelle que plus abstraite. La richesse et la complexité de cet ensemble postulaient sa diffusion: elles faisaient de lui . . . un langage mythique, une forme apte à recevoir toute espèce de contenu et à lui communiquer sa force.''[6] The poet's craft as imitation of Nature and through her of God realizes the conjunctive and disjunctive activities of Imitation. Imagination is thus the intimation of truth.

Guillaume de Lorris made Imagination suitable to the expression of *fin'amors*. To explicate and nuance abstract concepts consonant with *fin'amors,* the authors used personifications and figural allegory. The play of meaning and sentiment on the literal level elicits a more penetrating and refined understanding of the ideas the Images articulate, whether as metonymy or allegory. This allows for variation from one text or situation to another in accordance with semantic adaptation, authorial intention and understanding, and consequently choice of Images—in short, with authorial finesse. And it flies in the face of the oft-heard but superficial allegation that courtly poetry is monotonous and monolithic.

J'ay bien de besoingnes escriptes
Devers moy, de pluseurs manieres,
De moult de diverses matieres,
Dont l'une l'autre ne ressamble.
(Jugement Navarre, vv. 884–87)[7]

[As for me, I've written much, and in several different ways, on many diverse subjects which are not alike.]

This is not the verse of Deschamps or Jean de Meun, but of Machaut.

If the subject matter and Images of authors like Machaut and Froissart seem jejune or anemic to modern readers, perhaps we are victims of the historical blindness that caused Voltaire's animadversion to Shakespeare, his ghosts and barbarism. Shakespeare's first folio editors suggest that one must like their author in order to understand him. Must we like *fin' amors* to understand it?

Amours puet ses rais partout traire,
Mais qui n'a souffissant regart,
Dou regarder moult bien se gart.
(Alerion, vv. 3160–62)

[Love may dart his beams everywhere; but let those with weak eyes carefully avoid looking at them.]

The problem posed in the introduction to this study, and suggested by these lines of Machaut, is not an idle one.

D. Poirion has accurately summarized the thrust of courtly literature in the late Middle Ages. "Le lyrisme est d'abord entraîné vers un enrichissement des images sensibles, puis vers une réévaluation de l'amour en fonction de la vie concrète, vers un approfondissement de la vie intérieure dans le sens de la tristesse, enfin vers une sagesse éclairée par une culture morale plus humaniste mais toujours orientée vers Dieu."[8] This evolution raises important questions about historical mentalities and shifting human aspirations. Of course, words come and go, changing their meanings and their affective values like the leaves on Horace's tree or in Chaucer's wind. There is no doubt an inevitable embarrassment in taking courtly love seriously unless we are able, as for some Middle High German Minnesänger and Italian poets of the *dolce stil nuovo,* to link it to higher ideals or discover a more systematic conceptualization or striking metaphoric language. No doubt we also feel, albeit unconsciously, that to take Machaut seriously we should be willing to practice his arts. But surely this too is silly; it is certainly superficial. A Catholic can read Buddha with profit: "What was once joy and sorrow must now become knowledge."[9] Applying this suggestion from Cassirer, we may place ourselves in Machaut's and Froissart's position, and, like Christine de Pisan, observe and learn from the Imagination of others apparently unlike us. Chaucer's narrator in his love visions and romanticized narratives is not impossible to imitate. The combination of identification by rhetorical appeal and dramatic alienation because of the narrator's own intervention and chronological distance enhances the quality of our experience. This is precisely what the French word *appréciation* connotes.

But there are difficulties stemming from sources other than different historical mentalities. Even contemporary minds may fail to understand one another. Jean de Meun's brushing aside of *fin' amors* as an alternative to the love he describes and, more to the point, the dispute represented by the quarrel of the *Roman de la rose* are faults in the monolithic medieval mind as we tend to understand it today. We probably feel closer to the Humanists than to the courtiers in that controversy, and tend to share Robertson's and Fleming's preference for their reading of the *Rose* and see in Christine de Pisan's criticism nothing short of "frenzy."[10] This does not mean, however, that we must follow Jean de Meun and reduce the historical fact of *fin' amors* to absurdity and farce. The Court and the Church at any rate seem to have been on Christine's side, which both compounds the problem and gives us matter for reflection.

The writings of certain modern thinkers may enhance our appreciation of the phenomenon *fin' amors* in medieval literature. They wrote, in fact, under the influence of late medieval allegory and late medieval alchemy. C. G. Jung's concept of active imagination is directly inspired by esoteric thought on the nature of alchemical change. And we have seen in the *Echecs amoureux* Commentary that Imagination was a feature of alchemy and its conception of significant transformation. Tuve's and MacCaffrey's studies of the sources and origins of Spenser's poetry and Walter Benjamin's examination of the Baroque Trauerspiel identify Images and modes of representation proper to medieval Imagination. Thus the faculty of Imagination became a rich and varied mode to express human experience. And love has its place in that scheme. The fascinating diversity in Imagination referred to by Machaut in the passage cited above demands reassessment, indeed re-cognition, through a new reading of medieval literature on courtly love. Just as when Froissart reread Rose's poem after determining its intention, we too would benefit from such reconsideration. If writers like Jung, Tuve, Benjamin, Machaut, and Charles d'Orléans could derive as much profit from it as Froissart said he did, surely we too may learn something there. If all of them drew water from the same well, that water must be refreshing and restorative. It certainly calls for a reassessment of authors like Machaut and Froissart, of the personifications and gods and goddesses of courtly allegory who, like Pygmalion's statue, were constantly revitalized by the finesse of courtly Imagination.

The semantic variability of the literal level in allegory gives it an open potential for significance. It is amenable to diverse judgments depending on the meaning it is given and the context in which it is placed. Charles d'Orléans realized these possibilities and exploited them in his later poems. For the significance of other Images it is often necessary to make careful comparisons among different authors. Ultimately, the significance of the Images is recognizable through interrogation, the application in criticism of the topical formulae that the Middle Ages knew from Cicero and refurbished in the arts of poetry written by Matthew of Vendôme and Geoffrey of Vinsauf.

Jean de Meun, for example, used the Pygmalion story as an Image of idolatrous love at once foolish and sensual—"amour commune au monde," as the *Echecs* Commentator terms it. This did not prevent Machaut from using Pygmalion to represent the love of Jean de Berry for his wife in the *Fonteinne amoureuse*. The author of the *Ovide moralisé* read the same tale to show different scientific, historical, and religious truth *in bono* and *in malo*. Apollo could appear as Antichrist and Christ in successive, indeed parallel interpretations, then reappear in Froissart as lovesickness and good love in separate dits. The letter is neutral. The author's use of it, the *affectus sermocinantis,* endows the letter with intentionality. Our problem may be presented in a nutshell. In Baudouin de Condé's *Oliphant,* the traits of the Elephant show forth the virtues and qualities of Marguerite de Flandres. The incongruity of the two terms of comparison is a modern imposition that does not seem to have occurred to the medieval writer. For us the elephant is an animal; for him it was an Image.[11]

The adaptability of Images is evident in those which recur in different works with various significations. Thus, Machaut's Pygmalion in the *Fonteinne amoureuse* shows forth faithful conjugal love, the second type of love as outlined by the *Echecs* Commentator. But there was also a third kind: courtly love. Here there was no precedent or authority to fall back on within the sharp doctrinal separation between good and bad love. But this is a medieval problem, not a modern invention foisted onto the evidence. The phenomenon of *fin' amors,* outside and sometimes even opposed to marriage and conjugal love, maintained an ambiguous tie to the sexual urge, elicited fascination for almost half a millenium, even awe, but also a curious anguish, judging by the writings from that time. Anguish stemmed principally from the moral ambiguities and uncertainties inherent in a love lacking religious and social sanction. But that ambiguity was also a fruitful source of topical amplification and interpretation.

If Andreas Capellanus could separate love and conjugal affection by entirely extrinsic, imposed criteria such as suitability of jealousy, superiority of husband to wife, and necessity of fear, the *Echecs* Commentator, who did know a lot about French romance and lyric, felt free to assert that, despite external differences like the extramarital fact, the sentiment in *fin' amors* and conjugal love is of the same essence and quality. This idea, which he derives from Arthurian romance, is best illustrated in the writings of Chrétien de

Troyes, who makes conjugal and extraconjugal love share many of the qualities and activities typical of aristocratic love in medieval literature. Between the surface distinctions in Andreas and the essential sameness of Chrétien's conception of good love, lies the wide range of courtly writing. This is the *fin'amors* the poets sought to understand and realize in diverse Imaginations. They did so with a perseverence that the historical fact of courtly love makes evident, and for which Imagination and an aristocratic *esprit de finesse* provided means to investigate and explain. The combined arts of love, music, and poetry made their interpretations clear, credible, and meaningful. It was all good rhetoric.

Reference Matter

Appendix
Music and Poetry

IN THE ROMANCES AND DITS there are numerous contrived situations in which shorter poems and sometimes their music are introduced into the narrative. Although presumably fictional, or at least generalized to such an extent that biographical allusions are unrecognizable, these situations are close enough to actual practice to indicate the use made of short poems in contemporary society. It is thus possible to illustrate the principal uses of the poems and songs by these examples. We may begin with the trouvères in order to show the continuity and uniformity of practice.

THIRTEENTH-CENTURY ROMANCE: *GUILLAUME DE DOLE* AND THE *ROMAN DE LA VIOLETTE*

Union of text and music is evident from the end of the eleventh century.[1] The trouvères, like the troubadours, were poet-composers. Their manuscripts frequently (but not usually) contain both words and music.[2] Furthermore, in romance from the thirteenth century on, there is emphasis on the close relation between music as *chant* and word as *dit*.

> Il conte d'armes et d'amors
> Et chante d'ambedeus ensamble,
> S'est avis a chascun et samble
> Que cil qui a fet le romans
> Qu'il trovast toz les moz des chans,
> Si afierent a ceuls del conte.
> (*Guillaume de Dole,* vv. 24–29)[3]

This adaptability of the poem to suitable situations in the romance's narrative is common throughout the *Guillaume de Dole* and the *Roman de la violette*. These two thirteenth-century romances make extensive use of inserted poems and songs. Each poem is sung or recited for one purpose or another by the characters in the romances.[4]

Expression of joy is a common reason for singing, as Machaut, Froissart, and Deschamps had stated: "De la joie qui l'en rehete / Li est ciz chans dou cuer volez" (*Dole,* vv. 5104–5).[5] The Romantic notion of the wandering troubadour is not entirely inaccurate. And the joyful singer suits the medieval commonplace that constant sorrow is unbecoming to a nobleman. An opportune song may restore self-control and harmony.

239

Si s'en vet chans travers toz seuls,
Mout dolenz et mout angoisseus,
Tenant sa main a son arçon.
Des bons vers mon segnor Gasson
Li sovient, qui li font grant bien,
Que prodom ne gaaigne rien
En fere doel qui riens ne vaut.

(Dole, vv. 3617–23)[6]

Since the song is about disconsolate love, it can hardly be the words that relieve the sadness.

Music thus serves to assuage the sorrows of love and other emotions. Love itself, as a subject, may well suffice to lighten the heart, but rarely can it do so in the heavy atmosphere of most courtly songs—provided one pays careful attention to the words of those songs! In social surroundings, with dancing and singing, the music tends to outweigh the words in affective impact, just as today the most woebegone love song or the most trenchant social or political criticism may, through its music, be the occasion for dance and laughter.

L'empereres, por lui esbatre,
Le reveut de tant conforter
Qu'il veut ceste chançon chanter.

(Dole, vv. 1766–68)[7]

This will not happen, however, if the lover's sorrow is too great:

Tout ensi va Gerars chantant,
Qui conforter se cuide en tant;
Mais quant li menbre de s'amie,
Molt tenrement pleure et larmie
Et plaint son cors et sa biauté.

(Violette, vv. 1322–26)[8]

This touches on another commonplace of courtly poetry: the contrast between feelings and external obligations.[9] In the Violette, a parallel is made between the lover and the jongleur when Gerard disguises himself as a jongleur in order to see his lady.

Or puis jou bien por voir retraire
Que jougleres mal mestier a;
Que quant plus froit et mesaise a,
Tant le semont on plus souvent
De chanter et seïr au vent.

(Violette, vv. 1395–99)

The result may be unwillingness to sing or write, mutism, or self-forgetfulness.

D'une chambre ou li baron sont
Oï l'empereres cest vers.
Com ses pensers estoit divers
De ciaus qu'il avoit assamblez!
Si li est ses solaz emblez
Qu'il ne set qu'il die ne face.

(Dole, vv. 4594–99)

Or,

> Cil chanteor ne lor chançon
> Ne la poënt esleecier;
> Si oï ele conmencier
> Iceste chançon auvrignace.
> Se ne fust cil, cui Diex mal face,
> Qui la cuida desloiauter,
> Mout seüst bien cest vers chanter.
> (Dole, vv. 4646-52)

But then singing may also help one to forget sorrow:

> Oublïer se velt, si chanta
> Ceste chanchon, qui bon chant a;
> C'amours l'a mise en grant malage.
> (Violette, vv. 3120-22)[10]

Or it may serve as a remedy by releasing complaint and lamentation.

> Sospirant, plorant et plains d'ire,
> Com de traïtor et felon
> Se plaint es vers de sa chançon.
> (Dole, vv. 3748-50)

The song itself obviously had very strong, immediate expressive force.

The music could not but enhance the rhetorical impact of the words, which might recall past adventures or communicate a message or appeal. For memory:

> Pour chou qu'il me souvient ore
> De li, chanterai jou encore
> Ceste chançon, pas ne lairai.
> (Violette, vv. 234-36)[11]

For communication either explicit or implicit (here one finds again the argumentative intent of courtly poetry stressed by Brunetto Latini):

> Oïr porrés apertement
> Comment je vous escondirai
> En un vier que je vous dirai,
> C'aparmain porrés escouter.
> (Violette, vv. 437-40)[12]

The particular application of the words in context makes them explicit. Thus the contention, now generally regarded as merely Romantic, that the songs aptly express personal experience, is not wrong.

> Por le deduit des oisellons
> Que chascuns fet en son buisson,
> De joie ont comencié cest son.
> (Dole, vv. 1298-1300)[13]

More explicitly amorous:

> Mais amours, ki onques ne fine,
> Le semont que il chant encore

> Ceste cançonnete a karole,
> Ne li caut ki en ait envie.
>> *(Violette,* vv. 200–203)[14]

The personal application did not preclude a more aesthetic, dispassionate appreciation of the artistic qualities of song and word, especially if the words were difficult to understand.

> S'oïrent chanter un vallet
> La bone chançon le Vidame
> De Chartres. Onques mes nule ame,
> Ce li sambla en chevauchant,
> Miex ne dist cest vers ne cest chant.
>> *(Dole,* vv. 4122–26)

Nonetheless, the song could always receive a personal application. The artistry made such application more gratifying, and perhaps enriched the personal understanding: "Fet li rois: 'Juglet, a droiture / Fu ciz vers fet por moi sanz doute.'" *(Dole,* vv. 4132–33)[15]

Seven principal purposes for song and word are conspicuous in the two romances. The emphasis may shift from musical composition to poetic, even exclude one or the other entirely. The seven are: expression of joy; comfort in distress; inspiration by surrounding circumstances or settings; rapport with personal experience; communication of message or expression of feeling or thought; critical, aesthetic appreciation of artistry; expression of contrast between personal experience and poetic experience as failure, muteness or disinclination to perform. In short, the evidence of the *Guillame de Dole* and the *Roman de la violette* permits us to identify in a given poem (*chant* plus *dit*) music, poetry, personal experience, and intimate communication. No intention is exclusive; they may well play complementary or contrasting roles in a given setting. Certainly it is not possible to limit the use made of a given courtly poem in the Middle Ages to any one of these intentions.

These conclusions suggest why music could be used even by poets after Machaut, who were not composers. Since music could function independently of the words, poets like Froissart could either adapt the poem to a known melody or present it without music. In any event the evidence of late courtly poetry confirms the semantic and rhetorical intention of the poem discernible in *Guillaume de Dole* and the *Violette*. This may be illustrated by the *Cassidorus* and the *Chastelaine de Vergi*. Robert Bossuat has demonstrated how the former expands a *jeu-parti* into narrative, just as, reciprocally, a given situation may be abstracted and synthesized as a debate or analysis in any fixed form.[16] The *Chastelaine de Vergi* is the exemplification of the ideas expressed in one stanza of a *chanson* by the Châtelain de Couci.

> Si est en tel point autressi
> Com li chastelains de Couci,
> Qui au cuer n'avoit s'amor non,
> Dist en un vers d'une chançon:
> Par Dieu, Amors, fort m'est a consirrer
> Du dous solaz et de la compaingnie

> Et des samblanz que m'i soloit moustrer
> Cele qui m'ert et compaingne et amie.
> (vv. 291–98)[17]

The knight in love with the Châtelaine de Vergi finds a parallel to his own experience in the abstract language of the Châtelain de Couci. Thus his own actions become exemplary (see vv. 15–21, 951–55).

THE FOURTEENTH CENTURY: *MELIADOR* AND THE *VOIR-DIT*

Two fourteenth-century poems permit us to identify and appreciate the double function of the fixed form as poem and song: Froissart's *Meliador* and Machaut's *Voir-Dit*. First, they contrast the poet-composer and the poet who was not a composer. Second, the *Voir-Dit*, being at least pseudoautobiographical, allows us to understand the author's intention in writing both words and music, as well as the independent, complementary, or antithetical uses to which he puts them. The *Meliador*, an impersonal romance set in an Arthurian past, shows in an exemplary way how poem and song were written and used in a conventional setting. Finally, as with *Guillaume de Dole* and the *Violette*, the great number of illustrative passages vouchsafes the evidence. One finds the same separation between the musical and the verbal as in the thirteenth-century romances, and within each of these categories between public and private usage as described by Deschamps in the *Art de dictier*. I shall discuss each category in turn under the headings identified in the study of the thirteenth-century romances and in light of the possibilities for narrative amplification suggested by the function of the chanson in the *Chastelaine de Vergi*. The principal difference between the works of Machaut and Froissart and those of the thirteenth century is the preponderance of pieces allegedly written and composed by the characters in the works; that is, original invention predominates over borrowing. There is also greater use of the poem without music.

EXPRESSION OF JOY

The poem sung for festive occasions to accompany song and dance is evident in the following passage:

> Et Argentine, sans sejour,
> S'en part et en la sale vient,
> Et regarde, et voit c'on se tient
> Tout en carolant par le doy,
> Et que menestrel sont tout quoi,
> Et cantoient cil baceler
> Et ces damoiselles moult cler.
> Si vint la si a point Argente
> C'une pucelle jone et gente
> Avoit, comme lie et doucete,
> Commencié une cançonnete,
> Que sa dame ooit volentiers;
> Car moult li plaisoit li mestiers
> Dou canter, il n'est mies doubte.
> Argente se taist et escoute

243

> Que c'estoit uns rondelès gens,
> Qui doit bien plaire a jones gens
> Qui ont la pensée amoureuse.
> (*Meliador*, vv. 17122–39)

Music was appropriate at such times, as one personage asserts:

> Jamais ne vous deveriés taire,
> Mais toutdis dire telz paroles
> Ou a dances ou a caroles.
> (*Meliador*, vv. 19623–25)[18]

Even in small groups the practice obtained, although such performance is closer to Deschamps' *musique naturele*. This includes unaccompanied or solitary singing.

> Melyador comme amoureus,
> Lors qu'il fu partis de Housagre,
> De coer resjoÿ et halagre
> Commança .I. doulz rondelet
> A canter; c'est raisons c'on l'et,
> Car il fu amoureus et gens.
> (*Meliador*, vv. 19038–43)

This is the principal source of delight for Péronne d'Armentières in the *Voir-Dit:* "car c'est le plus grant esbatement que je aie, que de oÿr & de chanter bons dis & bonnes chansons, se je le savoie bien faire" (p. 48). Machaut avers the same for himself (p. 19). The *Voir-Dit* also contains scenes illustrating dance and song in large groups (vv. 3573–82).[19]

COMFORT IN DISTRESS

Intimate private reading or singing stresses the consolatory effect of poetry and music. The *Meliador* and the *Voir-Dit* contain numerous passages where consolation leads to joy.

> Je ne vous adiroie pas
> Le grant bien et le grant solas,
> Que vostre cançon m'a ci fait.
> Li parler en sont tres parfait,
> Et dame, qui ensi s'avance
> A parler, par bonne ordenance,
> Reconforte moult son ami.
> (*Meliador*, vv. 10136–42)

It is a constant theme in the exchanges described in the *Voir-Dit*, whether by Péronne or Machaut. Machaut: "Ma tres-chiere & souveraine dame, je vous remerci ... de vos douces, courtoises & amiables escriptures. Car vraiement, je y preng grant plaisance, grant confort & grant deduit, toutes les fois que je les puis veoir, oÿr & tenir; & certes je vous en doy bien mercier; car elles font & ont faict plus grans miracles à ma personne que je ne vi onques faire n'à saint n'à sainte qui soit en paradis. Je estoie assourdis, arrudis, mus, impotens, par quoy joie m'avoit de tous poins guerpi & mis en oubli; mais vos douces escriptures me font oÿr & parler, venir & aler, & m'ont rendu joie qui ne savoit mais où je demouroie" (*Voir-Dit*, p. 41). Péronne: "je ne preng confort ne esbatement fors en veoir & en lire" (p. 57). *Meliador* is in no way different.

> Pour solaciier Phenonée,
> La fu une feste ordonnée,
> Belle et courtoise, a ceste fois,
> Apriès souper, dedens le bois.
> Et la fu au chanter premiere
> Une pucelle coustumiere
> De dire motès et cançons.
> (*Meliador*, vv. 22856–62)[20]

This in no way conflicts with the expression and evocation of joy. Even sad or disconsolate themes may dissolve into joy in song.[21]

INSPIRATION FROM SURROUNDING CIRCUMSTANCES OR SETTINGS

Entirely external circumstances may lead to the composition or the performance of a poem or song. Traditional in courtly poetry was competition between poets, as in the *puys*. In the *Voir-Dit* there is a poetic debate for a public contest.[22] Or a poem may serve as a gift;[23] here, however, the distinction between personal and public intention is maintained: "&, par ma foi, il ne me desplaist point se vous envoiés à autres qu'à moy; car chose qui vous plaist ne me porroit desplaire. Mais qu'il vous plaise que je les aie la premiere" (*Voir-Dit*, p. 194). Less intimate but equally personal is this example from *Meliador:* "C'une cançon soit chi cantée / En l'onneur de vostre cousine" (vv. 8447–48). Conventional motifs may serve as inspiration, like the song of birds that reminds one of the beloved.[24] This procedure is prominent in Oton de Grandson, Alain Chartier, and Charles d'Orléans for May Day, Spring, Saint Valentine's, etc.

RAPPORT WITH PERSONAL EXPERIENCE

External considerations, although they have their place in inspiration, are secondary to the intention to communicate, as Brunetto Latini and Deschamps point out. Communication is by far the most frequent use made of the poems except for the simple expression of joy. It is the justification for speaking or singing *de sentement*, "Car qui de sentement ne fait, / Son ouevre et son chant contrefait" (*Remede de Fortune*, vv. 407–8).

Sentement is the principal concern of the poets. Without it, Machaut insists, no genuine poetry is written. Love is the inspiration,[25] the sentiment in need of expression:

> Amours m'a mis et met en voie,
> Et chi le sentement m'envoie
> De faire .I. rondelet joli,
> Et tout pour l'amour de celi,
> Que tu me dis et si m'afferme
> Que je verai dedens brief terme.
> (*Meliador*, vv. 11970–75)[26]

245

Similarly in the *Voir-Dit:* "Mon chier amy je vous envoie ce virelay qui est fait de mon sentement, & vous pri que vous me vueilliez envoier des vostres. Car je sçay bien que vous en avez fait depuis que je n'oÿ nouvelles de vous. Et j'ay veu une balade en laquelle il a *En lieu de bleu dame vous vestez vert,* & si ne sçay pour qui vous la féistes; se ce fu pour moy, vous avez tort" (pp. 346–47). This includes both words and song.

> Amours voelt que droit ci j'approce
> A faire .I. rondelet joli,
> Et je voir, pour l'amour de li,
> Li ferai tout presentement
> Et canterai de sentement.
> *(Meliador,* vv. 18450–54)

The musical *sentement* was then "grafted" onto the poem for communication to the lady.

> Adont s'esmut a haute vois
> De chanter .I. seul rondelet,
> Et croi qu'il le fist tout a fet
> Qu'il le canta, car il fu cours,
> Mais uns grans sentemens d'amours
> Estoit ou rondelet entés.
> *(Meliador,* vv. 9782–87)

This realizes the dual function of the poem: expression of the *sentement* to the loved one and appreciation of its quality by third parties. The former is, of course, the more important purpose: "Je vous suppli tant humblement comme je puis & de tout mon cuer que vous me vueilliez envoier l'une des choses que vous mettés plus près de vostre cuer, par quoy je la puisse mettre si près du mien comme je porray" *(Voir-Dit,* p. 191).[27]

Others may adapt the song to their own experience.

> En cantant volt les mos haper,
> Car pas a oubliier ne fait,
> Car il touchent moult a son fait.
> *(Meliador,* vv. 23011–13)

This is typical in courtly love.

> Argente se taist et escoute
> Que c'estoit uns rondelès gens,
> Qui doit bien plaire a jones gens
> Qui ont la pensée amoureuse.
> *(Meliador,* vv. 17136–39)

It provides lovers with agreeable pastime, food for thought, and instruction for improvement *(Meliador,* vv. 19585–605). The poetic and epistolary exchanges between Flos and Rose in Froissart's *Prison amoureuse,* as was shown in chapter 7, also illustrate acceptance and adaptation to personal circumstances of the emotions and thoughts of others.

Love in the heart is deemed essential to the composition and appreciation of courtly song and verse; it is a traditional requirement in courtly poetry by the fourteenth century.[28] In Froissart and Machaut it includes Imagination as the Image of the lady or the qualities associated with her in the mind's eye.

> Lors me pria que je préisse
> Matere en moy dont je féisse
> Chose de bonne ramembrance.
> *(Voir-Dit,* vv. 2184–86)

The *Meliador* is even more explicit.

> Tout ce qui au chanter m'encline,
> Ce fait li amour d'Ermondine
> Pour qui je sui jolis et gais.
> Li doulz pensers m'est grans souhais;
> A lui il n'est si vraie cose,
> Et parmi tant moult bien je m'ose
> Fiier d'un seul rondelet dire,
> Car j'ai matere qui m'i tire.
> *(Meliador,* vv. 7744–51)

And her qualities are the source of another composition.

> Or me dittes a la parclose
> Se vous avés a vo retour,
> En considerant la valour
> D'Ermondine et son gent maintien,
> Fait aucune cose de bien,
> Rondelet, balade ou cançon.
> *(Meliador,* vv. 17777–82)

He proposes to compose by putting down "ce qu'en samblance / M'en venra" (vv. 17792–93). The following passage, which refers to a lady's composition, sums up best the entire process of composition in relation to Imagination.

> Ymaginations le vinrent,
> Qui en .I. tel pourpos le tinrent
> Que chi vous m'orés regarder.
> Elle prist a considerer
> L'arroy, le maintien, la samblance
> Et la jolie contenance
> De Melyador le vassal,
> Et comment il est a cheval
> Et a piet gratïeus et frices.
> Ces pensers [li] furent si riches
> Que la belle adont s'eslargi,
> A tout ce que elle entendi,
> A faire .I. petit rondelet
> Et, de corage joliet,
> Elle en entra en ordenance,
> Et prist ens es mos tel plaisance
> Qu'elle les recorda .III. fois;
> Puis le canta a clere vois
> En la cambre toute seulete.

247

> Si fu tele la cançonnete
> Et faite de bon sentement
> Que vous orés presentement.
> *(Meliador,* vv. 17843–64)

More succinctly in the *Voir-Dit,* Machaut recapitulates the same steps in describing the composition of a poem: "je ne le sceusse faire se il ne venist de vous" (p. 369).

COMMUNICATION OF MESSAGE OR EXPRESSION TO THE BELOVED OF FEELING OR
THOUGHTS

Brunetto Latini emphasizes the communicative intention of the poem, to which all rhetorical embellishment is subservient. This obtains in all courtly poetry, and is especially conducive to the intimacy of this abstract poetry.[29] Of course, the *Voir-Dit* makes narrative use of the communicative intention, not only through the epistles but also through the direct exchange of poems between the lovers. "Je vous envoie aussi une balade de mon piteus estat qui a esté.... Si verrez comme je prie aus dames qu'elles se vestent de noir, pour l'amour de moi. J'en feray une autre où je leur prieray que elles se vestent de blanc pour ce que vous m'avez gari" *(Voir-Dit,* p. 42). There is thus in each poem both a public posture and a private intent comprehensible to the addressee. But the private intention may also be imposed independently of the author.

> Siques quant la dame ot canté,
> Li rois, a ce motet hapé,
> A Melyador dist en l'eure:
> "Biaus cousins, certes, je couleure
> Ceste parole ou nom de vous."
> Et Melyador, qui fu tous
> Apparilliés que de respondre,
> Dist: "Sire, on le poet bien expondre
> En quelque maniere c'on voet.
> Se ma souveraine se muet
> Au canter tout ce pour m'amour,
> Ossi tent mon coer sans demour
> A faire tout a sa plaisance."
> *(Meliador,* vv. 30138–50)[30]

The application of the poem to Meliador himself conforms to the listener who adapts the poem's contents to his or her circumstances. Such imposition was apparently taken for granted.[31] While serving as straightforward proof of love *(Meliador,* vv. 916–22, 6201–21), the validity, the *sentement* of such imposition could also provoke quarrels by misunderstandings or facilitate reconciliations *(Voir-Dit,* vv. 5770–73, 8618–35).[32]

CRITICAL AND AESTHETIC APPRECIATION OF ARTISTRY

However easily some of the poems seem to have been written (especially the rondeaux[33]), they were still subject to critical scrutiny. The poet sought perfection as proof of his sincerity and worthiness. *Meliador* contains many illustrations of the relation between artistry and sentiment.

> C'est pour la parfaite
> Ma dame, que je tieng a dame.
> Se ne voudroie pas, par m'ame,
> Ou cas que pour l'amour de li
> Le fay, que g'i eusse falli.
> (*Meliador*, vv. 15894–98)

And:

> Car, s'elle n'estoit amoureuse
> Et en cel estat virtueuse,
> Elle ne poroit tout ce faire.
> (vv. 28687–89)[34]

The sentiment thus enhanced the artistry of the poem.

> Moult bien me plaist li rondelés,
> Car il est de bon sentement,
> Et assés amoureusement
> L'avés fait selonc vo matere.
> (vv. 17806–9)[35]

It was possible to judge the verisimilitude of the sentiments expressed: "nous les volons oïr / Pour vos parolles averir" (*Meliador*, vv. 21409–10), or to choose among different poems in accordance with the nature and quality of one's own love: "Ceste parole n'est pas mienne, / Car onques n'amai par tel art" (*Meliador*, vv. 20353–54).[36]

The variety of *sentement* accounts as well for the diversified epithets used to designate and judge different poems: "pas rudes ne let" (*Voir-Dit*, v. 152), "belle et gratïeuse, / Et moult grandement amoureuse" (*Meliador*, vv. 15672–73), "Femininement dit et fet" (*Meliador*, v. 19605),[37] "De biau langage tres courtois" (*Meliador*, v. 23631), "Biaus et jolis" (*Meliador*, v. 23659),

> Car il est fors entrelaciés
> De parlers doulz et gracïeus
> Et moult grandement amoureus.
> (*Meliador*, vv. 23692–94)

"Bien fais, oultre l'ensengne" (*Meliador*, v. 25082), "bien fais / Et amoureusement retrais" (*Meliador*, vv. 25133–34), "ce doulz rondelet, / Amoureusement dit et fet" (*Meliador*, vv. 25591–92), "moult grandement fu prisiés" (*Meliador*, v. 29162), etc.

The marked awareness of artistry accounts for the frequent emphasis on correction and imitation. Péronne d'Armentières is especially anxious to have Machaut improve what she has written. "Et sur ce, je vous envoie un virelay, lequel j'ay fait; & se il y a aucune chose à amender, si le vueilliés faire, car vous le sarés mieus faire que je ne fais; j'ay trop petit engien pour bien faire une tele besongne, & aussi n'eus-je onques qui rien m'en aprenist" (*Voir-Dit*, p. 48).[38] Machaut did regard instruction as part of his obligation to her, and treated her poems accordingly. "Les .ij. choses que vous m'avés envoiées sont tres-bien faites à mon gré: mais se j'estoie .j. jour avec vous, je vous diroie & apenroie ce que je n'apris onques à créature; par quoy vous les feriés

249

mieus" (*Voir-Dit*, p. 21).[39] She does improve with practice and instruction, as a good student would under a beloved master.[40]

> Et elle fist ce rondelet
> Qui ne me semble mie let,
> Car il n'i ha rien que reprendre.
> (*Voir-Dit*, vv. 3632–34)

Machaut himself does not always measure up to his own standards. This may be because of some disturbance unrelated to his love (the *diversa* and *alienatio* of the *Epistolae duorum amantium*), internal stress, or illness (*Voir-Dit*, vv. 826–28).[41] In composing the *Voir-Dit* itself, Péronne becomes authority and corrector.[42] Judgment and correction are alluded to in the *Meliador* as well.[43]

Imitation was one means of developing skill and acquiring taste.[44]

> Cousine, cilz m'agrée
> Assés mieus que cilz de devant.
> J'en prise mieulz le couvenant,
> Les paroles et la façon.
> (*Meliador*, vv. 19653–56)[45]

But there was also substance—*sens*—to the poems, which acquired a rhetorical intent when expressed through appropriate Imagination.

> Pour ses pensées mieulz pollir
> Commença la .I. rondelet
> A faire, et ançois que fait l'et
> Eut mainte imagination.
> (*Meliador*, vv. 18823–26)

Particularly sought after was what may be called the moral improvement derived from writing and reading the poem. "Et comment que je ne vaille riens & sache moins, elles me font amer honneur & haÿr deshonneur, & fuir vice, pechié & toute villenie" (*Voir-Dit*, p. 19). The point is worth dwelling upon, given the current tendency to minimize the significance of the message in courtly poetry or to deny its redeeming value. "Et de ce que vous dites que chose qui vient de vous ne me puet amender, je di que, sauve vostre grace, qu'elle m'a amendée & amende de jour en jour; car je me paine de faire chose à mon pooir de quoy il aille bonnes nouvelles par devers vous; et vostre bonté me fait amer tous les bons & eslongnier tous les autres" (*Voir-Dit*, pp. 28–29). This is what distinguishes *fin'amors* from *fole amour* in Guillaume de Lorris and in the Commentary on the *Echecs amoureux*. It is an old idea constantly revitalized since the earliest courtly writers.[46]

> Li oïrs m'en a fait grant bien.
> Si vous en remerci .c. fois,
> Il m'en souvenra tout ce mois
> Et si en vaurrai assés mieulz.
> (*Meliador*, vv. 7553–56)

The source of worth is love. Upon hearing a balade, someone in the *Meliador* exclaims:

> Sire, c'est uns grans biens
> D'estre ensi jolis et joieus.
> Point ne prise ces anoieus,
> Qui ne font toutdis que muser.
> Amours voelent bien d'el user,
> Canter, jouster et tournoiier.
> Trop bien affiert a chevalier
> D'estre ou parti ou je vous voi,
> Et ossi dire le vous doi
> Puis que je sui de vo conseil;
> Siques, sire, je vous conseil
> Que toutdis tenés cel argu,
> Par quoi devant le roy Artu
> Viennent de vous bonnes nouvelles.
> *(Meliador, vv. 13880–93)*

This expands the discussion to include the advantages gained by participation in courtly life, including love and poetry. Thus the interrelationship between poet and prince that Poirion has described shows itself in the commissioned poem. The link with Arthur's court conforms to the special mission of Arthurian literature in the propagation of *fin' amors* that we read of in the *Echecs amoureux* and in Watriquet de Couvin.

Thus, even the commissioned poem is not ipso facto artificial, vain, or insincere. Requests to write and sing are frequent in *Meliador*. Froissart's use of the poems of Wenceslas de Brabant as the fixed forms in the romance[47] illustrates this on a large scale. In the *Parfait du paon* the participants in the contest are said to be sincere, even though writing on command for a public performance. Their production is thus on a par with the execution of the oaths in the *Paon* sequence. The aristocratic "word of honor" guarantees their integrity. As long as the poem expresses a real sentiment there need be no discrepancy between the *poème d'occasion,* even when paid for or otherwise rewarded, and the poem written for personal reasons. The ideal combination is the poem written at the loved one's behest.

> Mais ma dame qui commande ha
> Seur moy, me dist & commanda
> Qu'aucune chose li déisse,
> Ou que de nouvel la féisse;
> Si fis cecy nouvellement
> A son tres-dous commandement.
> *(Voir-Dit, vv. 3605–10)*

There is nothing untoward or false in the situation. The *sentement* confirms the sincerity. The poet merely rises to the occasion, and the lady will recognize the *sentement* in the poem and apply it to herself. This is part of love's discrimination. Froissart's use of Wenceslas' poems in the *Meliador* in no way falsifies or perverts their purposes, but merely recognizes their excellence and appropriateness. This explains why poetic contests were possible.[48]

EXPRESSION OF CONTRAST BETWEEN PERSONAL EXPERIENCE AND THE POEM'S SENTIMENTS

The contrast between public and private posture could be exploited for rhetorical effect in composition. Dragonetti has shown to what extent the pathos in the trouvères' chansons derives from antithetical demands:[49] the lover must express joy, and do so *de sentement,* yet he may feel only sorrow, even despair. The conflict finds its way into the verse. The poets of the Second Rhetoric also use this conceit, though perhaps less self-consciously than the trouvères in their opening stanzas. It certainly could occur in romances and dits. Muteness and self-forgetfulness become important arguments in the elaboration of conflicting demands. The most striking example is the effect of Machaut's reading of the lai to his lady in the *Remede.*

Sickness and love may go together: *Amor est passio.* Machaut links them as the point of departure for the *Voir-Dit.* Péronne writes to him at the outset:

> On li a dit & raconté
> Qu'un yver & près d'un esté
> Avez esté griefment malades:
> Et que, toudis, faisiés balades,
> Rondeaus, motés & virelais,
> Complaintes & amoureus lais.
> Dont elle dit que c'est trop fort
> D'avoir en un cuer tel confort,
> Et qu'avoir puist pensée lie,
> Tant soit chargiés de maladie.
> (vv. 86–95)

On the other hand, Meliador cannot write because "droitement tous pesans sui" (v. 17814). Here however the *maladie* is love sickness. For earlier Meliador had composed a balade "Moiiennement lié et malade" (v. 17442). Sickness and joy evoke sympathy, as they counterpoint one another and ultimately harmonize like the Romantic blending of sweet song and sad thought. Péronne proclaims to Machaut: "je vous envoie ceste balade que j'ay puisie en la fontaine de larmes où mes cuers se baingne, quant je vous voy à tel meschief; car par Dieu je ne porroie ne vorroie bien ne joie avoir, puis que je vous saroie en doleur & en tristesce. Et, pour ce, ay fait ceste balade,—de cuer plourant en corps malade" (*Voir-Dit,* pp. 186–87). The prospect of writing while in such a state leaves the poet with two alternatives: consolation or impotence. We have examined the consolatory effect above, and refer to it only in passing here. It may happen in group singing and dance.

> Mais pour trouver aucun moiien
> Entre amour et ses maladies,
> Plusieurs damoiselles jolies
> Y ajoustent bien telz parolles,
> Pour plus resjoïr les carolles
> Et les festes ou elles vont.
> (*Meliador,* vv. 28626–31)

For Machaut, consolation is a private, solitary matter.

> Lors pour allegier ma dolour,
> Qui taint & palit ma colour,
> Je fis ceste balade-ci
> A cuer taint & malade, si
> Plein d'amoureuse maladie,
> Que meure en est la melodie.
> *(Voit-Dit,* vv. 7638–43)[50]

However, the effort may be too great. Sagremor must interrupt the composition of a balade because of his "coer... malade" (*Meliador,* vv. 26110–22). Even inspirational impotence may result from love sickness. Machaut's silence in the *Remede de Fortune* when his lady asks who wrote the lai recurs elsewhere when inspiration and will flag. Péronne is so griefstricken that she can complete only two of three stanzas to a virelai.

> Helas! la douce debonnaire,
> Le tiers ver ne pot onques faire,
> Tant estoit lasse & adolée,
> Triste dolente & esplourée.
> *(Voir-Dit,* vv. 8534–37)

Machaut stresses the debilitating effect of melancholy in the discussion of music in the *Prologue* (V, vv. 85–90).

SONG AND WORD

The most persistent problem in courtly poetry is the relationship of song to word. The manuscripts only compound the dilemma. Although Machaut is everywhere singled out as the last great poet to write his own music and set his verse to song,[51] it is a fact that most of the short pieces in his manuscripts are not set to music. Froissart was no composer, but he did set some poems to known melodies. His manuscripts B. N. fr. 830 and 831 contain no musical notation, nor space for it.[52] But Froissart assigns a known melody to one piece in the *Meliador* (vv. 28640–45). This is composition based on the use of *contrafacta,* or imposed melody. The melodic structure of most forms in the Second Rhetoric is well known,[53] and Froissart's use of music is in its way a more rigorous imposition of musical structure on form, one that parallels the development of the rondeau and the balade into regular forms. The use of *contrafacta* did not begin with Froissart. Machaut, for all his ability as a composer, did not hesitate on occasion to set his poems to music written by others. The *Voir-Dit* contains two examples. "J'ay fait le chant sur *Le grand desir que j'ay de vous véoir,* ainsi comme vous le m'aviez demandé & j'ay fait ainsi comme un *Rés d'Alemaigne*" (*Voir-Dit,* p. 55). This does not mean that no significant relation exists between word and song. In one place Machaut speaks as if there were some affinity between the kind of poem and the music and instrumentation and makes specific recommendations regarding voices, tempo, and choice of instruments. "Je vous envoie mon livre de *Morpheus,* que on appelle la *Fontaine amoureuse,* où j'ay fait un chant à vostre commandement & est à la guise d'un rés d'Alemaigne; & par Dieu longtemps ha que je ne fis si bonne chose à mon gré; & sont les tenures aussi doulces comme pappins dessalés...; & se veut dire de bien longue mesure; & qui la porroit mettre sus les orgues, sus cornemuses ou aultres instrumens, c'est sa droite nature" (p. 69). Thus while the music fixes form it also fits the sentiment expressed in the poem. In short, the music was chosen for the words. Note once again that Machaut's music is a *contrafactum*.

Music could get in the way of comprehension. This is obvious in two- and three-part polyphonic pieces where the words for all parts are sung at once, instead of having one part sung while leaving the others instrumental. The combination of religious, courtly, and scabrous verse in some of these compositions would hardly be conducive to sustained *sentement* or serious attention to content. Special effort was needed to catch (*haper*) the words when sung in this way.

> En cantant volt les mos haper,
> Car pas a oubliier ne fait,
> Car il touchent moult a son fait.
> (*Meliador*, vv. 23011–13)

The problem of comprehension multiplied with the increase in simultaneous singers.

> Là fumes servi de dous lais,
> D'entremés, & de virelais,
> Qu'on claime chansons baladées,
> Bien oÿes, bien escoutées,
> Et de tout le fait de musique,
> Tres-bien & tres-proprement; si, que
> On ne savoit auquel entendre.
> Là pooit-on assés aprendre;
> Car chascuns faisoit son effort
> De chanter bien, & bel & fort.
> (*Voir-Dit*, vv. 3573–82)

Accordingly, general festivities tended to stress the music rather than the substance of the poem.

> On doit de tant, vous voel je aprendre,
> Toutes cançons en bon gré prendre,
> Car on les fait seul pour esbatre,
> Non pour argüer ne debatre.
> (*Meliador*, 28657–60)

If the substance of the poem was important, song and word were separated in performance: "Le dit vous en dirai ançois / Que je ne vous face le chant" (*Meliador*, vv. 23912–13). And even in the foregoing example, the rondeau supposedly meant only for amusement shows certain qualities in its verbal expression.

> quant de bouce de dame ist
> Si plaisant mot, au dire voir,
> On l'en doit moult grant gré savoir;
> Car, s'elle n'estoit amoureuse
> Et en cel estat virtueuse,
> Elle ne poroit tout ce faire.
> (*Meliador*, vv. 28684–89)

Obviously the meaning of the words counted for something more than passing consideration in the speaker's mind. Péronne frequently requests music for the poems Machaut sends her. She wishes to sing what she enjoyed reading. The poem almost always precedes the "version notée." "Car en cas qu'elle la liroit, / Assez mieus l'en entenderoit" (Voir-Dit, vv. 2215-16). However a given piece may be performed, two distinct intentions are discernible in the romances and dits: lyrical and rhetorical. The former stresses music and is conducive to dance. The latter emphasizes thought and is conducive to reflection on the sentiments and ideas treated in the poem. The difference is, in medieval language, the same as that between *chanson* and *dit*. Deschamps' distinction in the *Art de dictier* is therefore a fundamental one: *musique artificiele* leads to dance, *musique naturele* to communication. Lack of joy and hopelessness were therefore real inhibitions to composition.

POETRY AS RHETORIC:
THE DISTINCTION BETWEEN SONG AND VERSE

Rhetoric fixed modes of thought governing the criticism of poetry. A good illustration is found in the poetic contest that concludes Jean de la Mote's *Parfait du paon*. The contest includes balades, some of which are set to music and some not.[54] Although one participant asserts that "balade vault trop peu quant elle n'est chantee" (v. 1211), the sentiments of the authors are the ultimate guarantee of its worth (v. 1214), since they vouchsafe the sincerity of the poem.[55] The judgments are based solely on the text of the poem, and are in no way determined by accompaniment (there is none) or singing (of which there is some). This corresponds to what Deschamps says in the *Art de dictier* on *musique naturele* and the poem's contents: "les faiseurs d'icelle ne saichent pas communement la musique artificiele ne donner chant par art de notes a ce qu'ilz font, toutesvoies est appellée musique ceste science naturele, pour ce que les diz et chançons par eulz faiz ou les livres metrifiez se lisent de bouche, et proferent par voix non pas chantable, tant que les douces paroles ainsis faictes et recordées par voix plaisent aux escoutans qui les oyent, si que au *Puy d'amours* anciennement et encores est acoustumez en pluseurs villes et citez des pais et royaumes du monde."[56] In the *Parfait du paon*, the decision follows a careful and repeated reading of the eight balades offered in competition: "Cascune des balades fu assez regardee, / Lute plus de .x. fois et bien consideree" (vv. 1396-97). And there is some difference of opinion (vv. 1398-1408).

The final decision is based on considerations of versification, correctness and elegance of expression, and understanding of good love. Specifically, these qualities or defects are noted:

1. Incorrect pronunciation ("ou secont ver....i. faus ronmant," v. 1412): note "avision" (v. 1326) in three syllables, whereas all corresponding rimes give full syllabic value to *i* before *o*
2. Repetition ("redicte en sens," v. 1414): "consideré"/"pensant" (vv. 1246-47).[57]
3. Grammatical error ("un genoul," v. 1415): perhaps "Et bien fais" (v. 1156), which is ambiguous, serving either as noun object to "donne," or as first person verb, neither of which is meaningful.
4. Subject and/or style not sufficiently elevated ("point tres hautement parlant," v. 1419).

5. Boast ("un poi va vantant," v. 1421).
6. Inappropriate treatment of good love ("dist qu'elle a nouvel amant / Li mot ne sont pas haut," vv. 1422–23). This does not mean that the words are not "plaisant," v. 1423.
7. A cheville ("piler," v. 1425).

The judgment confirms the impression obtained from the romances and dits that the poem is either song or word. The two may be complementary or they may fulfill independent functions, either when the words are not sung or when the notes are played without verbal accompaniment. One fundamental distinction accounts for this. The music was conducive to joy, and thus to dance and entertainment. The words were conducive to self-expression within established forms and conventions, were essentially rhetorical, and therefore demanded appreciation of the art and the message of the poem.[58] The norms were grammatical correctness, rhetorical excellence, and elevation of Imagination. The highest art of the Second Rhetoric is the fixed form, as it had earlier been the chanson, and its message is *fin' amors*.

It is therefore entirely correct to study courtly poetry, even the fixed forms, independently of the music—where there is music! And if Robert Guiette's thesis that courtly poetry was written for a discriminating, refined, and perceptive public capable of appreciating formal excellence is correct, it is now evident that the public was also discriminating in matters of love and courtliness. With respect to the latter, readers could recognize the author's sincerity and accommodate their sentiments to his or hers wherever this seemed appropriate. Art of poetry and art of love are therefore integrated and must be studied together. Music is an independent aspect of composition in most cases, or, where it is not, is adapted to authorial intention as expressed verbally.

Notes

INTRODUCTION

1 Arnaut Daniel, *Canzoni,* ed. G. Toja (Florence, 1960), II, 10–15 [I hear the song and the warbling in the woods; therefore, lest I be put to blame, I forge and file words of quality with Love's art, from which task I have no desire to withdraw]; Charles d'Orléans, *Poésies,* ed. Pierre Champion, Classiques français du moyen âge, 2 vols. (Paris, 1966), Rondeau CCLXXVI [An old relic in old satin].

2 See Daniel Poirion, *Le Poète et le prince: L'Évolution du lyrisme courtois de Guillaume de Machaut à Charles d'Orléans* (Paris, 1965), pp. 173–77.

3 Geoffrey Chaucer, *Works,* ed. F. N. Robinson, 2nd ed. (Boston, 1957, 1961), HF 725–28.

4 Paul Zumthor, *Langue et techniques poétiques à l'époque romane (XIe–XIIIe siècles)* (Paris, 1963), pp. 7–8. Cf. Pierre Bec, "Quelques réflexions sur la poésie lyrique médiévale: Problèmes et essai de caractérisation," *Mélanges offerts à Rita Lejeune,* 2 vols. (Gembloux, 1969), II, 1320–21.

5 Such matters are often problems more of fashion than of mentality or discrimination; one of the finest modern descriptions of courtly love is contained in the review of a modern work in *L'Express* (no. 1236, p. 52): "Cette suite de poèmes constitue un étonnant monument baroque, où la difficulté d'exprimer clairement des détails scabreux oblige le poète à des acrobaties verbales, à d'ingénieuses métaphores, dont la tradition remonte à Michel-Ange et à Shakespeare. Une tradition qui n'est autre que celle de l'amour dit courtois, fait d'interdits, de raffinement et de mystère."

6 "Three Meanings of Symbolism," *Yale French Studies* 9 (n.d.), 13.

7 See most recently Ulrich Mölk, *Trobar clus trobar leu: Studien zur Dichtungstheorie der Trobadors* (Munich, 1968); L. M. Paterson, *Troubadours and Eloquence* (Oxford, 1975).

8 See S. J. Williams, "An Author's Role in Fourteenth-Century Book Production: Guillaume de Machaut's *Livre ou je met toutes mes choses,*" *Romania* 90 (1969), 446.

9 Jean de Garencières, *Le Chevalier poète Jean de Garencières: Sa vie et ses poésies complètes,* ed. Y. A. Neal, 2 vols. (Paris, 1953), II, 103.

10 Robert Guiette, "D'une poésie formelle en France au moyen âge," *Revue des sciences humaines* (1949), pp. 61–68 [reprint in *Questions de littérature,* in *Romanica Gandensia* 8 (1960), 9–23; and in Paris 1972 under the original title in

a separate volume]; Silvio d'Arco Avalle, "Variazioni su tema obbligato," in *Antologia dei 'Saggi di Umanismo Cristiano'* (Pavia, 1973), pp. 371–80.

11   Bec in "Réflections," p. 1323; further, "les mots significatifs... qui reviennent constamment, jouissent d'une richesse sémantique particulière, d'une pluralité de valeurs, d'une puissance allusive, qui font le désespoir du philologue, mais étendent très loin le message poétique et compensent par là la pauvreté numérique des unités lexicales. Et c'est bien sûr dans la poésie 'savante', essentiellement mais non exclusivement, que ces *mots allusifs* se présentent en plus grand nombre: consacrés qu'ils sont par la maturité d'une tradition et cette *connivence* implicite entre poète et auditeur dont nous avons parlé." Thus lexicography becomes fundamental to understanding the poetic message; see G. M. Cropp, *Le Vocabulaire courtois des troubadours de l' époque classique* (Geneva, 1975). The demise of such poetry occurs when the polysemous abstraction and its qualifiers lose their nuances; see Richard Glasser, *"Abstractum agens* und Allegorie im älteren Französisch," *Zeitschrift für romanische Philologie* 69 (1953), 101–4. Lexicographical discrimination no doubt facilitated the reading of extensive manuscripts containing great numbers of chansons or balades; Zumthor, in the passage cited above, refers to the medievalist reading a single poem.

12   Ed. P. V. Mengaldo (Padua, 1968), II.ii.7 (pp. 35–36).

13   Daniel Poirion, *Le Moyen âge. II. 1300–1480, Littérature française,* ed. Claude Pichois, vol. II (Paris, 1971), p. 55.

CHAPTER 1

1   Ernest Langlois, *Recueil d'arts de Seconde Rhétorique* (Paris 1902), pp. vii–viii; W. F. Patterson, *Three Centuries of French Poetic Theory: A Critical History of the Chief Arts of Poetry in France (1328–1630),* 2 vols. (Ann Arbor, 1935), I, 9–10.

2   Douglas Kelly, "The Scope of the Treatment of Composition in the Twelfth- and Thirteenth-Century Arts of Poetry," *Speculum* 41 (1966), 261–78; and "Theory of Composition in Medieval Narrative Poetry and Geoffrey of Vinsauf's *Poetria Nova," Mediaeval Studies* 31 (1969), p. 144, n. 65. See also Eustache Deschamps, *L'Art de dictier,* in his *Œuvres complètes,* ed. A. Queux de Saint-Hilaire and G. Raynaud, 11 vols., (Paris, 1878–1904), XI, 291–92.

3   Heinrich Lausberg, *Handbuch der literarischen Rhetorik: Eine Grundlegung der Literaturwissenschaft,* 2 vols. (Munich, 1960), §§ 1–8; Hennig Brinkmann, *Zu Wesen und Form mittelalterlicher Dichtung* (Halle, 1928), pp. 12–13.

4   *Œuvres,* ed. E. Hoepffner, 3 vols. (Paris 1908–21). Cf. the *Fonteinne amoureuse,* vv. 1505–7.

5   Hoepffner, ed., *Œuvres,* I, lv.

6   See the anonymous *Règles de la Seconde Rhétorique,* in Langlois, *Recueil,* p. 12; and especially Patterson, *Three Centuries,* I, 82.

7   Brunetto Latini, *Li Livres dou tresors,* ed. F. J. Carmody, (Berkeley and Los Angeles, 1948), p. 319; and his *La rettorica,* ed. Francesco Maggini (Florence, 1915), pp. 36–37.

8   See Nigel Wilkins, ed., *La Louange des dames* (Edinburgh and London, 1972), pp. 15–16.

9 *Chansons of the Troubadours and Trouvères: A Study of the Melodies and Their Relation to the Poems* (Utrecht, 1972), p. 33.

10 Friedrich Gennrich, *Grundriß einer Formenlehre des mittelalterlichen Liedes als Grundlage einer musikalischen Formenlehre des Liedes* (Halle, 1932, and Darmstadt, 1970), pp. 26-27; *Musikwissenschaft und romanische Philologie* (Halle, 1918), p. 1.

11 Kenneth Varty, "Deschamps's *Art de dictier,*" *French Studies* 19 (1965), 164-65. But see Nigel Wilkins, ed., *One Hundred Ballades, Rondeaux and Virelais from the Late Middle Ages* (Cambridge, 1969), pp. 39-40; N. E. Wilkins, "The Post-Machaut Generation of Poet-Musicians," *Nottingham Mediaeval Studies* 12 (1968), 40-84.

12 See V. Chichmaref, ed., Guillaume de Machaut, *Poésies lyriques,* 2 vols. (Paris, 1909), I, lxxviii; Wilkins, *Louange,* pp. 26-43, and *One Hundred Ballades,* p. 2; Friedrich Ludwig, ed., Machaut, *Musikalische Werke,* 4 vols. (Leipzig, 1926-54), II, 7; L. Schrade, *Polyphonic Music of the Fourteenth Century: Commentary to Volume II and III* (Monaco, 1956), pp. 21-23.

13 Pierre Champion, ed., Charles d'Orléans, *Poésies,* I, xxxiv; Wilkins, *One Hundred Ballades,* p. 106. See also Isidore Silver, *The Intellectual Evolution of Ronsard,* 2 vols. (St. Louis, 1969-73), I, 75-76, and his "The Marriage of Poetry and Music in France: Ronsard's Predecessors and Contemporaries," in *Poetry and Poetics from Ancient Greece to the Renaissance* (Ithaca and London, 1975), pp. 152-84.

14 *La Prison amoureuse,* ed. Anthime Fourrier (Paris, 1974), vv. 337-41.

15 Machaut did the same occasionally: "*J'ay fait le chant sur Le Grand desir que j' ay de vous veoir,* ainsi comme vous me l'aviez demandé & j'ay fait ainsi comme un *Res d'Alemaigne,*" in *Le Livre du Voir-Dit,* ed. Paulin Paris (Paris, 1875), p. 55. See also pp. 68-69 in the *Voir-Dit.*

16 See the detailed discussion in the Appendix to this volume. Similar distinctions are evident in Middle High German literature; see Brinkmann, *Wesen,* pp. 17-18.

17 See also the *Prologue* V, vv. 1-8 and 159-68.

18 Cf. Balade CCXXX, v. 22: "Einsois les vueil toutes pour une amer."

19 *De amore libri tres,* ed. E. Trojel (Copenhagen, 1892), p. 18.

CHAPTER 2

1 *Epistolae duorum amantium: Briefe Abaelards und Heloises?* ed. Ewald Könsgen, Mittellateinische Studien und Texte, 8 (Leiden and Cologne, 1974), Letter LXXV [We did love wisely, which is, however, rare, given the fact that someone has asked: "who ever loved wisely?" We did indeed love wisely]; John Gower, *Confessio amantis,* in *The Complete Works,* ed. G. C. Macaulay, 4 vols. (Oxford 1899-1902), I, 18.

2 See Henri de Lubac, *Exégèse médiévale,* 4 vols. (Paris, 1959-64), especially the chapter "Symbolisme," II, pt. 2, 125-262. For the problem in courtly literature, see *Critical Approaches to Medieval Literature,* ed. Dorothy Bethurum (New York and London, 1960), especially the papers on "Patristic Exegesis in the

Criticism of Medieval Literature" by E. T. Donaldson (pp. 1-26), R. E. Kaske (pp. 27-60), and C. Donahue (pp. 61-82).

3 As well as *amours par amours*, or *bone, vraie, honeste amours*, etc. Cf. Jean Frappier, " 'D'amors,' 'par amors,' " *Romania* 88 (1967), 433-74. On the origins of the expression *amour courtois*, see Frappier, "Amour courtois," in *Mélanges Jean Boutière*, 2 vols. (Liège 1971), I, 243-52. Both articles are reprinted in Frappier's *Amour courtois et Table Ronde* (Geneva, 1973). The OED dates the earliest English example 1896; Frappier identifies the oldest French instance as G. Paris' in 1883.

4 Since the semantic field of *fin'amors* was broader than what courtly love normally connotes, the modern expression, despite its ambiguities, will be preferred in the present studies.

5 *The Consaus d'amours*, ed. W. M. McLeod, in *Studies in Philology* 32 (1935), 12 (§ 19). Cf. also Franz Quadlbauer, *Die antike Theorie der 'genera dicendi' im lateinischen Mittelalter* (Vienna, 1962), pp. 150-57; and Werner Ziltener. *Studien zur bildungsgeschichtlichen Eigenart der höfischen Dichtung: Antike und Christentum in okzitanischen und altfranzösischen Vergleichen aus der unbelebten Natur*, Romanica Helvetica 83 (Bern, 1972), p. 36, especially note 7.

6 In part because Gaston Paris introduced it as such in his early study of Chrétien's *Charrette;* see his "Etudes sur les romans de la Table Ronde: Lancelot du Lac," especially *Romania* 12 (1883), 518-24, 532-34. J. F. Benton has rightly observed that Paris misdirected our thinking about courtly love by his tendency to systematization and codification; see Benton's "Clio and Venus: An Historical View of Medieval Love," in F. X. Newman, ed., *The Meaning of Courtly Love* (Albany, 1968), pp. 19-20, 36-37. See J. M. Ferrante and G. D. Economou, eds., *In Pursuit of Perfection: Courtly Love in Medieval Literature* (Port Washington and London, 1975), p. 3-4.

7 D. W. Robertson, Jr., *A Preface to Chaucer: Studies in Medieval Perspectives* (Princeton, 1962), especially pp. 391-503; and his "The Concept of Courtly Love as an Impediment to the Understanding of Medieval Texts," in Newman, *Meaning*, pp. 1-18. However, the impediment may be in the eye of the beholder rather than in the object under consideration. Cf. Frappier's review of this and other articles in "Sur un procès fait à l'amour courtois," *Romania* 93 (1972), 145-93 (reprinted in *Amour courtois et Table Ronde*).

8 See Moshé Lazar, *Amour courtois et fin'amors dans la littérature du XIIe siècle* (Paris, 1964): "Plutôt que de vouloir tenter une définition sèche (et forcément incomplète) de la *fin'amors*, nous essayerons de capter l'atmosphère dans laquelle elle se développe, l'ambiance poétique dans laquelle elle s'inscrit" (p. 55).

9 Ernst Sieper, *"Les Echecs amoureux": eine altfranzösische Nachahmung des Rosenromans und ihre englische Übertragung*, (Weimar, 1898), p. 30 (punctuation mine). Sieper's resumé of Diane's words reveals the distinction: "Natürlich war eine Liebe dieser Art nicht nach dem Sinne der Venus." For the passages referred to in Geoffrey of Monmouth and Wace, see, respectively, the *Historia regum Britanniae* in Edmond Faral, *La Légende arthurienne*, 3 vols. (Paris, 1929), III, 246; *Le Roman de Brut*, ed. Ivor Arnold, 2 vols. (Paris 1938-40), vv. 10493-520. See Jean Frappier, "Le Concept de l'amour dans les romans arthu-

riens,'' *Bulletin bibliographique de la Société Internationale Arthurienne* 22, (1970), 119-36 (reprinted in *Amour courtois et Table Ronde*).

10 B.N. fr. 9197, fol. 225v. Cf. especially: ''Comme l'acteur dit en son livre rymé dont nous parlons des dammes de Bretaigne, qui ancyennement au temps du roy Artu ne daignoient amer nul chevalier quelconcques s'il n'estoit avant esprouvé estre preux et vaillant aux armes atout le mains troix fois. Ilz ne fu pas bon doncques telz dammes assaillir ne trop y mettre son cuer quant on voit qu'elles sont de tel fierté et de si grant orgueil, mais les doit on laissier a leurs pareilz'' (fol. 222r). Additional discussion of love ''in Arthur's time'': fols. 293r, 296r-v, 384r. The Commentator can be referring only to the Vulgate cycle or earlier works. Cf. Chrétien de Troyes, *Le Chevalier au lion (Yvain)*, ed. Mario Roques (Paris, 1971), vv. 13-32. The Post-Vulgate cycle extends explicitly the condemnation in the *Queste* over the entire cycle; see Fanni Bogdanow, *The Romance of the Grail: A Study of the Structure and Genesis of a Thirteenth-Century Arthurian Prose Romance* (Manchester and New York, 1966), pp. 208-15. René d'Anjou also closely associates Arthurian subjects with love, in a manner reminiscent of the Brito episode in Andreas Capellanus; see the *Livre du cuer d'amours espris,* ed. Ottakar Smital and Emil Winkler, 3 vols. (Vienna, 1926), §§ 40-58 and 275.

11 On the universality of the Commentator's classification, see Egidio Gorra, ''La Teorica dell'amore e un antico poema francese inedito,'' in *Fra drammi e poemi* (Milan, 1900), pp. 201-56. On marriage and love see in particular Richart de Fornival's *Consaus,* p. 15, § 25.

12 Ed. Georg Wimmer, Ausgaben und Abhandlungen aus dem Gebiete der romanischen Philologie, 76 (Marburg, 1888).

13 Huon followed his acknowledged forerunner, Raoul de Houdenc, who also made love integral to courtesy; see the latter's *Romans des eles,* in *Trouvères belges (nouvelle série),* ed. Auguste Scheler (Louvain, 1879), vv. 486-632.

14 The expression ''passe rose'' is the pseudonym for the author's lady in the *Partonopeu de Blois* continuation, eds. Leon Smith and Joseph Gildea, 2 vols. (Villanova, 1967-70), v. 3927; see also the dictionaries of Godefroy (X, 291) and Tobler and Lommatzsch (VII, col. 453).

15 Cf. Bohors in *The Vulgate Version of the Arthurian Romances,* ed. H. O. Sommer, 8 vols. (Washington, 1909-16), V, 332, ll. 21-26; ''Mes bohort fu mut pensis & dolenz de co que lancelot auoit conte de la fille al roi brangorre qui auoit eu enfant de li . & se uns autres en eust autresint parle . il ne lamast iames . car mout en auoit honte de co que la damoisele se pleingnoit de li . Mes pur co que lancelot est ses sires & ses cosins sen test il a itant . & nepurquant il bee ben a gabber lo de la fille al roi pescheur quant il uerra leu & tens.''

16 Douglas Kelly, ''Courtly Love in Perspective: The Hierarchy of Love in Andreas Capellanus,'' *Traditio* 24 (1968), 136 and 140-41, n. 49 (p. 141).

17 See the *Vulgate Arthurian Romances,* V, 82-84.

18 *La Mort le Roi Artu,* ed. Jean Frappier, 3rd ed. (Geneva, 1964), § 4 (pp. 3-4).

19 *Vulgate Arthurian Romances,* V, 105-12. The daughter ''seduces'' Lancelot even after conceiving Galaad (V, 379-80), which recalls Jean de Meun's conclusion to the *Rose;* see Winthrop Wetherbee, ''The Literal and the Allegorical: Jean de Meun and the *de Planctu Naturae*,'' *Mediaeval Studies* 33 (1971), 285-86.

20 See the *Queste del saint graal,* ed. Albert Pauphilet (Paris, 1949), p. 129; and *La Mort le Roi Artu,* pp. 264-66.

21 *Queste,* pp. 251-52.

22 See note 10 above; cf. Frappier, "Concept," pp. 119-36. Jehannot de Lescurel has poems expressing the thoughts of the *ami* and *amie* separated by considerable distance (XXXII, pp. 49-56) or by marriage (XXXIII, pp. 57-66), in *Chansons, ballades et rondeaux,* ed. Anatole de Montaiglon (Paris, 1855).

23 C. F. Ward, ed., *The Epistles on the "Romance of the Rose" and Other Documents in the Debate* (Chicago, 1911), pp. 94-95, ll. 463-66. See also Pierre-Yves Badel, "Pierre d'Ailly auteur du *Jardin amoureux,*" *Romania,* 92 (1976), 369-81. Robertson, *Preface,* pp. 361-64, and J. V. Fleming, *The "Roman de la rose": A Study in Allegory and Iconography* (Princeton, 1969), pp. 47-48 et passim, support the Humanists' reading of Jean de Meun against the objections of Christine de Pisan and Jean Gerson. They do not deal fairly with Jean de Meun's critics. There was a certain amount of bad rhetoric on both sides, and ignorance and misunderstanding of what both Guillaume de Lorris and Jean de Meun intended. But Christine's argument in Ward's Document XIII, far from being frenzied (see Robertson, p. 364), is eloquent and, at many points, offers a considered, credible critique of the thought and taste of the *Rose* continuation. For a more balanced assessment of the two sides and their argumentation, see Peter Potansky, *Der Streit um den Rosenroman,* (Munich, 1972). The debate is typical of acrimonious disagreement in any time of change (see Potansky, pp. 19-22). Rosemond Tuve herself shares Christine's perplexity at Jean's "loveless" poem in *Allegorical Imagery: Some Mediaeval Books and Their Posterity* (Princeton, 1966), pp. 261-62 and 274, n. 19. But Jean may not have been quite so cynical about courtly love as Robertson, Fleming, and Tuve present him; see Wetherbee, "Literal," pp. 264-91, and his *Platonism and Poetry in the Twelfth Century* (Princeton, 1972), pp. 220-41, 255-66; and Douglas Kelly, "'Li chastiaus... Qu'Amors prist puis par ses esforz': The Conclusion of Guillaume de Lorris' *Rose,*" in *A Medieval French Miscellany,* ed. N. J. Lacy, (Lawrence, Kansas, 1972), pp. 72-77.

24 Kelly, "Courtly Love," pp. 125-28; cf. Potansky, *Streit,* pp. 140-42.

25 Ernest Langlois, ed., "Le Traité de Gerson contre le Roman de la rose," *Romania* 45 (1918-19), 47; cf. Ward, *Epistles,* p. 54, ll. 678-86 for the Latin translation and Potansky, *Streit,* pp. 101-2.

26 On the court, see Poirion, *Poète,* pp. 24-37. It plays a role in the debate about Machaut's love in the *Voir-Dit.*

27 Marc-René Jung, "Gui de Mori et Guillaume de Lorris," *Vox Romanica* 27 (1968), 107-10; Kelly, "Chastiaus," p. 75.

28 See Andreas Capellanus, pp. 10 and 106. Thus love may be an improvement on nature; see Jehan Acart de Hesdin, *La Prise amoureuse,* ed. Ernest Hoepffner, (Dresden, 1910), vv. 337-50; cf. also vv. 745-49 and 1254-62.

29 See Guillaume de Lorris and Jean de Meun, *Le Roman de la rose,* ed. Ernest Langlois, 5 vols. (Paris 1914-24), vv. 2057-62 [2055-60]). Lines in brackets refer to the edition by Félix Lecoy, 3 vols. (Paris 1965-70). The translation

referred to is Charles Dahlberg's *The Romance of the Rose* (Princeton, 1971). Nicole de Margival made the same recommendation about one hundred years earlier than the verse *Echecs* in the *Dit de la Panthère d'amours,* ed. H. A. Todd (Paris, 1883), vv. 1032–37: "Qui veult d'amors a chief venir, / Dedens le rommant de la Rose / Trouveras la science enclose. / La porras, se tu veus, aprendre / Comment vrais amans doit entendre / A servir Amors sans meffaire." Did Nicole know Jean's continuation? He also recommends Drouart la Vache's adaptation of Andreas Capellanus (vv. 1707–26); this passage corroborates the qualitative distinctions in love based on nobility and the implications of material style. The verse adaptation of Richart de Fornival's *Bestiaires* also seems to utilize Guillaume de Lorris, but not Jean de Meun; see *Le Bestiaire d'amour rimé,* ed. A. Thordstein, (Lund, Copenhagen, [1941]), pp. xxx–xxxi and passim in the notes. It also takes up nobility and equality based on lineage and love; see vv. 2788–818. See also René d'Anjou's *Livre du cuer d'amours espris,* § 263, vv. 8–17.

30   See Kelly, "Chastiaus," pp. 77–78.

31   *Epistolae dourum amantium.* The definition is contained in Letter XXIV, with reference to its sources or analogues on p. 14, notes 1 and 2; the equality of lovers is alluded to in that letter and in Letter LXXII. Their love is described as *integra caritas* in Letter XXV. *Amicitia* may be good or bad (Letter L). Cf. also Jean Leclercq, "L'Amitié dans les lettres au moyen âge: autour d'un manuscrit de la bibliothèque de Pétrarque," *Revue du moyen âge latin* 1 (1945), 391–410. Richart de Fornival also struggled with the definition of different kinds of love; see Ernest Langlois, "Quelques œuvres de Richard de Fournival," *Bibliothèque le l'Ecole des chartes* 65 (1904), 103–11; and also his *Consaus d'amours,* pp. 6–10.

32   *"Li Bestiaires d'amours" di Maistre Richart de Fournival e "Li Response du Bestiaire,"* ed. Cesare Segre, (Milan, Naples, 1957), pp. 88, l. 5–90, l. 8; the argument is founded on the authority of Ovid and an unidentified Poitevin writer.

33   "Sur le mot 'raison' dans le *Tristan* de Thomas d'Angleterre," in *Linguistic and Literary Studies Helmut A. Hatzfeld* (Washington, 1964), pp. 171–76.

34   Wace, *Brut,* vv. 10733–72. Cf. Gauvain's response to Cador's condemnation of *uisdive:* "Bone est la pais emprés la guerre, / Plus bele e mieldre en est la terre; / Mult sunt bones les gaberies / E bones sunt les drueries. / Pur amistié e pur amies / Funt chevaliers chevaleries" (vv. 10767–72). Useful discussions of the relation of love to prowess in arms: R. W. Hanning, "The Social Significance of Twelfth-Century Chivalric Romance," *Medievalia et Humanistica,* n.s. 3 (1972), 3–29; Georges Duby, "Dans la France du Nord-Ouest au XIIe siècle: Les 'Jeunes' dans la société aristocratique," *Annales: économies sociétés civilisations* 19 (1964), 835–46; Erich Köhler, "Über das Verhältnis von Liebe, Tapferkeit, Wissen und Reichtum bei den Trobadors," in *Trobadorlyrik und höfischer Roman* (Berlin, 1962), pp. 73–87; A. J. Denomy, *"Jovens:* The Notion of Youth among the Troubadours, Its Meaning and Source," *Mediaeval Studies* 11 (1949), 1–22; Köhler, "Sens et fonction du terme *jeunesse* dans la poésie des troubadours," in *Mélanges René Crozet* (Poitiers, 1966), pp. 569–83; Lazar, *Amour,* pp. 33–43.

35 See Mölk, *Trobar,* pp. 15-39; Lazar, *Amour,* pp. 47-55. Also useful is Sebastian Neumeister, *Das Spiel mit der höfischen Liebe: das altprovenzalische Partimen* (Munich, 1969).

36 See Gervase Mathew, "Ideals of Friendship," in *Patterns of Love and Courtesy: Essays C. S. Lewis* (London, 1966), pp. 45-53.

37 Paul Nève, "L'Anti-intellectualisme de Pascal," *Annales de l'Institut Supérieur de Philosophie: Louvain* 5 (1924), 428; cf. Marie-Dominique Chenu, "Spiritus: Le Vocabulaire de l'âme au XIIe siècle," *Revue des sciences philosophiques et théologiques* 12 (1957), 210.

38 See Richart de Fornival's *Consaus,* p. 19, §§ 35-36.

39 "Contes d'amours," vv. 313-18, in *Dits et Contes de Baudouin de Condé et de son fils Jean de Condé,* ed. Auguste Scheler, 3 vols. (Brussels, 1866-67). See also Jean de Condé's "Dis de la pelote," vv. 1-6. See von Wartburg *Französisches etymologisches Wörterbuch,* s.v. *finis,* II, 563 and 567-68; Littré, III, 1606-7; also Robert Javelet, *Psychologie des auteurs spirituels du XIIe siècle* (Strasbourg, 1959), pp. 118-25.

40 *Le Recueil Trepperel,* ed. Eugénie Droz and Halina Lewicka, 2 vols. (Paris 1935-61).

41 Neumeister, *Spiel,* pp, 82-101.

42 *Epistolae,* pp. 88-91; see especially Letters XLIX, L, LVII, LXXV, CIX.

43 An addition to ms D (14th century) of Andreas distinguishes between the *honestus amor* of Books 1 and 2 and the *inhonestus amor* of Book 3; see the *De amore,* p. xxv. On eloquence and love in Andreas and among the troubadours, see Mölk, *Trobar clus,* pp. 44-45. On *honestus* as a category of beauty implying discrimination, see Brinkmann, *Wesen,* p. 4.

44 *De vulgari eloquentia,* II.ii.7. Cf. M. L. Colish, *The Mirror of Language: A Study in the Medieval Theory of Knowledge* (New Haven, 1968), pp. 269-73.

45 " 'Courtly Love' as a Problem of Style," in *Chaucer und seine Zeit: Symposion für Walter F. Schirmer,* ed. Arno Esch (Tübingen, 1968), pp. 1-33; R. O. Payne, *The Key of Remembrance: A Study of Chaucer's Poetics* (New Haven and London, 1963), pp. 180-82 and 189-90; Colish, *Mirror,* pp. 269-70. See also Peter Ochsenbein, *Studien zum "Anticlaudianus" des Alanus ab Insulis* (Bern and Frankfurt, 1975), pp. 158-60, 182-83.

46 *Frauendienst,* ed. Reinhold Bechstein, (Leipzig, 1888), 49.24-29 [I.56] [And if I should, like you, be near my dear, noble lady, I would not exchange my place for the grail which the bold, valiant Perceval achieved with such difficulty and knightly effort].

47 J. B. Allen, *The Friar as Critic: Literary Attitudes in the Later Middle Ages* (Nashville, 1971); also Poirion, *Poète,* pp. 93-95; Paule Demats, *Fabula: Trois études de mythographie antique et médiévale* (Geneva, 1973); Lubac, *Exégèse,* II.ii, 233.

48 M. W. Bloomfield, "Symbolism in Medieval Literature," *Modern Philology* 56 (1958-59), 78 [reprinted in *Essays and Explorations: Studies in Ideas, Language, and Literature* (Cambridge, Mass., 1970]. See also Payne, *Key,* pp. 24-27. For Middle High German literature, see Brinkmann, *Wesen,* pp. 27-28, and Rudolf Krayer, *Frauenlob und die Natur-Allegorese: Motivgeschichtliche Untersuch-*

ungen—ein Beitrag zur Geschichte des antiken Traditionsgutes (Heidelberg, 1960).

49 Ed. C. de Boer, *Verhandelingen der koninklijke Akademie van Wetenschappen*, Amsterdam. Afdeeling Letterkunde, n.s. 15 (Amsterdam, 1915).

50 See the discussion of imposed allegory in Tuve, *Imagery*, pp. 219–333; Walter Haug, "Struktur und Geschichte: Ein literaturtheoretisches Experiment an mittelalterlichen Texten," *Germanisch-romanische Monatsschrift*, n.s. 23 (1973), 129–52.

51 Tuve, *Imagery*, p. 239.

52 See Alain Chartier, *La Belle dame sans mercy et les poésies lyriques*, ed. A. Piaget and R. L. Wagner, 2nd ed. (Paris, 1949). Line numbers are the same for the more recent edition by J. C. Laidlaw, *The Poetical Works of Alain Chartier* (Cambridge, 1974). Fornival's lady is not so uncompromising in her *Response* as the Belle Dame; she shows intelligent judgment regarding the conduct suitable to sincere and insincere love (*Response*, p. 129, l. 14–130, l. 11); she suggests in conclusion that her love is not unattainable, "tant que par raison merchis ara son lieu" (p. 136, l. 17).

53 Erich Köhler, "Zur Selbstauffassung des höfischen Dichters," in *Trobadorlyrik*, pp. 13–14, 17–20.

54 Cf. H. R. Jauss in the *Grundriß der romanischen Literaturen des Mittelalters* (Heidelberg, 1968), VI.1, 150–51.

55 Jauss, *Grundriß*, VI.1, 226.

56 Cf. the examples cited in Lausberg, *Handbuch*, I, 292–95. Another indication of the proximity of the two kinds of trope is Conrad of Hirsau's teaching that Prudentius' *Psychomachia* is to be read "Tropice, id est per figuram metonomiam" in the *Dialogus super auctores*, ed. R. B. C. Huygens, (Brussels, 1955), p. 38, l. 863. However, the anonymous accessus to Avianus' fables describes their *materia* as "ipse fabule et commune proficuum allegorie" in *Accessus ad auctores*, ed. Huygens, (Brussels, 1954), p. 17, l. 12. Cf. Conrad of Hirsau: "Est enim fabula res ficta, non facta, animum legentis oblectans et sententiam ex ipsa rerum comparatione commendans. uerum omissis monstris fabulosis diuinis intendamus oraculis, quibus ut inest sensus geminus, sic duplex fructus lectionis eius est quantum ad litere ueritatem et intelligentiam spiritalem" (p. 27, ll. 506–11). See Marc-René Jung, *Etudes sur le poème allégorique en France au moyen âge*, (Bern, 1971), pp. 31–33; and W. T. H. Jackson, "Allegory and Allegorization," *Research Studies Washington State University* 32 (1964), 163–64.

57 *Ars versificatoria*, in Edmond Faral, *Les Arts Poétiques du XIIe et du XIIIe siècle* (Paris, 1924, 1958). Translation by Ernest Gallo, "Matthew of Vendôme: Introductory Treatise on the Art of Poetry," *Proceedings of the American Philosophical Society* 118 (1974), 51–92. See also John of Garland, *The "Parisiana Poetria,"* ed. Traugott Lawler (New Haven and London 1974), p. 126, ll. 286–88.

58 The distinction between *tota allegoria* and *permixta apertis allegoria* is discussed in Lausberg, *Handbuch*, I, 442 (§ 897). See as well Wetherbee, *Platonism*, p. 143 and (on Jean de Meun) 260; on allegory and metonymy, see L. J. Friedman's review of Jung, *Etudes* in *Speculum* 47 (1972), 319.

59 See Matthew of Vendôme, *Ars versificatoria*, pp. 150, §§ 114–15; 154, § 10; 185–87.
60 *The Allegory of Love* (Oxford, 1936), pp. 364–66.
61 M. F. Nims, *"Translatio:* 'Difficult Statement' in Medieval Poetic Theory," *University of Toronto Quarterly* 43 (1974), 219–21; Ochsenbein, *Studien*, pp. 135–36. For the *Liber in distinctionibus dictionum theologicalium*, see Migne, *PL* 210, cols. 685–1012.
62 *Imagery*, p. 132. Cf. also Lubac, *Exégèse*, II.ii, 180.
63 Jauss, *Grundriß*, VI.1, 228–29; Poirion, *Poète*, pp. 466–473.

CHAPTER 3

1 *Georgics*, III. 242–44 [Thereupon every species of men and beast on land, every aquatic kind, flocks and brightly colored birds, hurl themselves into madness and combustion. Love is the same to all].
2 See especially *Image et ressemblance au XIIᵉ siècle: De Saint Anselme à Alain de Lille*, 2 vols. (n.p., 1967); "La Réintroduction de la liberté dans les notions d'image et de ressemblance, conçues comme dynamisme," in *Der Begriff der 'repraesentatio' im Mittelalter: Stellvertretung, Symbol, Zeichen, Bild*, ed. A. Zimmermann (Berlin and New York, 1971), pp. 1–34. The seminal studies are Marie-Dominique Chenu's *"Imaginatio:* Note de lexicographie philosophique médiévale," in *Miscellanea Giovanni Mercati*, 6 vols. (The Vatican, 1946), II, 593–602; and his *"Spiritus,"* pp. 209–32. Other important studies are: M. W. Bundy, *The Theory of Imagination in Classical and Mediaeval Thought* (Urbana, 1927): Pierre Michaud-Quantin, "La Classification des puissances de l'âme au XIIᵉ siècle," *Revue du moyen âge latin* V (1949), 15–34; Marie-Dominique Chenu, *La Théologie au douzième siècle* (Paris, 1966); F. A. Yates, *The Art of Memory* (London, 1966), especially pp. 50–104. Yates argues that the subjects of memory and Imagination have hardly begun to be studied (p. 104); she and Bundy discuss the Scholastic adaptation of memory and Imagination to philosophical thought (see Yates, pp. 66, 81, 84–85). She stresses their significance for "order" and arrangement (p. 99). See also Harry Caplan, *"Memoria:* Treasure-House of Eloquence," in his *Of Eloquence: Studies in Ancient and Medieval Rhetoric* (Ithaca, 1970), pp. 196–246. There is also some useful material in Johan Huizinga, *The Waning of the Middle Ages* (New York, 1954), although the appreciations are often vitiated by Huizinga's disapprobation, indeed suspicion of the excesses of artistic and religious Imagination. Three recent studies, which reached me too late for extensive discussion here, make important contributions to the study of medieval notions of Imagination. They are Peter Dronke, *Fabula: Explorations into the Use of Myth in Medieval Platonism* (Leiden and Cologne, 1974); and W. P. Wetherbee, "The Theme of Imagination in Medieval Poetry and the Allegorical Figure of 'Genius,'" *Medievalia et Humanistica* 7 (1976), 45–64; Barbara Nolan, *The Gothic Visionary Perspective* (Princeton, 1977). There have also been a number of studies of Imagination in medieval and Renaissance English literature: M. W. Bloomfield, *"Piers Plowman" as a Fourteenth-Century Apocalypse* (New Brunswick, 1961), especially "The Problem of Imaginatif", pp. 170–74; C. S. Lewis, *The Discarded Image: An Introduction to*

Medieval and Renaissance Literature (Cambridge, 1967), especially pp. 152–69; B. J. Harwood, "Imaginative in *Piers Plowman,*" *Medium Ævum* 44 (1975), 249–63; V. A. Kolve, "Chaucer and the Visual Arts," in D. Brewer, ed. *Geoffrey Chaucer* (Athens, Ohio, 1975), pp. 290–320; and I. G. MacCaffrey, *Spenser's Allegory: The Anatomy of Imagination* (Princeton, 1976). None of these studies deals significantly with either the medieval poetic tradition represented by the twelfth- and thirteenth-century arts of poetry, nor with French sources and traditions.

3   Javelet has brought his knowledge to bear on the phenomenon of courtly love in troubadour poetry; his discussion is worthy of Gilson's earlier treatment of the subject in relation to Saint Bernard, and therefore deserves to be better known. See "L'Amour spirituel face à l'amour courtois," in *Entretiens sur la renaissance du XIIe siècle,* ed. Maurice de Gandillac and Edouard Jeauneau (Paris and The Hague, 1968), pp. 309–36. Cf. Etienne Gilson, "Saint Bernard et l'amour courtois," in *La Théologie mystique de Saint Bernard,* 3rd ed. (Paris, 1969), pp. 193–215. Cf. also Chenu, *Théologie,* pp. 178–80.

4   Brian Stock, *Myth and Science in the Twelfth Century: A Study of Bernard Silvester* (Princeton, 1972); Marie-Thérèse d'Alverny, *Alain de Lille: Textes inédits avec une introduction sur sa vie et sur ses œuvres* (Paris, 1965), pp. 166–80; Marian Kurdziałek, "Der Mensch als Abbild des Kosmos," in *Der Begriff der repraesentatio im Mittelalter,* pp. 37–75.

5   See *ThLL,* s.v. *imaginatio,* VII.1, cols. 402–3, and s.v. *imago,* col. 412, ll. 47–67; Albert Blaise, *Dictionnaire latin-français des auteurs chrétiens* (Strasbourg, 1954), s.v. *imaginatio,* pp. 405–6; Lubac, *Exégèse,* II.2, 135; Colish, *Mirror,* pp. 75–79; Theodore Silverstein, "The Fabulous Cosmogony of Bernardus Silvestris," *Modern Philology* 46 (1948–49), 97–98; Ulrich Wienbruch, " 'Signum,' 'significatio' und 'illuminatio' bei Augustin," in *Der Begriff der repraesentatio im Mittelalter,* pp. 81–84.

6   *The Consolation of Philosophy,* in *The Theological Tractates,* eds. H. F. Stewart and E. K. Rand (Cambridge, Mass. and London, 1968), V.Pr iv. 82–91. Translation from this edition. Cf. Wetherbee, *Platonism,* pp. 74–82. For a general survey of Boethius' influence in the twelfth century, see Chenu, *Théologie,* pp. 142–58. For the importance of his hierarchy of cognitive functions, see Michaud-Quantin, "Classification," p. 16; Tullio Gregory, *Anima mundi: La filosofia di Guglielmo di Conches e la scuola di Chartres* (Florence, 1955), pp. 167–68. Bernardus Silvestris explicitly adopts Boethius' scheme in his commentary on Vergil; see the *Commentum Bernardi Silvestris super sex libros Eneidos Virgilii,* ed. Wilhelm Riedel (Greifswald, 1924), p. 44, ll. 2–4. On the relation of the perception of form to the objects of sense as an aesthetic principle, see Edgar de Bruyne, *Etudes d'esthétique médiévale,* 3 vols. (Bruges, 1946), I, 26–28.

7   *Commentarii in Somnium Scipionis,* ed. Jakob Willis (Leipzig, 1963), I.ii.14: W. H. Stahl, trans., *Commentary on the Dream of Scipio* (New York, 1952).

8   *Alain de Lille: Poète du XIIe siècle* (Montreal and Paris, 1951), p. 145. The general considerations are developed in the *artes dictaminis* under sender, recipient, and subject of the epistle; cf. John of Garland, especially on *genus* and *species, Parisiana Poetria,* I.124–134 (p. 10), II.44–50 (p. 34), and II.83–86 (p.

36). See also Nims, *"Translatio,"* pp. 215–30; Mölk, *Trobar clus,* pp. 177–99; Paterson, *Troubadours.*

9 But that prefigure his own experiences to follow; see vv. 4098–99 [4068–69]. Also Alain de Lille, *De planctu Naturae,* ed. Thomas Wright (London, 1872, Wiesbaden, 1964), p. 471; D. M. Moffat, trans., *The Complaint of Nature* (New York, 1908), p. 46.

10 "Amour, se bien sui apensee, / C'est maladie de pensee / Entre deus persones annexe, / Franches entre eus, de divers sexe, / Venant aus genz par ardeur nee / De vision desordenee, / Pour acoler e pour baisier, / Pour aus charnelment aaisier" (vv. 4377–84 [4347–54]). Jean's conclusion—"Amanz autre chose n'entent, / Ainz s'art e se delite en tant" (vv. 4385–86 [4355–56])—is not entirely faithful to Andreas, who makes significant distinctions regarding the object of love; nor does Jean translate the latter's "et omnia de utriusque voluntate in ipsius amplexu amoris præcepta compleri" (p. 1), which would have taken the reader back to the god of Love's instruction in Guillaume de Lorris, as recommended by the *Echecs* Commentator for "good" lovers. Cf. Drouart la Vache, *Li Livres d'amours,* ed. Robert Bossuat (Paris, 1926), vv. 142–43: "Et de commun assent connexe, / Ainsi com Venus le commande." Richart de Fornival also uses the combination of definition and description in the *Consaus d'amours;* see p. 6 (§ 3) and p. 9 (§ 11). However, Richart denies that love can be bad: "Amours male n'est pas amours, ains est niens," p. 6 (§ 3); cf. p. 10 (§ 12). Evils, or rather "maladies," may befall it (p. 15, §§ 26–28), for which there are remedies that do not destroy the love (pp. 15–16, § 29).

11 On thinkers between Boethius and the twelfth century, see the works cited in note 2 above; and Stock, *Myth,* pp. 41–42.

12 *Didascalicon: De studio legendi,* ed. C. H. Buttimer (Washington, 1939), p. 29; trans. Jerome Taylor (New York and London, 1961). Hugh places *intelligentia* ("de solis rerum principiis, id est, Deo, ideis, et hyle, et de incorporeis substantiis, pura certaque cognitio") above Imagination, and the senses below ("passio animae in corpore ex qualitatibus extra accidentibus"). There may be five cognitive functions. But the actual kinds are unimportant here, as all classifications are essentially parallel and hierarchic, and include Imagination. In general, see Taylor, trans., *Didascalicon,* p. 201, note 37. Cf. also Bundy, *Imagination,* pp. 200–207; and de Bruyne, *Etudes,* II, 218–28.

13 Wetherbee, *Platonism,* p. 5. See in general de Bruyne, *Etudes,* II, 255–301. Bundy, *Imagination,* and Yates, *Memory,* do not discuss the Chartrains; however, Bundy discusses Hugh of Saint Victor and Dante. The authors we are concerned with here are mostly representative of or analogous to the writers in the so-called School of Chartres, as it had a decisive influence on the arts of poetry. About a "Chartrain" school in the twelfth century there is some controversy. For recent views, see R. W. Southern, "Humanism and the School of Chartres," in his *Medieval Humanism and Other Studies* (Oxford, 1970), pp. 61–85; and Jean Châtillon, "Les Ecoles de Chartres et de Saint-Victor," in *La Scuola nell' Occidente latino dell' alto medioevo* 2 vols. (Spoleto, 1972), II, 795–804; N. Häring, "Chartres and Paris Revisited," *Essays in Honour of Anton Charles Pegis* (Toronto, 1974), pp. 268–317. Cf. also Gregory, *Anima,* pp. 247–78.

14 Wetherbee, *Platonism,* pp. 4–5, 66–73; Lubac, *Exégèse,* II.2, 158 and 188. On the limits of reason, Lubac, *Exégèse,* II.2, 151.

15 Edouard Jeauneau, "L'Usage de la notion d'*integumentum* à travers les gloses de Guillaume de Conches," *Archives d'histoire doctrinale et littéraire du moyen âge* 32 (1957), 37–39; Jean Seznec, *The Survival of the Pagan Gods: The Mythological Tradition and Its Place in Renaissance Humanism and Art,* trans. B. F. Sessions (New York, 1953), especially pp. 11–147. Cf. also Chenu, *Théologie,* pp. 165–66.

16 *Eclogues,* VI. 35–36 [Then did the earth begin to harden and to separate itself from the sea, and gradually to assume the forms of things].

17 For texts and discussion, see Lausberg, *Handbuch,* §§ 812, 815–16; a useful survey is in Ziltener, *Studien,* pp. 54–71.

18 See *Thesaurus Linguae latinae,* VII.1, cols. 404–14. Cf. the following passage from Alain de Lille, cited in Jung, *Etudes,* p. 68, n. 8: "Imaginaria vero visio est quando per unum comprehendimus aliud, ut: quia in Partenopeo pulcritudo Atalante resultat; in eo matris videmus pulcritudinem. A simili, per eo que facta sunt, invisibilia Dei conspiciuntur." See also F. P. Pickering, *Literature and Art in the Middle Ages* (Glasgow, 1970), especially pp. 75–121.

19 *Rhetorica ad Herennium,* ed. Harry Caplan (Cambridge, Mass. and London, 1968); translation from this edition. Cf. Ziltener, *Studien,* pp. 54–55.

20 Lausberg, *Handbuch,* § 812.

21 *Ars versificatoria,* p. 151, § 1. Cf. *visio* in Macrobius, *Somnium:* "Cum id quis videt quod eodem modo quo apparuerat eveniet" (p. 10, ll. 15–16). It is as such one kind of poetic *visio;* see Lausberg, *Handbuch,* §§ 811 and 1089. The *De planctu* is a *visio imaginaria* (p. 522).

22 Priscian, *Praeexercitamina,* in Heinrich Keil, ed., *Grammatici latini,* 7 vols. (Leipzig, 1857–80), III, 430.

23 Michele Bevilacqua, *Introduzione a Macrobio* (Lecce, 1973), especially pp. 51–52 and 173; Jung, *Etudes,* pp. 292–93.

24 Alain de Lille, *Anticlaudianus,* ed. Robert Bossuat (Paris, 1955); trans. J. J. Sheridan (Toronto, 1973).

25 Brinkmann, *Wesen,* pp. 29–33; Faral, *Arts poétiques,* pp. 99–102; Stock, *Myth,* p. 275; Wetherbee, *Platonism,* pp. 145–51.

26 See note 6 above for Bernardus' *Commentum;* also the "Traité des cinq puissances de l'âme," in d'Alverny, *Alain,* pp. 313–17.

27 See Ochsenbein, *Studien,* p. 89. Cf. Huizinga, "Über die Verknüpfung des Poetischen mit dem Theologischen bei Alanus de Insulis," in his *Verzamelde Werken,* 9 vols. (Haarlam 1948–53), IV, 31. Ochsenbein expresses astonishment that the *Anticlaudianus* does not use the word *imaginatio* (pp. 91 and 108); the word is missing for metrical reasons. The process is obvious in the conception of the work itself, and its representations are usually designated by *pictura.* "In dieser bunten Hülle ringt ein ernster Geist mit seinem tiefsten Bedürfnis: der zentralen Wahrheit, wie er sie schaut, Ausdruck zu verleihen; und er greift zum Bilde, wo der Begriff versagt" (Huizinga, "Verknüpfung," p. 31). Useful discussion of the allegorical function of the concept (*Begriff*) is found in Walter Benjamin, *Ursprung des deutschen Trauerspiels* (Frankfurt, 1963).

28 *De mundi universitate libri duo,* ed. Carl S. Barach and Johann Wrobel (Innsbruck, 1876, Frankfurt 1964); Winthrop Wetherbee, trans., *The Cosmographia of Bernardus Silvestris* (New York and London, 1973). On *silva,* see J. Reginald O'Donnell, "The Meaning of 'Silva' in the Commentary on the *Timaeus* by Chalcidius," *Mediaeval Studies* 7 (1945), 1–20.

29 The passage thus adapts cogently Vergil's *vocis imago, Georgics* IV, v. 50; cf. Macrobius, *Saturnalia,* ed. Jakob Willis (Leipzig, 1963), 6.6.7.

30 See notes 6 and 26 above; also Alain's "Sermo de sphaera intelligibili," in d'Alverny, *Alain,* pp. 302–3.

31 Marie-Thérèse d'Alverny, "Maître Alain—'Nova et vetera,'" in *Entretiens sur la renaissance du XIIe siècle,* p. 132.

32 Cf. Macrobius, *Somnium,* pp. 6–7. Also Raynaud de Lage, *Alain,* pp. 92–93.

33 In Faral, *Arts poétiques;* trans. M. F. Nims (Toronto, 1967). Cf. Payne, *Key,* pp. 16–17. The *Epistolae duorum amantium* links the Image to the realization of love in Letter LXXXVIII. On the "prudent" artist, note that in the *Anticlaudianus* Nature sends Prudence to God to propose the fashioning of the New Man.

34 See de Bruyne, *Etudes,* III, 114–5; L. J. Friedman, "'Jean de Meung,' Antifeminism, and 'Bourgeois Realism,'" *Modern Philology* 57 (1959–60), 14–16, 21–23; Fritz Peter Knapp, "Vergleich und Exempel in der lateinischen Rhetorik und Poetik von der Mitte des 12. bis zur Mitte des 13. Jahrhunderts," *Studi medievali* ser. 3, 14 (1973), 464–66.

35 See Brinkmann, *Wesen,* pp. 80–81; Huizinga, "Verknüpfung," pp. 3–84; Wetherbee, *Platonism,* pp. 187–241; Lubac, *Exégèse,* II.ii, 208–33.

36 *Schemata dianoeas quae ad rhetores pertinent,* in Karl Felix von Halm, ed., *Rhetores latini minores* (Leipzig, 1863), p. 71 (§ 1); cf. Brinkmann, *Wesen,* p. 66; and Lausberg, *Handbuch,* pp. 399–402. On medieval versions of the *praeexercitamina,* see Edmond Faral, "Le Manuscrit 511 du 'Hunterian Museum' de Glasgow: notes sur le mouvement poétique et l'histoire des études littéraires en France et en Angleterre entre les années 1150 et 1225," *Studi medievali,* n.s. 9 (1936), 18–121; and Bruce Harbert, ed. *A Thirteenth-Century Anthology of Rhetorical Poems: Glasgow Ms. Hunterian V.8.14* (Toronto, 1975).

37 Cited from Achard de Saint-Victor's *De discretione animae* in Chenu, "*Spiritus,*" p. 212; see also Knapp, "Vergleich," pp. 468–69; and Ochsenbein, *Studien,* p. 89.

38 On the sense of *conorare,* see Könsgen's "Anhang," p. 64.

39 P. clvi.

40 See Erich Köhler, "Zur Entstehung des altprovenzalischen Streitgedichts," *Zeitschrift für romanische Philologie* 75 (1959), 53–54; Rupprecht Rohr, "Zur Skala der ritterlichen Tugenden in der altprovenzalischen und altfranzösischen höfischen Dichtung," *Zeitschrift für romanische Philologie* 78 (1962), 320. Cf. also Christiane Leube-Fey, *Bild und Funktion der "dompna" in der Lyrik der Trobadors* (Heidelberg, 1971).

41 *Prudentius,* ed. H. J. Thomson, 2 vols. (Cambridge, Mass. and London, 1962), I, 274–343; translation from this edition.

42 Payne, *Key,* p. 182.

43 D'Alverny, *Alain*, p. 316. See also Yates, *Memory*, especially pp. 20–21; and Ochsenbein, *Studien*, pp, 80–108, 160, 174; Richard H. Green, "Alan of Lille's *Anticlaudianus:* Ascensus mentis in Deum," *Annuale Mediaevale* 8 (1967), 14–16.

44 Letters XXIV and CVIII (v. 13); see *Statius*, ed. J. H. Mozley, 2 vols. (Cambridge, Mass., and London, 1961); translation from this edition. Mozley translates *laetus horror* (I.493–94) as "a thrill of joy;" it is an omen from the gods.

45 Payne, *Key*, p. 183, n. 27.

46 The terms *static* and *dynamic* are borrowed from Jung, *Etudes*, p. 20. Cf. the *imagines agentes* in memory (Yates, *Memory*, p. 30). See also Paul Zumthor, *Langue, texte, énigme* (Paris, 1975), pp. 253–56.

47 See the *Echecs* Commentator's inclusion of Renart tales under Imagination, cited above, p. 33. Also Hans Robert Jauss, *Untersuchungen zur mittelalterlichen Tierdichtung* (Tübingen, 1959); and the *Grundriß der romanischen Literaturen des Mittelalters*, VI.1, 247–49.

48 *Le Roman de Renart*, ed. Ernest Martin, 3 vols. (Straßburg and Paris, 1882–87; Berlin and New York, 1973); cross-references to Mario Roques' edition (Paris 1948–63) are in brackets. For a different invention on Adam and Eve, see the *Queste del saint graal*, pp. 210–19, and *Li Response du Bestiaire*, pp. 107–9 and 136.

49 In Faral, *Arts poétiques;* trans. R. P. Parr (Milwaukee 1968). Cf. Brinkmann, *Wesen*, pp. 71 and 76–77.

50 Faral, *Arts poétiques*, p. 67.

51 Cf. Stock, *Myth*, pp. 155–57.

52 Stock, *Myth*, p. 275.

53 *Arts poétiques*, p. 67. Cf. Rohr, "Skala," p. 302: "So läßt sich mit Sicherheit annehmen, daß von ihm [Marcabru] das Tugendsystem nach dem Prinzip der Emanation—bzw. des Immanentseins aller Tugenden in einer, der Liebe—als absteigend schöpfend und als aufsteigend heranziehend, von der Liebe aus und zur Liebe hin durch deren Kräfte, Freude und Hoffnung und Gnade und Gabe, aufgefaßt wurde."

54 V. 1251. See the *Ad Herennium*, IV.xlv.58 - li.65.

55 See pp. 71–74.

56 Lubac, *Exégèse*, II.ii, 41–60; Kelly, "Theory," pp. 126–27.

57 Cf. Wetherbee, *Platonism*, p. 255.

58 "Imitari, imitatio," *ALMA (Bulletin Du Cange)* 15 (1940–41), 151. Cf. Brinkmann, *Wesen*, pp. 8–10; Lubac, *Exégèse*, II.i, 323–28; Huizinga, "Verknüpfung," p. 50; C. O. Brink, *Imagination and Imitation* (Liverpool, 1953); Green, "Alan of Lille's *Anticlaudianus*," pp. 7–9; Bernardus Silvestris, *Commentum:* "Emulatio autem loco poesis intelligitur quia tota est in imitatione" (p. 74, ll. 28–29; see also p. 75, l. 3).

59 *Rhetorica ad Herennium* IV.xxviii.39 [A poem ought to be a painting that speaks; a painting ought to be a silent poem]; *Epistolae*, Letter LXXVIII [He who does not possess writes assiduously in order to find what he does not possess].

60 See Chenu, "*Spiritus*," pp. 210–12, 213–14, 223, 230–32.

61 Heinrich Bechtoldt, "Der französische Wortschatz im Sinnbezirk des Verstandes. (Die geistliche und lehrhafte Literatur von ihren Anfängen bis zum Ende des 12.

Jahrhunderts.)," *Romanische Forschungen* 49 (1935), 21-180; Daniel Koenig, *"Sen" / "sens" et "savoir" et leurs synonymes dans quelques romans courtois du 12ᵉ et du début du 13ᵉ siècle* (Bern and Frankfurt, 1973). Cf. Hans-Georg Koll, *Die französischen Wörter "langue" und "langage" im Mittelalter* (Geneva and Paris, 1958).

62 "Wortschatz," p. 141. Some of his texts, or others contemporary with them, do use *image* and its derivatives; see the examples in Godefroy, the FEW, and Tobler-Lommatzsch.

63 See Rohr, "Skala," pp. 292-325. There is some evidence that Alain de Lille was acquainted with courtly literature; see d'Alverny, "Maitre Alain—'Nova et vetera'," in *Entretiens sur la renaissance du XIIᵉ siècle*, pp. 126-27 and 142-43.

64 Bernart de Ventadorn, *Seine Lieder*, ed. Carl Appel (Halle, 1915).

65 *Les Fragments du Roman de Tristan*, ed. B. H. Wind (Geneva and Paris, 1960).

66 *Œuvres poétiques*, ed. H. Suchier, 2 vols. (Paris, 1885), II, 214.

67 Alain de Lille, *Textes*, p. 315.

68 Glasser, "Abstractum," pp. 101-4. On the possible influence of Aristotelian Scholasticism on this development, see Chenu, *Théologie*, pp. 184-85.

69 See *Le Commentaire de Copenhague de l' "Ovide moralisé,"* ed. J. T. M. van 't Sant (Amsterdam, 1932).

70 Langlois, *Recueil*, pp. viii-x; Patterson, *Three Centuries*, I, 10-12. Sermons and the *artes praedicandi* may have had an influence on such collections; see Ziltener, *Studien*, pp. 45-49.

71 Homage is an Image frequently used for topical amplification in conformity with authorial intention. Pygmalion's homage in Machaut's Balade CCIII has different readings in the *Fonteinne amoureuse*, vv. 963-67, and in Jean de Meun's *Rose*, vv. 20811-21214 [20781-21184].

72 See William Calin, *A Poet at the Fountain: Essays on the Narrative Verse of Guillaume de Machaut* (Lexington, 1974), pp. 197-98.

73 On "stamps" in allegory, see Lausberg, *Handbuch*, § 901.

74 Ed. M. L. de Mas Latrie (Geneva, 1877). See also Calin, *Poet*, pp. 213 and 218.

75 A number of contemporary and near-contemporary works blend exceptional historical biography and marvelous narrative: *Jehan de Saintré, Fouke Fitz Waren, Prise d'Alexandrie, Jean de Paris,* and some of the *Cent nouvelles nouvelles*. See for example Charles A. Knudson, "The Prussian Expedition in *Jehan de Saintré,"* in *Etudes Félix Lecoy* (Paris, 1973), pp. 271-77; Knudson, "The Two Saintrés," *Romance Studies Edward Billings Ham* (Hayward, Cal., 1967), pp. 73-80; A. H. Diverres, "The Irish Adventures in Froissart's *Meliador,"* in *Mélanges Jean Frappier*, I, 235-51.

76 Newman, *Meaning*, pp. 3-4.

77 See Machaut, *Voir-Dit*, p. 20, and vv. 3948, 5687-89, 6785-88; *Confort d'ami*, vv. 2185-90. The nobleman in the *Fonteinne amoureuse* reads the Pygmalion story in bono to figure himself (vv. 955-70). For Froissart, see the *Paradys d'amour*, vv. 1119-35. Froissart there contrasts Pygmalion—"Quoique le fol crie et braie... Il n'est rien qu'il en extraie / Fors imagination" [*confusa imaginatio*]—with himself; but his lady at least offers him solace: "ma querelle gaie / Qui a la fois me resgaie." Similarly, Machaut (Balade notée XXXVIII,

vv. 9–12). In the *Tresor amoureux*, uncertainly attributed to Froissart: "La pensée et l'intencion / Ymaginative que j'ay / Mueent en moy l'impression / De ma dame, quant je visay / A sa beauté et advisay / Son bel et gracieux atour" (Froissart, *Œuvres*, III, 81: V, vv. 9–14). The idea is commonplace in courtly literature; see Lazar, *Amour*, pp. 67–70.

78 *Remede*, vv. 3189–3351. See also the *Voir-Dit*, p. 55: "Se je avoie vostre douce ymage, après Dieu & vous je l'ameroie, serviroie & obéiroye, & feroie maintes choses nouvelles en l'onneur de vous & de li;" cf. also vv. 1362–1401, where the prayer is assimilated to a feudal oath of allegiance. There are numerous examples in Machaut, especially among the fixed forms (e.g., Lai IX, vv. 125–27).

79 Cf. the *Voir-Dit*, vv. 5088–93; *Confort d'ami*, vv. 1287–1311 (where Pygmalion's statue is called an "image," v. 1303) and 1369. One exception, which is made explicitly so, are Manasseh's "fausses ymages et ydoles" (v. 1307). See as well Lai XV, v. 134, and Motet VIII, v. 9. I have found no example in Froissart. An *ydole* in this sense falls under Macrobius' *insomnium*.

80 *In Anticlaudianum Alani commentum*, ed. Jan Sulowski (Wrocław, 1972), pp. 55–57.

81 *Voir-Dit*, pp. 193–94, 202, 367.

82 *Confort d'ami*, vv. 3903–24 on the hierarchy of God and honor.

83 See pp. 132–35. See also the appreciation of Machaut's conception of love in Robertson, *Preface*, pp. 233–36; his reservations concerning the *Voir-Dit* will not hold, since the conception of love it propounds is the same as that offered in Machaut's other dits beginning with the *Remede* and the *Jugement Navarre*, as is shown in Chapter 6.

CHAPTER 4

1 *Amour courtois et Table Ronde*, p. 138.

2 The recovery is effected by a return to "memoire" (v. 1665), the healing influence of the dream and courtly qualities, including "avis," "sens et raison" (vv. 1113–14), as delineated in the anonymous mid fourteenth-century *Songe vert*, which may have influenced the composition of Chaucer's *Book of the Duchess;* ed. Léopold Constans, *Romania* 33 (1904), 490–539. Cf. also the anonymous fifteenth-century *Roman du comte d'Artois*, ed. Jean-Charles Seigneuret (Geneva and Paris, 1966), p. 1, ll. 3–7: "Pour ce que huiseuse traveille lez cuers humains par diversez ymaginacions et merancolies, est pourffitable et bonne chose a oÿr lez plaisantez lectures dez anchiennes histoires pour passer le tempz en joye et fuir lez fantaziez quy trop grievent Nature."

3 See Charles Dahlberg, "Macrobius and the Unity of the *Roman de la rose*," *Studies in Philology* 58 (1961), 573–82. It is therefore not "a phantasm, a nightmare," as Fleming asserts (*Rose*, p. 54). The sole distinction between *somnium* and *insomnium* is truth—and Guillaume affirms the veracity of his dream. Cf. also Radulphe, *In Anticlaudianum*, p. 54: "Si vero spiritus illi aliquid obscure denuntient tectum figuris, velatum ambagibus, nec nisi interpretatione intelligendum, somnium stricto vocabulo dicitur." A *somnium* may be a nightmare as much as an *insomnium*, prior to its elucidation; and if that interpretation is foreboding, it is no less nightmarish!

4 See also v. 2066 [2064]: "la matire en est novele."
5 See Jackson, "Allegory," p. 171; Kelly, "Chastiaus," p. 62–64.
6 A. M. F. Gunn provides a brief resumé of the varieties of amplification used here and elsewhere in the *Rose,* including Jean de Meun's part, in *The Mirror of Love: A Reinterpretation of "The Romance of the Rose"* (Lubbock, 1952), pp. 76–94, 509–22. There is little thorough analysis of the description as such, due to Gunn's emphasis on structure and his acceptance of Faral's conception of amplification as dilation for its own sake. In fact, amplification is the final step in the invention of topoi; see Ernest Gallo, *The "Poetria Nova" and Its Sources in Early Rhetorical Doctrine* (The Hague and Paris 1971), pp. 150–66, and "Matthew," pp. 53–58. This is no criticism of Gunn's study; he was well ahead of his time in taking amplification in the *Rose* seriously.
7 See Gérard Marie Paré, *Les Idées et les lettres au XIIIᵉ siècle: Le "Roman de la rose"* (Montreal, 1947), p. 311; and Friedman, "Jean," pp. 17–18. The notion appears in Chaucer, HF 853–69. By contrast, see the discussion of the *doctus lector* required for Alain de Lille in Ochsenbein, *Studien,* pp. 73 and 75.
8 See Dagmar Thoss, *Studien zum locus amoenus im Mittelalter,* (Vienna and Stuttgart, 1972), pp. 117–18. It is confirmed in the *Echecs* Commentary: "Pour ce fu il ainsi faint au commenchement du *Rommant de la rose* qu'elles [the Images in the wall] estoyent pourtraittes entour et au dehors des murs du vergier de Deduit, ou Amours et ses gens repairent voulentiers pour ce que chilz qui sont de leur condition ne sont pas bien seant en l'amoureuse vie, ne Amours aussi n'a cure de tel gent. Car Amours et Deduit ne ayment que joye et delectation; pour ce est il la dit que tel gent ne sont pas de entrer ou vregier dignes pour ce qu'ilz sont de toutte tristour signe" (fol. 275 r).
9 See Langlois, *Rose,* II, v. 205 note (pp. 296–97).
10 Cf. the god of Love's words when Guillaume pays him homage later: "Si me baiseras en la bouche, / A cui nus vilains on ne touche. / Je n'i laisse mie touchier / Chascun vilain, chascun bouchier, / Ainz doit estre cortois e frans / Cil que j'ensi a ome prens" (vv. 1935–40 [1933–38]). On these lines and vv. 469–70 [467–68]), see Kelly, "Chastiaus," pp. 70–71.
11 It is therefore inaccurate to speak of "une grande variété dans le détail de ces descriptions" (Daniel Poirion, *Le Roman de la rose,* (Paris, 1973), p. 29.
12 This is true for Guillaume as well, at the beginning of the *Rose,* vv. 87–102 [ibid.].
13 The commonplace of love alternately ennobling and vilifying dates from the first known troubadour; see Guillaume d'Aquitaine, *Chansons,* ed. A. Jeanroy (Paris, 1927), IX.25–30. It remained alive throughout the Middle Ages, with a tendency to stress either the ennobling or the villainous features exclusively. Cf. Jean de Condé, "Dis de la pelote," *Dits,* II, 259–64 and 436.
14 FEW, s.v. *ríki,* XVI, 712–13; Tobler-Lommatzsch, s.v. *richece,* VIII, cols. 1268–70. It is thus related to *dangier,* either in the good sense of seigniorial authority or in the narrower sense of wealth pure and simple. Jean de Meun emphasizes the latter in his relatively brief return to Richesse; see *Rose,* vv. 7943–60 [7913–30], 10051–267 [10021–237]. Cf. also Glynnis Cropp, *Le Vocabulaire courtois des troubadours de l'époque classique* (Geneva, 1975), pp. 93–96.

15   See Köhler, "Reichtum und Freigebigkeit in der Trobadordichtung," *Trobador-lyrik*, pp. 45–72; and "Über das Verhältnis," *Trobadorlyrik*, pp. 73–87. Also Lazar, *Amour*, pp. 41–42, 44–45.

16   But Arthur's largesse makes such knights possible; thus he exemplifies Richesse in practice. The dire consequences of Arthur's neglect of largesse are evident in Marie de France's *Lanval* and the *Perlesvaus*. Arthur is referred to in v. 1177 [1175] of Guillaume's description.

17   Cf. the *Roman des eles*, where Largesse and Cortoisie lift up Prowess.

18   Franchise's companion is "Fiz au seignor de Guindesores" (v. 1228 [1226]). The allusion to Windsor may mean an actual duke of Windsor, Arthur himself, or both (see Langlois, *Rose*, II, v. 1228 note [p. 306]). The uncertain distinction between Franchise and Cortoisie—and for that matter Richesse—is apparent in the identification of Love's third arrow in the 'good' quiver: "Franchise . . . empenee / De . . . cortoisie" (vv. 942–43 [ibid.]). It is later named Cortoisie (v. 1767 [1765]). Guillaume is exploiting overlapping semantic fields, allegorically tagging the arrows and personifications as seems contextually suitable in a given passage.

19   She is "envoisiee e gaie" (v. 1265 [1264]).

20   *The Battle of the Seven Arts*, ed. Louis John Paetow (Berkeley, 1914), vv. 12–13.

21   Geoffrey's *Documentum*: "Sed, cum commune est describere pulchritudinem, ponamus difficiliores et minus usitatas, ut diversitas exemplorum tollat fastidium et nova difficultas, tanquam cibus aurium, invitet auditorem" (p. 272, § 5). Geoffrey's remarks are not strictly speaking a condemnation; he merely points out that such descriptions are common and easy enough to preclude extensive illustration.

22   Douglas Kelly, *"Sens" and "Conjointure" in the "Chevalier de la charrette"* (The Hague and Paris, 1966), pp. 204–205.

23   Thoss, *Locus amoenus*, pp. 118–27.

24   As defined by Faral, "les théoriciens du XIIe et du XIIIe siècle entendent [by amplification] 'développer, allonger (un récit)' " (*Arts poétiques*, p. 61). The explanation is vague and incomplete. See Brinkmann, *Wesen*, pp. 47–48; Payne, *Key*, pp. 46–47; Gallo, *Poetria Nova*, pp. 159–66; and Knapp, "Vergleich," pp. 460–68. A useful survey of the nature and kinds of topical description from classical times through Provençal and French literature (to about 1250) and German literature appears in Brinkmann, *Wesen*, pp. 103–84; also Alice M. Colby, *The Portrait in Twelfth-Century French Literature: An Example of the Stylistic Originality of Chrétien de Troyes* (Geneva, 1965).

25   Emphasis mine. See also Gervais of Melkley, *Ars poetica*, ed. Hans-Jürgen Gräbener (Münster, 1965), pp. 201–2.

26   Tobler-Lommatzsch does not contain any examples; in Godefroy (s.v. *psychologie*, X, 443) and FEW (s.v. *psyche*, IX, 502) the earliest instance is 1588 in the sense of "science de l'apparition des esprits." Ernst Gamillscheg's *Etymologisches Wörterbuch der französischen Sprache*, 2nd ed. (Heidelberg, 1969), p. 732, describes it as Neo-Latin, derived from the Greek by Melanchton. See also Brinkmann, *Wesen*, pp. 85–95. However, the anonymous "Traité des cinq puissances de l'âme" uses the root to designate *anima*, in connection with *imaginatio*: "Quare iam *non in istis est*, id est in visibilibus, a quibus, visu cessante, discessit, *sed est secundum ista*, id est in istorum ymaginibus, dum ad

eorum comparationem notiones ymaginarias motus recordationis in animam re-
spergit. Verum diuinam psichen, hoc est creature rationalis animam longe
perspicacius diuinitatis iubar illustrat, cui ad ymaginationis et sensus obtusi pur-
gandum iudicia ignes impassibilis perhenitatis intenduntur, quorum alter circa
alterum, et uterque circa predictas anime valetudines, diffusis fulgoribus, imperat
tenebris, cecitate fugata, et in natura priora, que rerum sunt cause formales, viam
pandit anime'' (d'Alverny, *Textes,* pp. 315-16).

27 *Le Jardin de plaisance et fleur de rethorique,* eds. E. Droz and A. Piaget (Paris,
1910–25), fol. cii r.

28 Cf. also *Ars versificatoria,* pp. 133-34, §§ 64-71.

29 Payne, *Key,* p. 191, note 35. See especially the *Scholia Vindobonensia ad Horatii
Artem Poeticam,* ed. Joseph Zechmeister (Vienna, 1877), pp. 9-10: "*Colores o.*,
id est, proprietates unicuique rei attribuendas (quia, sicut colores variant et distin-
guunt picturam, ita proprie describere quamque rem distinguit et ornat rem de-
scriptam)." Cf. C. O. Brink, *Horace on Poetry,* 2 vols. (Cambridge, 1963-71),
II, 173.

30 *Maneries* = "genus"; see Eberhard of Béthune, *Graecismus,* ed. Johann Wrobel
(Warsaw, 1887), p. 287; and Alexander of Villedieu, *Doctrinale,* ed. Dietrich
Reichling (Berlin, 1893), v. 315, note (p. 23). Cf. also Kelly, "Fortune and
Narrative Proliferation in the *Berinus,*" *Speculum* 51 (1976), 7, note 5.

31 See Isidore of Seville, *Etymologiarum sive originum libri XX,* ed. W. M.
Lindsay, 2 vols. (Oxford, 1911), 1.29.1.: "Etymologia est origo vocabulorum,
cum vis verbi vel nominis per interpretationem colligitur," which may include
human, and thus poetic, invention: "Quaedam non secundum qualitatem, qua
genita sunt, sed iuxta arbitrium humanae voluntatis vocabula acceperunt"
(1.29.3). Cf. Eberhard de Béthune, *Graecismus,* 10.70–71: "Etymologia tantum
lingua tibi sit in una, / At uariis linguis interpretatio fiet." See Faral, *Arts
poétiques,* pp. 65-67; and especially Roswitha Klinck, *Die lateinische Etymologie des Mittelalters* (Munich, 1970); and Yates, *Memory,* p. 30. G. Raynaud de Lage studies similar contextual adaptation of personifications in Alain
de Lille; see his *Alain,* especially pp. 88, 99–100, 119-21; see also Richard
H. Green, "Alan of Lille's *De planctu Naturae,*" *Speculum* 31 (1956), 649-74.
Like the seven liberal arts in the chariot that bears Prudence to the limits of
Heaven, "que uultum sub septem uultibus unum / Reddunt" (*Anticlaudianus* II.
326-27), the personifications in the garden of Deduit display distinct qualities
with the same features.

32 Gunn, *Mirror,* pp. 76, 110-13. The identification of different "traditions" by
Thoss (*Locus amoenus*) does not invalidate the formal principle.

33 Brinkmann, *Wesen,* pp. 58-65; Gallo, *Poetria,* pp. 150-76.

34 See Langlois, *Rose,* v. 78 note (II, 294-95).

35 Thoss, *Locus amoenus,* pp. 128-33.

36 *Locus amoenus,* pp. 132-33. Such topical adaptations are of obvious significance
for correct iconographic readings of the *Rose* and other allegorical poems.

37 Ed. Léopold Constans, 6 vols. (Paris, 1904–12), vv. 14631–958.

38 On Papelardie, cf. the *Rose,* vv. 434-35 [432-433]: "A li e as siens iert la
porte / Deveee de parevis."

39 See Leo Spitzer, *Classical and Christian Ideas of World Harmony: Prolegomena to an Interpretation of the Word "Stimmung"* (Baltimore, 1963), pp. 54–58, 175–78; James Wimsatt, *Chaucer and the French Love Poets: The Literary Background of the "Book of the Duchess"*, (Chapel Hill, 1968), pp. 16–20; Werner Ross, "Rose und Nachtigall: Ein Beitrag zur Metaphorik und Mythologie des Mittelalters," *Romanische Forschungen* 67 (1955), 55–82; Dragonetti, *Technique*, pp. 181–83. For the *Rose* in particular, see Thoss, *Locus amoenus*, pp. 122–23, 130–31.

40 Obviously an indication of talent and artistry. To the examples cited in Spitzer, *Classical Ideas*, add: Peire d'Alvernha, *Liriche*, ed. Alberto del Monte (Turin, 1955), XII.1–6 and 79–81; Wace, *Brut*, vv. 10421–24; *Durmart le galois*, ed. Joseph Gildea, 2 vols. (Villanova, 1965–66), vv. 3226–30. Finally, cf. the *Rose*, vv. 675–77 [673–75]: "A chanter furent ententif / Li oiselet, qui aprentif / Ne furent pas ne non sachant." See Calin, *Poet*, pp. 227–28.

41 In vv. 902–3 [ibid.], the god of Love "sembloit que ce fust uns anges / Qui fust tot droit venuz dou ciel." Fleming's ironic commentary on this passage (*Rose*, p. 69) is undercut by the frequency of the comparison in courtly literature before Guillaume. Benoît de Saint-Maure uses the same expressions to describe the *chambre de beautés* in the *Troie*—a place of retreat in an extraordinary setting and an atmosphere of courtliness (vv. 14786–90, 14911–13); see also vv. 18027, 20799–805, 24001–2, 28845. Similarly, Messire Thibaut, *Li Romanz de la poire*, ed. Friedrich Stehlich (Halle, 1881), vv. 27 and 403. Lancelot himself, according to Chrétien de Troyes, "n'est mie moins biax d'un ange": *Le Chevalier de la charrete (Lancelot)*, ed. Mario Roques (Paris, 1958), v. 6670. René d'Anjou refers to the island of love that "mieulx sembloit estre chose espirituelle que terrienne" in his *Cuer*, § 139, l. 85; see also ll. 106–7, and § 234, ll. 13–14.

42 Erich Köhler, "Narcisse, la fontaine d'Amour et Guillaume de Lorris," in *L'Humanisme médiéval dans les littératures romanes du XIIᵉ au XIVᵉ siècle*, ed. Anthime Fourrier (Paris, 1964), pp. 151–52.

43 And as may indeed take place at the conclusion of the romance; see Wetherbee, "Literal," pp. 285–86. A child also results from the consummation of Pygmalion's love, *Rose*, v. 21184 [21154].

44 Cf. Peter Dronke's parallels in *Medieval Latin and the Rise of European Love-Lyric*, 2nd ed., 2 vols. (Oxford, 1968), I, 1–56.

45 Cf. Erec's father-in-law in *Erec et Enide*, ed. Mario Roques (Paris, 1966), vv. 509–17; and *Lanval* in Marie de France's *Les Lais*, ed. Jean Rychner (Paris, 1968), vv. 30–38. It was an old concern; see, for example, the *Charroi de Nîmes*, ed. Duncan McMillan (Paris, 1972), vv. 637–57. Guillaume's promise of booty inspires the exploits of his knights in subsequent branches of the cycle. In general see Köhler, *Ideal*, pp. 1–36; and Karl-Heinz Bender, *König und Vasall: Untersuchungen zur Chanson de geste des XII. Jahrhunderts* (Heidelberg, 1967), pp. 118–22; Ochsenbein, *Studien*, pp. 149–51.

46 Cf. C. S. Lewis, *Allegory*, pp. 103–4.

47 The *Echecs* Commentator reads Covoitise in the garden wall as lechery; see fol. 245 r. Gerson allies Oiseuse with it when the subject is melancholy, not when it is *deduit:* "De ce avient que une personne melencolieuse et maladive et de chetive

277

complexion sera a la fois plus ardemment temptee de charnalité que une personne saine et sanguine, riant et se jouant, et tout vient de fantasie" ("Traité," p. 46). Guillaume represents the latter type both when he begins his morning promenade and when he enters the Garden of Deduit.

48 *De oratore,* I.i.1, ed. A. S. Wilkins, in Cicero, *Rhetorica,* 2 vols. (Oxford, 1902). Hugh of Saint Victor's qualification of *otium* is also adaptable to Gauvain's context as set forth in Wace's *Brut:* "Vitae quies . . . exterior, ut otium et opportunitas honestis et utilibus studiis suppetat" (*Didascalicon,* p. 67).

49 Christine de Pisan, *Le Livre de la mutacion de Fortune,* ed. Suzanne Solente, 4 vols. (Paris, 1959–66). This is true for Gerson as well; see his "Traité," p. 46.

50 Renon and Los are attributed to Compaignie (vv. 449–55), as with good love in the *Echecs* Commentary; see above pp. 14–15.

51 René d'Anjou, *Cuer,* § 241, l. 30. Oyseuse is thus distinguishable from Paresse, whose sloth is of no avail in the defense of the Château du Tertre deveé d'amours, held by its lord and lady Courroux and Tristesse (§ 51). René's Oyseuse has only a slight defect: "Elle estoit, a bien veoir et congnoistre ses façons et manieres d'elle agenser, ung bien peu nonchalante" (§ 241, ll. 26–28). She is thus akin to Charles d'Orléans' Nonchaloir; see Shigemi Sasaki, *Sur le thème de Nonchaloir dans la poésie de Charles d'Orléans* (Paris, 1974).

52 Cf. The *Bestiaire d'amour rimé:* "Ne pas ne vous sieu pour oidive, / Pour ce que je n'ai riens que faire; / Ains ai laissié tout autre afaire / Pour vous servir" (vv. 3368–71). See also Arno Esch, "John Gowers Erzählkunst," in *Chaucer und seine Zeit,* pp. 210–18. Gower, like the writer in the *Epistolae duorum amantium,* foresees *pes* or *quies* as the full realization of love; see J. A. W. Bennett, "Gower's 'Honeste Love' ", in *Patterns of Love and Courtesy,* p. 120.

53 Charlton Thomas Lewis and Charles Short, *A Latin Dictionary* (Oxford, 1879), s.v. *otium,* p. 1285, for its position and negative sense in classical Latin; cf. also Alexander Souter, *A Glossary of Later Latin to 600 A.D.* (Oxford, 1949), s.v. *otiositas,* p. 281: "Idleness, laziness; leisure . . . ; fruit of leisure (i.e. authorship)." The *Echecs* Commentator has Fleming's distinction for the verse *Echecs* (fol. 277 v), but adapts it for the *Rose* to Oiseuse's brief role as gatekeeper: "Pour ce briefment voult faindre ainsi l'acteur du *Romant de la rose* que Oyseuse estoit portier du vregier de Deduit et qu'elle lui ouvry la porte et le mist ens premier. Et aussi fait l'acteur samblablement du livre rymé dessusdit dont nous devons parler" (fols. 278v–279 r). But the *Echecs* lover had already met Venus; Guillaume is not yet in love, or in lust for that matter, when he meets Oiseuse; see Kelly, "Chastiaus," pp. 65–66.

54 Cf. H. R. Jauss, "Form und Auffassung der Allegorie in der Tradition der *Psychomachia* (von Prudentius zum ersten *Romanz de la Rose*)," in *Medium Aevum Vivum: Festschrift Walther Bulst* (Heidelberg, 1960), pp. 202–3; Thoss, *Locus amoenus,* pp. 117–18.

55 Faral, *Arts poétiques,* p. 61; Gallo, *Poetria,* p. 166.

56 Köhler, "Narcisse," p. 151.

57 *Studien,* pp. 144–45. Ochsenbein's discussion of the Vices and Virtues in the *Anticlaudianus* is a model for analysis of such Images, because of its careful attention to adaptation, semantic range, and context. Benjamin also discusses the

distinction between treatise and allegorical literature, distinguishing between the concept (*Begriff*) that characterizes the former, and the idea that informs the latter (*Ursprung,* pp. 7–22).

58 Gunn, *Mirror,* p. 186, n. 67 [p. 187].

59 Fleming, *Rose,* p. 238.

60 See Jean Batany, "Paradigmes lexicaux et structures littéraires au moyen âge," *Revue d'histoire littéraire de la France* 70 (1970), 819–35, and Paul Zumthor, *Essai de poétique médiévale* (Paris, 1972), p. 82. Also, in general, his "Note sur les champs sémantiques dans le vocabulaire des idées," *Neophilologus* 39 (1955), 175–83, 241–49; and "Pour une histoire du vocabulaire français des idées," *Zeitschrift für romanische Philologie* 72 (1956), 340–62. Also P. A. Messelaar, *Le Vocabulaire des idées dans le "Tresor" de Brunet Latin* (Assen, 1963).

61 That is, the suborners of Richesse; see vv. 1034–52 [1034–50].

62 This will change in Jean de Meun, where Male Bouche "envenime e... entouche / Touz ceus don il fait sa matire" (vv. 4102–3 [4072–73]), thus enabling him to specialize her description as a "fausse devote" and a hypocrite—"Par langue les livre a martire" (v. 4104 [4074]).

63 Gustav Gröber, *Grundriß der romanischen Philologie,* 2 vols. (Straßburg, 1897–1906), II.i, 737; Friedman, "Jean," p. 16; Fleming, *Rose,* p. 112. Baudouin de Condé makes the intervention of Reason a valid response to a hopeless love, and one which Love himself, given the desperate circumstances, will not object to; see his *Prisons d'amours* in the *Dits,* vv. 1813–43. Machaut does the same, especially in the *Dit de l'alerion.* Letter CVII of the *Epistolae duorum amantium* relates the vision of the Mulier in which a lady who ressembles Guillaume's Reason upbraids her for loving the Vir. The Mulier attributes this to her preoccupation with distracting cares. Her response is unfortunately excerpted in the manuscript, but it is preceded by her return to harmony and unity in her soul (*animus*); the letter concludes with her still in love.

64 Nims, "*Translatio,*" p. 216.

65 See Huizinga's "Verknüpfung," pp. 3–4. Definition is more appropriate to logic than to rhetoric, he argues (pp. 49–50); however, definition is one formula for topical invention.

66 Kelly, "Chastiaus," pp. 66–67.

67 Cf. vv. 2486–87 [2472–73]: "Car miauz vaut de li uns regarz / Que d'autre li deduiz entiers."

68 Machaut will imitate Guillaume's sequence in the *Dit de la rose;* see Calin, *Poet,* pp. 232–33.

69 Pp. 364–66.

70 P. 365.

71 P. 124.

72 In *Medium Aevum Vivum,* pp. 204–5.

73 Choice of epithets is important; see Jauss, "La Transformation de la forme allégorique entre 1180 et 1240: d'Alain de Lille à Guillaume de Lorris," in *Humanisme médiéval,* pp. 125–26. Cf. "Malveis dangier" in *L'Histoire de Guillaume le maréchal,* ed. Paul Meyer, 3 vols. (Paris, 1891–1901), v. 11075; Jean

de Garencières says of Dangier: "Qui bien sembloit estrange valeton, / Ung grant villain fier d'orrible visaige," and "il semble bien mau sire" (ed. Neal, II, 100, vv. 22-23, 26). For positive examples, see Tobler-Lommatzsch, s.v. *dangier,* II, especially cols. 1190-91. Note also *mauvais dangier,* cols. 1193-94. Cf. Sasaki, *Thème,* pp. 216-23.

74 *Allegory,* p. 365.

75 *Allegory,* pp. 365-66.

76 This is material style, wherein epithets conform to the class of the person, thing, or action represented; see Franz Quadlbauer, *Genera dicendi.*

77 Nims, *"Translatio,"* p. 216. Cf. the *Bestiaire d'amour rimé,* vv. 3657-60. See also Peter F. Dembowski, "Vocabulary of Old French Courtly Lyrics—Difficulties and Hidden Difficulties," *Critical Inquiry* 2 (1976), 763-79.

78 See Fleming's enlightening argument that gender is a superficial consideration for personifications, *Rose,* pp. 44-46.

79 Jean de Meun will turn Bel Acueil into a minx under the Vieille's influence.

80 Cf. the thorns surrounding the Rose, vv. 1675-80 [1673-78].

81 Felix Schlösser, *Andreas Capellanus: Seine Minnelehre und das christliche Weltbild um 1200* (Bonn, 1960), pp. 97-114; Kelly, *Sens,* p. 46.

82 But how should one explain the closed bud ("boutons") at the beginning of Guillaume's adventures, vv. 1666 [1664]? See also vv. 3363-70 [3345-52].

83 This is Reason's concern; see vv. 2853-62 [2837-46].

84 See the *Echecs* Commentary, cited above, pp. 18-19.

85 In German, *Bild* as *Einbildung* allies *imaginatio* as used here with *Bildung,* or "education."

86 Jauss, "Transformation," p. 142.

87 In the *Queste,* on the other hand, the grail is made to modify its attributes at each appearance.

88 See in general Köhler, *Ideal und Wirklichkeit in der höfischen Epik: Studien zur Form der frühen Artus- und Graldichtung,* (Tübingen, 1970), pp. 102-6, 267; Kelly, *"Matiere,"* pp. 148-50. Also Harry Caplan, ed. and trans., Gianfrancesco Pico della Mirandola, *On the Imagination,* (New Haven, 1930), pp. 2, 4-6; Jeauneau, "Usage," pp. 85-86; Lubac, *Exégèse,* II.2, 196; and Wolfram von den Steinen, "Les Sujets d'inspiration chez les poètes latins du XIIe siècle," *Cahiers de civilisation médiévale* 9 (1966), 374. Compare these studies with Erich Neumann, *The Origins and History of Consciousness,* trans. R. F. C. Hull (Princeton, 1954), pp. 7-8, and his collection *Art and the Creative Unconscious,* trans. Ralph Manheim (Princeton, 1959).

89 Cf. for example Gerhard Adler, *The Living Symbol: A Case Study in the Process of Individuation* (Princeton, 1961), p. 410: "I have attempted to follow the process as it went along and to describe what took place. If I started the treatment with certain theoretical premises it has been my endeavor not to let them intrude into the actual observations; in fact, one's own point of view is constantly transformed by observations and experiences like those discussed here. The true function of the analyst is exactly this: to help the patient understand and accept what is taking place in him without interfering with the unique process that unfolds itself according to its own rhythm and inner law." Adler also points out that "every

actual experience contains at least two aspects: the archetypal image and the evoking factor, which in their interpenetration form the imago" (p. 13). C. G. Jung's concept of "active imagination" derives from alchemy, and is thus allied to our subject; see his *Psychologie und Alchimie* (Zürich, 1944). In the *Rose,* the "evoking factor" is the context imposed by Guillaume de Lorris: the art of love. The Image is the Rose. Cf. Lubac, *Exégèse,* II.2, 180: "Moins le symbole est traduisible en langage clair, plus il arrive que se pressent les inventions allégoriques en vue de le cerner ou de le suggérer." In connection with these considerations, one may also cite Benjamin's discussion of the relationship between symbol and allegory in his *Ursprung des deutschen Trauerspiels;* Benjamin's discussion is influenced by Plato. The fascination of medieval Images is their *merveille;* see Morton W. Bloomfield, "Episodic Motivation and Marvels in Epic and Romance," in *Essays and Explorations,* pp. 96–128; and Kelly, *"Matiere,"* pp. 148–50.

90 "The Rhetoric of Sincerity in the *Roman de la rose,"* in *Romance Studies Edward Billings Ham,* pp. 116–18. See Zumthor, *Langue, texte, énigme,* pp. 258–59.

91 See Jeauneau, "Usage," p. 87; Wetherbee, *Platonism,* pp. 6 and 43–45.

CHAPTER 5

1 See chapter 3 for the adaptation of Imagination to the poetics of the Second Rhetoric in the writings of Machaut.

2 Jauss, *Grundriß,* VI.1, 228–29, 232–33.

3 Pierre Le Gentil, "Réflexions sur la création littéraire au moyen âge," in *Chanson de geste und höfischer Roman* (Heidelberg, 1963), especially p. 19.

4 Ed. Stehlich, vv. 2016–2251. On this work, see Jung, *Etudes,* pp. 310–17. Cf. also the *Bestiaire d'amour rimé,* vv. 1994–2014.

5 *Preface,* p. 233. See also Poirion, *Poète,* p. 204: "Il [Machaut] a aménagé les débats traditionnels en longs inventaires des idées conduisant au jugement formulé au nom de la raison." But the combination was not new.

6 See Hoepffner, ed. *Œuvres,* I, lvi–lvii.

7 *Ars d'amour, de vertu et de boneurté,* ed. Jules Petit, 2 vols. (Brussels, 1867–69), I, 199–200. Imagination thus belongs for Jehan le Bel to that part of rhetoric treated under memory; see Caplan, *Of Eloquence,* pp. 202–3, 210–12.

8 Caplan, *Of Eloquence,* pp. 228–40; Yates, *Memory,* p. 7.

9 *Le Roman de Cassidorus,* ed. Joseph Palermo, 2 vols. (Paris, 1963–64), § 54. This is not wish-fulfillment, the *insomnium* of Macrobius. An example of the latter occurs in the dreams of a maiden who tries to seduce Helcanor, unaware that the latter is a young man only in disguise: "Il sambloit a la damoisele par ymagination que Helcanor fust avec lui charnelment" (§ 296).

10 The *Kanor* is the last branch in the cycle.

11 Ed. Hermann Breuer (Dresden, 1915).

12 The device of writing for the lady occurs in other romances, notably in *Le Bel Inconnu, Partonopeu de Blois, Florimont,* and *Joufroi de Poitiers;* see John L. Grigsby, "The Narrator in *Partonopeu de Blois, Le Bel Inconnu,* and *Joufroi de Poitiers,"* *Romance Philology* 21 (1967–68), 536–43.

13 Ed. Segre, pp. viii–ix.
14 Cf. Colby, *Portrait;* Dragonetti, *Technique,* pp. 248–72; Cropp, *Vocabulaire,* pp. 141–42.
15 *Maniere, port,* and *maintieng* (vv. 197–216) are grouped together, as are *honneur* and *courtoisie* (vv. 239–56) in this catalogue.
16 This is the typical movement of love from dissemblance to resemblance, from exile to approximation; see Javelet, in *Entretiens,* p. 316.
17 See also vv. 336–42.
18 In the classical sense of using figural ornamentation to enhance and embellish the thought, while preserving clarity of expression; see Erich Auerbach, *Literatursprache und Publikum in der lateinischen Spätantike und im Mittelalter* (Bern, 1958), p. 153; Dragonetti, *Technique,* p. 15.
19 See Dragonetti, *Technique,* pp. 32–35; Quadlbauer, *Genera,* p. 109; Kelly, "Theory," pp. 136–43. Auerbach (*Literatursprache*) does not consider the medieval terminology.
20 The sole exception so far identified is Abaelard; see Javelet, *Entretiens,* p. 319.
21 See chapter 2, note 34.
22 E.g. Chichmaref, ed., Balade notée XXXIII. Of course, he wrote some about a love not at all courtly: Appendix I, VII–X, XV.
23 I see no reason to change my reading of Andreas or the Vulgate cycle, although I am now convinced that the attempt to account for gradualism in part by reference to Thomist thought was unfortunate (see "Courtly Love," p. 135). The lack of a philosophical foundation for gradualism, or at least our ignorance of that foundation, does not do away with its obvious place in Andreas' *De amore,* or in the poets and romancers; cf. Köhler, "Entstehung," pp. 43–49, 64–70. A more likely source for the notion of gradualism is Chartrain thought, especially because of its influence on poetics and literature; see Wetherbee, *Platonism,* pp. 70–71. The abrupt introduction of a new or broader perspective is a kind of *ordo artificialis* on the level of exposition that occurs not only in Andreas and the Vulgate cycle, but, as we shall see below, in Froissart, in the parts of the Alexander cycle containing the *Iter ad paradisum* episode, and in Gautier de Châtillon's *Alexandreis* with the intervention of Nature. In general, see Haug, "Struktur," pp. 129–52.
24 Cf. the censure of love Machaut places in the mouth of the French king in the *Voir-Dit,* pp. 224–32. It is part of a debate about how reasonable Machaut's love for Péronne is.
25 *Preface,* p. 48.
26 See Dieter Schaller, "Probleme der Überlieferung und Verfasserschaft lateinischer Liebesbriefe des hohen Mittelalters," *Mittellateinisches Jahrbuch* 3 (1966), 25–36.
27 See Robertson's "Some Medieval Literary Terminology, with Special Reference to Chrétien de Troyes," *Studies in Philology* 48 (1951), 669–92.
28 Fleming, *Rose,* p. 76.
29 Jeauneau, "Usage," pp. 43 and 47.
30 *Rose,* pp. 95 and 97.

31 *Preface,* pp. 61–62. See Watriquet de Couvin, *Dits,* ed. Auguste Scheler (Brussels, 1868).

32 *Preface,* p. 232.

33 See also the "Dis des huit couleurs," vv. 101–5, 329–34.

34 See Ward, ed., *Epistles,* p. 26, ll. 274–80. Cf. also Chaucer, "The Miller's Prologue," vv. 3167–86. This is a traditional medieval notion: "Fabulas poetae quasdam delectandi causa finxerunt, quasdam ad naturam rerum, nonnullas ad mores hominum interpretati sunt. Delectandi causa fictas, ut eas, quas vulgo dicunt, vel quales Plautus et Terentius conposuerunt" (Isidore of Seville, I.xl.3). Cf. also Macrobius, *Commentarii,* I.ii.7–9; and L. T. Topsfield, *Troubadours and Love* (Cambridge, 1975), pp. 24–40.

35 See especially vv. 121–51. Also Jehan Maillart's *Le Comte d'Anjou,* ed. Mario Roques (Paris, 1931), vv. 1–3, 19–22.

36 Jacques Ribard, *Un Ménestrel du XIVᵉ siècle: Jean de Condé* (Geneva, 1969), p. 172.

37 Ribard, *Ménestrel,* pp. 172–96.

38 Cf. Andreas Capellanus: "Semper amorem crescere vel minui constat" (*De amore,* p. 310), and, in general, pp. 238–50.

39 Andreas, p. 17: "Doctus enim amans vel docta deformem non reiicit amantem, si moribus intus abundet"—no doubt salutary for knights who participated in tournaments and fought wars!

40 See Ernst Robert Curtius, *Europäische Literatur und lateinisches Mittelalter,* 2nd ed. (Bern, 1954), pp. 214–17, on the overlapping meanings of Poetry and Philosophy. In Froissart's *Joli buisson de jonece,* "Philozophie" (v. 191) exhorts the poet to arise from melancholy and lethargy and to continue writing. See also Marie de France, *Lais,* prologue vv. 9–22.

41 Baudouin de Condé equates *connissance* and *entendement* in the *Prisons d'amours,* vv. 342–45: "Entendemens et connissance: / Par ce set de cascun l'afaire, / C'on doit laisier ne c'on doit faire, / Ne coi furnir ne coi eslire."

42 P. 432. Cf. Love in Christ's army in Huon de Mery's *Tornoiement.*

43 Cf. the lover's homage to the god of Love in Guillaume de Lorris, *Rose,* vv. 1927–2042 [1925–2040].

44 See Jean Froissart, *Œuvres,* III, 52–281.

45 "Sed qui Domino contendunt perfecte servire, eius prorsus debent obsequio mancipari et iuxta Pauli sententiam nullo saeculari debent adimpleri negotio. Ergo, si servire Deo tantum vultis eligere, mundana vos oportet cuncta relinquere et coelestis patriae solummodo contemplari secreta. Non enim Deus voluit, aliquem dextrum in terris pedem et in coelo tenere sinistrum, quia nemo potest duorum intendere competenter obsequiis" (pp. 161–162); see in general the *De amore,* pp. 159–63.

46 See also Baudouin de Condé's "Contes d'amours," vv. 169–75.

47 Cf. v. 258; and p. 121: XLIV, vv. 9–16.

48 See the beginning to Machaut's *Voir-Dit,* vv. 39–47, and p. 20: "Vous m'avez ressuscité & rendu mon sentement que j'avoie tout perdu: & jamais par moi ne fust fais chans ne lais, se vous ne fussiez."

49 On *humilité,* see Richart de Fornival's *Consaus d'amours:* "Humilités fait gens molt gracieus, ne il n'a riens en homme ki tant soit haie comme orguix" (p. 12, § 19).

50 I.e. an idol. Cf. Machaut's Motet VIII, vv. 9-13 (ed. Chichmaref): "Une ydole est de fausse portraiture, / Où nuls ne doit croire ne mettre cure; / Sa contenance en vertu pas ne dure, / Car c'est tous vens, ne riens qu'elle figure / Ne puet estre fors de fausse figure." It is an *insomnium,* a meaningless fantasy in false Imagination.

51 See Jean de Condé's emphatically affirmative response in "Li Recors d'armes et d'amours"; and Ribard, *Ménestrel,* p. 186. See Froissart, "Cour de may", vv. 1004-24.

CHAPTER 6

1 *Troilus* II.25-28.

2 Lionel J. Friedman, "Gradus amoris," *Romance Philology* 19 (1965-66), 167-77. The "typical" did not preclude adaptive variations, as in Matthew of Vendôme's "ordinaria successio" of six steps described in the *Ars versificatoria,* p. 183, § 13; see Friedman, "Gradus," pp. 170-71.

3 Cf. Machaut's *Dit de la harpe,* v. 259, Karl Young, ed., in *Essays Albert Feuillerat,* ed. H. Peyre (New Haven, 1943). See also Calin, *Poet,* p. 228.

4 Cf. also "niceté" (v. 847) and irrational love (vv. 856-62), suggesting the *Rose's* description of love by oxymoron (vv. 4293-358 [4263-328]) and that in the *Remede* (vv. 1129-60).

5 The lover's "idolatry," kneeling before his lady's mansion to beseech aid and encouragement from Amour and Esperance, corresponds to the lover offering homage to the god of Love in the *Rose* (vv. 1932-58 [1930-56]). See Wimsatt, *Chaucer,* pp. 110-12.

6 *Ursprung,* p. 16: "Und zwar liegen jene Elemente, deren Auflösung aus den Phänomenen Aufgabe des Begriffes ist, in den Extremen am genauesten zutage. Als Gestaltung des Zusammenhanges, in dem das Einmalig-Extreme mit seinesgleichen steht, ist die Idee umschrieben. . . . Das Empirische . . . wird um so tiefer durchdrungen, je genauer es als ein Extremes eingesehen werden kann. Vom Extremen geht der Begriff aus."

7 Åke Blomqvist, ed. (Karlshamn, 1951), v. 4991.

8 Eds. John E. Matzke and Maurice Delbouille, (Paris, 1936), vv. 1-2; cf. vv. 3-74.

9 Köhler, *Ideal,* pp. 187-88. See also Raymond Lincoln Kilgour, *The Decline of Chivalry as Shown in the French Literature of the Late Middle Ages* (Cambridge, Mass., 1937).

10 Jauss, *Grundriß,* VI.1, 150-151, 163-64.

11 Cf. the *Fonteinne amoureuse,* ed. Hoepffner, *Œuvres,* III, xxv-xxviii; and Froissart's *Bleu Chevalier.* On the latter, see Normand R. Cartier, "Le Bleu chevalier," *Romania* 87 (1966), 289-314.

12 In the *Remede* Complainte, Machaut refers to Boethius as a useful aid in resisting Fortune, vv. 982-84.

13   It is also emphasized in Alain Chartier's *Traité de l'esperance*. See *Les Œuvres,*
     ed. André du Chesne (Paris, 1617), pp. 277 ff. It thus corrects a state of melan-
     choly analogous to Chaucer's in the *Book of the Duchess:* "En ceste dolente &
     triste pensee, qui tousiours se presente a mon cueur, & m'accompaigne au leuer &
     au coucher, dont les nuiz me sont longues, & ma vie ennuyeuse; ay long temps
     trauaillé & foullé mon petit Entendement, qui tant est surpris & enuironné de
     desplaisans frenesies, que ie ne le puis exploictier à choses dont me viegne liesse
     ne confort. Et comme n'agueres la memoire des choses passees, l'expouentement
     des dispositions presentes, & l'orribleté des perilz auenir eussent reueillé tous mes
     douloureux regraiz, mes adoulees imaginations, & ma paour deffiee de seureté; ie
     demouray comme homme esperdu, le visage blesme, le sens troublé, & le sang
     meslé ou corps" (p. 263).

14   This is not dissimilar to Tristan's use of the "salle aux images" in Thomas
     d'Angleterre. But Tristan's Images lead to "errance" and jealousy rather than
     reasonable expectation (see Turin[1], vv. 14–17).

15   Machaut cites his authority again in the *Voir-Dit*, v. 5447.

16   The following discussion owes much to Martha Wallen's unpublished Ph.D.
     minor thesis (University of Wisconsin, 1971) "The Illumination of Guillaume de
     Machaut's *Confort d'ami*."

17   Here self-knowledge is awareness of one's duties.

18   Cf. Robertson, *Preface,* pp. 233–34: for Machaut, "love should be allied with
     virtue rather than with Fortune, so that its aims are consonant with the principle
     that true happiness rests in God". Similarly, Froissart has Love proclaim, "après
     Dieu je puis sur tous" ("Cour de may," v. 963).

19   In Balade CCIII, the poet complains that his "idol," unlike Pygmalion's, does
     not become "une vive creature" (vv. 15–16).

20   Cf. the reference to Morpheus' importance—and thus the significance of dream
     visions in the *Fonteinne amoureuse* and the *Voir-Dit*—in the latter dit's allusions
     to the former; see Hoepffner, ed., Machaut, *Œuvres,* III, xxi–xxii.

21   On Machaut's borrowings from Boethius in the *Remede,* see Hoepffner, ed.
     Œuvres, II, xix–xxxii; and Calin, *Poet,* pp. 57–62. Esperance's independence
     from Fortune is perhaps adumbrated in passages from the *Consolation* like "Quid
     si haec ipsa mei mutabilitas iusta tibi causa est sperandi meliora?" (II Prose
     ii.43–44) *Spes* is elsewhere described as "lubrica" (IV Metrum ii.8). Machaut's
     adaptation is neither profound nor servile; one may indeed apply to Machaut what
     Edward Kennard Rand has written of Boethius' own art of adaptation. It "is not a
     thing of shreds and patches, of clippings and pilferings, of translatings and ex-
     tractings, but springs from two main sources, *ingenium* and *memoria*" *Founders
     of the Middle Ages,* p. 164. This is applicable to Machaut's conception of art as
     expressed in the *Remede,* vv. 1–44, and the *Prologue;* for the art of love, see the
     Remede, vv. 61–86, 135–66.

22   Cf. such passages as "O felix hominum genus, / Si uestros animos amor / Quo
     caelum regitur regat" (II Metrum viii.28–30); "Sic aeternos reficit cursus /
     Alternus amor" (IV Metrum vi. 16–17); or "Hic est cunctis communis amor /
     Repetuntque boni fine teneri, / Quia non aliter durare queant, / Nisi conuerso

rursus amore / Refluant causae quae dedit esse'' (IV Metrum vi. 44–48). See Rand, *Founders*, p. 169.

23 *De amore*, p. 1 [p. 28]. Both extant Old French translations of the definition, by Jean de Meun and Drouart la Vache, retain only carnal desire. Drouart, vv. 143–46: "Ainsi com Venus le commande, / Par qui chascuns amans demande / Plus l'acoler et le baisier / Que lui d'autre chose aaisier." Jean, *Rose*, vv.4381–86 [4351–56]: "ardeur nee / De vision desordenee, / Pour acoler et pour besier / Pour els charnelment aesier. / Amant autre chose n'entent, / Ains s'art et se delite en tant." Jean then adds by way of clarification: "De fruit aveir ne fait il force; / Au deliter senz plus s'efforce" (vv. 4387–88 [4357–58]). As such the definitions include only what Andreas classifies as love for peasants, *nimia voluptatis abundantia*, or, at best, a hasty *amor simplex*. No time is left for hope, or for inquiring into Love's *praecepta*. This is the reason for Christine de Pisan's attack on Jean de Meun's inadequate survey of love.

24 On these distinctions, see my article "Courtly Love," pp. 119–47. Also, on the prominence of the distinction before Andreas, see Cropp, *Vocabulaire*, pp. 253–74; and Topsfield, *Troubadours*, passim.

25 In Guillaume's *Rose*, vv. 3959–4058 [3931–4028]. His lover fluctuates between hope for love and unrequited desire.

26 See Howard R. Patch, *The Goddess Fortuna in Medieval Literature* (Cambridge, Mass., 1927), pp. 90–98; Chrétien de Troyes, *Der Percevalroman*, ed. Alfons Hilka (Halle, 1932), vv. 4646–47 note (p. 715); Hoepffner, ed., *Œuvres*, II, xvii–xviii; Pickering, *Literature*, pp. 168–222.

27 See also the lady in the *Fonteinne amoureuse*, vv. 2207–10. The *Bestiaires d'amours* also equates death with despair (p. 29, ll. 3–6).

28 Especially vv. 1619–26, 1701–6, 2403–10; and *De consolatione*, I Prose vi.39–62. The lai, like the other fixed forms in the *Remede*, provides a thematic structure for the discursive and narrative elaboration in the octosyllabic couplets; see Calin, *Poet*, p. 71; Robertson, *Preface*, p. 233.

29 Vv. 2467–71; and *De consolatione*, II Prose iv.79–84.

30 *De consolatione*, IV Prose iii. See as well Richart de Fornival's *Consaus d'amours*, pp. 6–7 (§§ 3–4).

31 C. S. Lewis, *The Discarded Image* (Cambridge, 1964), p. 86.

32 Note the lady's allusion to the ambiguity of *bien* in *La Belle Dame sans mercy*, v. 425.

33 Cf. again *La Belle Dame sans mercy*, vv. 569–76.

34 Poirion, *Poète*, p. 131. Cf. *Remede*, vv. 347–51.

35 Richart de Fornival makes the same case, stressing at the same time that *seignorie* has no place in good love (*Bestiaires*, p. 89, ll. 1–2). The problem comes up in Chrétien's *Erec* as well; see Douglas Kelly, "La Forme et le sens de la quête dans l'*Erec et Enide* de Chrétien de Troyes," *Romania* 92 (1971), 343, n. 1, and 349–52.

36 *De consolatione* III Prose ix.80–98.

37 The use of *sublimatio* in a parallel sense is attested in Chenu, "*Imaginatio*," pp. 595–96; and in his "*Spiritus*," p. 232, n. 79.

38 *De amore,* p. 10; Wace, *Brut,* vv. 10513-20.

39 See Hoepffner, ed. *Œuvres,* II, xiv n. 2; Brinkmann, *Wesen,* pp. 89-90; Wimsatt, *Chaucer,* p. 174, n. 6. Machaut makes the same assertion in the *Lyon,* vv. 1136-44, and in Balade CCLXXII. Richart de Fornival also stresses the significance of appearances, both in the *Consaus* (pp. 17-18, § 33), and in the *Bestiaires* (pp. 22, l. 5-23, l. 1; 71, l. 1-72, l. 7). See also the *Response du Bestiaire* (pp. 129, l. 14-130, l. 11). Note as well the distinctions made in the *Epistolae duorum amantium:* "Raro quenquam invenimus in hoc salo tam composite felicitatis, tam perfecte virtutis, quin corpus eius non bene politum, deesse sibi peniteat multum, nisi tu solus, qui per omnia et in omnibus extas virtuosus" (Letter LXXXVIII); see also Letter CIX.

40 Wimsatt, *Chaucer,* p. 111. Cf. the judicious remark of Calin (*Poet,* p. 28): "The semantic range of courtly vocabulary is sufficiently wide, especially in the late Middle Ages, to allow for a sensual or a chaste interpretation of *joie* and *don.* I believe that readers or listeners were free to interpret such words each in his own way, according to his own temperament." See also p. 61.

41 On this subject see Steadman, "Courtly Love," pp. 20-26; Robertson, *Preface,* pp. 108-10, 457-60; and Calin, *Poet,* p. 245.

42 Cf. von den Steinen, "Sujets," p. 171, on Hildebert de Lavardin: "Hildebert est évêque de tout son cœur; il n'en revient pas moins toujours à la figure idéale du sage, épris de vertu et du désir de connaître, donc à l'abri des coups de la Fortune." There is thus common ground in Hildebert's and Machaut's love poetry. The Vir in the *Epistolae duorum amantium* also distinguishes his and his lady's love from the kind subject to Fortune (Letter L). The exchange between the Vir and the Mulier, tentatively attributed to Abaelard and Heloise by the editor, Ewald Könsgen (pp. 93-103), is markedly similar to that evinced in the letters of Machaut and Péronne d'Armentières in the *Voir-Dit.*

43 See the *Jugement Behaingne,* vv. 938-47, 989-99, 1941-56, and especially 1934-35: "Que cils amans est plus loing de confort / Que la dame ne soit, que Dieus confort."

44 See for example Love's companions in the *Vergier,* vv. 613-14, 621-22. In the *Jugement Behaingne,* see vv. 896-99; the counsellors in debate include Desirs (v. 1482, 1991), and it is obvious that love may be hopeless. The *Vergier* was greatly influenced by Guillaume's *Rose;* see Hoepffner, ed. *Œuvres,* I, lvi-lvii. Machaut does not acknowledge explicitly his debt to Guillaume de Lorris; however, he alludes to the *Rose* in the *Prise d'Alexandrie,* vv. 8492-93, and the *Voir-Dit,* p. 28. In both the *Vergier* and the *Jugement Behaingne,* the lover has at least a modicum of hope while suffering from desire: the promise of reward sometime in the future. The same is true in Guillaume's *Rose* (vv. 2765-67 [2745-47]).

45 Hoepffner, ed., *Œuvres,* I, lxix. Calin, *Poet,* p. 45, correctly points out that the roles could easily be reversed, and thus do not depend on the litigants' sex.

46 There is no general agreement on the precise chronology of the two *Jugement* poems and the *Remede,* but the sequence *Jugement Behaingne, Remede, Jugement Navarre* enjoys favor. It seems certain that the last two follow the first and are nearly contemporary with each other.

47 The theme acquired a certain actuality in the Hundred Years War; see Chartier's *Livre des quatre dames* and the evocation of the plague at the beginning to the *Jugement Navarre*. Cf. Robertson, *Preface*, p. 236, n. 158.

48 See vv. 1989–95, where however Noblesse is missing.

49 Appears later, v. 1597.

50 Is Machaut adapting Andreas' definition?

51 For example, at the end of Chaucer's *Troilus;* and, with slight variations to account for aging, in Gower's *Confessio amantis*, Froissart's *Joli buisson de jonece*, and Charles d'Orléans' *Songe en complainte*.

52 *Poète*, p. 101; see also pp. 102–3.

53 "Ce que je di n'est pas contrueve, / Car chascuns le dit et apprueve; / Et pour ce que chascuns le dit, / L'ay je recordé en mon dit" (*Jugement Navarre*, vv. 3055–58); cf. Jean de Meun, *Rose*, vv. 15222–32 [15192–202].

54 In the *Remede*, see vv. 653–80. The lover's service in the last part of the dit exemplifies this.

55 *Fonteinne amoureuse*, vv. 2267–70, 2335–50. The change is striking, since these lines are in the complainte, which thus corrects the *Remede's* complainte.

56 This is related to the conflict between astrological determinism and human freedom. Bernardus Silvestris accorded it special emphasis; see Stock, *Myth*, pp. 26–30, 164–67, and Wetherbee, *Platonism*, pp. 153–58.

57 *Rose*, vv. 21573–82 [21543–52]. Cf. Paré, *Idées*, pp. 31–32. It is current; cf. Ernst Cassirer, *Philosophie der symbolischen Formen* (Darmstadt, 1964), I, 58–59.

58 By analogy, survival of the plague corresponds to passing through the misfortunes of love; only death is irremediable, for death dissipates all love. On the analogy between the poem's subject and its melancholy introduction, see Robertson, *Preface*, pp. 235–36.

59 See especially pp. 141–42. On p. 167 and following, Esperance intervenes as a personification, reminding the lover of the "Lay de l'esperance" alluded to in the *Confort*, and inserted here in its entirety (pp. 172–80). See especially strophe 10: "Si, n'est vie / Si jolie / Com de desiree amie, / En espoir / Qui chastie / Et maistrie / Desir, si qu'il n'ait maistrie / Ne pooir, / Qu'il detrie. / Vie lie, / Quant Espoirs ne l'amolie" (pp. 178–79). There is an allusion to Boethius in v. 5447 (p. 231), and Fortune and Souffissance are contrasted further on: "si vivrons en joie & en plaisance, & si aurons parfaite souffisance. Et aussi, nous serons hors des dangiers de Fortune" (p. 367). In general, see pp. 352–60 of the *Voir-Dit;* also Calin, *Poet*, p. 233.

60 See especially Chichmaref, ed. Lais VIII–IX, XIII–XIV, XVII–XXI. In XXI, the "Lay de la rose," the rose represents hope. Even in lais in which despair prevails, it is because of death, as in the *Jugement Navarre*. Cf. the "Lay dou plour" at the end of the *Jugement Navarre* and the "Lay mortel," XII, vv. 171–79: "Si prent la venjence / De m'outrecuidence / Amours qui me lance / De mortel fer da sa lance; / C'est desesperence / En lieu d'esperance." On the lai, Deschamps notes in the *Art de dictier:* "C'est une chose longue et malaisée a faire et trouver" (*Œuvres*, VII, 287).

61 Ed. Gaston Raynaud (Paris, 1905).

62. Johannes de Hauvilla, *Architrenius,* ed. Paul Gerhard Schmidt (Munich, 1974), VII, vv. 416–18 (p. 247).
63 Vv. 1520–26, 2195–286.
64 Vv. 1863–934. See Poirion, *Poète,* pp. 63–66.
65 See also vv. 1776–804, 3837–40.
66 De Boer, ed., *Ovide moralisé,* XV, 28–43; Froissart, *Espinette,* p. 33 and passim in notes.
67 Demats, *Fabula.*
68 Marc-René Jung "*Poetria:* Zur Dichtungstheorie des ausgehenden Mittelalters in Frankreich," *Vox Romanica* 30 (1971), 44–64.
69 *Joli buisson,* vv. 1554–707, 5078–438. Cf. Froissart's *Espinette,* v. 125, and vv. 402–4, note (p. 175).
70 For example, Machaut's *Dit dou Lyon* and *Dit de l'alerion.*
71 Jauss, *Grundriß,* VI.1, 179–80.
72 As in Gace de la Buigne's *Deduis,* ed. Blomqvist, pp. 9–12.
73 *Imagery,* pp. 21–22.
74 The distinction *argument-exemplaire* is rhetorical. An argument is the substance of topical amplification at a suitable place (*locus,* here "point") in the *matière.* One means to amplify is exemplification, another is discursive analysis. See Lausberg, *Handbuch,* pp. 197–236.
75 On the recurrent inspiration of the lady's Image, see the *Vergier,* vv. 193–95; *Jugement Behaingne,* vv. 409–15; *Jugement Navarre,* vv. 4150–56; *Voir-Dit,* passim.
76 On the interchangeable pair external *grace* = inner *vertu,* see the *Remede* and *The Marguerite Poetry of Guillaume de Machaut,* ed. James I. Wimsatt (Chapel Hill, 1970), where the two are used interchangeably in the "Dit de la fleur de lis et de la marguerite."

CHAPTER 7

1 *Faust,* vv. 5531–34 [For we are Allegories, and so you should recognize us. *Herald:* I wouldn't know what to name you. Rather, I could describe you].
2 Cf. also the *Orloge amoureus,* vv. 19–36. The debate in the *Plaidoirie de la rose et de la violette* takes place "Devant Imagination, / Où on doit par droite action / Mettre memoires et escris" (vv. 1–3). Scheler comments on these lines: "*Imagination,* dans le sens de Froissart, signifie réflexion, examen.—Les vers 2 et 3 sont de pur remplissage, dont le sens ne ressort pas trop clairement" (II, 456, note). Froissart rarely resorts to "remplissage"; rather, vv. 2–3 make the figurative sense of Imagination explicit: a courtly problem is resolved by personifications in debate. Cf. Kolve, "Chaucer," p. 304.
3 Cf. the hair-pulling incident in the *Espinette,* vv. 3774–93.
4 Bellorophus is likened to Narcissus as a scornful lover, vv. 159–83. Like Guillaume de Lorris, Froissart distinguishes his case from theirs (vv. 184–94). See also Normand R. Cartier, "Froissart, Chaucer and Enclimpostair," *Revue de littérature comparée* 38 (1964), 18–34.
5 *Œuvres,* I, 394–95; cf. Fourrier, ed. *Prison amoureuse,* pp. 18–19.
6 Fourrier, ed. *Espinette,* p. 36.

7   *Voyage en Béarn,* ed. A. H. Diverres (Manchester, 1953), pp. 84–85. See also Christine de Pisan, *Mutacion de Fortune,* vv. 1025–416, especially vv. 1025–42, 1343–400.

8   Tuve, *Imagery,* p. 26.

9   In the "Cour de may," vv. 1529–46, Froissart asserts that Orgueil is good in battle and in a lady's response to a villainous request. *Bon orgueil* is also esteemed prudent and admirable in a woman in the *Response au Bestiaire,* pp. 128, l. 10–129, l. 3.

10 *Œuvres,* I, 399. On the following see I, 400–401, and Fourrier, ed., *Prison amoureuse,* pp. 20–28.

11 Scheler, ed., *Œuvres,* I, 401.

12 Fourrier, ed., *Espinette,* vv. 2473–74 note (pp. 180–81).

13 Idem, vv. 3129–31 note (p. 182).

14 See Fourrier, ed., *Espinette,* p. 32.

15 Tuve, *Imagery,* p. 425.

16 Idem, pp. 21–22.

17 In Machaut's *Lyon,* the *médisants* are the swarms of vile creatures that plague the noble lion because of his love.

18 *De amore,* p. 3 [p. 28].

19 *De amore,* pp. 5–6 [p. 29]. Cf. Andreas' prologue: "Asseris te namque novum amoris militem novaque ipsius sauciatum sagitta illius nescire apte gubernare frena caballi nec ullum posse tibi remedium invenire" (p. 1). See also the *rage,* the immoderate haste of Guillaume's first attempt to pluck the Rose, discussed in Kelly, "Chastiaus," pp. 65–66.

20 Outrage produces a similar effect in Rose's dream; see vv. 2760–72. Cf. also p. 154, ll. 130–38. Even a lover as purified of desire as the one Machaut exemplifies in the *Remede* is not safe from slander; see *Remede,* vv. 4195–216.

21 Cf. Andreas Capellanus: "Qui enim probus invenitur et prudens, nunquam facile posset in amoris semita deviare vel suum coamantem afficere turbatione" (p. 17).

22 *Dialogus super auctores,* ed. R. B. C. Huygens (Brussels, 1955), p. 16, ll. 123–24.

23 *Accessus ad auctores,* ed. Huygens (Brussels, 1954), p. 14, ll. 15–17; see also p. 23, l. 8 in the "Accessus Seduli," note. Cf. Zumthor, *Essai,* pp. 73–74.

24 *Accessus,* pp. 23–24, ll. 11–14.

25 *Accessus,* p. 14, ll. 7–9.

26 *Accessus,* p. 26, ll. 19–26.

27 See Bogdanow, *Romance,* pp. 194–96; Roger Lathuillère, *Guiron le courtois: Étude de la tradition manuscrite et analyse critique* (Geneva, 1966), pp. 16–17. It might be that the title is chosen not for the prominence of Palamède in the narrative, but for the excellence of his courtesy alone—courtesy being the source of the romance: "Quel non li porrai je donner? Tel comme il plera a mon seigneur le roy Henri. Il vuelt que cestui mien livre, qui de courtoisie doit nestre, soit apelés Palamedes pour ce que si courtois fu toutesvoies Palamedes que nus plus courtois chevalier ne fu au temps le roy Artus et tel chevalier et si preu comme l'estoire vraie tesmoigne" (*Guiron,* p. 180).

28 Fourrier, ed., *Espinette,* v. 385, note (p. 175).

29 Here is the origin of the sequel to the *Espinette*, the *Joli buisson de jonece*.
30 The reference makes plausible the analogy between the *espinette* and the rose the lover gives his lady, vv. 981–1007.
31 *Espinette*, v. 4198, note (p. 184).
32 Similarly, in Richart de Fornival's *Consaus d'amours*, p. 11 (§ 14); this justifies the encouragement he gives his sister to realize a good love now that she is of the right age (pp. 5–6, § 1).
33 *Espinette*, v. 402–4, note (p. 175).
34 "Ensi maintinrent cele vie, / Sans jalousie et sans envie, / Sans visce et sans iniquité, / D'une amour et d'une unité / Sans mestrie et sans signourie / Il nouris et elle nourie" (*Prison amoureuse*, vv. 1374–79; cf. also vv. 820–21).
35 See pp. 247–48.

CHAPTER 8

1 *Bestiaires d'amours*, p. 54, ll. 1–4 [I say the same thing about myself, beautiful and beloved lady: I believe there is a medicine by which you can restore me to life, but I don't know what the medicine is. I know only that by the nature of one beast one may know the nature of another]. *Le Roman de Laurin, fils de Marques le sénéchal*, ed. Lewis Thorpe (Cambridge, 1958), ll. 8502–5 [And what do you know, fair maid?—In truth, my lord, he made it clear to me yesterday when he forcefully abducted me. For you may be certain that he would not have done such a thing to me if he had loved me as he said he did].
2 Fleming, *Rose*, p. 30; see Robertson, *Preface*, pp. 231–33.
3 Curtius, *Europäische Literatur*, p. 92.
4 See Cropp, *Vocabulaire*, pp. 312–15; Friedman, "Jean," pp. 15–16.
5 *Oton de Grandson, sa vie et ses poésies*, ed. Arthur Piaget (Lausanne, 1941).
6 Maurice Roy, ed., *Œuvres poétiques*, 3 vols. (Paris, 1886–96): Cent balades I, III, V–XX.
7 Henry A. Todd, ed. (Paris, 1883), pp. xxv and 113–15.
8 For example, Machaut's *Remede, Fonteinne amoureuse*, and *Voir-Dit;* Froissart's *Espinette amoureuse*.
9 Also in Jean de Garencières, ed. Neal, II, xx–xxii. It is characteristic of the times, as one may observe in Christine de Pisan's and Chartier's political and social writings. On John Gower as well, see John H. Fisher, *John Gower: Moral Philosopher and Friend of Chaucer* (New York, 1964), p. 3: "Gower's continued cultivation of complaint," and cf. pp. 36, 153–54, 206–7.
10 *Gace Brulé trouvère champenois: Édition des chansons et étude historique*, ed. Holger Petersen Dyggve (Helsinki, 1951), LIV, vv. 1–7.
11 Jean Frappier, "Variations sur le thème du miroir de Bernard de Ventadour à Maurice Scève," *Cahiers de l'Association Internationale des Etudes Françaises* 11 (1959), 134–58; Frederick Goldin, *The Mirror of Narcissus in the Courtly Love Lyric* (Ithaca, 1967).
12 *Ideal*, p. 90; cf. Payne, *Key*, pp. 222–25.
13 Ed. Alexander Bell (Oxford, 1960). See Maria Luisa Meneghetti, "L''Estoire des Engleis' di Geffrei Gaimar fra cronaca genealogica e romanzo cortese," *Medioevo romanzo* 2 (1975), 232–46.

14 See Kelly, *"Matiere,"* pp. 155-56.

15 Cf. Chenu, *Théologie,* p. 181: "A tourner la réalité en pure figure, la tropologie s'anémie d'elle-même." In the sequence of lovers exemplified in Machaut's *Alerion* each love is qualitatively distinct, as the separate bird Images indicate. Péronne herself readily sings songs written by Machaut for his former lady. This identifies her with the public lady, as it were, and everyone may sing about her. However, by making a song for a former lady over to Péronne, Machaut is eliminating or blurring distinctions.

16 Wetherbee, *Platonism,* pp. 7-8.

17 Ed. Neal, II, 109. The threat appears in Garencières' complaintes, II, 72-84. *L'amant martyr* is a favorite Image; see Neal, I, 93-94.

18 See Paul Zumthor, "Le Carrefour des Rhétoriqueurs: intertextualité et rhétorique," *Poétique* 27 (1976), 317-37; N. Wilkins, "Post-Machaut," pp. 80-82; R. Deschaux, *Un Poète bourgignon du XVe siècle: Michault Taillevent (édition et étude)* (Geneva, 1975).

19 Daniel Poirion, "L'Allégorie dans le *Livre du cuer d'amours espris,* de René d'Anjou," *Travaux de linguistique et de littérature* 9, no. 2 (1971), 62-64.

20 Love's arrows are fired at random, and without aim (§ 241, ll. 100-102).

21 On the *Hospital d'amours* by Achille Caulier, see Arthur Piaget, "La *Belle dame sans merci* et ses imitations," *Romania* 34 (1905), 561-62.

22 How this is possible is taken up in § 226.

23 This contrasts with Guillaume de Lorris' adaptation of feudal homage to love in the *Rose.*

24 *Studies in French Poetry of the Fifteenth Century* (The Hague, 1970), pp. 32-120.

25 Poirion, *Poète,* pp. 48, 260-65; and Normand R. Cartier, "Oton de Grandson et sa princesse," *Romania* 85 (1964), 1-16.

26 *De amore,* pp. 150-52, 280-82, 290.

27 Poirion, *Poète,* p. 10. Cf. Christine de Pisan's *Mutacion de Fortune,* vv. 771-1024.

28 Cf. Kenneth Varty, ed., in Christine de Pisan, *Ballades, Rondeaux, and Virelais: An Anthology* (Leicester, 1965), p. 152 (to Poem LXX): "It is impossible to say whether or not the *doulx ami* of l. 2 is husband or lover."

29 Thomas Malory, *The Works,* ed. Eugène Vinaver, 2nd ed., 3 vols. (Oxford, 1967), III, 1161.

30 *Key,* pp. 20-21; see also pp. 209-31.

31 *Key,* pp. 90-91.

32 On Chaucer, see Derek S. Brewer, ed., *Geoffrey Chaucer* (Athens, Ohio, 1975), pp. 346-47; Payne, *Key,* pp. 51-57, and his "Chaucer and the Art of Rhetoric", in Beryl Rowland, ed., *Companion to Chaucer Studies* (Toronto, New York, and London, 1968), pp. 38-57. On Gower, James J. Murphy, "John Gower's *Confessio amantis* and the First Discussion of Rhetoric in the English Language," *Philological Quarterly* 41 (1962), 401-11; Götz Schmitz, *"The middel weie":* *Stil- und Aufbauformen in John Gowers "Confessio amantis"* (Bonn, 1974). Chaucer's "remembraunce" (see Payne, *Key,* especially pp. 63-80) is obviously fundamental to Imagination. My comments here serve to link Payne's analysis of

Chaucer to the specifically French literary tradition based on that cognitive faculty as a function and expression of memory.

33 See Ian Robinson, *Chaucer and the English Tradition* (Cambridge, 1972); Derek Brewer, ed., *Chaucer and the Chaucerians: Critical Studies in Middle English Literature* (London, 1966).

34 Cf. HF Prologues II and III.

35 Like Machaut's sequence: *voir-imaginer-concevoir.*

36 See Steadman "Courtly Love," pp. 25-33.

37 Steadman, "Courtly Love," p. 21.

38 Payne, *Key,* pp. 63-64.

39 Cf. the contemporary statement by Jean Gerson: "Et yci garda mal l'acteur [i.e. Jean de Meun] les regles de mon escole, les regles de rethorique, qui sont de regarder cil qui parle, et a qui on parle, et pour quel temps on parle. Et n'est pas le deffault yci seulement, car es autres lieux pluseurs il attribue a la personne qui parle ce qui ne lui doit appartenir, comme il entroduit Nature parlant de paradis et des misteres de nostre foy, et Venuz qui jure par la char Dieu" ("Traité," p. 46).

40 Payne, *Key,* pp. 142-44.

41 See in general C. S. Lewis, *Allegory,* pp. 232-96; and the papers in Brewer, ed., *Chaucer and the Chaucerians.*

42 The *Mirour de l'omme* utilizes Imagination, but it is not treated here because the principal context is neither love nor *fin'amors.* Cf. however the description of Imagination, vv. 14773-84, as well as the diverse situations possible in *fin'amors* in Gower's French Balades, I, 343-73 and in the ensuing *Traitié,* I, 379-92.

43 Schmitz, *Middel weie,* pp. 90-91; Fisher, *Gower,* pp. 70-85. Marriage was the only union really suitable to good love for Gower; see Bennett, "Gower's 'Honneste Love'," in *Patterns of Love,* pp. 107-21.

44 Lewis, *Allegory,* pp. 217-18; Fisher, *Gower,* pp. 162, 214, 220-23, 227. The squire-knight sequence anticipates the two parts of *Jehan de Saintré* (pp. 258-59).

45 Lewis, *Allegory,* pp. 199, 213-14.

46 Cf. 6.1266-87.

47 I, 392 (translation based on Macauley I, 473).

48 Chrétien stressed this in *Erec.*

CHAPTER 9

1 Migne, *Patrologia latina,* CCX, col. 577. [A new trope in the figure makes a new metaphor; a new property in a combination produces a new construction. In this union of the Word, every rule is bereft of sense]. This chapter on Charles d'Orléans does not pretend to review all the scholarship on the poet prince. The two most important works are by Poirion (*Poète,* especially the final chapters) and John Fox (*The Lyric Poetry of Charles d'Orléans,* Oxford, 1969. The important study by Alice Planche reached me too late for use in this chapter: *Charles d'Orléans, ou la recherche d'un langage* (Paris, 1975).

2 On these designations, see Adolf Hofmeister, "*Puer, iuvenis, senex:* Zum Verständnis der mittelalterlichen Altersbezeichnungen," in *Papsttum und Kaisertum: Festschrift Paul Kehr,* ed. A. Brackmann (Munich, 1926), pp. 287-316. The

passage from Youth to Age is thus applicable to Froissart's turning from love when he perceives his gray hair in the mirror. See also Sergio Cigada, *L'Opera poetica di Charles d'Orléans* (Milan, 1960).

3 Unless the untagged "vent" is a personal allusion, perhaps to an expected envoy, friend, or messenger to be sent to England.

4 The English contains an envoy missing in the French: "More riche of weele was neuyr noon then y / Alle though my good resemble vnto Iope / My myrroure hit shalle riche me to y dy / In abidyng my gladsom in good hope" (vv. 1277-80).

5 See Ann Tukey Harrison, *Charles d'Orléans and the Allegorical Mode* (Chapel Hill, 1975), pp. 56-57; see also pp. 103-17.

6 This occurs even in the poems whose meaning is clear both on the abstract level of courtly love, and on the concrete level of his captivity in England; see Balade LXXX, where the first stanza is framed by "Je fu en fleur ou temps passé d'enfance" (v. 1) and the slightly mocking refrain "Mis pour meurir ou feurre de prison."

7 The method is adumbrated by Richart de Fornival, in the conclusion to the *Consaus*. It contains, like the *Lai du trot* and the Brito episode in Andreas Capellanus, a questing knight who finds the Palace of Love (pp. 19-21, §§ 37-45); but the adventure is transposed into a vision: "Si m'amena aventure a celui voiage en le forest de longue pensée ú je trouvai assés de beles et de mervelleuses aventures. Et entre les autres aventures que je trouvai en cele forest me mena aventure en le court le dieu d'amours" (p. 19, § 37). However, Richart there feigns to be a knight who does not love.

8 Poirion, "Allégorie," pp. 54-56.

9 Reffus was originally Dangier in the manuscripts; see Poirion, "Allégorie," p. 54, n. 4.

10 Glasser, "Abstractum," p. 105.

11 Norma Goodrich, *Charles of Orleans: A Study of Themes in His French and in His English Poetry* (Geneva, 1967).

12 Ed. G. Ouy, "Un Poème mystique de Charles d'Orléans: le *Canticum Amoris,*" *Studi francesi* 7 (1959), 64-84.

13 Ouy, "Poème," p. 67.

14 On the *anima* as seat of the Imagination, see Chenu, "*Spiritus,*" passim.

15 Cf. Gérard Defaux, "Charles d'Orléans ou la poétique du secret: À propos du Rondeau XXXIII de l'édition Champion," *Romania* 93 (1972), 194-243.

16 See Cigada, *Opera,* pp. 72-74.

17 Glasser, "Abstractum," pp. 101-4; cf. the discussion of "allegorical renewal" in Hans Heinz Holz, "Prismatisches Denken," in *Über Walther Benjamin* (Frankfurt, 1968), pp. 75-79. Cf. also Paul Zumthor, "Charles d'Orléans et le langage de l'allégorie," in *Mélanges Rita Lejeune,* II, 1481-502 (Reprinted in *Langue, texte, énigme,* pp. 197-213).

CONCLUSION

1 Plato, *The Symposium,* trans. W. Hamilton (Baltimore, 1951), p. 78.

2 Poirion, *Littérature française,* pp. 56-57.

3 Tuve, *Imagery,* p. 21.

4 In contrast to Jean de Meun's *reductio amoris ad absurdum*.
5 "Recherches sur les topiques dans la poésie lyrique des XII ͤ et XIIIͤ siècles," *Cahiers de civilisation médiévale* 2 (1959), 420.
6 *Langue et techniques*, p. 154.
7 Not of course to furnish biographical information. See also Calin, *Poet*, pp. 239–46. One frequents *fins amants* "nompas pour savoir leurs secrez / Selonc especialité, / Mais en la generalité / De ce qu'on porroit bonnement / Dire a tous bons generalment" (*Alerion*, vv. 222–26). *Soutileté* appears frequently in the sense of finesse. See also Köhler's discussion of *sen* and *saber* in "Zum Begriff des Wissens im höfischen Kulturbild," in *Trobadorlyrik*, pp. 29–43.
8 Poirion, *Poète*, p. 10.
9 From Jakob Burckhardt as cited in Ernst Cassirer, *An Essay on Man* (New Haven and London, 1944), p. 206.
10 Robertson, *Preface*, p. 364; Fleming (*Rose*) brands her a "minor" poet whose "part in the Quarrel has been rather inflated, one suspects [?], by modern feminists [!] and should probably not be taken too seriously [!]" (p. 47).
11 It seems to me that this corrects Calin's condemning the use of hunting imagery and falconry in the *Alerion*, in *Poet*, p. 101–2.

APPENDIX
1 Van der Werf, *Chansons;* Gennrich, *Grundriß einer Formenlehre.*
2 Gennrich, *Musikwissenschaft*, p. 1; van der Werf, *Chansons*, p. 13, and especially p. 24: "Almost all of the chansons in fixed form from the 13th century have been preserved either without music or with a polyphonic setting." On the poetic pieces in the prose *Tristan*, see Jean Maillard, "Lais avec notation dans le *Tristan en prose*," in *Mélanges Rita Lejeune*, II, 1347–64; *Les Lais du roman de "Tristan" en prose d'après le manuscrit de Vienne 2542*, ed. Tatiana Fotitch and Ruth Steiner (Munich, 1974); Emmanuèle Baumgartner, *Le 'Tristan en prose': Essai d'interprétation d'un roman médiéval* (Geneva, 1975), pp. 298–307.
3 Jean Renart, *Le Roman de la rose ou de Guillaume de Dole*, ed. Félix Lecoy (Paris, 1962). See also Gerbert de Montreuil, *Le Roman de la violette ou de Gerart de Nevers*, ed. Douglas L. Buffum (Paris, 1928), vv. 36–41: "Et s'ert li contes biaus et gens, / Que je vous voel dire et conter, / Car on i puet lire et chanter; / Et si ert si bien acordans / Li cans au dit, les entendans / En trai a garant que di voir."
4 Only one passage in the *Violette* is ambiguous as to whether the poem is read aloud or sung (vv. 132–33): "A dit ceste canchon nouviele, / Car ele amoit bien par amor." In any case, this example illustrates Deschamps' poem sung or read in private, or for private reasons; see the *Art de dictier*, p. 272.
5 Cf. vv. 1451–55.
6 See Machaut's Prologue, V, 167–68. Chrétien de Troyes and others express similar opinions, so that we may take it to be a consolatory commonplace in aristocratic literature; see *Erec et Enide*, vv. 6466–69.
7 Cf. vv. 3878–82; *Violette*, vv. 1260–65, 1312–13, 2336–38, 3137–40.
8 *Dole*, vv. 4594–99, 4646–47, 4660–63.
9 See Dragonetti, *Technique*, pp. 183–93. The subject is taken up in Guillaume de Lorris' *Rose*, vv. 2257–83 [2245–71], and Chartier's *Belle dame*, vv. 81–112.

10 Cf. vv. 3324–26.
11 Also vv. 317–23, 3637–39.
12 Also vv. 3329–37, 3648–52, 4167–70.
13 Also vv. 3175–79.
14 Also *Violette,* vv. 317–23, 4182–86, 4342–43, 4472–76, 4618–23.
15 *Violette,* vv. 6121–24, 6612–15.
16 See Bossuat, "Un Débat d'amour dans le roman de *Cassidorus,*" *Etudes Mario Roques* (Paris, 1946), pp. 69–75.
17 Ed. Frederick Whitehead, 2nd ed. (Manchester, 1951).
18 *Meliador,* vv. 28626–33, 29138–53, 30331–38.
19 See Machaut's *Remede,* vv. 3359–71.
20 See also *Meliador,* vv. 12565–69, 14792–98, 26144–50.
21 See Machaut's *Prologue* V, vv. 91–94.
22 See Poirion, *Poète,* pp. 266 and 276.
23 *Meliador,* vv. 2143–45.
24 *Meliador,* vv. 3600–607, 18809–31; cf. Poirion, *Poète,* pp. 95–96.
25 *Meliador,* vv. 7505–8, 14792–98; *Voir-Dit,* vv 5542–45.
26 *Meliador,* vv. 4173–77, 4348–56, 6524–29, 13705–11, 26110–22, 28305–21, 28706–8.
27 *Voir-Dit,* vv. 6749–51.
28 Dragonetti, *Technique,* pp. 21–30.
29 See Deschamps, *Art de dictier,* p. 272.
30 Cf. *Meliador,* vv. 30344–47.
31 *Voir-Dit,* vv. 2153–63, 4491–504.
32 The author could also use his poem to transmit bits of news and information interspersed in the amorous argument (*Meliador,* vv. 25114–18).
33 See *Meliador,* vv. 5609–15, 18445–56.
34 *Meliador,* vv. 17877–80.
35 *Meliador,* 21393–407 (where Imagination is the source).
36 *Meliador,* vv. 9805–7.
37 *Meliador,* v. 20332.
38 *Voir-Dit,* pp. 48, 58, 276–77.
39 *Voir-Dit,* pp. 48 and 279.
40 See the *Remede,* vv. 1–166.
41 Cf. the description of the plague in the *Jugement Navarre,* 1–540; and the *Remede,* vv. 689–1495.
42 *Voir-Dit,* vv. 4065–72, and pp. 259 and 314.
43 *Meliador,* vv. 8463–67, 9723–26.
44 *Voir-Dit,* vv. 444–47, 2715–18, 5935–39, 6738–52.
45 *Meliador,* vv. 25080–84, 25131–34, 30385–87.
46 See Marie de France, *Lais,* prologue vv. 23–27.
47 See Auguste Longnon, ed., I, lxiii.
48 Poirion, *Poète,* pp. 37–43, and on the *Parfait du paon,* pp. 255–56.
49 Dragonetti, *Technique.*
50 Cf. *Meliador,* 12528–69, 26144–50.
51 Varty, "Deschamps," pp. 164–68.

52 Based on examination of microfilms of the manuscripts.
53 See Gennrich, *Grundriß*, pp. 60-80; Nigel Wilkins, "Structure of Ballades, Rondeaux and Virelais in Froissart and in Christine de Pisan," *French Studies* 23 (1969), 337-48; Frank M. Chambers, "Imitation of Form in the Old Provençal Lyric," *Romance Philology* 6 (1952-53), 104-20; Friedrich Gennrich, *Die Kontrafaktur im Liedschaffen des Mittelalters,* (Langen bei Frankfurt, 1965).
54 Cf. vv. 1209 and 1371, in R. J. Carey, ed. (Chapel Hill, 1972). There is no music in the extant manuscripts.
55 *Parfait,* vv. 1137-39, 1143.
56 *Art de dictier,* p. 271.
57 Cf. Langlois, *Recueil,* p. 49: "que sur tout son sens il se garde de redites finables en bout de ligne."
58 See A. Henry, ed. *Les Œuvres d'Adenet le Roi,* 5 vols. (Brussels, 1951-71), V, 681-83.

Works Consulted

PRIMARY SOURCES

WORKS IN FRENCH

Acart de Hesdin, Jehan. *La Prise amoureuse*. Edited by Ernest Hoepffner. Gesellschaft für romanische Philologie, 22. Dresden: Gesellschaft für romanische Philologie, 1910.

Adenet le Roi. *Œuvres*. Ed. Albert Henry. 5 vols. Bruges: De Tempel; Brussels: Presses universitaires, 1951–71. [Vol. V: *Cleomades*.]

Andeli, Henri d'. *The Battle of the Seven Arts*. Edited by Louis John Paetow. Memoirs of the University of California, 4. Berkeley: University of California Press, 1914.

Beaumanoir, Philippe de Remi, sire de. *Œuvres poétiques*. Edited by Hermann Suchier. Société des anciens textes français (SATF). 2 vols. Paris: Firmin Didot, 1884–85.

Benoît de Sainte-Maure. *Le Roman de Troie*. Edited by Léopold Constans. SATF. 6 vols. Paris: Firmin Didot, 1904–12.

Buigne, Gace de la. *Le Roman des deduis*. Edited by Åke Blomqvist. Karlshamn, 1951.

Charles d'Orléans. *Poésies*. Edited by Pierre Champion. Classiques français du moyen âge (CFMA). 2 vols. Paris: Champion, 1966.

———. *The English Poems*. Edited by Robert Steele and Mabel Day. Early English Text Society, 215 and 220. London: Early English Text Society; Oxford: University Press, 1941–46.

Chartier, Alain. *La Belle dame sans mercy et les poésies lyriques*. Edited by Arthur Piaget and R.-L. Wagner. Textes littéraires français. Lille: Giard; Geneva: Droz, 1949.

———. *Les Œuvres*. Edited by André du Chesne. Paris: Thiboust, 1617.

———. *The Poetical Works*. Edited by J. C. Laidlaw. Cambridge: University Press, 1974.

———. *Le Quadrilogue invectif*. Edited by Eugénie Droz. CFMA. Paris: Champion, 1950.

Chrétien de Troyes. *Le Chevalier au lion (Yvain)*. Edited by Mario Roques. CFMA. Paris: Champion, 1971.

———. *Le Chevalier de la charrete (Lancelot)*. Edited by Mario Roques. CFMA. Paris: Champion, 1958.

————. *Erec et Enide*. Edited by Mario Roques. CFMA. Paris: Champion, 1966.

————. *Der Percevalroman*. Edited by Alfons Hilka. Halle: Niemeyer, 1932.

Christine de Pisan. *Ballades, Rondeaux, and Virelais: An Anthology*. Edited by Kenneth Varty. Leicester: University Press, 1965.

————. *Le Livre de la mutacion de Fortune*. Edited by Suzanne Solente. SATF. 4 vols. Paris: Picard, 1959–66.

————. *Œuvres poétiques*. Edited by Maurice Roy. SATF. 3 vols. Paris: Firmin Didot, 1886–96.

Condé, Baudouin and Jean de. *Dits et contes*. Edited by Auguste Scheler. 3 vols. Brussels: Devaux, 1866–67.

Deschamps, Eustache. *Œuvres complètes*. Edited by A. Queux de Saint-Hilaire and Gaston Raynaud. SATF. 11 vols. Paris: Firmin Didot, 1878–1903.

Drouart la Vache. *Li Livres d'amours*. Edited by Robert Bossuat. Paris: Champion, 1926.

Fornival, Richart de. *"Li Bestiaires d'amours" di Maistre Richart de Fornival e "Li Response du Bestiaire."* Edited by Cesare Segre. Documenti di filologia, 2. Milan and Naples: Ricciardi, 1957.

————. *"The Consaus d'amours."* Edited by William M. McLeod. *Studies in Philology*, 32 (1935), 1–21.

Froissart, Jean. *L'Espinette amoureuse*. Edited by Anthime Fourrier. Paris: Klincksieck, 1963.

————. *Meliador*. Edited by Auguste Longnon. SATF. 3 vols. Paris: Firmin Didot, 1895–99.

————. *Œuvres*. Edited by Auguste Scheler. 3 vols. Brussels: Devaux, 1870–72.

————. *La Prison amoureuse*. Edited by Anthime Fourrier. Paris: Klincksieck, 1974.

————. *Voyage en Béarn*. Edited by A. H. Diverres. Manchester: University Press, 1953.

Gace Brulé. *Gace Brulé trouvère champenois: Édition des chansons et étude historique*. Edited by Holger Petersen Dyggve. Mémoires de la Société Néophilologique de Helsinki, 16. Helsinki: Société Néophilologique, 1951.

Gaimar, Geffrei. *L'Estoire des Engleis*. Edited by Alexander Bell. Oxford: Blackwell, 1960.

Garencières, Jean de. *Le Chevalier poète Jean de Garencières: Sa vie et ses poésies complètes*. Edited by Young Abernathy Neal. 2 vols. Paris: Nizet, 1953.

Gerbert de Montreuil. *Le Roman de la violette ou de Gerart de Nevers*. Edited by Douglas L. Buffum. SATF. Paris: Champion, 1928.

Gerson, Jean. *"Le Traité de Gerson contre le Roman de la rose."* Edited by Ernest Langlois. *Romania* 45 (1918–19), 23–48.

Huon de Mery. *Le Tornoiemenz Antecrit*. Edited by Georg Wimmer. Ausgaben und Abhandlungen aus dem Gebiete der romanischen Philologie, 76. Marburg: Elwert, 1888.

Jakames. *Le Roman du Castelain de Couci et de la Dame de Fayel*. Edited by John E. Matzke and Maurice Delbouille. SATF. Paris: Société des anciens textes français, 1936.

Jean le Seneschal. *Les Cent ballades: Poème du XIVᵉ siècle*. Edited by Gaston Raynaud. SATF. Paris: Firmin Didot, 1905.

La Sale, Antoine de. *Jehan de Saintré.* Edited by Jean Misrahi and Charles N. Knudson. Textes littéraires français. Geneva: Droz; Paris: Minard, 1965.

Latini, Brunetto. *Li Livres dou tresor.* Edited by Francis J. Carmody. University of California Publications in Modern Philology, 22. Berkeley and Los Angeles: University of California Press, 1948.

Le Bel, Jehan. *Le Ars d'Amour, de vertu et de boneurté.* Edited by Jules Petit. 2 vols. Brussels: Devaux, 1867–69.

Lescurel, Jehannot de. *Chansons, ballades et rondeaux.* Edited by Anatole de Montaiglon. Paris: Jannet, 1855.

Lorris, Guillaume de, and Jean de Meun. *Le Roman de la rose.* Edited by Ernest Langlois. SATF. 5 vols. Paris: Firmin Didot, 1914–24.

——. *The Romance of the Rose.* Translated by Charles Dahlberg. Princeton: University Press, 1971.

——. *Le Roman de la rose.* Edited by Félix Lecoy. CFMA. 3 vols. Paris: Champion, 1965–70.

Machaut, Guillaume de. *Dit de la harpe.* Edited by Karl Young. *Essays in Honor of Albert Feuillerat.* New Haven: Yale, 1943. Pp. 1–20.

——. *La Louange des dames.* Edited by Nigel Wilkins. Edinburgh: Scottish Academic Press; London: Chatto and Windus, 1972.

——. *The Marguerite Poetry.* Edited by James I. Wimsatt. University of North Carolina Studies in the Romance Languages and Literatures, 87. Chapel Hill: University of North Carolina Press, 1970.

——. *Musikalische Werke.* Edited by Friedrich Ludwig. 4 vols. Leipzig: Breitkopf und Härtel, 1926–54.

——. *Œuvres.* Edited by Ernest Hoepffner. SATF. 3 vols. Paris: Firmin Didot, 1908–21.

——. *Œuvres.* Edited by Prosper Tarbé. Rheims and Paris: Techener, 1849.

——. *Poésies lyriques.* Edited by V. Chichmaref. 2 vols. Paris: Champion, 1909.

——. *La Prise d'Alexandrie, ou Chronique du roi Pierre de Lusignan.* Edited by M. L. de Mas Latrie. Publications de la Société de l'Orient latin, série historique, 1. Geneva: Fick, 1877.

——. *Le Livre du Voir-dit.* Edited by Paulin Paris. Paris: Société des bibliophiles françois, 1875.

Maillart, Jehan. *Le Roman du Comte d'Anjou.* Edited by Mario Roques. CFMA. Paris: Champion, 1931.

Margival, Nicole de. *Le Dit de la panthère d'amours.* Edited by Henry A. Todd. SATF. Paris: Firmin Didot, 1883.

Marie de France. *Les Lais.* Edited by Jean Rychner. CFMA. Paris: Champion, 1968.

Meun, Jean de. See Lorris, Guillaume de, and Jean de Meun.

Mote, Jean de la. *Le Parfait du paon.* Edited by Richard J. Carey. University of North Carolina Studies in the Romance Languages and Literatures, 118. Chapel Hill: University of North Carolina Press, 1972.

Oton de Grandson. *Oton de Grandson, sa vie et ses poésies.* Edited by Arthur Piaget. Lausanne: Payot, 1941.

Raoul de Houdenc. "Li Romans des eles." *Trouvères belges (nouvelle série).* Edited by Auguste Scheler. Louvain: Lefever, 1879. Pp. 248–71.

Renart, Jean. *Le Roman de la rose ou de Guillaume de Dole*. Edited by Félix Lecoy. CFMA. Paris: Champion, 1962.

René d'Anjou. *Livre du cuer d'amours espris*. Edited by Ottakar Smital and Emil Winkler. 3 vols. Vienna: Österreichische Staatsdruckerei, 1926.

———. *Le Mortifiement de vaine plaisance*. Edited by Frédéric Lyna. New York: Stechert, 1926.

Thibaut. *Li Romanz de la poire*. Edited by Friedrich Stehlich. Halle: Niemeyer, 1881.

Thomas d'Angleterre. *Les Fragments du Roman de Tristan*. Edited by Bartina H. Wind. Textes littéraires français. Geneva: Droz; Paris: Minard, 1960.

Wace. *Le Roman de Brut*. Edited by Ivor Arnold. SATF. 2 vols. Paris: Société des anciens textes français, 1938–40.

Watriquet de Couvin. *Dits*. Edited by Auguste Scheler. Brussels: Devaux, 1868.

Anonymous Works

Le bestiaire d'amour rimé. Edited by Arvid Thordstein. Etudes romanes de Lund, 2. Lund: Gleerup and Copenhagen: Munksgaard, [1941].

Le Roman de Cassidorus. Edited by Joseph Palermo. SATF. 2 vols. Paris: Picard, 1963–64.

Le Charroi de Nîmes: Chanson de geste du XIIe siècle. Edited by Duncan McMillan. Paris: Klincksieck, 1972.

La Chastelaine de Vergi. Edited by Frederick Whitehead. 2nd ed. Manchester: University Press, 1951.

Le Roman du Comte d'Artois (XVe siècle). Edited by Jean-Charles Seigneuret. Textes littéraires français. Geneva: Droz; Paris: Minard, 1966.

Cristal et Clarie. Edited by Hermann Breuer. Gesellschaft für romanische Literatur, 36. Dresden: Gesellschaft für romanische Literatur, 1915.

Durmart le galois: Roman arthurien du treizième siècle. Edited by Joseph Gildea. 2 vols. Villanova: Villanova University Press, 1965–66.

Livre des eches amoureux ou des eches d'amours [Commentary on the *Echecs amoureux*]. Manuscript Bibliothèque Nationale, Paris. French 9197.

L'Histoire de Guillaume le Maréchal, comte de Striguil et de Pembroke. Edited by Paul Meyer. 3 vols. Paris: Renouard, 1891–1901.

Le Jardin de plaisance et fleur de rethorique. Edited by Antoine Vérard, Eugénie Droz, and Arthur Piaget. SATF. 2 vols. Paris: Firmin Didot and Champion, 1910–25.

Le Roman de Laurin, fils de Marques le sénéchal. Edited by Lewis Thorpe. University of Nottingham Research Publication, 2. Cambridge: Heffer, 1958.

La Mort le roi Artu: Roman du XIIIe siècle. Edited by Jean Frappier. Textes littéraires français. 3rd ed. Geneva: Droz and Paris: Minard, 1964.

Le Lai de l'oiselet. Edited by Raymond Weeks. *Mediaeval Studies in Memory of Gertrude Schoepperle Loomis*. Paris: Champion; New York: Columbia, 1927. Pp. 341–53.

L'Ovide moralisé. Edited by Cornelis de Boer. Verhandelingen der koninklijke Akademie van Wetenschappen te Amsterdam. Afdeeling Letterkunde, n. s. 15, 21, 30.3, 37, 43. Amsterdam: Müller, 1915–36.

Le Commentaire de Copenhague de l'"Ovide moralisé", avec l'édition critique du Septième Livre. Edited by Jeannette T. M. van 't Sant. Amsterdam: Paris, 1929.

Partonopeu de Blois. Edited by Leon Smith and Joseph Gildea. 2 vols. Villanova: Villanova University Press, 1967–70.

La Queste del saint graal: Roman du XIIIe siècle. Edited by Albert Pauphilet. CFMA. Paris: Champion, 1949.

Le Roman de Renart. Edited by Ernest Martin. 3 vols. Strassburg: Trübner, Paris: Leroux: 1882–87.

————. Edited by Mario Roques. CFMA. 6 vols. Paris: Champion, 1948–63.

Le Songe vert. Edited by Léopold Constans. *Romania* 33 (1904), 490–539.

Le Recueil Trepperel. Edited by Eugénie Droz and Halina Lewicka. 2 vols. Paris and Geneva: Droz, 1935–61.

Les Lais du roman de "Tristan" en prose d'après le manuscrit de Vienne 2542. Edited by Tatiana Fotitch and Ruth Steiner. Münchener romanistische Arbeiten, 38. Munich: Fink, 1974.

The Vulgate Version of the Arthurian Romances. Edited by H. Oskar Sommer. 8 vols. Washington, D.C.: Carnegie, 1909–16.

Anthologies

Langlois, Ernest. *Recueil d'arts de Seconde Rhétorique.* Paris: Imprimerie Nationale, 1902.

Schrade, Leo. *Polyphonic Music of the Fourteenth Century.* 12 vols. Monaco: L'oiseau-lyre, 1956–76.

Ward, Charles F., ed. *The Epistles on the Romance of the Rose and Other Documents in the Debate.* Chicago: University of Chicago, 1911.

Wilkins, Nigel, ed. *One Hundred Ballades, Rondeaux and Virelais from the Late Middle Ages.* London and Cambridge: Cambridge University Press, 1969.

WORKS IN LATIN

Alain de Lille. *Anticlaudianus.* Edited by Robert Bossuat. Textes philosophiques du moyen âge, 1. Paris: Vrin, 1955.

————. *Anticlaudianus, or the Good and Perfect Man.* Translated by James J. Sheridan. Toronto: Pontifical Institute, 1973.

————. *De planctu Naturae.* Edited by Thomas Wright. *The Anglo-Latin Satirical Poets and Epigrammatists of the Twelfth Century.* Rolls Series, 59. 2 vols. London: Her Majesty's Stationery Office, 1872; reprint Wiesbaden: Kraus, 1964. Vol. II, pp. 429–522.

————. *The Complaint of Nature.* Translated by Douglas M. Moffat. Yale Studies in English, 36. New York: Holt, 1908.

————. *Liber in distinctionibus dictionum theologicalium.* Migne, *Patrologia latina.* Vol. 210, cols. 685–1012.

————. *Alain de Lille: Textes inédits, avec une introduction sur sa vie et ses œuvres.* Edited by Marie-Thérèse d'Alverny. Etudes de philosophie médiévale, 52. Paris: Vrin, 1965.

Alexander of Villedieu. *Das Doctrinale.* Edited by Dietrich Reichling. Monumenta Germaniae paedagogica, 12. Berlin: Hofmann, 1893.

Andreas Capellanus. *De amore libri tres.* Edited by E. Trojel. Copenhagen: Gadiana, 1892.

——. *The Art of Courtly Love.* Translated by John J. Parry. New York: Columbia, 1941.

Bernardus Silvestris. *Commentum super sex libros Eneidos Virgilii.* Edited by Wilhelm Riedel. Greifswald: Abel, 1924.

——. *De mundi universitate libri duo, sive Megacosmus et Microcosmus.* Edited by Carl S. Barach and Johann Wrobel. Innsbruck: Wagner, 1876; reprint Frankfurt: Minerva, 1964.

——. *The "Cosmographia."* Translated by Winthrop P. Wetherbee. New York, London: Columbia, 1973.

Boethius. *The Consolation of Philosophy.* Edited by H. F. Stewart and E. K. Rand. *The Theological Tractates.* Cambridge, Mass.: Harvard; London: Heinemann, 1968. Pp. 128–411.

Charles d'Orléans. "Un Poème mystique de Charles d'Orléans: Le *Canticum amoris.*" Edited by Gilbert Ouy. *Studi francesi* 7 (1959), 64–84.

Cicero. *Rhetorica.* Edited by A. S. Wilkins. 2 vols. Oxford: Clarendon, 1902–3.

Conrad of Hirsau. *Dialogus super auctores.* Edited by R. B. C. Huygens. Collection Latomus, 17. Brussels: Latomus, 1955.

Dante Alighieri. *De vulgari eloquentia.* Edited by Pier Vincenzo Mengaldo. Vulgares eloquentes, 3. Vol. I. Padua: Antenore, 1968.

Eberhard of Béthune. *Graecismus.* Edited by Johann Wrobel. Warsaw: Koebner, 1887.

Gervais of Melkley. *Ars poetica.* Edited by Hans-Jürgen Gräbener. Forschungen zur romanischen Philologie, 17. Münster: Aschendorff, 1965.

Hugh of Saint Victor. *Didascalicon: De studio legendi.* Edited by Charles Henry Buttimer. Washington, D.C.: Catholic University of America Press, 1939.

——. *Didascalicon: A Medieval Guide to the Arts.* Translated by Jerome Taylor. New York, London: Columbia, 1961.

Isidore of Seville. *Etymologiarum sive originum libri XX.* Edited by Wallace Martin Lindsay. 2 vols. Oxford: Clarendon, 1911.

Johannes de Hauvilla. *Architrenius.* Edited by Paul Gerhard Schmidt. Munich: Fink, 1974.

John of Gárland. *The "Parisiana Poetria."* Edited by Traugott Lawler. Yale Studies in English, 182. New Haven, London: Yale, 1974.

Macrobius. *Commentarii in Somnium Scipionis.* Edited by Jakob Willis. Leipzig: Teubner, 1963.

——. *Commentary on the Dream of Scipio.* Translated by William Harris Stahl. New York: Columbia, 1952.

——. *Saturnalia.* Edited by Jakob Willis. Leipzig: Teubner, 1963.

Pico della Mirandola, Giovanni. *On the Imagination.* Edited by Harry Caplan. Cornell Studies in English, 16. New Haven: Yale; London: Milford, 1930.

Prudentius. *Prudentius.* Edited by H. J. Thomson. 2 vols. Cambridge, Mass.: Harvard; London: Heinemann, 1949–53. [*Psychomachia,* vol. II, pp. 274–343.]

Radulphe de Longchamps. *In Anticlaudianum Alani commentum.* Edited by Jan Sulowski. Wrocław: Zakład Narodowy Imienia Ossolínskich, 1972.

Statius. *Statius*. Edited by J. H. Mozley. 2 vols. Cambridge, Mass.: Harvard; London: Heinemann, 1961. [*Thebaid*, vol. I, p. 339-vol. II, p. 505.]

Anonymous

Accessus ad auctores. Edited by R. B. C. Huygens. Collection Latomus, 15. Brussels: Latomus, 1954.

Epistolae duorum amantium: Briefe Abaelards und Heloises? Edited by Ewald Könsgen. Mittellateinische Studien und Texte, 8. Leiden and Cologne: Brill, 1974.

Rhetorica ad Herennium. Edited by Harry Caplan. Cambridge, Mass.: Harvard; London: Heinemann, 1968.

Scholia Vindobonensia ad Horatii Artem poeticam. Edited by Joseph Zechmeister. Vienna, 1877.

Anthologies

Faral, Edmond. *Les Arts poétiques du XIIe et du XIIIe siècle: Recherches et documents sur la technique littéraire du moyen âge*. Paris: Champion, 1924. [Contains Matthew of Vendôme, *Ars versificatoria* (pp. 109-93); Geoffrey of Vinsauf, *Poetria Nova* (pp. 197-262); Geoffrey of Vinsauf, *Documentum de modo et arte dictandi et versificandi* [short version] (pp. 265-320.)

Gallo, Ernest, trans. "Matthew of Vendôme: Introductory Treatise on the Art of Poetry." *Proceedings of the American Philosophical Society* 118 (1974), 51-92.

Nims, Margaret F., trans. Geoffrey of Vinsauf. *Poetria Nova*. Toronto: Pontifical Institute, 1967.

Parr, Roger P., trans. *Documentum (Instruction in the Method and Art of Speaking and Versifying)*. Milwaukee: Marquette, 1968.

Halm, Karl Felix von, ed. *Rhetores latini minores*. Leipzig: Teubner, 1863. [*Schemata dianoeas quae ad rhetores pertinent*, pp. 71-77.]

Harbert, Bruce, ed. *A Thirteenth-Century Anthology of Rhetorical Poems: Glasgow Ms. Hunterian V.8.14*. Toronto: Pontifical Institute, 1975.

Keil, Heinrich, ed. *Grammatici latini*. 7 vols. Leipzig: Teubner, 1857-70 [Priscian, *Praeexercitamina*, vol. III, pp. 430-40].

Arnaut Daniel. *Canzoni*. Edited by Gianluigi Toja. Florence: Sansoni, 1960.

Bernart de Ventadorn. *Seine Lieder*. Edited by Carl Appel. Halle: Niemeyer, 1915.

Chaucer, Geoffrey. *The Works*. Edited by F. N. Robinson. 2nd ed. Boston: Houghton Mifflin, 1957, 1961.

Gower, John. *The Complete Works*. Edited by G. C. Macaulay. 4 vols. Oxford: Clarendon, 1899-1902.

Guillaume d'Aquitaine. *Les Chansons*. Edited by Alfred Jeanroy. CFMA. Paris: Champion, 1927.

Latini, Brunetto. *La rettorica*. Edited by Francesco Maggini. Florence: Galletti e Cocci, 1915.

Malory, Thomas. *The Works*. Edited by Eugène Vinaver. 2nd ed. 3 vols. Oxford: Clarendon, 1967.

Peire d'Alvernha. *Liriche*. Edited by Alberto del Monte. Turin: Loescher-Chiantore, 1955.

Plato. *The Symposium*. Translated by W. Hamilton. Baltimore: Penguin, 1951.

Ulrich von Liechtenstein. *Frauendienst*. Edited by Reinhold Bechstein. Deutsche Dichtungen des Mittelalters, 6-7. Leipzig: Brockhaus, 1888.

DICTIONARIES

Blaise, Albert. *Dictionnaire latin-français des auteurs chrétiens*. Strasbourg: Le Latin chrétien, 1954.

Gamillscheg, Ernst. *Etymologisches Wörterbuch der französischen Sprache*. 2nd ed. Heidelberg: Winter, 1969.

Godefroy, Frédéric Eugène. *Dictionnaire de l'ancienne langue française, et de tous les dialectes du IXe au XVe siècle*. Paris: Vieweg-Bouillon, 1880-1902.

Lewis, Charlton Thomas, and Charles Short. *A Latin Dictionary*. Oxford: Clarendon, 1879.

Poirion, Daniel. *Le Lexique de Charles d'Orléans dans les Ballades*. Geneva: Droz, 1967.

Souter, Alexander. *A Glossary of Later Latin to 600 A.D.* Oxford: Clarendon, 1949.

Thesaurus linguae latinae. Leipzig: Teubner, 1900-.

Tobler, Adolf, and Erhard Lommatzsch. *Altfranzösisches Wörterbuch*. Berlin: Weidmann; Wiesbaden: Steiner, 1915-.

Wartburg, Walther von. *Französisches etymologisches Wörterbuch: Eine Darstellung des galloromanischen Sprachschatzes*. Bonn: Klopp; Basel: Zbinden, 1928-.

SECONDARY SOURCES

Adler, Gerhard. *The Living Symbol: A Case Study in the Process of Individuation*. Princeton: University Press, 1961.

Allen, Judson B. *The Friar as Critic: Literary Attitudes in the Later Middle Ages*. Nashville: Vanderbilt, 1971.

Auerbach, Erich. *Literatursprache und Publikum in der lateinischen Spätantike und im Mittelalter*. Bern: Francke, 1958.

Badel, Pierre-Yves. "Pierre d'Ailly auteur du *Jardin amoureux*." *Romania* 97 (1976), 369-81.

Batany, Jean. "Paradigmes lexicaux et structures littéraires au moyen âge." *Revue d'histoire littéraire de la France* 70 (1970), 819-35.

Baumgartner, Emmanuèle. *Le "Tristan en prose" : Essai d'interprétation d'un roman médiéval*. Geneva: Droz, 1975.

Bec, Pierre. "Quelques réflexions sur la poésie lyrique médiévale: Problèmes et essai de caractérisation." *Mélanges offerts à Rita Lejeune*. 2 vols. Gembloux: Duculot, 1969. Vol. II, pp. 1309-29.

Bechtoldt, Heinrich. "Der französische Wortschatz im Sinnbezirk des Verstandes (Die geistliche und lehrhafte Literatur von ihren Anfängen bis zum Ende des 12. Jahrhunderts)." *Romanische Forschungen*, 49 (1935), 21-180.

Bender, Karl-Heinz. *König und Vasall: Untersuchungen zur Chanson de geste des XII. Jahrhunderts*. Heidelberg: Winter, 1967.

Benjamin, Walter. *Ursprung des deutschen Trauerspiels*. Frankfurt: Suhrkamp, 1963.

Bennett, J. A. W. "Gower's 'Honneste Love.'" *Patterns of Love and Courtesy: Essays in Memory of C. S. Lewis*. London: Arnold, 1966. Pp. 107–21.

Benton, John F. "Clio and Venus: An Historical View of Courtly Love." *The Meaning of Courtly Love*. Edited by F. X. Newman. Albany: State University of New York, 1968. Pp. 19–41.

Bethurum, Dorothy, ed. *Critical Approaches to Medieval Literature*. New York and London: Columbia, 1960.

Bevilacqua, Michele. *Introduzione a Macrobio*. Lecce: Milella, 1973.

Bloomfield, Morton W. "Episodic Motivation and Marvels in Epic and Romance." *Essays and Explorations: Studies in Ideas, Language, and Literature*. Cambridge, Mass.: Harvard, 1970. Pp. 96–128.

———. *"Piers Plowman" as a Fourteenth-Century Apocalypse*. New Brunswick: Rutgers, 1961. ["The Problem of the Imaginatif," pp. 170–74.]

———. "Symbolism in Medieval Literature." *Modern Philology* 56 (1958–59), 73–81. Also in *Essays and Explorations*, pp. 82–95.

Bogdanow, Fanni. *The Romance of the Grail: A Study of the Structure and Genesis of a Thirteenth-Century Arthurian Prose Romance*. Manchester: University Press; New York: Barnes and Noble, 1966.

Bossuat, Robert. "Un Débat d'amour dans le roman de *Cassidorus*." *Etudes romanes dédiées à Mario Roques*. Paris: Droz, 1946. Pp. 63–75.

Brewer, Derek S. ed. *Chaucer and the Chaucerians: Critical Studies in Middle English Literature*. London: Nelson, 1966.

Brink, Charles O. *Horace on Poetry*. 2 vols. Cambridge: University Press, 1963–71.

———. *Imagination and Imitation*. Liverpool: University Press, 1953.

Brinkmann, Hennig. *Zu Wesen und Form mittelalterlicher Dichtung*. Halle: Niemeyer, 1928.

Bundy, Murray W. *The Theory of Imagination in Classical and Mediaeval Thought*. University of Illinois Studies in Language and Literature, 12.2–3. Urbana: University of Illinois, 1927.

Calin, William. *A Poet at the Fountain: Essays on the Narrative Verse of Guillaume de Machaut*. Lexington: University Press of Kentucky, 1974.

Caplan, Harry. "*Memoria:* Treasure-House of Eloquence." *Of Eloquence: Studies in Ancient and Mediaeval Rhetoric*. Ithaca: Cornell, 1970. Pp. 196–246.

Cartier, Normand R. "Le Bleu chevalier." *Romania* 87 (1966), 289–314.

———. "Froissart, Chaucer and Enclimpostair." *Revue de littérature comparée* 38 (1964), 18–34.

———. "Oton de Grandson et sa princesse." *Romania* 85 (1964), 1–16.

Cassirer, Ernst. *An Essay on Man*. New Haven and London: Yale, 1944.

———. *Philosophie der symbolischen Formen*. 3 vols. Darmstadt: Wissenschaftliche Buchgesellschaft, 1954–64.

Chambers, Frank M. "Imitation of Form in the Old Provençal Lyric." *Romance Philology* 6 (1952–53), 104–20.

Châtillon, Jean. "Les Ecoles de Chartres et de Saint-Victor." *La scuola nell'Occidente latino dell'alto medioevo*. Settimane di studio del Centro italiano di studi sull'alto medioevo, 19. (15–21 April, 1971). 2 vols. Spoleto: Centro, 1972. Vol. II, pp. 795–839.

Chenu, Marie-Dominique. "*Imaginatio:* Note de lexicographie philosophique médié-vale." *Miscellanea Giovanni Mercati.* 6 vols. The Vatican: Biblioteca Apostolica, 1946. Vol. II, pp. 593–602.

――――. "*Spiritus:* Le Vocabulaire de l'âme au XIIᵉ siècle." *Revue des sciences philosophiques et théologiques* 41 (1957), 209–32.

――――. *La Théologie au douzième siècle.* Etudes de philosophie médiévale, 45. 2nd ed. Paris: Vrin, 1966.

Cigada, Sergio. *L'Opera poetica di Charles d'Orléans.* Milan: Vita e pensiero, 1960.

Colby, Alice M. *The Portrait in Twelfth-Century French Literature: An Example of the Stylistic Originality of Chrétien de Troyes.* Geneva: Droz, 1965.

Colish, Marcia L. *The Mirror of Language: A Study in the Medieval Theory of Knowledge.* New Haven: Yale, 1968.

Cropp, Glynnis M. *Le Vocabulaire courtois des troubadours de l'époque classique.* Geneva: Droz, 1975.

Curtius, Ernst Robert. *Europäische Literatur und lateinisches Mittelalter.* 2nd ed. Bern: Francke, 1954.

Dahlberg, Charles. "Love and the *Roman de la rose.*" *Speculum* 44 (1969), 568–84.

――――. "Macrobius and the Unity of the *Roman de la rose.*" *Studies in Philology,* 58 (1961), 573–582.

D'Alverny, Marie-Thérèse. "Maître Alain—'Nova et vetera.'" *Entretiens sur la renaissance du XIIᵉ siècle.* Edited by Maurice de Gandillac and Edouard Jeauneau. Paris and The Hague: Mouton, 1968. Pp. 117–45.

D'Arco Avalle, Silvio. "Variazioni su tema obbligato." *Antologia dei "Saggi di umanismo cristiano."* Pavia: Saggi, 1973. Pp. 371–80.

De Bruyne, Edgar. *Etudes d'esthétique médiévale.* 3 vols. Bruges: De Tempel, 1946.

Defaux, Gérard. "Charles d'Orléans ou la poétique du secret: À propos du Rondeau XXXIII de l'édition Champion." *Romania* 93 (1972), 194–243.

Demats, Paule. *Fabula: Trois études de mythographie antique et médiévale.* Geneva: Droz, 1973.

Dembowski, Peter F. "Vocabulary of Old French Courtly Lyrics—Difficulties and Hidden Difficulties." *Critical Inquiry* 2 (1976), 763–79.

Denomy, A. J. "*Jovens:* The Notion of Youth among the Troubadours, Its Meaning and Source." *Mediaeval Studies* 11 (1949), 1–22.

Deschaux, Robert. *Un Poète bourguignon du XVᵉ siècle: Michault Taillevent (édition et étude).* Geneva: Droz, 1975.

Diverres, A. H. "The Irish Adventures in Froissart's *Meliador.*" *Mélanges de langue et de littérature du moyen âge et de la Renaissance offerts à Jean Frappier.* Geneva: Droz, 1970. Vol. I, pp. 235–51.

Dragonetti, Roger. *La Technique poétique des trouvères dans la chanson courtoise: Contribution à l'étude de la rhétorique médiévale.* Bruges: De Tempel, 1960.

Dronke, Peter. *Fabula: Explorations into the Use of Myth in Medieval Platonism.* Mittellateinische Studien und Texte, 9. Leiden, Cologne: Brill, 1974.

――――. *Medieval Latin and the Rise of European Love-Lyric.* 2nd ed. 2 vols. Oxford: Clarendon, 1968.

Duby, Georges. "Dans la France du Nord-Ouest au XIIᵉ siècle: Les 'Jeunes' dans la société aristocratique." *Annales: Économies sociétés civilisations* 19 (1964), 835–46.

Esch, Arno. "John Gowers Erzählkunst." *Chaucer und seine Zeit: Symposion für Walter F. Schirmer.* Edited by Arno Esch. Buchreihe der Anglia: Zeitschrift für englische Literatur, 14. Tübingen: Niemeyer, 1968. Pp. 207–39.

Faral, Edmond. *La Légende arthurienne: Études et documents.* 3 vols. Paris: Champion, 1929.

————. "Le Manuscrit 511 du 'Hunterian Museum' de Glasgow: Notes sur le mouvement poétique et l'histoire des études littéraires en France et en Angleterre entre les années 1150 et 1225." *Studi medievali,* n. s. 9 (1936), 18–121.

Ferrante, Joan M., and George D. Economou, eds. *In Pursuit of Perfection: Courtly Love in Medieval Literature.* Port Washington, New York, and London: Kennikat, 1975.

Fisher, John H. *John Gower: Moral Philosopher and Friend of Chaucer.* New York: University Press, 1964.

Fleming, John V. *The "Roman de la rose": A Study in Allegory and Iconography.* Princeton: University Press, 1969.

Fox, John. *The Lyric Poetry of Charles d'Orléans.* Oxford: Clarendon, 1969.

Frappier, Jean. *Amour courtois et Table Ronde.* Geneva: Droz, 1973.

————. "Le Concept de l'amour dans les romans arthuriens." *Bulletin bibliographique de la Société Internationale Arthurienne* 22 (1970), 119–36.

————. "D'amors,' 'par amors.'" *Romania* 88 (1967), 433–74.

————. "Notes lexicologiques: I. 'Gole'—II. 'Amour courtois.'" *Mélanges de philologie romane dédiés à la mémoire de Jean Boutière.* 2 vols. Liège: Soledi, 1971. Vol. I, pp. 233–52.

————. "Sur le mot 'raison' dans le *Tristan* de Thomas d'Angleterre." *Linguistic and Literary Studies in Honor of Helmut A. Hatzfeld.* Washington, D.C.: Catholic University of America Press, 1964. Pp. 163–76.

————. "Sur un procès fait à l'amour courtois." *Romania* 93 (1972), 145–93.

————. "Variations sur le thème du miroir de Bernard de Ventadour à Maurice Scève." *Cahiers de l'Association Internationale des Etudes Françaises* 11 (1959), 134–58.

Friedman, Lionel J. "Gradus amoris." *Romance Philology* 19 (1965–66), 167–77.

————. "'Jean de Meung,' Antifeminism, and 'Bourgeois Realism.'" *Modern Philology* 57 (1959–60), 13–23.

————. Rev. M.-R. Jung, *Etudes. Speculum* 47 (1972), 316–20.

Frye, Northrop. "Three Meanings of Symbolism." *Yale French Studies* 9 [1952], 11–19.

Gallo, Ernest. *The "Poetria Nova" and Its Sources in Early Rhetorical Doctrine.* The Hague, Paris: Mouton, 1971.

Gennrich, Friedrich. *Grundriß einer Formenlehre des mittelalterlichen Liedes als Grundlage einer musikalischen Formenlehre des Liedes.* Halle: Niemeyer, 1932; Darmstadt: Wissenschaftliche Buchgesellschaft, 1970.

————. *Die Kontrafaktur im Liedschaffen des Mittelalters.* Summa musicae medii aevi, 12. Fundamenta, 2. Langen bei Frankfurt, 1965.

————. *Musikwissenschaft und romanische Philologie: Ein Beitrag zur Bewertung der Musik als Hilfswissenschaft der romanischen Philologie.* Halle: Niemeyer, 1918.

Ghellinck, Jean de. "Imitari, imitatio." *ALMA (Bulletin du Cange)* 15 (1940-41), 151-59.

Gilson, Etienne. *La Théologie mystique de Saint Bernard.* Etudes de philosophie médiévale, 20. Paris: Vrin, 1934, 1969.

Glasser, Richard. "Abstractum agens und Allegorie im älteren Französisch." *Zeitschrift für romanische Philologie* 69 (1953), 43-122.

Goldin, Frederick. *The Mirror of Narcissus in the Courtly Love Lyric.* Ithaca: Cornell, 1967.

Goodrich, Norma L. *Charles of Orleans: A Study of Themes in His French and in His English Poetry.* Geneva: Droz, 1967.

Gorra, Egidio. *Fra drammi e poemi: Saggi e ricerche.* Milan: Hoepli, 1900.

Green, Richard H. "Alan of Lille's *Anticlaudianus:* Ascensus mentis in Deum." *Annuale mediaevale* 8 (1967), 3-16.

―――. "Alan of Lille's *De planctu Naturae.*" *Speculum* 31 (1956), 649-74.

Gregory, Tullio. *Anima mundi: La filosofia di Guglielmo di Conches e la scuola di Chartres.* Pubblicazioni dell'Istituto di Filosofia dell'Università di Roma, 3. Florence: Sansoni, 1955.

Grigsby, John L. "The Narrator in *Partonopeu de Blois, Le Bel Inconnu,* and *Joufroi de Poitiers.*" *Romance Philology* 21 (1967-68), 536-43.

Gröber, Gustav. *Grundriß der romanischen Philologie.* 2 vols. Straßburg: Trübner, 1897-1906.

―――. *Grundriß der romanischen Philologie, neue Folge: Geschichte der mittelfranzösischen Literatur.* Edited by Stefan Hofer. 2 vols. 2nd ed. Berlin and Leipzig: Gruyter, 1933-37.

Grundriß der romanischen Literaturen des Mittelalters. Edited by Hans Robert Jauss and Erich Köhler. Heidelberg: Winter, 1968-.

Guiette, Robert. "D'une poésie formelle en France au moyen âge." *Revue des sciences humaines* (1949), pp. 61-68. Reprint I: *Questions de littérature. Romanica Gandensia* 8 (1960), 9-23 Reprint II: *D'une poésie formelle en France au moyen âge.* Paris: Nizet, 1972.

Gunn, Alan M. F. *The Mirror of Love: A Reinterpretation of "The Romance of the Rose."* Lubbock: Texas Tech, 1952.

Hanning, Robert W. "The Social Significance of Twelfth-Century Chivalric Romance." *Medievalia et humanistica,* n. s. 3 (1972), 3-29.

Häring, Nikolaus. "Chartres and Paris Revisited." *Essays in Honour of Anton Charles Pegis.* Toronto: Pontifical Institute, 1974. Pp. 268-329.

Harrison, Ann Tukey. *Charles d'Orléans and the Allegorical Mode.* University of North Carolina Studies in the Romance Languages and Literatures, 150. Chapel Hill: University of North Carolina, 1975.

Harwood, Britton J. "Imaginative in Piers Plowman." *Medium Ævum* 44 (1975), 249-63.

Haug, Walter. "Struktur und Geschichte: Ein literaturtheoretisches Experiment an mittelalterlichen Texten." *Germanisch-romanische Monatsschrift,* n. s. 23 (1973), 129-52.

Hofmeister, Adolf. "*Puer, iuvenis, senex:* zum Verständnis der mittelalterlichen Altersbezeichnungen." *Papsttum und Kaisertum: Forschungen zur politischen Ges-*

chichte und Geisteskultur des Mittelalters Paul Kehr dargebracht. Munich: Verlag der Münchener Drucke, 1926. Pp. 287–316.

Holz, Hans Heinz. "Prismatisches Denken." *Über Walter Benjamin.* Frankfurt: Suhrkamp, 1968. Pp. 62–110.

Huizinga, Johan. "Über die Verknüpfung des Poetischen mit dem Theologischen bei Alanus de Insulis." *Verzamelde Werken.* 9 vols. Haarlem: Tjeenk, 1948–53. Vol. IV, pp. 3–84.

――――. *The Waning of the Middle Ages: A Study of the Forms of Life, Thought and Art in France and the Netherlands in the Dawn of the Renaissance.* New York: Doubleday, 1954.

Jackson, W. T. H. "Allegory and Allegorization." *Research Studies Washington State University* 32 (1964), 161–75.

Jauss, Hans Robert. "Form und Auffassung der Allegorie in der Tradition der *Psychomachia* (von Prudentius zum ersten *Romanz de la Rose*)." *Medium Aevum vivum: Festschrift für Walther Bulst.* Heidelberg: Winter, 1960. Pp. 179–206.

――――. "La Transformation de la forme allégorique entre 1180 et 1240: D'Alain de Lille à Guillaume de Lorris." *L'Humanisme médiéval dans les littératures romanes du XIIᵉ au XIVᵉ siècle.* Edited by Anthime Fourrier. Paris: Klincksieck, 1964. Pp. 107–46.

――――. *Untersuchungen zur mittelalterlichen Tierdichtung.* Beihefte zur Zeitschrift für romanische Philologie, 100. Tübingen: Niemeyer, 1959.

Javelet, Robert. "L'Amour spirituel face à l'amour courtois' " *Entretiens sur la renaissance du XIIᵉ siècle.* Edited by Maurice de Gandillac and Edouard Jeauneau. Paris and The Hague: Mouton, 1968. Pp. 309–46.

――――. *Image et ressemblance au XIIᵉ siècle: De Saint Anselme à Alain de Lille.* 2 vols. Paris: Letouzey et Ané, 1967.

――――. *Psychologie des auteurs spirituels du XIIᵉ siècle.* Strasbourg: [the author], 1959.

――――. "La Réintroduction de la liberté dans les notions d'image et de ressemblance, conçues comme dynamisme." *Der Begriff der repraesentatio im Mittelalter: Stellvertretung, Symbol, Zeichen, Bild.* Edited by Albert Zimmermann. Miscellanea mediaevalia, 8. Berlin and New York: Gruyter, 1971. Pp. 1–34.

Jeauneau, Edouard. "L'Usage de la notion d'*integumentum* à travers les gloses de Guillaume de Conches." *Archives d'histoire doctrinale et littéraire du moyen âge* 32 (1957), 35–100.

Jung, Carl Gustav. *Psychologie und Alchimie.* Zurich: Rascher, 1944.

Jung, Marc-René. *Etudes sur le poème allégorique en France au moyen âge.* Romanica helvetica, 82. Bern: Francke, 1971.

――――. "Gui de Mori et Guillaume de Lorris." *Vox romanica* 27 (1968), 106–37.

――――. "*Poetria:* Zur Dichtungstheorie des ausgehenden Mittelalters in Frankreich." *Vox romanica* 30 (1971), 44–64.

Kelly, Douglas. " 'Li chastiaus . . . Qu'Amors prist puis par ses esforz': The Conclusion of Guillaume de Lorris' *Rose.* " *A Medieval French Miscellany.* Edited by Norris J. Lacy. University of Kansas Humanistic Studies, 42. Lawrence: University of Kansas, 1972. Pp. 61–78.

————. "Courtly Love in Perspective: The Hierarchy of Love in Andreas Capellanus." *Traditio* 24 (1968), 119–47.

————. "La Forme et le sens de la quête dans l'*Erec et Enide* de Chrétien de Troyes." *Romania* 92 (1971), 326–58.

————. "Fortune and Narrative Proliferation in the *Berinus.*" *Speculum* 51 (1976), 6–22.

————. "*Matiere* and *genera dicendi* in Medieval Romance." *Yale French Studies* 51 (1974), 147–59.

————. "The Scope of the Treatment of Composition in the Twelfth- and Thirteenth-Century Arts of Poetry." *Speculum* 41 (1966), 261–78.

————. "*Sens*" and "*Conjointure*" in the "*Chevalier de la charrette.*" The Hague and Paris: Mouton, 1966.

————. "Theory of Composition in Medieval Narrative Poetry and Geoffrey of Vinsauf's *Poetria Nova.*" *Mediaeval Studies* 31 (1969), 117–48.

Kilgour, Raymond Lincoln. *The Decline of Chivalry as Shown in the French Literature of the Late Middle Ages.* Harvard Studies in Romance Languages, 12. Cambridge, Mass.: Harvard, 1937.

Klinck, Roswitha. *Die lateinische Etymologie des Mittelalters.* Medium Aevum: philologische Studien, 17. Munich: Fink, 1970.

Knapp, Fritz Peter. "Vergleich und Exempel in der lateinischen Rhetorik und Poetik von der Mitte des 12. bis zur Mitte des 13. Jahrhunderts." *Studi medievali,* n.s. 3, 14 (1973), 443–511.

Knudson, Charles A. "The Prussian Expedition in *Jehan de Saintré.*" *Etudes de langue et de littérature du moyen âge offertes à Félix Lecoy.* Paris: Champion, 1973. Pp. 271–77.

————. "The Two Saintrés." *Romance Studies in Memory of Edward Billings Ham.* Hayward: California, 1967. Pp. 73–80.

Köhler, Erich. *Ideal und Wirklichkeit in der höfischen Epik: Studien zur Form der frühen Artus- und Graldichtung.* Beihefte zur Zeitschrift für romanische Philologie, 97. 2nd ed. Tübingen: Niemeyer, 1970.

————. "Narcisse, la fontaine d'Amour et Guillaume de Lorris." *L'Humanisme médiéval dans les littératures romanes du XIIe au XIVe siècle.* Ed. Anthime Fourrier. Paris: Klincksieck, 1964. Pp. 147–66.

————. "Sens et fonction du terme 'jeunesse' dans la poésie des troubadours." *Mélanges offerts à René Crozet.* 2 vols. Poitiers: Société d'Etudes Médiévales, 1966. Vol. I, pp. 569–83.

————. *Trobadorlyrik und höfischer Roman: Aufsätze zur französischen und provenzalischen Literatur des Mittelalters.* Berlin: Rütten und Loening, 1962.

————. "Zur Entstehung des altprovenzalischen Streitgedichts." *Zeitschrift für romanische Philologie* 75 (1959), 37–88.

Koenig, Daniel. "*Sen*" / "*sens*" et "*savoir*" et leurs synonymes dans quelques romans courtois du 12e et du début du 13e siècle. Bern: Herbert Lang; Frankfurt: Peter Lang, 1973.

Koll, Hans-Georg. *Die französischen Wörter "langue" und "langage" im Mittelalter.* Geneva: Droz, 1958.

Kolve, V. A. "Chaucer and the Visual Arts." *Geoffrey Chaucer.* Edited by Derek Brewer. Athens, Ohio: Ohio University Press, 1975. Pp. 290–320.

Krayer, Rudolf. *Frauenlob und die Natur-Allegorese: Motivgeschichtliche Untersuchungen—ein Beitrag zur Geschichte des antiken Traditionsgutes.* Heidelberg: Winter, 1960.

Kurdziałek, Marian. "Der Mensch als Abbild des Kosmos." *Der Begriff der repraesentatio im Mittelalter: Stellvertretung, Symbol, Zeichen, Bild.* Edited by Albert Zimmermann. Miscellanea Mediaevalia, 8. Berlin and New York: Gruyter, 1971. Pp. 35–75.

Langlois, Ernest. "Quelques œuvres de Richard de Fournival." *Bibliothèque de l'Ecole des Chartes* 65 (1904), 101–15.

Lathuillère, Roger. *Guiron le courtois: Étude de la tradition manuscrite et analyse critique.* Geneva: Droz, 1966.

Lausberg, Heinrich. *Handbuch der literarischen Rhetorik: Eine Grundlegung der Literaturwissenschaft.* 2 vols. Munich: Hueber, 1960.

Lazar, Moshé. *Amour courtois et fin'amors dans la littérature du XIIe siècle.* Paris: Klincksieck, 1964.

Leclercq, Jean. "L'Amitié dans les lettres au moyen âge: Autour d'un manuscrit de la bibliothèque de Pétrarque." *Revue du moyen âge latin* 1 (1945), 391–410.

Le Gentil, Pierre. "Réflexions sur la création littéraire au moyen âge." *Chanson de geste und höfischer Roman: Heidelberger Kolloquium 30. Januar 1961.* Studia romanica, 4. Heidelberg: Winter, 1963. Pp. 9–20.

Leube-Fey, Christiane. *Bild und Funktion der "dompna" in der Lyrik der Trobadors.* Studia romanica, 21. Heidelberg: Winter, 1971.

Lewis, C. S. *The Allegory of Love: A Study in Medieval Tradition.* Oxford: Oxford University Press, 1936, 1958.

———. *The Discarded Image: An Introduction to Medieval and Renaissance Literature.* Cambridge: University Press, 1964.

Lubac, Henri de. *Exégèse médiévale: Les quatre sens de l'Ecriture.* 4 vols. Paris: Aubier, 1959–64.

MacCaffrey, I. G. *Spenser's Allegory: The Anatomy of Imagination.* Princeton: University Press, 1976.

Maillard, Jean. "Lais avec notation dans le *Tristan* en prose." *Mélanges offerts à Rita Lejeune.* 2 vols. Gembloux: Duculot, 1969. Vol. II, pp. 1347–64.

Mathew, Gervase. "Ideals of Friendship." *Patterns of Love and Courtesy: Essays in Memory of C. S. Lewis.* London: Arnold, 1966. Pp. 45–53.

Meneghetti, Maria Luisa. "L'Estoire des Engleis' di Geffrei Gaimar fra cronaca genealogica e romanzo cortese." *Medioevo romanzo* 2 (1975), 232–46.

Messelaar, Petrus Adrianus. *Le Vocabulaire des idées dans le "Tresor" de Brunet Latin.* Assen: Van Gorcum, 1963.

Michaud-Quantin, Pierre. "La Classification des puissances de l'âme au XIIe siècle." *Revue du moyen âge latin* 5 (1949), 15–34.

Mölk, Ulrich. *Trobar clus trobar leu: Studien zur Dichtungstheorie der Trobadors.* Munich: Fink, 1968.

Murphy, James J. "John Gower's *Confessio amantis* and the First Discussion of Rhetoric in the English Language." *Philological Quarterly* 41 (1962), 401–11.

Neumann, Erich. *Art and the Creative Unconscious: Four Essays.* Translated by Ralph Manheim. Princeton: University Press, 1959.

————. *The Origins and History of Consciousness.* Translated by R. F. C. Hull. Princeton: University Press, 1954.

Neumeister, Sebastian. *Das Spiel mit der höfischen Liebe: Das altprovenzalische Partimen.* Munich: Fink, 1969.

Nève, Paul. "L'Anti-intellectualisme de Pascal." *Annales de l'Institut Supérieur de Philosophie: Louvain* 5 (1924), 423–45.

Nichols, Stephen G., Jr. "The Rhetoric of Sincerity in the *Roman de la rose.*" *Romance Studies in Memory of Edward Billings Ham.* Hayward: California, 1967. Pp. 115–29.

Nims, Margaret F. "*Translatio:* 'Difficult Statement' in Medieval Poetic Theory." *University of Toronto Quarterly* 43 (1974), 215–30.

Nitzsche, Jane Chance. *The Genius Figure in Antiquity and the Middle Ages.* New York and London: Columbia, 1975.

Nolan, Barbara. *The Gothic Visionary Perspective.* Princeton: University Press, 1977.

Ochsenbein, Peter. *Studien zum "Anticlaudianus" des Alanus ab Insulis.* Bern: Herbert Lang; Frankfurt: Peter Lang, 1975.

O'Donnell, J. Reginald. "The Meaning of 'Silva' in the Commentary on the *Timaeus* of Plato by Chalcidius." *Mediaeval Studies* 7 (1945), 1–20.

Paré, Gérard Marie. *Les Idées et les lettres au XIIIe siècle: Le "Roman de la rose."* Montreal: Centre de psychologie et de pédagogie, 1947.

Paris, Gaston. "Etudes sur les romans de la Table Ronde. Lancelot du Lac, I. Le *Lanzelet* d'Ulrich de Zatzikhoven. II. Le *Conte de la charrette.*" *Romania* 10 (1881), 465–96; 12 (1883), 459–534; 16 (1887), 100–101.

Patch, Howard R. *The Goddess Fortuna in Medieval Literature.* Cambridge, Mass.: Harvard, 1927.

Paterson, Linda M. *Troubadours and Eloquence.* Oxford: Clarendon, 1975.

Patterson, Warner F. *Three Centuries of French Poetic Theory: A Critical History of the Chief Arts of Poetry in France (1328–1630).* 2 vols. Ann Arbor: University of Michigan Press, 1935; New York: Russell and Russell, 1966.

Payne, Robert O. "Chaucer and the Art of Rhetoric." *Companion to Chaucer Studies.* Edited by Beryl Rowland. Toronto, New York and London: Oxford University Press, 1968. Pp. 38–57.

————. *The Key of Remembrance: A Study of Chaucer's Poetics.* New Haven and London: Yale, 1963.

Piaget, Arthur. "La *Belle dame sans merci* et ses imitations: XI. L'*Hôpital d'amour* par Achille Caulier." *Romania* 34 (1905), 559–65.

Pickering, F. P. *Literature and Art in the Middle Ages.* Glasgow: University Press; Coral Gables: Miami, 1970.

Planche, Alice. *Charles d'Orléans, ou la recherche d'un langage.* Paris: Champion, 1975.

Poirion, Daniel. "L'Allégorie dans le *Livre du cuer d'amours espris,* de René d'Anjou." *Travaux de linguistique et de littérature,* 9.2 (1971), 51–64.

_____. *Le Moyen âge. II: 1300–1480. Littérature française.* Edited by Claude Pichois. Paris: Arthaud, 1971.

_____. *Le Poète et le prince: 'Evolution du lyrisme courtois de Guillaume de Machaut à Charles d'Orléans.* Paris: Presses universitaires, 1965.

_____. *Le "Roman de la rose."* Paris: Hatier, 1973.

Potansky, Peter. *Der Streit um den Rosenroman.* Münchener romanistische Arbeiten, 33. Munich: Fink, 1972.

Quadlbauer, Franz. *Die antike Theorie der genera dicendi im lateinischen Mittelalter.* Österreichische Akademie der Wissenschaften. Philologische-historische Klasse. Sitzungsberichte, 241.2. Viennä: Böhlaus, 1962.

Rand, Edward Kennard. *Founders of the Middle Ages.* Cambridge, Mass.: Harvard, 1928.

Raynaud de Lage, Guy. *Alain de Lille: Poète du XIIe siècle.* Montreal: Institut d'Etudes médiévales; Paris: Vrin, 1951.

Ribard, Jacques. *Un Ménestrel du XIVe siècle: Jean de Condé.* Geneva: Droz, 1969.

Robertson, D. W., Jr. "The Concept of Courtly Love as an Impediment to the Understanding of Medieval Texts." *The Meaning of Courtly Love.* Edited by F. X. Newman. Albany: State University of New York, 1968. Pp. 1–18.

_____. *A Preface to Chaucer: Studies in Medieval Perspectives.* Princeton: University Press, 1962.

_____. "Some Medieval Literary Terminology, with Special Reference to Chrétien de Troyes." *Studies in Philology* 48 (1951), 669–92.

Robinson, Ian. *Chaucer and the English Tradition.* Cambridge: University Press, 1972.

Rohr, Rupprecht. "Zur Skala der ritterlichen Tugenden in der altprovenzalischen und altfranzösischen höfischen Dichtung." *Zeitschrift für romanische Philologie* 78 (1962), 292–325.

Ross, Werner. "Rose und Nachtigall: Ein Beitrag zur Metaphorik und Mythologie des Mittelalters." *Romanische Forschungen* 67 (1956), 55–82.

Sasaki, Shigemi. *Sur le thème de nonchaloir dans la poésie de Charles d'Orléans.* Paris: Nizet, 1974.

Schaller, Dieter. "Probleme der Überlieferung und Verfasserschaft lateinischer Liebesbriefe des hohen Mittelalters." *Mittellateinisches Jahrbuch* 3 (1966), 25–36.

Schlösser, Felix. *Andreas Capellanus: Seine Minelehre und das christliche Weltbild um 1200.* Bonn: Bouvier, 1960.

Schmitz, Götz. *"The middel weie": Stil- und Aufbauformen in John Gowers "Confessio amantis."* Bonn: Bouvier, 1974.

Seznec, Jean. *The Survival of the Pagan Gods: The Mythological Tradition and Its Place in Renaissance Humanism and Art.* New York: Harper, 1953.

Shapley, C. S. *Studies in French Poetry of the Fifteenth Century.* The Hague: Nijhoff, 1970.

Sieper, Ernst. *"Les Echecs amoureux": Eine altfranzösische Nachahmung des Rosenromans und ihre englische Übertragung.* Litterarhistorische Forschungen, 9. Weimar: Felber, 1898.

Silver, Isidore. *The Intellectuel Evolution of Ronsard.* 2 vols. St. Louis: Washington University, 1969–73.

————. "The Marriage of Poetry and Music in France: Ronsard's Predecessors and Contemporaries." *Poetry and Poetics from Ancient Greece to the Renaissance: Studies in Honor of James Hutton.* Ithaca and London: Cornell, 1975. Pp. 152–84.

Silverstein, Theodore. "The Fabulous Cosmogony of Bernardus Silvestris." *Modern Philology* 46 (1948–49), 92–116.

Southern, Richard W. "Humanism and the School of Chartres." *Medieval Humanism and Other Studies.* Oxford: Blackwell, 1970. Pp. 61–85.

Spitzer, Leo. *Classical and Christian Ideas of World Harmony: Prolegomena to an Interpretation of the Word "Stimmung."* Edited by Anna Granville Hatcher. Baltimore: Johns Hopkins, 1963.

Steadman, John M. " 'Courtly Love' as a Problem of Style." *Chaucer und seine Zeit: Symposion für Walter F. Schirmer.* Edited by Arno Esch. Buchreihe der Anglia: Zeitschrift für englische Literatur, 14. Tübingen: Niemeyer, 1968. Pp. 1–33.

Steinen, Wolfram von den. "Les Sujets d'inspiration chez les poètes latins du XIIe siècle." *Cahiers de civilisation médiévale* 9 (1966), 163–75, 363–83.

Stock, Brian. *Myth and Science in the Twelfth Century: A Study of Bernard Silvester.* Princeton: University Press, 1972.

Thoss, Dagmar. *Studien zum locus amoenus im Mittelalter.* Wiener romanistische Arbeiten, 10. Vienna and Stuttgart: Braumüller, 1972.

Topsfield, L. T. *Troubadours and Love.* Cambridge: University Press, 1975.

Tuve, Rosemond. *Allegorical Imagery: Some Mediaeval Books and Their Posterity.* Princeton: University Press, 1966.

Van der Werf, Hendrik. *The Chansons of the Troubadours and Trouvères: A Study of the Melodies and Their Relation to the Poems.* Utrecht: Oosthoek, 1972.

Varty, Kenneth. "Deschamps's *Art de dictier.*" *French Studies* 19 (1965), 164–67.

Wallen, Martha. *The Illumination of Guillaume de Machaut's "Confort d'ami."* M. A. thesis: University of Wisconsin, 1971.

Wetherbee, Winthrop P. "The Function of Poetry in the 'De planctu Naturae' of Alain de Lille." *Traditio* 25 (1969), 87–125.

————. "The Literal and the Allegorical: Jean de Meun and the *de Planctu Naturae.*" *Mediaeval Studies* 33 (1971), 264–91.

————. *Platonism and Poetry in the Twelfth Century: the Literary Influence of the School of Chartres.* Princeton: University Press, 1972.

————. "The Theme of Imagination in Medieval Poetry and the Allegorical Figure of 'Genius.'" *Medievalia et Humanistica* 7 (1976), 45–64.

Wienbruch, Ulrich. "'Signum,' 'significatio' und 'illuminatio' bei Augustin." *Der Begriff der repraesentatio im Mittelalter: Stellvertretung, Symbol, Zeichen, Bild.* Edited by Albert Zimmermann. Miscellanea Mediaevalia, 8. Berlin and New York: Gruyter, 1971. Pp. 76–93.

Wilkins, Nigel E. "The Post-Machaut Generation of Poet-Musicians." *Nottingham Mediaeval Studies* 12 (1968), 40–84.

————. "Structure of Ballades, Rondeaux and Virelais in Froissart and in Christine de Pisan." *French Studies* 23 (1969), 337–48.

Williams, Sarah Jane. "An Author's Role in Fourteenth-Century Book Production: Guillaume de Machaut's 'Livre ou je met toutes mes choses'." *Romania* 90 (1969), 433–54.

Wimsatt, James I. *Chaucer and the French Love Poets: The Literary Background of the "Book of the Duchess."* University of North Carolina Studies in Comparative Literature, 43. Chapel Hill: University of North Carolina Press, 1968.

Yates, Frances A. *The Art of Memory.* London: Routledge and Paul, 1966.

Ziltener, Werner. *Studien zur bildungsgeschichtlichen Eigenart der höfischen Dichtung: Antike und Christentum in okzitanischen und altfranzösischen Vergleichen aus der unbelebten Natur.* Romanica Helvetica, 83. Bern: Francke, 1972.

Zumthor, Paul. "Le Carrefour des Rhétoriqueurs: Intertextualité et rhétorique." *Poétique* 27 (1976), 317–37.

———. "Charles d'Orléans et le langage de l'allégorie." *Mélanges offerts à Rita Lejeune.* 2 vols. Gembloux: Duculot, 1969. Vol. II, pp. 1481–502.

———. *Essai de poétique médiévale.* Paris: Seuil, 1972.

———. *Langue et techniques poétiques à l'époque romane (XIe-XIIIe siècles).* Paris: Klincksieck, 1963.

———. *Langue, texte, énigme.* Paris: Seuil, 1975.

———. "Note sur les champs sémantiques dans le vocabulaire des idées." *Neophilologus* 39 (1955), 175–83, 241–49.

———. "Pour une histoire du vocabulaire français des idées." *Zeitschrift für romanische Philologie* 72 (1956), 340–62.

———. "Recherches sur les topiques dans la poésie lyrique des XIIe et XIIIe siècles." *Cahiers de civilisation médiévale* 2 (1959), 409–27.

Index

(All titles not anonymous are listed under the author)

COMPOSED BY THE COMPOSING ROOM, INC., GRAND RAPIDS, MICHIGAN
MANUFACTURED BY CUSHING-MALLOY, INC., ANN ARBOR, MICHIGAN
TEXT IS SET IN TIMES ROMAN, DISPLAY LINES IN WEISS

Library of Congress Cataloging in Publication Data
Kelly, Douglas.
Medieval imagination.
Bibliography: p.
Includes index.
1. French poetry—To 1500—History and criticism.
2. Love poetry, French—History and criticism.
3. Courtly love. I. Title.
PQ155.L7K44 1978   841'.1   78-3522
ISBN 0-299-07610-5

DATE DUE

MAY 15		
NOV 15		

821.09
K29

97180

AUTHOR		
Kelly, Douglas		
TITLE		
Medieval Imagination		
DATE DUE	**BORROWER'S NAME**	
MAY 15	H. Whiteman 83	
NOV 15	Harriet Whiteman	

GAYLORD 45

821.09
K29

97180